THE RISE OF THE ARAB AMERICAN LEFT

JUSTICE, POWER, AND POLITICS

Coeditors
Heather Ann Thompson
Rhonda Y. Williams

Editorial Advisory Board
Peniel E. Joseph
Matthew D. Lassiter
Daryl Maeda
Barbara Ransby
Vicki L. Ruiz
Marc Stein

The Justice, Power, and Politics series publishes new works in history that explore the myriad struggles for justice, battles for power, and shifts in politics that have shaped the United States over time. Through the lenses of justice, power, and politics, the series seeks to broaden scholarly debates about America's past as well as to inform public discussions about its future.

More information on the series, including a complete list of books published, is available at http://justicepowerandpolitics.com/.

PAMELA E. PENNOCK

THE RISE OF THE ARAB AMERICAN LEFT

Activists, Allies, and Their Fight against Imperialism and Racism, 1960s–1980s

The University of North Carolina Press
Chapel Hill

© 2017 The University of North Carolina Press
All rights reserved

Designed and set in Scala and Scala Sans by Rebecca Evans
Manufactured in the United States of America

The University of North Carolina Press has been a member of the
Green Press Initiative since 2003.

Cover illustration: Arab Americans in the Southend of Dearborn, Michigan,
rally in support of Arab forces during the October War in 1973. *AAUG
Newsletter*, December 1973, AAUG Papers, Eastern Michigan University,
Special Collections Library.

Library of Congress Cataloging-in-Publication Data
Names: Pennock, Pamela E., author.
Title: The rise of the Arab American left : activists, allies, and their fight
   against imperialism and racism, 1960s–1980s / Pamela E. Pennock.
Other titles: Justice, power, and politics.
Description: Chapel Hill : The University of North Carolina Press, [2017] |
   Series: Justice, power, and politics | Includes bibliographical references
   and index.
Identifiers: LCCN 2016019559| ISBN 9781469630977 (cloth : alk. paper) |
   ISBN 9781469630984 (pbk : alk. paper) | ISBN 9781469630991 (ebook)
Subjects: LCSH: Arab Americans—Politics and government—20th century. |
   United States—Politics and government—20th century.
Classification: LCC E184.A65 P46 2017 | DDC 305.892/7073—dc23 LC record
   available at https://lccn.loc.gov/2016019559

Portions of chapter 2 were previously published as "Third World Alliances:
Arab American Activists at American Universities, 1967–1973," *Mashriq &
Mahjar: Journal of Middle East Migration Studies* 2, no. 2 (2014): 55–78.

CONTENTS

Acknowledgments ix

Introduction 1

PART ONE
THE IMPACT OF THE 1967 ARAB-ISRAELI WAR ON
ARAB AMERICAN ORGANIZING AND THE AMERICAN LEFT

1 Progressive Activism after the June War 21
   The Association of Arab American University Graduates

2 Arab Students and the Politics of Palestine 47
   The Organization of Arab Students and the Arab American Left

3 Intersections 79
   Palestine, Arab Americans, and the Movements of the Sixties

PART TWO
A HOSTILE CLIMATE FOR ACTIVISM

4 "A Disturbed Individual, not a Martyr" 121
   Sirhan Sirhan's Impact on Arab American Activism

5 "Enemies Within" 143
   Operation Boulder and Infringements of Civil Liberties

PART THREE
AMERICANIZATION OF ACTIVISM: LOCAL ORGANIZING
AND NATIONAL INTEGRATION

6 Traversing Arab and American Spaces 167
   Community and Labor Organizing in the Southend

7 Seeking Integration 201
   Arab American Political Organizing in the 1980s

Conclusion 230

Notes 239   *Bibliography* 283   *Index* 303

ILLUSTRATIONS

Organization of Arab Students, University of Michigan, flyer advertising march and rally, 1969 58

Organization of Arab Students, University of Michigan, flyer advertising film about Palestinian commandos, 1969 59

Nabeel and Sameer Abraham picketing Yitzhak Rabin appearance, Oak Park, Michigan, 1969 62

Protesters at University of Colorado–Boulder, October 1973 74

Shirley Chisholm and Abdeen Jabara, 1972 92

Cover of "The Lost Significance of Sirhan's Case," pamphlet by Organization of Arab Students, University of Southern California, 1968 131

Southend residents protest in Dearborn, 1971 173

Southend Dearborn Community Council members 179

October War rally in the Southend of Dearborn, 1973 181

American Arab Coordinating Committee, protest advertisement in the *Detroit Free Press*, 1973 186

ACKNOWLEDGMENTS

Teaching at the University of Michigan–Dearborn over the past fourteen years has been a wonderfully enriching experience. Interacting with a student body composed of a substantial population of Arab Americans and working in a community steeped in Arab American culture and politics has profoundly affected my worldview as well as my understanding of American society and history. When teaching my courses in twentieth-century U.S. history, including my course on the sixties in America, I now think about diversity, inclusion, and exclusion in a different and deeper way than I had previously. Several years ago it occurred to me that the only Arab American who appears in most of the history texts I assign in my classes is Sirhan Sirhan. The genesis of this book was my interest in learning more about his place in American history, a pursuit that evolved into my captivation with the connections between the Arab world and American activism of the 1960s and 1970s. Growing increasingly cognizant of the silences and distortions surrounding Arab Americans in the field of American history, I was motivated to remedy my own ignorance and communicate my findings to other American historians who study this period. The more I investigated—discovering archival collections, learning from people on campus and in the community—the more I realized the richness and strength of decades of Arab American activism all around me. Thus, I first want to acknowledge the tremendous impact of my UM-Dearborn students, colleagues, and community on the development of both my research and my consciousness.

I also thank UM-Dearborn for awarding me a research grant that served as the catalyst for this project and providing me with the funds to hire my marvelous student Benjamin Jenkins as my research assistant. In my first interview for this project, the fascinating stories of UM-Dearborn associate provost Ismael Ahmed opened my eyes to the extent and power of the history I would encounter and made me think, for the first time, "there might be a book in this." I have benefited from the support of so many colleagues, especially my fellow history and Arab American studies faculty members, including Hani Bawardi and Ron Stockton. Most instrumental in helping me research and write this book has been my colleague and friend Sally Howell. She has generously imparted her considerable expertise in the field of Arab American and Muslim American studies, providing me indispensable insights, countless leads, astute critiques of my drafts, and, perhaps most important, encouragement when I needed it most. Words cannot adequately convey my profound gratitude to her.

The cheerful and adept assistance of many librarians and archivists made my research as well as the gathering of images for the book possible. In particular I thank Matt Stiffler and Elyssa Bisoski at the Arab American National Museum, Alexis Marks and Amber Davis at Eastern Michigan University Archives, and Malgosia Myc, Karen Wight, and many other staff members at the Bentley Historical Library for being so accommodating during my many visits. Meghan Lee-Parker at the Richard Nixon Presidential Library, David Langbart at the National Archives, Kathy Lafferty at the University of Kansas's Spencer Research Library, Edward Fields at the UC-Santa Barbara Library, Cathy Dorin-Black at the North Carolina State University Archives, and Casey Westerman at the Walter P. Reuther Library all helped me locate significant and unique sources. Special thanks go to Mohammad Hassan Bakhti at the University of Utah's Marriott Library for his tireless assistance in providing me with materials from the Fayez Sayegh Papers. The University of Michigan–Dearborn's interlibrary loan staff helped me procure many materials, including microfilm collections, in a smooth and timely manner. I am indebted to Marlene Gordon, UM-Dearborn's skilled visual resources curator, for helping me in a pinch when I needed a high-quality scan of a photograph for the book.

My conversations and correspondence with many activists and scholars have been invaluable in tracking down and fleshing out information for the book. Many thanks to Hatem Abudayyeh, Carol Haddad, Therese Saliba, Michael Fischbach, Randall Sarafa, Warren David, Lealan Swanson, David Good, and Joe Borrajo for providing me with useful leads and encouragement. Akram Khater, Matt Stiffler, Maurice Jr. Labelle, and Barbara Aswad gave their time and expertise in commenting on earlier drafts of conference papers or chapters. Louise Cainkar's comments on the entire manuscript were very helpful. I am deeply indebted to Salim Yaqub not only for his exhaustive and perceptive review of my manuscript but also for generously sharing sources and vital observations with me.

I am enormously grateful to all the activists who granted me interviews and deepened my understanding of this period. In particular, I could not have written this book without the assistance and encouragement of Nabeel

Abraham and Abdeen Jabara, whose stories, struggles, and commitments are woven throughout this research. Both were unfailingly helpful and open-handed with their time, experience, and personal source material.

Brandon Proia at the University of North Carolina Press has been incredibly attentive and supportive. I could not ask for a better editor in guiding me through this process. Thanks also to Jay Mazzocchi, Jad Adkins, and other production and editorial staff members at UNC Press for their professionalism.

This book has been immeasurably improved by the skilled editing and conscientious counsel of my dear old friend and brilliant editor Charlotte Weber. Charlotte, I cannot thank you enough for your steadfast friendship and wisdom. Many other good friends supported me during this labor of love, especially Victoria Clement, Jill Engel, Carla Vecchiola, Henry Healey, and Melissa Stull. My devoted, talented husband, Bob, and our teenaged sons, Isaac and Sam, provided me with needed distractions and much laughter and love. As always, I deeply appreciate my parents' unflagging love and support.

Introduction

Carrying signs and banners proclaiming "Jewish People Yes, Zionism No," in November 1973 hundreds of Arab American autoworkers and their supporters picketed an event in Detroit at which the Jewish organization B'nai B'rith was honoring United Auto Workers' president Leonard Woodcock. Plans for the protest had been building for several weeks, emanating from demonstrations held in reaction to the war fought between Israel and several Arab nations in October 1973. The October demonstrations that took place in Dearborn, Michigan, home to the largest concentration of Arab Americans in the United States, focused on championing the Arabs' fight along with protesting American support for Israel. In Dearborn and across the country, Arab American political mobilization on behalf of Palestine had escalated since the Arab-Israeli War of 1967, when Israel had defeated its Arab opponents and displaced hundreds of thousands of Palestinians.

Arab American autoworkers now charged their own union with complicity in Israeli actions. In the course of the protests held in October 1973, demonstrators revealed that the United Automobile Workers (UAW)—the union to which many Arab American workers belonged—had invested in Israeli bonds. Building on the momentum generated by the October War demonstrations, Arab American activists organized the protest against the B'nai B'rith fund-raising event to pressure the UAW to both divest its Israeli bonds and recognize the pro-Palestinian position held by its Arab American workers. Seeking to appeal to African Americans, whom organizers considered allies in the struggle to protect minority workers' rights in the auto plants as well as the broader struggle for Third World liberation from capitalism and imperialism, the American Arab Coordinating Committee ran an advertisement in Detroit's leading black newspaper explaining that "purchase of Israeli bonds is regarded by these [Arab] workers similarly as a UAW investment in racist South Africa would be regarded by black workers." The ad, which also ran in other media outlets, invited all rank-and-file union members and anyone opposing the UAW's holding of Israeli bonds to join the demonstration.[1]

The protest was a success. After substantial media attention in Detroit, the UAW local in Dearborn divested its Israeli bonds. For the activists, however, this was only the beginning. Those involved in the Arab Workers Caucus (AWC) kept up their agitation against the UAW by drawing connections between Israel's treatment of Palestinians, U.S. corporations' exploitation of the Arab world, and Arab workers' experience in the United States. The AWC called on Arab Americans to mobilize against "big Auto companies and sell-out union officials," just as Palestinians were fighting Zionists. AWC activists reached out to African American and leftist labor organizations in an attempt to build a dissident coalition and proposed a set of resolutions advocating the rights of Arab American workers and the liberation of Palestine at the national UAW convention in 1974. Although the AWC's challenge at the convention failed, the national UAW eventually sold portions of its Israeli bonds and took steps to improve relations with Arab American workers.

This book tells the story of the rise of Arab American radical activism that these protests exemplified. Characteristic of this wave of activism, mainly taking place in the wake of the Arab-Israeli War of 1967, was the attempt to draw a connection between conflicts in the Arab world and injustice in the United States, and efforts to construct alliances with non-Arab activist groups. The ideas and strategies of key Arab American organizations and activists—primarily in support of Palestine but also on behalf of their own rights in the United States—help illuminate the emerging alliances between Arab American and other anti-imperialist and antiracist movements of the late 1960s through late 1970s. Building on activist and scholar Michael Suleiman's important essay "The Arab American Left," this book concentrates on a fusion of first-, second-, and third-generation Arab Americans who were nationalist, leftist, and secular in orientation, placing the development of a transnationalist Arab American Left in the context of "the movements" of the sixties and seventies.[2]

While most Arab Americans in the 1950s and 1960s were not visibly active on Arab issues, Arab American mobilization around a shared Arab identity and political concerns preceded the 1967 Arab-Israeli War. The earliest Arab American organizations dated back to the early twentieth century and included the New Syria Party (1926–30s), the Arab National League (1936–39), and the Institute of Arab American Affairs (1944–50). These groups attempted to unify Americans of Arab origin and mobilize their political action, chiefly in support of Arab (or Syrian) nationalism and Palestinian independence. Historian Hani Bawardi demonstrates that global and domestic developments during World War II were particularly instrumental in forming a political identity that linked Arab and American spaces. The swell of activism after the 1967 war thus built upon an ongoing history of Arab American political consciousness.[3]

I necessarily use an expansive definition of "politics" when considering Arab American activism in this period. The number of Arab Americans was quite small in the 1960s—estimates range from 1 to 1.5 million (about 0.5 percent of the U.S. population)—making it impractical to effectively translate their activism into electoral politics.[4] My study of politics thus emphasizes Arab Americans' collective action and consciousness-raising, which they directed both to their own communities and to the larger American public. Undertaken by activists who established national and local Arab American organizations, this form of activism encompassed public demonstrations, distribution of advocacy literature, and, in a more local context, a neighborhood struggle against urban renewal along with labor union agitation. Their main objective was to mobilize Arab American communities in support of an Arab political or humanitarian cause, usually connected to the Palestinian resistance movement. But some Arab Americans overlaid American class and racial justice politics onto their larger project of advocating for justice in the Arab world, emphasizing the transnational nature of their radical activism.[5]

Some Arab American organizations also sought to influence American public opinion and policy making outside of Arab American communities by promoting general awareness of Arab political perspectives. Although radical activists aimed to raise the consciousness of all Americans, their principal strategy was to generate support among their likeliest and potentially strongest allies: other American leftist groups. They hoped support from the Left would validate their evolving anti-imperialist, antiracist ideology. Recognizing the small size of the Arab American population, they believed that strength in numbers, represented by these leftist coalitions, would eventually translate into meaningful changes in American attitudes and policies toward Arabs throughout the diaspora.

Keenly attuned to the twists, turns, and tragedies of Middle East politics, Arab American activists were thus shaped both by events overseas and by cultures of protest within the United States. As a consequence, the activists' attachment to the Arab world could prove internally divisive and debilitating, especially when Arab countries and parties clashed with one another.[6] Nevertheless, the issue that most united and galvanized Arab Americans—across differences of generation, social class, religion, and national origin—was their shared outrage over the dispossession of Palestinian Arabs through the establishment of the state of Israel.[7] Viewing Zionism as a form of European colonialism, most Arabs considered the U.N. partition of Palestine and subsequent creation of Israel as an intolerable usurpation of Palestinian Arabs' right to self-determination. After the *Nakba* (catastrophe) of 1948, in which nearly 700,000 Palestinian Arabs were forcibly expelled or fled from their homes during the first Arab-Israeli war, Arabs throughout the diaspora continually called for Palestinian refugees' right of return and the replacement of the Jewish state with a secular state for Palestinians and Jews.[8] Zionists and their supporters countered with a powerful message that reminded the world of the historic persecution suffered by Jews—most recently and horrifically in the Nazi Holocaust—and defended their right to establish their own nation in the Holy Land, where they had maintained a presence for thousands of years. They rejected Palestinian Arab claims to the land (if they recognized their existence in the first place) and portrayed the refugee problem as a consequence of the decision by surrounding Arab nations to declare war on the nascent state rather than accept partition.

For reasons that are complex and varied, most Americans have found the Israeli narrative more compelling. As John B. Judis writes, "Israel occupied a special place in America's moral imagination."[9] Anti-Semitism in the United States declined markedly after World War II, while support for Israel surged as Americans became aware of the horrors of the Holocaust and viewed the new Israeli state as an underdog, surrounded by multitudes of threatening Arabs bent on the destruction of Jews. Although pernicious stereotypes of Jews dissipated, negative depictions of Arabs, circulating since at least the 1920s in American popular culture, persisted and magnified. As the Cold War intensified and America became increasingly dependent on oil from the Middle East, Americans tended to view Israel as its only reliable ally in a region they considered vulnerable to Soviet influence. When Israelis handily beat Arab military forces in the 1967 war and occupied new territory, displacing hundreds of thousands more Palestinians, the vast majority of Americans cheered their victory, and Presidents Lyndon Johnson and Richard Nixon increased American military support for Israel. Harsh denunciation of Israel by activists opened them to the charge of anti-Semitism, often estranging them from American progressives who had been very welcoming to American Jews. Headline-grabbing incidents of Palestinian terrorism and the Arab oil embargo fueled anti-Arab sentiment. Throughout this period, widespread sympathy for Israel in the United States resulted in the suppression of Arab political perspectives from mainstream discourse and the proliferation of negative perceptions of Palestinians and their supporters.[10]

At the same time that the increasingly pro-Israeli climate produced a hostile environment for supporters of Palestine in the United States, sympathy for their cause increased elsewhere in the world. After the 1967 war, radical Arab American activists advocated Palestinian liberation in solidarity with the Palestinian resistance groups (fedayeen) operating abroad. Simultaneously, the fedayeen were forming alliances with Third World liberation groups in places such as Algeria and Cuba, while most American-based leftist groups were also growing more oriented toward Third World struggles. Through ideological and personal connections, the Arab American Left became plugged in to the global Third World Left.[11] However, while their unequivocal support for Palestinian liberation situated the Arab Left and, by extension, the Arab American Left, at the center of the global Third World Left of the period, they were relegated to the periphery of the American political arena in the late 1960s and 1970s.

Although this book focuses on "radical" activism—which I define as supporting leftist governments throughout the Arab world and armed guerrilla revolution to establish one secular state in all of Palestine, as well as advocating coalitions with other groups and movements aligned with Third World nationalism—diverse political ideologies existed among Arab Americans. In the decade after the 1967 war, radical activism was most prominent, but there were Arab American activists and organizations that held more moderate positions in support of Palestinian self-determination and Arab progress, distancing themselves from revolutionary Marxist and nationalist movements in the United States and globally. Generally mirroring the trajectory of radicalism in the civil rights era, the Arab American Left waned over the ensuing decades, and this more moderate, yet still assertive and progressive, approach to Middle East politics and Arab American civil rights came to characterize most Arab American advocacy. Between this deradicalization and developments in the Middle East, by the 1990s Arab American political organizations began to win more support among mainstream liberals, broadening their support beyond the Far Left.

DESPITE THE MARGINALIZATION OF Arab Americans during the 1960s and 1970s, this era was pivotal to the production of their political consciousness, as well as the ongoing formation of Arab American identity out of diverse generational, geographic, and religious strands. During these years, Arab Americans were also developing new conceptions of citizenship, claiming the full rights and sense of belonging as citizens of the United States in relation to their conceptions of themselves as citizens of the Arab world seeking justice in their homelands.[12] Understanding this diasporic sense of citizenship among a growing number of Arab Americans in the 1960s and 1970s crucially engages the emerging field of comparative civil rights scholarship, in which Arab Americans have thus far been invisible.[13]

Arab American political action should be understood as part of the American experience of flourishing racial and ethnic minority rights activism of the 1960s and 1970s, especially as it converged with anti-imperialist ideology. However, as has been emphasized by scholars who have studied the civil rights movements of groups such as Puerto Rican and Asian Americans, it is important to recognize that Arab Americans' particular history of racialization and distinctive experiences of injustice in their homelands and in the United States shaped a form of activism that was distinct, especially in their focus on developments in the Arab world and their confrontation with Orientalist stereotyping.[14] Nevertheless, their practice of oppositional politics in various arenas across the United States and attempts to form alliances with non-Arab activist groups marked the beginning of their integration into the political culture that surrounded American communities of resistance.[15] By examining the ways that Arab American organizations situated themselves in civil rights and anti-imperialist discourses of the 1960s, this book seeks to bridge the gap between the particularized history of Arab Americans and the broader history of American social movements.

Before I go further, it is important to recognize the internal differences and inconsistencies in the constructed category "Arab American." In fact, before the 1960s, most Americans of Arab heritage rejected the term, and even now the label is problematic for many who prefer to identify with a specific national, ethnic, or religious community or who reject association with any identity other than "American."[16] Scholars have carefully examined how multiple factors, such as the time period of settlement in the United States along with particular class, national, kinship, and religious backgrounds, have shaped the diverse orientations and experiences of peoples who emigrated to America from Arab nations.[17] Nevertheless, I am going to use the term "Arab American" with the acknowledgment that I am simplifying a complex reality.

In defining radical Arab American activists as the subject of my study, I am focusing on people of Arab heritage who resided permanently in the United States and were secular, ideologically leftist, and avidly pro-Palestinian. They were a mixture of people from Christian and Muslim traditions, but religion was not a prominent feature of Arab or Arab American nationalist activism in this period.[18] With some important exceptions, they were well-educated elites. Admittedly, these characteristics meant that they constituted a subset of the Arab American population, but the phenomenon of a small, politicized minority operating at the forefront of activism has been true of most communities with an activist tradition.[19]

While my emphasis is on politically active Arab immigrants who settled in the United States and their descendants, I recognize that the boundaries between the categories "Arab" and "Arab American" are sometimes indistinct. In the second half of the twentieth century, Arab migrants often journeyed back and forth between the Arab world, the United States, and other nations. This movement throughout the diaspora invigorated Arab American activism but makes a precise definition of "Arab American" difficult. Some groups of immigrants, especially Yemenis, never intended to stay in the United States and resisted an identity as hyphenated Americans, but most nevertheless remained and became settlers, not "sojourners."[20] Arab students who attended American universities comprise the most significant "in-between" group in my study. While some did remain in the United States for a substantial period, if not permanently, most of them intended to return to the Arab world after completing their education.[21] Still, during the time they did spend in the United States, many were politically active, and some interacted with Arab Americans as well as other American activists. Thus, I include Arab students at American universities in my examination of Arab American activism.[22]

IMMIGRANTS FROM THE Arab world first came to the United States in noteworthy numbers in the late nineteenth century. Chiefly from the area called Greater Syria, they were overwhelmingly Christian (of Greek Orthodox and Eastern Catholic sects) and from peasant backgrounds. Many became peddlers as they settled in the United States, while some found industrial work in factories, such as those of the Ford Motor Company, and others made a living as farmers. Early scholarship on this first wave of Arab immigrants asserted that they and their children did not publicly claim an Arab American identity, portraying them as largely assimilated into American culture, generally straightforward in their adoption of a white racial identity, and readily following a path of upward socioeconomic mobility.[23]

This depiction of the first wave has been revised by scholars who have documented the existence of early politicization and attention to Arab nationalism among many Arab immigrants, seen especially in their formation of short-lived organizations in the 1910s–50s that were entirely directed to homeland politics, principally advocating Syrian nationalism and Palestinian independence.[24] Sarah Gualtieri challenges the overriding narrative that holds that the early wave of Arab immigrants uniformly claimed a white racial identity and easily assimilated into white American culture, arguing instead that the immigrants (largely Syrians) experienced a fluid racial identity "in between" white and nonwhite and that their experience of acculturation was complicated and selective and involved a complex "interplay of homeland and migratory identities."[25] In her study of the Palestinian community in Chicago, Louise Cainkar identifies a pattern of partial assimilation, or "measured adjustment to American life," as immigrants who had arrived before World War II began experiencing upward social mobility in the 1950s and 1960s.[26]

The next wave of Arab immigrants came to the United States during the twenty years following World War II. These were primarily university students and professionals who thus entered American society with a more privileged position than had the previous wave. They came mainly from Lebanon, Syria, Iraq, and Egypt, and more Muslims were represented in this migration. This wave also included substantial numbers of Palestinian refugees from the *Nakba* of 1948. Politically, many of these migrants had a close affinity with Arab nationalist movements and were especially supportive of Egyptian president Gamal Abdel Nasser, who promoted Arab independence and challenged Western powers in the Arab world. Although they maintained these perspectives, most Arabs who came to the United States in the 1950s and early 1960s were integrating into American professions and institutions—at least until the 1967 war, which generated surprise and resentment among them at Americans' enthusiastic support for Israel and disdain for Arabs.[27] Simultaneously alienated, disillusioned, and moved to action by the Arab loss in the war, many Arab Americans in the second wave became instrumental in the formation of the Association of Arab American University Graduates, the principal organization of this period, and other manifestations of secular, progressive activism in the 1960s and 1970s.[28]

Yet another wave of Arab migrants began arriving in the United States in the late 1960s, usually fleeing wars and other disruptions in the Arab world, especially the 1967 Arab-Israeli War, subsequent Israeli occupation of Arab territories, the civil wars in Yemen (1962–70) and Lebanon (1975–90), and the Iran-Iraq War (1980–88). Their emigration was greatly facilitated by the Immigration and Nationality Act of 1965, a major shift in America's immigration policy which significantly increased immigration to the United States from countries outside of western Europe. Ethnically, economically, and religiously diverse, they included professionals and peasants, Yemenis, Palestinians, Iraqis, Lebanese, and other national groups. Many more Muslims were represented in this wave than in previous emigrations from the

Arab world. In general, they were more apt to maintain their cultural and religious traditions and political affinities to their homelands than had earlier waves, and some felt so alienated from American society that they resisted any assimilative tendencies. Their open assertion of their Arabness (and/or Muslim identity) was enabled by the changing environment in American society which was much more conducive to authentic expressions of cultural nationalism and ethnic identity.[29]

The post-1967 wave's immediate experiences with upheaval and struggle in the Arab world facilitated a stronger bond with the diaspora while injecting both radicalism and a sense of urgency into the Arab American community. By this time, the grandchildren of the first wave were largely disconnected from their Arab origins, but in the wake of the 1967 war, which occurred at the same time that Americans of diverse races and ethnicities were embracing a hyphenated identity, some members of the third generation rediscovered their roots and embraced an Arab political consciousness.[30] Arab students at American universities comprised an important bridge group in this political and cultural exchange. Although the older Arab American communities remained largely separate from the second and third waves of newcomers, when interactions did occur, they often produced a heightened sense of Arab American identity and attendant political activism.[31] In turn, second- and third-generation Arab Americans provided the recent Arab immigrants an entrée into American political culture and, in some cases, afforded contact with non–Arab American activist organizations and communities. These collaborations were instrumental in producing a loose Arab American advocacy movement starting in the late 1960s and continuing through today.

Many politically active Arab Americans in the 1960s through the 1980s tended to fall into two categories. One group was entirely focused on Arab world issues, detached from American political life, and convinced that Americans would never support Arab positions. The other was so assimilated into American culture that they lobbied for Arab issues without grasping the extent of American anti-Arab bias. Anthropologist Nabeel Abraham has labeled these two categories of activists "isolationists" and "integrationists" and argues that both approaches proved ineffective and reinforced the marginalization of Arab Americans in American society and politics.[32]

While accepting this delineation and recognizing that some of the activists I study tended toward isolationism in their insularity and confined attention to their Arab homelands, I posit that a middle space between these two categories existed and grew over time. Several key activists in this period maintained their focus on the Arab world, principally Palestine, and engaged in a fundamental critique of America's anti-Arab attitudes and practices, while at the same time becoming quite involved in non-Arab political issues in the United States in an attempt to build anti-imperialist, antiracist coalitions. Furthermore, they became increasingly attentive to the problems and interests of Arab Americans in America ("here") and merged those concerns with their activism on Arab world issues ("over there") to develop their transnational political practice. Although I cannot claim that this strategy was effective in transforming American foreign policy or overturning most Americans' anti-Arab prejudices, I do argue that Arab American activists who endeavored to bridge Arab and American political spaces did make meaningful strides in generating support for Palestine and other Arab positions, at least from many Americans on the Left, and thereby diminished (without erasing) their marginalization in American political culture. Over time, many activists toned down their radical, revolutionary rhetoric and adopted more moderate positions on Middle East peace, advocating some compromise with Israel, which gained them more integration into mainstream American politics by the early 1990s.

DESPITE THE DIVERSITY OF Arab Americans' identities and politicization, they have in common the experience of anti-Arab stereotyping and persecution. A long history of distorted Orientalist discourse has depicted Arabs as variously exotic, erotic, savage, uncivilized, and incapable of autonomy.[33] Culturally based stereotypes of Arab peoples, deployed in the service of Western hegemony, were amplified in the last third of the twentieth century as Americans increasingly viewed Arab nations as enemies to the United States and Israel. While anti-Arab prejudice became especially pervasive and damaging after September 11, 2001, the stigmatization heightened in the aftermath of the 1967 war when many Americans increasingly grouped people of Arab heritage together, regardless of their citizenship or whether they resided in Arab nations or in the United States, and viewed them as threatening and suspicious. When factions of Palestinian guerrilla fighters, namely, Black September and the Popular Front for the Liberation of Palestine, undertook terrorist actions abroad in the 1970s, many Americans reacted by stereotyping all Arabs as terroristic. Because the Arab American population was small and largely unnoticed, the attitudes of other Americans toward people of Arab descent were rarely shaped by actual interaction but instead by Americans' perceptions of Arabs in the Arab world.[34]

Ironically, when disparate groupings of Arabs in America encountered the larger culture's scrutiny and homogenization of them, they were increasingly brought together in solidarity as Arab Americans to contest the dominant paradigm. Even many Americans of Arab heritage who had largely assimilated over generations found themselves subject to insults and stigmatization, which intensified their consciousness of their Arab identity and cognizance of Arab political conflicts. Increasingly, the Arab world, especially Palestine, formed an important part of their ideological geographies. For some, an enhanced appreciation of Arab American identity in the midst of intimidation and prejudice also served to escalate their political activism as Arab Americans, collaborating with more recent Arab immigrants and, to a lesser extent, with non-Arab anti-imperialists to advocate for justice throughout the diaspora.[35]

Several writers use the word "racism" to describe the prejudice and discrimination experienced by Arabs and Arab Americans. Many Arab Americans dispute that the label applies to them, first because Arab is not a racial category but a "cultural and linguistic group," and second because of their historically ambivalent relationship to whiteness.[36] Some Arab Americans have embraced a racially white identity in certain contexts yet rebuffed it in contexts when whiteness is associated with "cultural loss."[37] As with other groups in the United States, their racial identity has constantly shifted. Arab Americans' malleable racial identity, along with their relationship to nonwhite groups in America, is complicated by the circumstance that the U.S. Census Bureau considers people of Arab heritage to be Caucasian, yet other Americans tend to regard Arab Americans as not wholly white.

The process of racialization, however, is different from that experienced by most other minority groups in the United States because Arab Americans' racial "otherness" has been more firmly associated with geopolitical relations between the United States and the Arab world. More recently, especially since the Islamic Revolution in Iran in the late 1970s, the racialization by Americans of people from the Arab world has been intertwined with widespread negative perceptions of Muslims.[38]

Essentially, Arab Americans have not fit neatly into America's racial categories. As Louise Cainkar has observed, their experience of being "not quite white" has caused Arab Americans to experience "the double burden of being excluded from whiteness and from mainstream recognition as people of color."[39] Nevertheless, as demonstrated in this book, many Arab American activists in the 1960s and 1970s did perceive themselves as racially nonwhite and viewed Arabs as victims of racism. They endeavored to make common cause with other racial minority groups in America in order to construct a broad civil rights coalition that also opposed U.S. and Israeli racism and imperialism in the Third World.

ALTHOUGH DIFFERENT HISTORIES, demographics, and processes of racialization produced stark disparities between Arab Americans and other ethnic minorities in the United States, Arab Americans' radical activism in the 1960s and 1970s shared significant similarities with the activism practiced by members of other racially marginalized groups during that era.[40] The 1967 war coincided with a period of intensifying ethnoracial nationalism and Third-Worldism in U.S. oppositional politics. Such groups as Latino Americans and Asian Americans, who, like Arab Americans, had histories of intermittent activism stretching back to the early twentieth century, approached their collective political work in the late 1960s with new vigor, influenced by black nationalism and an escalating ideology of global solidarity among people of color. In a process that paralleled the cultivation of an Arab American identity in this era, many groups were forging pan-ethnic identities out of isolated and sometimes antagonistic national identities, as seen, for example, in activists bringing together Japanese, Chinese, Korean, and Filipino peoples in pan-Asian organizing in several West Coast cities. These pan-ethnic identities were consciously situated in a Third World space and, according to Laura Pulido, "reinforced" the status of Asians and Latinos "as nonwhites."[41]

Like Arab American leftists, these Third World activist groups in the United States were antiracist, anti-imperialist, and usually Marxist. Furthermore, most of them confronted specific issues around which Arab Americans also organized, such as agitating for workers' rights in a racialized capitalist system, fighting urban renewal plans aimed at destroying ethnic neighborhoods, and protesting government surveillance and harassment as well as other violations of marginalized groups' civil liberties. Often they practiced their activism in a local context by forming community centers to serve ethnic neighborhoods, at which they met their people's needs with legal counseling, language classes, health clinics, and free breakfast programs—a phenomenon that evolved in a similar way among activists who formed the Arab Community Center for Economic and Social Services (ACCESS), a community center in an Arab immigrant neighborhood near Detroit in the early 1970s.[42] Activists in different communities were aware of the campaigns and rhetoric of other social movements and borrowed them freely. These community-based manifestations of activism demonstrate the power of the local to shape identities and social movements.

Many communities of color were not just localist but also transnationalist in their politics. For instance, Puerto Rican activists advocated for the independence of the island alongside their struggle for Puerto Ricans' civil and economic rights in the United States. In their study of the Asian American movement, Michael Liu, Kim Geron, and Tracy Lai explain that activists combined "homeland issues" with "collective action for labor rights in fields and factories, [and] efforts to end discrimination through the legal system" in the United States. They argue that the Vietnam War and "other international contests . . . drove Asian American activism."[43] Corresponding to the homeland orientation of some Arab American organizations, a few of these Third World groups, such as the Mexican American organization Centros de Accion Social Autonomo (CASA), were so focused on political justice in their respective homelands that their insularity cut them off from the organizing outreach of other ethnicities.[44]

Efforts at building coalitions among different minority groups often faltered on the shoals of exclusivist nationalism or competition between marginalized communities for limited resources. Comparative civil rights scholarship demonstrates that maintaining Third World alliances among disparate groups, even when they were committed to shared ideology, has proven difficult.[45] These patterns of intergroup friction or simple indifference also hindered Arab Americans' relationships with other progressive and minority groups in America.

Nevertheless, despite their tenuous nature, coalitions among American ethnoracial justice movements multiplied in the late 1960s and 1970s and, in the words of historian Sherry Smith, produced a powerful "cross-fertilization of ideas, techniques and partnerships." She continues: "Some historians will emphasize the limitations of these coalitions. I prefer to emphasize the remarkable fact of their existence at all."[46] Along with Smith's book on the coalescence of American Indian activism with other movements in the 1960s, more recent studies of American social movements emphasize flourishing connections between organizations representing different racial and ethnic groups, usually contingent on the determined work of individual activists who reached across racial lines and promoted cross-identification and collaboration. For instance, Johanna Fernández examines the critical role played by African American activist Denise Oliver in bringing together elements of the black and Puerto Rican movements. In similar fashion, Arab

Americans' networks with non-Arab organizations were also usually predicated on the outreach of individual activists. Fernández posits that "racial and ethnic crossover . . . may have been more common in the movements of the 1960s than we currently acknowledge, a mingling that is not yet reflected in the historiography of the Black Power movement." While extensive borrowing of discourse and tactics as well as demonstrations of mutual support occurred, rarely did activist groups merge into unified, multiracial organizations. Instead, organizations tended to maintain their distinct ethnic or racial identities as they formed coalitions with one another.[47]

Besides providing spaces for interaction among like-minded people, a major impetus for establishing coalitions was cultivating strength in numbers so as to effect real change. For instance, Smith argues that "given Native Americans' relative demographic insignificance, they all realized they could not do it alone. . . . In short, the support and even active participation of sympathetic non-Indian people proved essential to any possible reform." Similarly, Pulido writes that Asian American activists "realized that given their group's size they had to forge coalitions with others to achieve anything."[48] Wide-ranging leftist alliances were manifest in the Puerto Rican solidarity movement, the Black Panther Party's Rainbow Coalition, anti–Vietnam War protests, Third World feminism, the movement for Native American rights, solidarity with the Cuban Revolution (the Venceremos Brigade), and the Third World Liberation Front at San Francisco State and other universities, among many other causes and issues. Although Arab American organizations were not closely involved in most of these alliances, several Arab American activists and their organizations positioned themselves in these networks, and by the mid-1970s, the Palestinian solidarity movement had begun to take its place in the milieu of American leftist coalitions.

Nevertheless, nearly all historical studies of American social and political movements of that period screen out Arab Americans and the Palestinian cause. Usually, the only Arab American who appears in historical accounts of the 1960s is Sirhan Sirhan, the Palestinian American who assassinated Robert F. Kennedy, and American historians typically omit a contextual discussion of the Arab-Israeli conflict when covering the assassination. Indeed, discussion of the 1967 war is absent from many American histories of the decade. Ethnic studies literature about that period dutifully examines African American, Latino American, Asian American, and Native American activism, inscribing those four groups as the ethnoracial categories requiring analysis and comparison. In her book *Soul Power: Culture, Radicalism, and the Making of a U.S. Third World Left*, Cynthia Young "analyzes the ideas, art forms, and cultural rituals of a group of African Americans, Latino/as, Asian Americans, and Anglos who, inspired by events in the decolonizing world, saw their own plight in global terms." Young does not, however, include the Arab-Israeli conflict as part of the anticolonial struggle that contributed to this emerging Third World perspective, nor does she consider Arab Americans as one of the groups also experiencing this awakening.[49] Laura Pulido's important book *Black, Brown, Yellow, and Left: Radical Activism in Los Angeles* exclusively focuses on the same ethnoracial groups as does Young, with fleeting recognition of Arab Americans' existence in Los Angeles in this time period.[50] Several studies have examined African Americans' relationships with Arabs in the Arab world, but they neglect consideration of African Americans' interaction with Arab Americans, rarely acknowledging that people of Arab origin lived in the United States and that some of them were active in U.S. organizations and mosques that advocated positions on Palestine shared by many African Americans.[51]

While Arab Americans constituted a small population and their activism was admittedly not as prominent as the activism of these other Third World groups in the United States, their almost complete omission from studies aimed at capturing the histories of marginalized communities is striking.[52] Although their invisibility in scholarship owes in part to their demography, I think it also derives from Americans' general antipathies toward Arabs, an attitude which is linked to discomfort with, if not outright opposition to, Arabs' and Arab Americans' support for Palestine and hostility to Israel. My book aims to begin filling in some of these silences and overcoming these disinclinations by integrating Arab Americans into the larger narrative of American progressive activism in the 1960s and 1970s and thereby closing the gap between Arab American history and American history.

IN THE 1960S AND 1970S, Arab Americans lived in every region of the United States and, like many twentieth-century immigrant groups, were concentrated in major urban areas. Key Arab American organizations, especially the Association of Arab American University Graduates (AAUG) and the Organization of Arab Students of the United States and Canada (OAS), were national in structure and had chapters in most American cities and universities. Therefore the scope of my study, especially as I concentrate on those organizations, is national; moreover, when I examine the interactions of activists with global issues, organizations, and leaders, my analysis is transnational. However, I also examine Arab American activism through a local lens by concentrating heavily on Detroit and its suburb Dearborn,

INTRODUCTION 15

Michigan. By the 1980s the Detroit area featured the largest concentration of Arab Americans, with the greatest number residing in Dearborn, and it was an internally diverse community, encompassing the multiple waves, generations, national origins, religions, and social classes that compose the unwieldy category "Arab American."[53] Although most Arab Americans in the area did not embrace the radical politics I highlight in my study, pockets of deeply committed Arab American activists and political organizations flourished in and near Detroit, making Arab American activism there arguably stronger than in any other area of the country.

Detroit as an epicenter of Arab American activism is reflected in archival collections in southeast Michigan libraries, principally the papers of several important Arab American activists, including Abdeen Jabara, held at the Bentley Historical Library at the University of Michigan in Ann Arbor; the papers of the AAUG, housed at the Special Collections Library at Eastern Michigan University in Ypsilanti; and papers at Wayne State University's Walter P. Reuther Library that document the activities of the Organization of Arab Students chapter at that university in the city of Detroit. I supplemented these rich archival collections by conducting interviews with Arab Americans and a few non–Arab American allies who had been active in the Detroit area in the 1960s and 1970s, including Abdeen Jabara, Ismael Ahmed, Barbara and Adnan Aswad, Nabeel Abraham, George Khoury, Mike Hamlin, Gloria House, and Joel Beinin. Many of these activists and archival collections, especially the AAUG papers, simultaneously reflect the national level of Arab American political activity. I located evidence of Arab student activity in a few university archives across the country, including the University of California at Berkeley and the University of Kansas, and I interviewed individuals who were active in localities outside of Detroit, such as Sheila Ryan and George Cavalletto in New York City and Khairy Abudayyeh and Ray Hanania in Chicago. Undoubtedly, much more documentary evidence and many more former activists' stories need to be captured to add to our understanding of Arab American activism in this period, especially in locales outside the Detroit area, but this book is intended to synthesize knowledge that has already been revealed about this era in Arab American studies literature, add more concrete details to fill out the historical record, and suggest some avenues for analysis that allow for integration with the broader comparative literature on American and global New Left activism.

The first part of this book explores the significance of the Palestinian-Israeli conflict to Arab American and American leftist activism, especially in the wake of the 1967 war. I begin in Part I with an analysis of the AAUG that concentrates on the organization's convergence with and divergence from Third World Left organizing and discourse. In the second chapter I conduct a similar analysis of the OAS's role in fostering the radical Arab American "movement" in connection to the Third World New Left, starting with a brief account of the organization's history in the 1950s and early 1960s. I focus on its activism and outreach in the late 1960s at several universities, with emphasis on the OAS chapter at Wayne State University in Detroit and its associations with other anti-imperialist groups. Chapter 3 delves further into the intersections among African American, New Left, and Palestinian ideologies and activism in this period, exploring not only the convergences but also emphasizing tensions and ambivalences.

Part II of the book concentrates on the increasingly hostile climate faced by Arab American activists in this period. First, I look specifically at Sirhan Sirhan and examine how his assassination of Robert F. Kennedy, his subsequent trial testimony about Palestine, and the U.S. media's treatment of Sirhan and the Israeli-Palestinian conflict affected the environment for pro-Palestinian activism in the United States. The case underlined the predicament of activist Arab Americans as they sought to generate sympathy for the Palestinian plight while growing numbers of Americans were equating "Palestinian" with "terrorist." Many Arab Americans, as well as much Arab American scholarship, responded to the thorny situation by screening Sirhan Sirhan out of their consciousness. The fifth chapter takes on the federal government's violations of Arab Americans' civil liberties in the 1960s and 1970s, with particular attention to the Nixon administration's program Operation Boulder, instituted in the wake of the murders by Palestinian commandos of Israeli athletes at the 1972 Olympics in Munich. Operation Boulder, which instituted rigorous checks on Arab immigrants' visas, operated under the auspices of the newly created Cabinet Committee to Combat Terrorism, which also ordered the Federal Bureau of Investigation and the Immigration and Naturalization Service to investigate dozens of Arab American activists as well as all Arab students in the United States for connections to terrorism.

Part III describes aspects of the gradual "Americanization" of Arab American activism as it moved beyond its initial "homeland" orientation to incorporate issues of local and national concern to Arab American communities. In chapter 6 I explore how a transnational Arab American political consciousness played out on the local level by examining a series of interrelated developments in Dearborn, Michigan, starting with a multiethnic movement involving Arab Americans that fended off the city's plans to destroy a working-class, immigrant neighborhood called the Southend, and the creation of ACCESS, a grassroots community center that served Arab Americans in the Southend and organized around Arab world issues. Out of these developments emerged a movement to protest the UAW's investments in Israeli bonds. Tied to these activities was the activism of the Arab Workers Caucus, a radical labor organization that continued the challenge to the UAW and combined the struggles for workplace justice and justice for Palestine.

The last chapter extends the story of Arab American activism through the 1980s and concentrates on its linkages to more mainstream progressive political organizing. The Palestine Human Rights Campaign, active in the late 1970s; the American-Arab Anti-Discrimination Committee (ADC), established in the early 1980s; and the Arab American Institute (AAI), formed in the mid-1980s, made concerted efforts to collaborate with liberal religious and political organizations, especially with moderate African Americans. The close work of the ADC and AAI with Jesse Jackson's Rainbow Coalition and his campaign for the Democratic Party presidential nomination signaled the inclusion of Arab Americans in mainstream civil rights coalitions.

Over time, by the early twenty-first century, most Arab American political organizations had grown less oppositional and more accommodationist to mainstream American political attitudes—but the history of Arab Americans' more radical activist past has not fully been told. This book will impart a better understanding of how, in the decade after the 1967 war, Arab Americans coalesced as communities, operated within the milieu of transnational leftist activism, asserted their identities as diasporic citizens, and campaigned for justice in the Arab world and in the United States.

PART ONE

THE IMPACT OF THE 1967
ARAB-ISRAELI WAR ON
ARAB AMERICAN ORGANIZING
AND THE AMERICAN LEFT

1 Progressive Activism after the June War
The Association of Arab American University Graduates

Two principal Arab American organizations, the Arab National League and the Institute of Arab American Affairs, had dissolved by 1950, but in the early 1950s the Organization of Arab Students of the United States and Canada (OAS) established chapters at many North American universities. As discussed in chapter 2, from its inception the OAS was political and secular in nature and promoted nationalism and socialism in Arab societies.[1] Along with the mainly foreign students in the OAS, many Arab Americans were inspired by Gamal Abdel Nasser's pan-Arab movement in the 1950s and 1960s. Transnational politics were kept alive in these years by a minority of Arab Americans who remained attentive to Palestine, a commitment that was further encouraged by recent immigrant arrivals who brought a keen awareness of Arab national issues.[2]

Thus, the political consciousness that would coalesce in the wake of the June War was not wholly new. Nevertheless, many Arab Americans remember 1967 as marking a critical turning point for the Arab diaspora. The establishment of the Association of Arab American University Graduates (AAUG) that year occurred against a backdrop of renewed organizational activity among Arab Americans. Of all the groups that mobilized Arab Americans' political sentiments in the 1960s and 1970s, the most visible with the most avowedly secular and pan-Arab foundation was the AAUG. In its radical advocacy of Palestinian nationalism, the nonsectarian AAUG quickly became the most influential organization on the Arab American Left.

IN JUNE 1967, Israel, with support from the United States, launched a preemptive strike against Arab troops who were massed on its borders in an apparent prelude to attack. Within a week, Israel had not only crushed the Egyptian, Syrian, and Jordanian forces but had captured sizable new swaths of Arab territory and displaced hundreds of thousands more Palestinians from their homes, adding to the already massive refugee population created by the 1948 Arab-Israeli War. The Arab-Israeli War of June 1967 was a devastating defeat for the Arab powers. While Israelis experienced a boost in power and morale, and enthusiasm for Zionism swelled throughout the Jewish diaspora, unity among Egypt, Syria, and Jordan collapsed. Both Gamal Abdel Nasser's leadership and the idea of pan-Arab nationalism were largely discredited in the eyes of most Arabs. In this difficult period of defeat and disillusionment, the Palestinian resistance movement became radicalized. In the newly occupied territories of the West Bank and Gaza Strip and especially in their bases inside Jordan, Palestinian resisters regrouped and vowed to undermine Israel with armed struggle to liberate all of Palestine and achieve Palestinians' right of return.[3]

The main Palestinian resistance group in this period was al-Fatah (the Palestinian National Liberation Movement), led by Yasser Arafat. Formed in 1959 by Palestinian exiles in the diaspora, Fatah believed that, to carry out genuine self-determination, Palestinians themselves must be at the forefront of the liberation struggle.[4] After the 1967 war, Fatah gained control of the Palestine Liberation Organization (PLO), and Arafat became the PLO's leader.[5] The PLO, an umbrella organization that encompassed many political groupings, coordinated the guerrilla resistance to Israel. It also struggled against neighboring Arab nations, first Jordan and then Lebanon, whose leaders sought to repress militant Palestinian activity within their territory. By the early 1970s, the PLO was advocating a one-state solution to the Palestinian question.[6]

The June War, the surge of the Palestinian resistance movement, and a subsequent war between Israel and Arab nations in October 1973 all galvanized Arab Americans and encouraged them, within both newly created and long-established organizations, to mobilize on behalf of Palestinian liberation. As one AAUG member characterized the impact of the 1967 war, the Arab defeat provided a "jolt" that caused Arab Americans who had arrived decades earlier to become more intimately connected with their identity as Arabs and the politics of "the Arab condition." According to AAUG leader Naseer Aruri, this awakening involved a realization that Americans were ignorant of Arab issues and viewpoints and a recognition that Arab Americans lacked "a forum from which to correct the information gap." Rashid Bashshur, a founding AAUG member, felt that the war "left the vast majority among us with a deep sense of deep frustration with the lame Arab response intellectually, militarily and politically as well as the lack of fairness in the U.S. media, the double standard of American policy, and the slanted public opinion." To Arabs throughout the diaspora who had advocated Arab nationalism in the 1950s and 1960s, the devastating loss represented a victory not only of U.S.-backed Israeli imperialism but also of conservative Arab regimes over the progressive tide in the Middle East.[7]

As the most significant and influential of the organizations founded shortly after the 1967 war, the AAUG was comprised of a select group of Arab Americans who formulated a sense of ethnic identity, fostered community solidarity, and practiced progressive and transnational politics. While it was not the only pan–Arab American political organization established in the wake of the war, the AAUG was distinguished by its commitment to an anti-racist, anti-imperialist analysis of Arab world problems and its adherence to an ideological orientation aligned with the global Left. The association's intellectual influence would outlast the organization itself.

The founding of the AAUG in the immediate aftermath of the 1967 war was a major advancement in Arab American organizing. The association was unique as an activist organization, for although it was a progressive group that represented an ethnic minority in the United States, it restricted its membership to college graduates in that community.[8] The AAUG's influence was most significant in its practice of activist scholarship that promoted an Arab, and usually leftist, perspective. This mission, as well as the AAUG's academic bent, was not unlike the political culture of the early New Left which largely originated and flourished within universities and among graduate students and professors. As historian Kevin Mattson demonstrates in his book *Intellectuals in Action: The Origins of the New Left and Radical Liberalism, 1945–1970*, activist scholars involved in endeavors such as the journal *Studies on the Left* continually grappled with the question, "What role should intellectuals play in effecting political change?" Their answer was that intellectuals should define a different kind of political engagement, one that provoked political change by engaging the American public in "deliberative and democratic" exchanges that provided citizens with the knowledge to confront the power structure. They intended their lectures and publications to be "forums for alternative politics," and the "teach-in" became an important tool in their activist approach to effecting change.[9] Arab American professionals and intellectuals at the forefront of the AAUG similarly participated in this tradition of the larger American Left (and its subset, the New Left) and likewise believed they had a responsibility to promote political progress by cultivating truthful understanding in the public sphere. This ambitious, idealistic undertaking made the AAUG the most important organization in the emerging Arab American Left. However, also like the wider Left, the maintenance of an intellectual stance and the use of largely academic discourse limited its audience and efficacy, instead fostering insularity.[10]

Although its main focus was solving Arab world conflicts, the AAUG also addressed issues faced by Arabs in America. By attempting to counter what its members saw as rampant misinformation about Arabs in American discourse, the organization confronted the heightened stereotyping and discrimination that many Arab Americans faced in the period after the 1967 war. The AAUG fostered a sense of Arab ethnic identity and pride across different generations and nationalities of Arab Americans at the same time that it helped integrate them into the American political arena and connect with organizations and leaders representing other American minority groups and positions.

The AAUG positioned its advocacy in the frameworks of the American and global anti-imperialist Left. Its aim was to show Americans that Zionism was a form of colonialism rather than a legitimate expression of Jewish nationalism, which many Americans presumed it to be. Year after year its members passed resolutions and produced literature supporting the Palestinian resistance movement led by the PLO and the formation of a single secular and democratic state in Palestine. Furthermore, the AAUG championed socialist nationalism and gender equality throughout the Arab world and saw the movement for Palestinian liberation as the vanguard of a wider transformation in the region. AAUG activists understood these as "people's struggles" emblematic of revolutionary movements throughout the Third World and regularly declared, as articulated in a typical resolution, "support for and solidarity with all other deprived and oppressed peoples everywhere struggling for their human rights."[11] One member, Ghada Hashem Talhami, later asserted: "Perhaps, the greatest success of the association was the establishment of the Palestine issue as the central question of the Arab liberation struggle, as well as one of the Third World's premier conflicts. The association helped elevate the Palestinian struggle to the status of a premier universal human rights issue."[12] This ideological position impelled AAUG leaders to reach out to eminent Third World leaders throughout the late 1960s and 1970s in a quest for solidarity and support. Although the AAUG's progressive focus on Palestinian and Arab world revolution in the context of global anti-imperialism served as the linchpin that mobilized Arab Americans in the organization, after several years of bitter conflicts between Arab nations, its transnational orientation also created friction among its members who hailed from different Arab states, disputes that became increasingly divisive by the 1980s and contributed to the organization's decline.

The Landscape of Arab American Organizations in the 1960s and 1970s

Although it would become the most significant, it is important to note that the AAUG was not the only organization devoted to promoting Arab perspectives in the United States. The other major Arab American organization established in the period between the 1967 and 1973 Arab-Israeli Wars was the National Association of Arab Americans (NAAA). In contrast to the AAUG, the NAAA intended to be explicitly political. Established in 1972, it was registered as a political lobbyist organization based in Washington, D.C., and sought to promote an "even-handed" U.S. policy toward the Middle East that would preserve Arab, Israeli, and American interests. Comprised mainly of Arab Americans who had come to the United States earlier in the twentieth century and dominated by prominent Arab American businessmen, many of whom were members of the Republican Party, the NAAA tended to promote more moderate positions than did the AAUG, marked by its advocacy of coexistence with Israel at its pre-1967 borders. Furthermore, its political style was decidedly less radical. It eschewed associations with leftist and minority activists in America and aimed to be the Arab counterpart to the American Israel Public Affairs Committee (AIPAC).[13] In its first few years, the NAAA did not make a major impact, and according to political activist Gregory Orfalea, who later worked for the NAAA, the organization was "not well-known by the community it claimed to serve."[14]

In addition to the pan-Arab AAUG and NAAA, numerous organizations existed at various points in the mid- to late twentieth century that specifically represented Palestinian Americans. Before the 1960s, most Palestinian groups in the United States had been small and narrow in scope, usually focused on village-based networks. The American Federation of Ramallah, founded in 1959, functioned mainly as a cultural and charitable organization for the thousands of Palestinians who had immigrated to the United States from the (then) largely Christian city of Ramallah, near Jerusalem in the West Bank. According to Rabab Abdulhadi, in the 1960s the federation "deliberately seemed nonpolitical on the surface," and although the federation preserved private expressions of Palestinian identity, it tried to blend into the "melting-pot" orientation dominant in American society. But over the course of the 1970s, the organization became more overtly political and nationalist in orientation, as well as more open in displays of Palestinian cultural heritage. Abdulhadi attributes the more public and political practices of "Palestinianness" to "the expanded U.S. space for oppositional and alternative Arab and Palestinian expressions." One marker of the organization's politicization in the 1970s was the appendage of "Palestine" to its title.[15]

Several other Palestinian American organizations were explicitly political from the beginning. The Arab American Congress for Palestine (AACP), founded in 1965 with chapters in Washington, D.C., Detroit, Chicago, and Los Angeles, was devoted to promoting American understanding of the Palestinian cause. It never attracted a substantial membership, and according to George Khoury, briefly a member of Detroit's AACP, it suffered from domination by recently arrived older Palestinian men whose political imagination was limited and whose public relations strategies were inadequate.[16] Additional Palestinian organizations with a nationalist political bent sprung up around the country after the 1967 war, such as the Palestine Committee in Boston, the Palestine House in Washington, D.C., and the Democratic Committee for Palestine in New York City.[17] A leftist pro-Palestinian newspaper, *Free Palestine*, was based in Washington, D.C., and edited by AAUG leader Abdeen Jabara in the early 1970s, although it was officially unaffiliated with the AAUG.[18] Many organizations with a humanitarian purpose also emerged in the few years following the 1967 war, chiefly to provide aid to Palestinian refugees. These included the United Holy Land Fund, originally based in Detroit, and the Palestine Arab Fund, based on the West Coast.[19] Other important sites for Arab and Palestinian American political communion were the Arab community centers that formed in several U.S. cities in the 1970s, such as Dearborn, Chicago, and San Francisco, where a bookstore specialized in Arabic leftist books. (Chapter 6 features an analysis of the Arab community center ACCESS in Dearborn.)[20]

Arab Americans affiliated with cultural and religious organizations also expressed political positions on Palestine and other Arab world issues during these years, though like the NAAA the stance of these groups was generally more moderate than that of the AAUG. The Midwest Federation of American Syrian-Lebanese Clubs, an organization that had traditionally concentrated on social and cultural activities, started to become more overtly political in the early 1970s. Its 1973 convention featured workshops about Arab American political influence and protection of Arab American civil rights, and in 1974 the federation, led by president Minor George, declared its support for the PLO. When the Cleveland chapter of the federation awarded its Distinguished

Service Award to Frank Maria, a moderate Arab American leader active in the Antiochian Orthodox Archdiocese of North America, Maria gave an address in which he sharply criticized America's support for Israel and called on federation members to be more politically involved.[21] Furthermore, the Antiochian Orthodox Christian Archdiocese, to which many Syrians and Lebanese in the United States belonged, began to convey its support of Palestine. After the 1967 war, the church's support was mostly confined to humanitarian aid, but in 1974 it echoed the Midwest Federation in calling for the United States government to recognize the PLO.[22]

Some Muslim mosques and organizations to which Arab Americans belonged similarly became more likely to issue positions on political matters, especially related to Palestine. Through their involvement in the Federation of Islamic Associations (FIA), an umbrella organization formed in 1952 by a number of American mosques, Arab American Muslims interacted with politically oriented Islamic organizations in the Arab world and were attentive to the plight of Palestinian refugees. In 1965, the FIA declared a position supporting Palestinians in the Israeli-Palestinian conflict but was careful to present its declaration as "not political but [a] humanitarian stand."[23] By the early 1970s, the FIA's main publication, the *Muslim Star*, was incorporating much more political content than it had in the 1960s, including an article by AAUG leader M. Cherif Bassiouni titled "The Arab-Americans: Future Political Force." Furthermore, the FIA joined secular Arab American organizations in sponsoring statements protesting U.S. policies in the Middle East and advocating Arab Americans' civil liberties.[24] Similarly, the Islamic Center in Washington, D.C., developed a political identity in the 1970s when its director, Dr. Muhammad Abdul Rauf, participated in a forum on the Palestinian-Israeli conflict and wrote a letter to the editor of the *New York Times* critical of Zionists.[25] In contrast, American Muslims associated with the Muslim Student Association, which was linked to the Muslim Brotherhood and later helped form the Islamic Society of North America, were unreceptive to Arab nationalism. Isolationist in their orientation toward American society, they purposefully avoided political action.[26]

The AAUG's Educational Approach

The AAUG took the lead in promoting Arab, and especially Palestinian, nationalism in the American public arena, particularly in intellectual circles. Its establishment is traced to an August 1967 meeting in Ann Arbor, Michigan, at which a small group of Arab American professionals and scholars agreed to channel their frustration over the June War into the founding of a new organization. They were most concerned with refuting what they saw as distorted and unfair depictions of Arabs in the American media and public discourse. During subsequent meetings that year in Chicago, they named the new organization the Association of Arab American University Graduates and elected its first slate of officers. The founders decided the AAUG's main objectives would be to generate scholarly study of Arab world issues, disseminate this information to an American audience, promote understanding between Americans and Arabs, and facilitate Arab American community building, particularly among Arab American intelligentsia and professionals. Some members also thought they should use their combined expertise to assist Arab countries with resource development.[27]

Psychologically and politically, the AAUG combatted the defeatism felt by its members, most of whom were recent immigrants, although more American-born Arabs joined over time. Most Arab professionals in America felt increasingly alienated from a country they perceived as anti-Arab, especially when they witnessed Americans' support for Israel in the June War. The AAUG provided a space for them to express themselves freely and interact with one another. In a transnational formulation, they linked the struggles of their peoples in their homelands for justice and self-determination to, in the words of AAUG leader Ibrahim Abu-Lughod, the emergence of Arab Americans "from oblivion to assert our rights to live in this country with dignity and freedom."[28] Lifting members' morale, the AAUG would allow them to move forward with an agenda promoting fair and constructive U.S. policy toward the Middle East, progress in the Arab world, and especially the liberation of Palestine from Israeli occupation. As the years went on, many AAUG members came to agree with fellow member and sociologist Elaine Hagopian, a daughter of Syrian immigrants who grew up in Cambridge, Massachusetts, that this agenda had been "utopian" because it naïvely assumed that by organizing themselves and providing accurate information on Middle East conflicts, the elite Arab Americans in the AAUG could effect substantial transformation in U.S. policy and within the Arab world.[29]

Its founders made three crucial decisions at the organization's inception. First, the AAUG would not be a political lobbyist organization; instead, as Abu-Lughod stated in his presidential address, it would "operate as an educational and cultural association," with the understanding that its "educational and cultural activities would and should have significant political implications and consequences." According to Bashshur, "the AAUG was established as a social movement, not a political platform."[30] Second, as indicated by the organization's title, its membership would be drawn from professionals and academics with Arab ethnic heritage, and thus it was not intended to be a grassroots organization seeking mass membership among all classes of Arab Americans. Third, the AAUG would be nonsectarian and secular in orientation, with a democratic structure and rotating leadership. The organization endeavored to maintain cohesion and unity among members who hailed from multiple Arab countries, principally Lebanon, Syria, Iraq, Egypt, Palestine, and Jordan, and religious faiths. Furthermore, it involved women in leadership positions from the beginning, and many members, including Janice Terry, claimed that it was not a patriarchal organization, although in the late 1970s an AAUG women's caucus contested that notion (as discussed later in this chapter).[31] Three years later, when AAUG membership had reached 700, organization president M. Cherif Bassiouni declared that the decision to maintain nonsectarianism and pursue pan-Arab solidarity had been vindicated, proclaiming: "The AAUG is . . . living proof that regionalism and ideological differences can be transcended. We are a microcosm of the ideal Arab society and stand as evidence that such a viable and unified society can exist." From its site in the diaspora, the AAUG was intended to provide leadership and serve as a paragon to the Arab world.[32]

The AAUG was oriented toward national and international levels of discourse and influence, rather than focusing locally. While it sought to establish active local chapters across the United States, it really set its sights on making an impact on national-level attitudes and policies. Indeed, the AAUG was the most active and visible national Arab American organization of the late 1960s and early 1970s.[33] Many former members emphasize the organization's significance in heightening diverse Arab Americans' consciousness of their Arabness and promoting a more cohesive sense of pan-Arabism in an atmosphere of openness and inclusiveness.[34] Nevertheless, when encouraging these identifications and ties, the AAUG did not actively recruit working-class and nonprofessional Arab Americans to its project or attend to the lived experiences of nonelite Arab Americans in their communities. Sociologist and former AAUG member Baha Abu-Laban has identified the unique, somewhat paradoxical nature of the organization, noting that it was clearly elitist in membership yet maintained a grassroots sensibility with its progressive stances and diversity of national origins, religions, academic disciplines, and professional pursuits.[35]

Although the AAUG founders' decision to restrict membership to college graduates became more controversial over time, most members initially accepted and even embraced the rationale. In their view, the organization would be most effective if it influenced other American elites. To command respect from such an audience, they believed, it must impart an air of professionalism and credibility. An organization of Arab American scholars and professionals would produce authoritative, well-reasoned arguments that persuasively promoted the Arab point of view and, in the words of Elaine Hagopian, would "challenge, by scholarly production and example, the Orientalist image of Arabs and Muslims as ignorant, conniving, lecherous, and bloodthirsty peoples." Some members may have thought that by counteracting prevalent stereotypes of Arabs, the AAUG could protect all Arabs—elite and nonelite, in the Arab world and throughout the diaspora—from American prejudice. Adnan Aswad, a founding member, was convinced that restricting membership to professionals was the best way to avoid debilitating sectarianism and counterproductive passions that he had experienced in other organizations, namely, the Organization of Arab Students. He wanted to maintain an atmosphere of high-toned, dispassionate professionalism. In a similar vein, AAUG member Fauzi Najjar argued that the distorted and demoralizing context of 1967 called for the "Arab American intelligentsia" to step up and play "a role of effective leadership" to reach American people "by calm, objective, and proper methods."[36]

Hagopian's impression was that useful, reliable knowledge about the Arab world was sorely lacking in the 1960s and that the "broader Arab-American community was itself ill-informed." Association members felt that as scholars and professionals in America, they were the best equipped to generate change by producing and disseminating knowledge. "We reasoned," Bashshur remembers, that "the road to justice is accurate information" and that well-educated Arab Americans possessed a "special obligation" to provide it. The AAUG, Hagopian maintains, was guided by the conviction that a national organization's deployment of Arab "brain power and talent" would be the only viable approach to "challenge and displace Zionist ideological tracts." "Hence," she continues, "a grassroots organization was not seen as the first step to take in Arab-American organizational efforts. Providing knowledge was."[37]

To accomplish this educational goal, some of the first actions the AAUG took were to create the Publications Committee as well as the Speakers Committee and organize a conference of scholarly presentations. The Speakers Committee worked with the Organization of Arab Students to identify speakers with authority on Palestine and the Arab world and to schedule their engagements at campuses and cities throughout the United States. These presentations were often part of "teach-in" forums that also addressed the Vietnam War and other imperialist conflicts. Several AAUG members frequently gave talks around the country in the late 1960s through 1970s to counter misinformation and inject the Arab point of view in scholarly and political debates. Former AAUG leader Fouad Moughrabi remembers, "For over twenty years most of us devoted a great deal of time and energy trying to mobilize Arab American communities and we crisscrossed the continent giving speeches. I think I probably spoke at every major University in North America and to nearly every Arab-American community, and so many churches." According to Abdeen Jabara, "These pioneers provided a cadre of campus speakers, writers, analysts and critics for a nascent group in the peace and antiwar movement in the United States that was raising questions about American policy toward the Middle East."[38] Additionally, the association's annual conventions provided an important forum in which scholars studying Arab and Arab American issues could present their work and interact with one another.

Many members consider the AAUG's support of research on Arab world issues to be, as Janice Terry has stated, the organization's "most enduring legacy." Because the AAUG's scholarship embraced a nationalist and often leftist perspective and was produced and disseminated with an overall purpose of provoking social justice and progressive policies, it represented a central component of the organization's activist agenda. In its ongoing effort to circulate its expertise, the AAUG published a newsletter and later an academic journal, *Arab Studies Quarterly*.[39] Furthermore, it established Medina University Press, which put out AAUG conference proceedings, information papers, and monographs on diverse Arab world topics. Not surprisingly, the topic most emphasized in Medina University Press publications was the Israeli-Palestinian conflict, and the analysis was usually critical not only of Israel and U.S. policy in the Middle East but also of conservative Arab states.[40] The AAUG also produced other types of materials, such as a filmstrip about Palestine, for distribution to universities, churches, and other organizations, and some local chapters engaged in projects to guide the educational curriculum in their school districts.[41]

The association's publications and projects intentionally challenged Orientalist and Zionist conceptions of the Arab world that were prevalent in academia as well as in other educational and media settings in the United States. It was joined in this endeavor by leftist scholars and activists, mainly of non-Arab descent, who founded the Middle East Research and Information Project (MERIP) in 1971 and began publishing *Middle East Report* (later *MERIP Reports*). The AAUG had a few members in common with MERIP, including activist and scholar Samih Farsoun, and in 1974 the AAUG decided to provide financial support to MERIP. Farsoun advocated this formal tie, explaining that MERIP "constituted [the AAUG's] major link to the American Left."[42]

The AAUG's promotion of this alternative literature helped to eventually break down barriers in the academic arena and by the 1980s achieved marked acceptance of the Arab perspective, at least in the field of Middle Eastern (or Near Eastern) studies. In Terry's view, the AAUG presented "material and analysis generally refused by mainstream publishers who tended to accept only manuscripts that agreed with narrow, Western oriented perceptions of the Middle East." Michael Suleiman reports that many AAUG members found the Middle East Studies Association (MESA) "not friendly or even hostile to Arab and Arab American issues." Similarly, Bassiouni considered the Middle Eastern studies field to have been "pre-empted by those favorable to Israel."[43] Barbara Aswad, professor of anthropology at Wayne State University, was one scholar of Middle East and Arab American studies who found a publication outlet in Medina University Press during the 1970s. Although Aswad was uncomfortable with the AAUG's elitist definition of itself as an organization confined to intellectuals and professionals, she understood that its focus on the academic arena provided an important function by helping scholars like herself succeed in universities and gain legitimacy for analysis which went against the grain and which could potentially influence U.S.-Arab relations.[44]

Advocacy of Palestinian Struggle and Third World Liberation

In much of its published scholarship, organizational resolutions, and other public statements since its founding in late 1967, the AAUG has adamantly supported the struggle for Palestinian nationalism and aligned itself with the PLO. However, the association never expressed affiliation with any of the fedayeen factions. Its first convention, held in Washington, D.C., in 1968, highlighted the theme "Arabs in America" and featured three presentations about Arab communities in the United States and Canada. The 1974 convention also focused on Arab Americans and their relationships with American society, especially in the wake of the October War of 1973. But most former AAUG members tend not to remember that early emphasis on Arab Americanism; in their minds it quickly became overshadowed by the AAUG's focus on Palestine. Indeed, prominent Palestinian spokesman Fayez Sayegh delivered the first convention's keynote speech, addressing the Palestinian armed struggle.[45] At the next year's convention, in Detroit, almost all the presentations were about Palestine, and at the conclusion of the meeting, AAUG members issued a resolution expressing strong support for the Palestinian resistance movement. The statement endorsed "the current necessary recourse of the Palestinian People to a war of national liberation of their historic homeland and their aspiration to liberate all sections of the Palestinian community from all manifestations of racial and national prejudice and other forms of human oppression." The statement went on to tie the Palestinian struggle to a more expansive Arab revolution as well as to liberation movements throughout the Third World.[46]

Despite the broad consensus within the AAUG about the importance of the Palestine question, its members disagreed over how radical a position to take. During a debate at the 1969 convention, some members expressed concern that an initial draft of the resolution was too "Marxist" and would alienate an American audience.[47] A member of the radical Committee to Support Middle East Liberation (CSMEL) who attended that convention perceived a split between radicals and moderates in the AAUG, with radicals advancing a Marxist analysis of Western oppression of the Arab world and the need for Arab socialist revolution in league with people's revolutions throughout the Third World. According to the CSMEL observer, the radicals viewed America as working closely with Israel to advance an imperialist design on the Arab world, whereas moderates in the AAUG believed that the United States had basically good relationships with Arab nations, relationships that were now threatened by Israel's actions. The CSMEL member noted that while the convention "reflected in many ways the militant spirit of the Palestinian guerrillas and their supporters" and featured speakers who passionately extolled the Palestinian resistance movement to enthusiastic applause, the AAUG leadership drew back from an indictment of U.S. imperialism. As a mark of their moderation, the leaders appealed to "the American liberal tradition" as the preferred approach for contesting Zionism.[48] A year later, a *New York Times* correspondent who attended the AAUG's 1970 convention noted disagreements among members over both Palestinian resistance methods and criticism of the United States; however, members were unified in their support for a Palestinian state that would include all the territory claimed by Israel.[49]

As time went on the AAUG became increasingly critical of Arab governments viewed as antiprogressive and as obstacles to the Palestinian cause. After the June War, Syria and Egypt demonstrably retreated from their commitment to pan-Arabism and Palestinian independence. Members of the AAUG were especially upset by King Hussein's expulsion of the PLO from Jordan in 1970–71. The AAUG's criticism of conservative Arab states can be seen in a series of telegrams Abdeen Jabara, president of AAUG in 1972, sent to Egyptian officials that year, criticizing their suppression of students' peaceful protest as well as the government's religious intolerance.[50] The organization's evolving position is also evident in its 1972 resolutions that "reaffirm[ed] its unconditional support of the Palestinian Revolution and the inalienable rights of the Palestinian people to engage in a war of national and social liberation for the establishment of a free, Democratic and secular state of Palestine" at the same time that it "condemn[ed] unequivocally the irresolution and the hypocrasy [sic] displayed by the regimes in the Arab States in conducting their struggle against Israel and its supporters." Thus the AAUG continued to voice its support for nationalist revolution not only in Palestine but also throughout the entire Arab world, calling for secular, "unified and progressive," and, in some members' hopes, socialist Arab states.[51]

Even more expansively, the AAUG stood in support of liberation movements around the world and wanted the Palestinian and Arab liberation movements to act in solidarity with peoples who were "committed to the destruction of colonialism." In taking this stance, it was echoing the PLO's position as it sought connections with anticolonial revolutionaries around the world. Although some ideological dissension existed among AAUG members on this point, in its resolutions and other public statements the association firmly positioned its support for Palestine in the context of Third World liberation, a cause that was becoming predominant among the American and global New Left at the end of the 1960s.[52] For many AAUG members, Third World anticolonialism was a genuine ideological commitment and reflected their analysis of how developments in Palestine, and more generally in the Arab world, were interconnected with global anti-imperialism in the second half of the twentieth century. Tactically, projecting the Palestinian struggle as an integral component of Third World revolution allowed the AAUG to attract broader support from the diverse anti-imperialist Left.

Following its declaration of support for the armed Palestinian resistance movement, the AAUG's 1969 convention resolution implored "all people of the world who believe in the right of national communities to determine their destinies and who are opposed to imperialism to rally behind the Palestinian Revolution." And to further promote a coalition with global anti-imperialist groups, the resolution declared: "Just as the Palestinian Revolution has publicly supported the just cause of the people of Asia, Africa, Latin America and the Black Community in the U.S., the Association registers its gratitude for the continuing support of these communities to the legitimate aspirations of the Palestinian People." Naseer Aruri remembers, "We perceived our own struggle for emancipation in the Arab world in the same context of the anti-colonialist movement in Vietnam and the struggle for equality in the United States. We often considered our movement as part and parcel of the fight for third world liberation."[53]

The leadership provided by two early presidents, Ibrahim Abu-Lughod and Abdeen Jabara, was crucial to shaping the AAUG's radical advocacy of a Third World stance. Many AAUG members attested to the importance of Abu-Lughod's guidance and vision, in particular. Born in British Mandate Palestine in 1929, as a young student Abu-Lughod had protested British control and Zionist incursion. He fled in 1948 and made his way to the United States, where he attended the University of Illinois and was active in the Organization of Arab Students. He eventually gained his Ph.D. in Middle East studies from Princeton and spent most of his career at Northwestern University as a professor of political science and founder of the Institute of African Studies.[54] Operating firmly within a leftist framework, Abu-Lughod's presidential address to the 1969 convention articulated the organization's allegiance to Third World anti-imperialism and placed the advocacy of Palestinian independence in the context of liberation movements across the globe as well as in the United States. He stated, "Though more of our activities have been concerned naturally with attaining equality for the Arab Americans and for Arabs in general, we have actively supported the just struggle of other groups to attain equality in systems where they are oppressed. We stand united with our Black Brothers in the United States, South Africa, Rhodesia and in Mozambique and Angola; we stand united with the gallant fighters of Vietnam and with all other groups valiantly struggling against all manifestations of human struggle." Near the end of his speech he asserted, "In our deliberations on the Palestinian Revolution we have perceived the inextricable link which the Revolution has with other wars of national liberation, particularly but not exclusively in the Third World."[55]

Three years later, in his presidential address to the convention, Abdeen Jabara echoed the principle of Third Worldism and went even further in encouraging the cultivation of coalitions with other marginalized groups in the United States. Jabara, born in northern Michigan to Lebanese immigrants, was keenly interested in social justice causes in the Arab world, the Third World, and the United States throughout his youth and college years at the University of Michigan. In the early 1960s he received his law degree from Wayne State University in Detroit, and he also spent a year working for the

Palestine Research Center in Beirut before joining a Detroit law firm dedicated to civil rights. Speaking at the 1972 AAUG convention, Jabara named "Black Americans, Chicanos, Oriental Americans, young people and civil libertarians" as "natural allies" who shared Arab Americans' experience of feeling "excluded from any meaningful participation in the American decision process." During his presidency of the organization, Jabara pursued an alliance with African American organizations over their common antipathy to South African–Israeli relations, thus combining the AAUG's dedication to Third World anti-imperialism with its support for oppressed minorities in the United States. He declared that the AAUG, like other activist groups in the United States and around the world, was engaged in a "struggle against racism."[56] As discussed further in chapters 3 and 7, these attempts to create common cause with African Americans and other marginalized groups were mildly successful and continued to solidify in the 1980s.

Equally as significant for signaling and propelling the association's radical "Third World credo" (as one observer termed it) was its invitation to prominent anti-imperialist and leftist leaders from around the world to speak at its annual conventions. Fouad Moughrabi recalls, "AAUG became the arena where activists from different parts of the world came to engage in solidarity work on the Palestine question. So many came from Latin America, South Africa, and elsewhere that AAUG conventions became the principal arena where these activists caucused to plan activities and strike alliances."[57] The 1969 convention featured guest speaker Ania Francos, a French writer known for her advocacy of revolutions in Africa, Asia, and Latin America; in her address she proclaimed, "We are all Palestinians." Another guest at the 1969 convention was Eqbal Ahmad, a Pakistani anti-imperial activist whose speech strongly criticized American foreign policy; according to the AAUG's Aruri, Ahmad's address "elicited thunderous applause from an audience well in tune with the radical politics of the sixties."[58] The next year, the keynote address was delivered by Indian leader Krishna Menon and titled "The Arabs and the Third World." Menon concentrated on the parallels between the Palestinian and Vietnamese struggles.[59] Subsequent conventions welcomed Algerian, Greek, Egyptian, and Libyan anticolonial leaders; Israeli human rights activists Israel Shahak and Felicia Langer; American peace activists Rev. William Sloan Coffin, Daniel Berrigan, and Noam Chomsky; and African American activists Shirley Graham DuBois and Stokely Carmichael, among many other anti-imperialist figures. Their appearances were augmented by presentations from AAUG members, such as Edward Said, who employed a Third World analysis of Arab nationalism.[60]

Activism in the Arab World

In addition to influencing American opinion and fostering Arab American cohesion, the association conceived part of its mission to be utilizing its members' expertise and resources to encourage socioeconomic development and justice in the Arab world. Early on, the AAUG established the Link Committee to serve as a bridge between Arab professionals residing in America and Arab professionals and leaders in the Arab world. It reached out to intellectuals, business, and political leaders in Arab countries who shared AAUG's progressive ideology and attempted to assist them in creating change in their societies. Jabara regards the AAUG as instrumental in providing "a forum for thinkers, scholars, political figures, and artists and activists from the Arab world where they might not have had such a forum in their home countries," many of which were controlled by conservative regimes.[61] The association sponsored meetings in Arab countries, established a relationship with the Beirut-based Institute for Palestine Studies, and held a conference in Kuwait in 1975 that featured the theme "issues in human resource development in the Arab World." Furthermore, the AAUG promoted engagement with the Arab world by supporting humanitarian projects for Palestinian refugees and raising funds for Birzeit University in Palestine.[62]

But some AAUG members grew disappointed over their interactions with their fellow Arabs, and by the end of the 1970s, the links had dwindled. For example, Elaine Hagopian's perception was that many Arabs who attended the AAUG's conference in Kuwait did not take it seriously, and she and other AAUG colleagues became disheartened by the corruption and sexism they encountered among supposedly progressive Arabs when they held meetings in the Arab world. Hagopian reflects: "The assumption that Arabs—even some allegedly progressive Arab Regimes—would welcome their politically progressive expatriates to help free them from Western neo-colonialism was utopian."[63] Jabara also grew frustrated by the lack of results produced by the dissemination of AAUG resources in Arab countries. When presented with a proposal in 1974 to establish an AAUG branch in the Arab world, the Link Committee declined with the explanation: "Arab countries are not concerned with the same problems we are."[64] There were thus limits, it seemed, to the AAUG's ability to promote a common vision of nonsectarian nationalist progress within the Arab world.

Political Activism: Influencing U.S. Policy

Despite its self-definition as an educational organization, the AAUG engaged in political activism to a considerable extent. Its intent was to push back against Zionist representations of Arabs that were circulating in American popular and policy-making discourse and thereby influence American leaders' perspectives and actions. For example, in 1969 the AAUG placed an advertisement in the *New York Times* in the form of a letter to President Nixon urging the U.S. government to support Palestinians. Also that year, AAUG leaders sent letters to Nixon and to members of Congress and met with the assistant secretary of state to press for alternative U.S. policies in the Middle East. In 1971, the association published another political advertisement, this time in the *Washington Post*, protesting the U.S. Senate's decision to sell fighter jets to Israel.[65] Association leaders, particularly Jabara and Bassiouni, also became politically involved in protesting the federal government's harassment of Arab Americans in 1972 through 1975, as detailed in chapter 6. But internal debate existed over how openly political the organization should become, and leaders were aware that too much political activity could jeopardize the AAUG's tax-exempt status.[66]

In 1973, the year after the National Association of Arab Americans formed, the AAUG paused to assess the implications of the new organization for the AAUG's mission and role. The AAUG formed the Committee on the Future of the Association to consider whether it should increase its level of formal political activity. Chaired by Ibrahim Abu-Lughod, the committee specifically took up the question of whether the AAUG should concentrate on "ethnic politics," which it defined as using the political process to "obtain gains for or reduction of grievances of a specific ethnic group," as well as if it should emulate the practice of Zionist lobbyist groups in the United States, as it thought the NAAA was trying to do. The committee ultimately determined that such an approach would be unproductive. Unlike the NAAA, AAUG members believed that "the breach between the U.S. and the countries of the Arab Middle East fundamentally emanates out of a systemic defect in the relationship and not out of the nonexistence of a pro-Arab political lobby." The AAUG's goal was more ambitious than traditional interest group pressure politics would contain, for its overriding mission was to shift all Americans' understanding of the nature of the Arab-Israeli conflict. Devoting resources to lobbying in the absence of this shift, the committee reasoned, would be futile.[67] Embedded in this justification of the AAUG's current modus operandi was an implicit critique of the NAAA's position and method.

Continuing the critique of the NAAA, Abu-Lughod sent a memo to the committee analyzing the differences between the two organizations. He began by recommending that the "AAUG welcomes NAAA and encourage members so inclined to join it and help it in implementing its goals" because "any effort that seeks to organize Arab Americans and thereby promote their interests in this country" should be supported. He thought that the NAAA's objective to support political campaigns was a "worthwhile goal" but not part of the AAUG's mission. Thus, in that realm the two organizations were complementary, not in conflict. But Abu-Lughod emphasized that the NAAA and the AAUG did clash over their policy orientation because the NAAA intended to promote, in its leaders' words, an "even-handed" U.S. policy toward the Middle East. Furthermore, the NAAA had stated its support for UN Security Council Resolution 242, which required Israel to give up the Arab territories it occupied in the 1967 war in exchange for Arab nations' recognition of Israel's existence. In contrast, the AAUG "does not accept the position of petitioning the United States government for an even-handed policy in the Middle East. What we want is a policy clearly in favor of liberation." Further demonstrating its location to the left of the NAAA, the AAUG had "denounced" Resolution 242, which it saw as counter to the goals of the "Palestinian Revolution and the Arab Liberation Movement" supported by the association. Abu-Lughod acknowledged that in these matters, the "fundamental difference [between the AAUG and NAAA] . . . bothers me."[68]

Furthermore, he expressed disappointment that the "NAAA is not a mass organization." Like the AAUG, the NAAA was exclusive, and he thought its membership dues were prohibitively high. To better distinguish the AAUG from the NAAA, he wondered, "should we rethink the structure of the AAUG and try to make it an Arab-American mass organization?" The AAUG envisioned itself as "educators of our own Arab American communities," but according to Abu-Lughod it needed to do a "better job and more diversified one" of establishing links to those communities, and to fulfill this mission it needed more funds.[69]

Meanwhile, even without extensive fund-raising, several local AAUG chapters tried to exert a presence in their cities and universities by engaging in ongoing events and pressure tactics. Some locals were clearly more active than others, but on the whole most of them regularly sponsored speakers on Arab world issues, wrote letters to the editor and letters to politicians, tried to have their editorials published in local media, and participated in radio programs. There was a sizable uptick in local AAUG activity coinciding with the October War in 1973, and many AAUG chapters joined with other Arab

American organizations in their area to stage demonstrations in support of the Arab countries and to protest U.S. support for Israel. Another period that saw a flurry of local AAUG activity came in May 1978 to mark the thirtieth year of the *Nakba*. For example, the Los Angeles chapter cosponsored the screening of the film *The Palestinian*, produced and narrated by British actress Vanessa Redgrave, and Redgrave herself attended and spoke to the audience of over 500 people. The next day, AAUG members and other supporters demonstrated outside the Academy Awards banquet to show support for Redgrave, who had been pilloried for her support of Palestine. Also that month, the New England chapter of AAUG worked with several organizations to sponsor such speakers as notable Palestinian writer Fawaz Turki at several universities in Massachusetts and Maine, held a conference on the Palestinian-Israeli conflict, and helped stage the "Day of the Palestinian Struggle" demonstration and teach-in at Cambridge Commons near Boston. Similar events were organized by AAUG chapters in New York City, Washington, D.C., Chicago, Madison-Milwaukee, Detroit, and Minneapolis-St. Paul.[70]

Internal Conflicts and Waning Influence

Despite this ongoing activism, as the 1970s wore on, many members became increasingly dissatisfied with the AAUG, and the crusading spirit it had embodied in the late 1960s and early 1970s began to wane. While the association lasted through the 1990s and continued its emphasis on Palestinian liberation in a Third World framework, it became a shadow of its former self, and most of its early leaders transferred their activism to other organizations and endeavors.[71] Various members became disenchanted with the AAUG for diverse reasons, and they offered numerous, and often clashing, diagnoses of the organization's weaknesses. Some believed that its exclusive membership prevented the AAUG from becoming a genuinely activist force in the Arab American community. To Arab Americans who sought grassroots activism, the AAUG seemed irrelevant and removed from most of the community. Further, the AAUG's elitism seemed to contradict the organization's leftist, anticolonial political stance which touted liberation for the Arab masses.

Some AAUG members argued that it could have broadened its membership and enhanced its momentum by more effectively appealing to young Arab Americans and including more women's voices and issues. Before the 1980s, only one woman, Elaine Hagopian, had served as president of the organization. Scholar Mervat Hatem has argued that the AAUG's focus on

Arab nationalism privileged a male-centered discourse and agenda.[72] In the late 1970s, the AAUG established the Committee on the Status of Women, which led to the formation of the Women's Caucus. In 1978 organizers of the caucus sent a questionnaire to women AAUG members, and most respondents believed that women were not adequately involved in decision making in the AAUG and that the caucus should endeavor to eliminate sexism in the AAUG. (Subsequent caucus meeting minutes stated that women had been relegated to clerical positions in the association.)[73] A few women responded that the AAUG was not sexist and that if some women felt they had been peripheral then they should make a greater effort to be involved. Some respondents agreed that sexism existed in the AAUG but that more pressing political and civil rights issues demanded attention. A year later, Women's Caucus organizer Noha Ismail acknowledged this point of view, stating, "The AAUG has certainly not been forceful in its commitment to the feminist cause. But my theory is that the cause for Palestine is so overwhelming and intense that it is difficult not to allow it to overshadow all other concerns." Nevertheless, she declared AAUG women need to "speak up and let our presence be recognized."[74]

Nearly all the women who responded to the questionnaire thought that the AAUG should feature at least one panel about the status of Arab women at its annual conventions and that the Women's Caucus should establish close ties with women's organizations in the Arab world. Active for a couple of years, the caucus circulated a newsletter, encouraged more women to submit scholarly papers to the AAUG, established child care at the conventions, and encouraged one another's efforts in publicizing mistreatment of Arab women (such as Arab women prisoners in Israel) and protesting offensive stereotypes of Arab women in American media.[75] In a letter to Noha Ismail, AAUG president Fouad Moughrabi welcomed the caucus at the same time as he defended the association's record of including women in leadership positions. Nevertheless, he agreed that "more women should be active and should be represented" in the AAUG.[76]

Another critique that had materialized by the late 1970s charged that the AAUG was too narrowly focused on the Palestinian cause. To some critics, the Palestinian emphasis was a detriment because they wanted a broader commitment to Arab world issues, while others wanted a mass-based movement concentrated on the development of the identity and rights of Arabs in America.[77] Relatedly, some members felt that the association was too closely aligned with the PLO and that this alliance hampered the organization's independence as well as its political influence in America.[78] Abdeen Jabara characterizes the organization as comprising recent Arab immigrants who were entirely focused on Arab world issues and out of touch with American culture and politics. Presumably excluding himself from this characterization, he claims AAUG members had "next to no concern about what was happening in this country other than thinking about producing accurate and scientific information about the Arab world[,] that this would somehow change the American perception about that region. In short these people had next to no . . . understanding about the American political system . . . . They did see America as an imperialist power and they did see America's involvement overseas as emanating out of its imperialist interests. But that's the only way they saw America, and it was basically a support movement for . . . Palestinian struggle." Political scientist and AAUG member Michael Suleiman concurs with some of this assessment but finds more variety among AAUG members and depicts the organization as a meeting ground for third- and fourth-generation Arab Americans with the recently arrived Arabs.[79]

The AAUG's engagement with Arab diaspora politics could prove divisive among its diverse membership, such as when the AAUG criticized the conservative forces in the Lebanese Civil War, causing some of its Lebanese members to resign. Elaine Hagopian remembers that at the height of the Syrian-Lebanese conflict in 1976 she felt "we were no longer Arab-Americans with the unitary goal of justice, but separate nationalities relating to events abroad."[80] In his retrospective look at the AAUG, Suleiman emphasizes Arab Americans' diverse origins and affiliations and notes that while the Palestinian focus was initially unifying, as time went on AAUG members became increasingly divided over solutions to the Palestinian-Israeli conflict. The organization's declaration of positions on Arab world issues could thus be quite complicated and contentious within the membership. Suleiman argues that the association facilely assumed the existence of a common bond uniting all Arabs without adequately understanding or acknowledging the variance among Arabs in its own membership and throughout the diaspora, ultimately to the detriment of the organization.[81] Accordingly, the AAUG's transnational political orientation served both as its energizing force and raison d'être after the 1967 war, as well as an eventual source of fragmentation.

Another source of fragmentation came from a contingent of members who thought the AAUG's political positions were too leftist and that its engagement with Third World anti-imperialism, along with its outreach to minority rights movements in the United States, was undermining the organization's ability to represent Arab Americans and make headway on Arab world conflicts. One such member was Rashid Bashshur, who later recalled: "I thought that seeking support from other disenfranchised groups and communities would dilute our effort, detract from our primary objectives and reduce the potential for success. Worse yet, it would dismiss the legitimacy of our perspective in mainstream American public opinion. Once we are smeared as a radical group –even by association—people would simply dismiss us." Bashshur argued, "We invited left-wing and fiery speakers to our national meetings who had their own agendas. Often, they alienated many of our own people, especially the professionals and some academicians who should have been the core of the membership." Indeed, some members who had initially joined the organization because they thought it would emphasize the provision of technical expertise in fields such as engineering and medicine to facilitate development in the Arab world ended up leaving the AAUG. Adnan Aswad, another founding member who held a Ph.D. in engineering, felt this disenchantment with what he viewed as the AAUG's overemphasis on leftist politics, particularly on Palestinian revolution, and its minimization of the organization's role in Arab resource development.[82]

Jabara dismisses this depiction of significant internal dissent over the AAUG's leftist stances, including its Third World orientation. He asserts that the association committed to these positions early on and they were maintained by the bulk of the membership; the minority of members who did not fully support the ideology left the organization, thus eliminating most dissent. If the AAUG had an identity crisis, it was over how much it should be an action-oriented organization focused on Arab Americans as opposed to an academic organization focused on Arab world issues.[83] As an early leader of the AAUG, Jabara had persistently advocated establishing coalitions with other oppressed minority groups in the United States as an effective strategy for gaining political visibility and a wider network of support for Arab Americans. Though some efforts had been made in this direction, by the late 1970s Jabara had become dissatisfied with the weakness of AAUG's ties to American groups he viewed as allies. He pressed the organization to pursue this strategy in order to combat Arab Americans' marginalization in American society and thereby exert more influence both on American policy in the Middle East and on American treatment of Arabs residing in the United States.[84] So while Bashshur thought that the AAUG had gone too far in building associations with persecuted groups such as African Americans, Jabara believed it had not gone far enough.

In the 1978 *AAUG Newsletter* article "Arab-Americans and the U.S. Policy

Process," Jabara asserted that the AAUG's initial assumption that its provision of credible and accurate information would lead to major improvements in U.S.-Arab relations was faulty and naïve. He also criticized the assumption he said was held by many Arab American intellectuals which identified the main culprit of America's biased Middle East policy as the Zionist lobby, positing that once an Arab lobby supplying correct information counteracted the Zionist lobby, American policy would become more favorable to Arab interests. Jabara countered that the most important factor in determining American foreign policy was not the influence of the Zionist lobby but America's definition and pursuit of its economic interests in the region. Once Arab Americans in the AAUG and other organizations understood the economic basis of American foreign policy, he argued, they could then operate more effectively as an interest group to influence that policy. Once more, he recommended working with other groups in American society as a valuable way to achieve influence. We should "seek to ally with groups which are organized to promote interests such as civil rights, disarmament, and opposition to the role of the US as a weapons supplier. Our concern about American foreign policy can be shared with other ethnic groups, like Black Americans, Irish-Americans, etc.," he wrote. If we get "Americans from all walks of life" to publicly support Arab Americans' positions, it will go a long way toward "break[ing] down the taboo that has been placed on our concerns generally."[85] Not long after penning this prescription for Arab American political action, Jabara helped launch new organizations to embody this approach (first the Palestine Human Rights Campaign, then the American-Arab Anti-Discrimination Committee, discussed in chapter 7) and began to drift away from the AAUG.

As often occurs in activist organizations, the AAUG had lost much of its early energy and optimism after a decade of scant tangible progress toward achieving its goals. Elaine Hagopian reflects: "We were faced with the stark reality of Israeli power and U.S. government complicity. The 'we can win' attitude we had in 1967 was melting before our eyes." Janice Terry also saw external developments thwarting the AAUG's objectives, noting: "The much anticipated political and social revolutions in Arab nations never materialized. Consequently, AAUG found itself in the impossible position of criticizing Arab regimes at the same time it attempted to lobby the U.S. government and society to adopt more objective, if not more favorable policies in the Arab world. . . . Indeed, some Arab regimes were hostile to the AAUG and its position; this again stands in notable contrast to the close cooperation of Zionist forces in the US and the state of Israel." Thus, some of the AAUG's failure to produce results could be attributed to the enormous obstacles it confronted in global politics and anti-Arab sentiment in the United States, as well as to its own lack of funding and resources. Hagopian and Baha Abu-Laban believe the organization was trying to address so many problems that it became overloaded.[86]

But many leaders, including Hagopian, Terry, and Suleiman, agreed with Jabara's assessment that much of the AAUG's impotence derived from its approach, particularly its naïve faith that Arab American professionals could generate meaningful political and social change through providing credentialed information. Jabara later wrote, "It has become abundantly clear that the idea that 'if Americans only know' is not enough to change the way the United States operated in the Middle East, or elsewhere in the world, for that matter." This idealistic but flawed assumption that knowledge would produce justice was exacerbated by fragmentation within the organization, such as between local chapters and the national board, and inadequate circulation of its research. Despite its conferences, speakers, and publications, the association had limited influence aside from Arab American elites and a few corners in the academic arena. Suleiman's final assessment of the AAUG, then, is that its accomplishments rested not in the policy arena but in the personal realm, insofar as participation in the organization enhanced its members' political consciousness and identity as Arab Americans. The AAUG, he states, "gave its members a feeling of personal satisfaction for doing something to advance issues important to them" and provided a nonsectarian space for critiquing American, Israeli, and Arab policies.[87]

Another significant legacy of the AAUG was that its "pathbreaking work," in Baha Abu-Laban's words, spawned new Arab American organizations that were better suited to the geopolitical realities that the AAUG had struggled to confront. These new organizations, most prominently the Palestine Human Rights Campaign, the American-Arab Anti-Discrimination Committee, and the Arab American Institute (AAI), operated as political action groups, and except for the AAI, they sought a mass base. Hagopian credits the AAUG for "plant[ing] many seeds" that sprouted into these new activist organizations in the 1980s; likewise, Jabara praises the association for helping to "pave the way for other Arab American organizations" and for "educat[ing] an entire generation of young Arab Americans" who then went on to lead the new groups. At the same time that the AAUG helped give birth to new Arab American organizations, competition from them for members and resources hastened the AAUG's decline.[88]

THE EMERGENCE OF THE AAUG in the months after the June War demonstrated that the organizational expression of political activism, distinguished by its transnationalism, became an increasingly important feature of the Arab American experience. Like other organizations representing marginalized racial and ethnic groups in the United States, the AAUG was not immune to divisiveness. Nevertheless, its role as a national-level organization representing Arab Americans, documenting their presence, and creating a constituency from them meant that, on the whole, the AAUG unified Arab Americans and promoted their political views in the American public and academic spheres. Despite the limitations on its membership and reach, the association fostered Arab American identity in the late 1960s and 1970s by strengthening Arab Americans' ties to one another and to the Arab world. Although Palestine was central to its politics, it also emphasized the rights of people of Arab origin in the United States, and the organization approached the two issues in concert. The AAUG thus laid the groundwork for organizations in the 1980s that were more attentive to Arab Americans' civil rights and participation in mainstream American politics.

Importantly, the AAUG's advocacy of Palestinian liberation, Arab nationalism, and Arab American dignity knitted together Arab world and Arab American radicalism in the framework of a Third World consciousness that also had a hold on much of the American and global New Left in the late 1960s and 1970s. According to Abu-Laban, the AAUG's activism made it "a political player forging alliances with other organizations to promote democratic development, fair play, and human rights," both in the United States and throughout the world.[89] These connections with other oppositional and Third World groups, constructed from their common overarching commitment to anti-imperialism and antiracism, constituted a key element of progressive Arab American organizing in those crucial years, a characteristic also shared by the even more radical Organization of Arab Students.

2 Arab Students and the Politics of Palestine
The Organization of Arab Students and the Arab American Left

The 1967 war not only galvanized the Arab American scholars and professionals who became active in the Association of Arab American University Graduates (AAUG) but also intensified the politicization of many Arabs and Arab Americans studying at American universities. In the midst of this ferment, politically conscious Arab and Arab American students connected their advocacy of Palestinian resistance to the activist style and ideologies practiced by other global and American anti-imperialist and antiracist struggles prominent in the New Left movement of the period. Most of these students were members of the Organization of Arab Students of the United States and Canada (OAS), the largest and most important activist Arab student group in the United States from the 1950s through the 1970s. Other organizations, such as the Palestine Human Rights Campaign, emerged later in the 1970s to mobilize Arab American students and their non-Arab student allies. These student groups translated Arab politics into the American protest arena and developed strategies to gain visibility, legitimacy, and support from anti-imperialist, antiracist Americans whom they imagined as natural allies. In some respects, the OAS and similar organizations served as cultural brokers between the politics of Arab decolonization and the American student movement.

The OAS was largely composed of foreign students, but it is important to recognize that some intended to remain in the United States and began to identify increasingly as Arab Americans, whereas a few OAS students were from Arab American families. For example, Ismael Ahmed, a third-generation Arab American, helped form chapters at two Detroit-area universities in the 1970s, and Ray Hanania, a second-generation Palestinian American born in Chicago, led a Chicago chapter of the OAS in the 1970s.[1] Thus, when I refer to the "Arab students" of the OAS, I am referencing a mixed composition of mostly Arab along with a few Arab American students.

As with the mixture of new immigrants and second- and third-generation Arab Americans in the AAUG, the confluence of these two groups in the OAS fostered the cross-fertilization of ideas and the production of a transnationalist Arab American identity, particularly in the climate after the 1967 war. At the same time, the mixture produced tensions between activists more deeply ingrained in American society and activists oriented toward Arab "homelands."

While the AAUG was vital in mobilizing Arab Americans and representing their political positions in the national arena, the OAS also played a significant role in advocating radical Arab perspectives on American campuses. For the most part, the OAS was edgier and more militant than the more professional and academic AAUG. One marker of the OAS's militancy was its embrace of the Palestinian fedayeen factions—chiefly Fatah, but also the Popular Front for the Liberation of Palestine and the Democratic Front for the Liberation of Palestine—as contrasted with the AAUG, which only officially supported the Palestine Liberation Organization and refrained from mentioning, let alone championing, the PLO's constituent factions (especially not the Marxist guerrilla groups).[2] Further, the students' activist style was generally more provocative and revolutionary than their more reserved (though still leftist and pro-Palestinian) elders in the AAUG, which followed the pattern of generational differences within most 1960s protest movements. Nevertheless, the two organizations often worked together because they held the same overall position supporting armed struggle to liberate Palestine, and they both championed Palestinian and Arab nationalism in the framework of anti-imperialist, Third World ideology. Additionally, both the AAUG and the OAS sought to promulgate the Palestinian-Arab perspective in certain sectors of American society, especially in left-wing circles.

The importance of organized students in what can loosely be described as an "Arab American movement" corresponds with the pivotal role that activist students occupied in the New Left and civil rights movements during this period. In what historian Terry Anderson calls the "student power" movement of the 1960s, organizations such as the Student Nonviolent Coordinating Committee (SNCC) and Students for a Democratic Society (SDS) were often in the vanguard of promoting progressive social change. These rebellious, idealistic, and intellectual student activists, although small in number and fairly elitist relative to the entire baby boom generation, were crucial in agitating against racism and war and for equality and peace. And it was not just in the African American and white New Left movements where the student voice was instrumental. Studies of the Puerto Rican and Asian American movements, among many others, demonstrate the key role of students both in mobilizing the larger immigrant communities and making connections with other movement organizations.[3]

By the end of the 1960s, student activists in many groups gravitated toward Marxist theory and a Third World perspective that condemned American imperialism and idolized Third World guerrilla fighters. The year 1968, in particular, signaled the emergence of a global student Left that involved radical students of virtually all races and ethnicities in the United States, along with students from Paris to Tokyo to Mexico City, in revolt against the establishment. Matthew Shannon's study of Iranian student protest in the United States sheds light on the importance of international students in shaping transnational activism in the "global sixties." Activist Iranian young people studying at American universities connected with other leftist groups on campus, such as SDS, and used "the language of the New Left" to protest the Shah's regime in Iran.[4]

Many Arab and Arab American students also participated in this swirl of global student activism. Although the OAS comprised mostly foreign students dedicated to foreign causes, they were assimilating into the American environment of campus activism, increasingly characterized by a culture of Third World protest, in the period that coincided with the aftermath of the 1967 Arab-Israeli War. Depending on their national origin, many of these Arab students were engaging in protest activities that would not have been permitted in their homelands. By the early 1970s, at least a few of these student activists were pushing beyond campuses to engage in political organizing in Arab American communities, seen, for example, in the relationship between OAS students at Wayne State University in Detroit and the large Arab American community in Dearborn, Michigan. In her study of Arab American activism in San Francisco, Nadine Naber notes that the Bay Area chapters of the OAS were instrumental in connecting politically active Arab immigrants with one another as well as leftist groupings in the Arab world, such as the Lebanese Communist Party, and with other global liberation movements.[5] In their vocal and sometimes brazen promotion of Palestinian and Arab nationalism in American campus and community arenas, Arab and Arab American students were critical to the mobilization of an active Arab American left.

The OAS as a Political Organization before 1967

The Organization of Arab Students formed in 1952 and held its first convention that year in Ann Arbor, Michigan, chaired by Kamal A. Shair, a Jordanian graduate student at Yale University. At its inception, the organization articulated three major aims: helping its members "achieve the main purpose of their presence in the U.S., that is, to acquire the best education"; facilitating relationships among Arab students so that when they return to their countries, "they can work together hand in hand, utilizing the knowledge . . . they acquired in the United States to develop their fatherland"; and improving the "understanding between Americans and Arabs."[6] Championing Arab nationalism, the OAS focused almost entirely on issues within the Arab world, and it developed close ties to and received funding from several Arab governments. According to Yvonne Haddad, "The campus OAS chapters were utilized by the Egyptian government to recruit supporters for Arab nationalism from among Arab students at various American universities," with the aim of preparing the students for leadership roles "they would undertake upon their return to their respective countries."[7] Similarly, Nabeel Abraham dubs the organization during this period the "Establishment OAS" or "shirt and tie OAS," which served the intentions of the established Arab regimes. A marker of this relationship was the OAS's affiliation with the Arab diplomatic missions located in New York City near its national office. In the 1950s, most Arab students in the United States came from wealthy families, and their studies were financed with petrodollar funds. They were almost exclusively young men studying technical fields and finance.[8] Over the next decade, however, both American institutions and Arab nations offered more scholarship funds to Arab students, enlarging access to an American university education. Most of the Arab students remained men, but some women also traveled to the United States for schooling; indeed, a few OAS chapters were led by Arab women students.[9]

An explicitly political organization, the OAS was oriented almost exclusively toward addressing Arab world problems by advocating a range of progressive solutions, including economic planning and political unity among the Arab states, educational development, land reform, and commitment to constitutional rights. It eventually developed the motto "One Arab Nation" to represent its overriding commitment to pan-Arab political unity. But the proceedings of the first convention stipulated that the primary crisis the students should confront was the subjugation of Palestine, which organization leaders declared was "the most important single problem in the minds of Arabs everywhere, overshadowing any other problem." Out of eight sets of resolutions on subjects ranging from Arab economic development to the status of women in the Arab world, the only resolutions receiving unanimous approval were those regarding Palestine. These Palestinian resolutions called for communicating the realities of the Palestinian situation to Americans and pressuring the United Nations to ameliorate the refugee problem and prevent Israeli settlement on Arab lands.[10]

Nine years after the founding of the OAS, its *Yearbook* demonstrated that active chapters existed on most major American university campuses and served both social and political purposes. In the early 1960s, the organization claimed a membership of five thousand students. Headquartered in New York City, the national office interacted with other foreign student organizations, such as the Pakistani Students Association, the Iranian Students Association, and the Pan-African Students Union, and in 1960 it joined the African Students Union in demonstrations supporting Algerian independence and protesting France for testing an atomic weapon in Algeria. Many of the OAS chapters across the country sponsored events to publicize the struggle for Algerian independence, such as the University of Chicago chapter that held Algerian Night at the Conrad Hilton Hotel and the Massachusetts Institute of Technology (MIT) chapter that hosted a speaker from the Algerian National Liberation Front in 1960. Many chapters also planned events involving speakers, films, and exhibits to mark United Arab Republic Day and Palestine Day. Their guest speakers were often representatives of the Arab Information Center, the propaganda arm of the League of Arab States, demonstrating OAS ties to Arab countries. The students themselves gave lectures on their campuses and to local civic groups and churches, such as the Louisiana State University chapter, whose members made forty-five presentations in 1960, and the Ohio State University chapter, whose president participated in two radio talk shows that year.[11]

The OAS also engaged in outreach through its publications. Initially, the OAS newsletter was printed in Arabic, but as time went on the leaders decided to publish it in English "to acquaint our American friends who are interested in our activities." The University of Indiana OAS was one chapter that published its own newsletter in English, pronouncing it "designed to acquaint the neighboring community with the Arab world."[12] Throughout most of the 1960s the OAS also published an academic journal, the *Arab Journal*, that featured articles by scholars at American universities, Arab government officials, socialist Jews, and its own members on Arab economic development, U.S.-Arab relations, and the Israel-Palestine conflict. Though it did not have the reach or impact of the AAUG's *Arab Studies Quarterly*, which began publication in the late 1970s, the *Arab Journal* provided an important venue for scholarship on the Arab world from a progressive standpoint.[13]

Occasionally the OAS's activities created tensions and resulted in conflicts. For example, members of the Sacramento, California, chapter organized a demonstration at the screening of the film *Exodus* which began peacefully but escalated into egg throwing between the Arab students and the Jewish B'nai B'rith members in attendance. According to the OAS *Yearbook*, as a result of the fracas, "Palestine and the Arab-Israeli friction became a major street topic in Sacramento. The students' stand has drawn attention to the Palestine question by the community, state legislators, and Arab diplomats, as well as the Israeli embassy and the Northwestern States American Zionist Council." At North Carolina State University in 1959, the school's administration grew upset with the student Arab Club (affiliated with the OAS), charging that maps and pictures displayed by the club during International Week "caused unhappy feelings between the Arab and the Israeli students."[14]

As further expression of its political project, the OAS occasionally staged public protests at events boosting Israel, such as when Arab students picketed a visit to New York City by Israel's prime minister David Ben-Gurion in 1960 and picketed a fund-raising dinner for Israeli bonds in Los Angeles in 1964. Some Zionist leaders were apprehensive about the organized Arab students and sought to discredit them. At a 1964 meeting in New York City, the head of the Israel Public Affairs Committee charged that Arab students sponsored by American Friends of the Middle East and the Arab Information Center were disseminating propaganda and indoctrinating "professors and fellow students against Israel." In contrast, he stated, his committee's information campaign sought only to circulate "factual information on events in Israel and the Middle East."[15]

In addition to their political activities, most OAS chapters hosted social and cultural events, both to foster community among their members and to expose Americans to aspects of Arab culture. Most popular were the "Arabian Nights" extravaganzas. These parties could be viewed as perpetuating Orientalist stereotypes of Arab culture, but combined as they were with the organization's fund-raising drives for Algeria and lectures on Palestinian liberation, they likely contained political undertones. Some of the chapters assimilated into the social climate of American campuses, such as the University of Texas-Austin chapter, which won the campus award for most active student organization, and the University of Florida chapter whose mascot was the "Arabgator" and whose float won second prize in the 1960 homecoming parade. In its 1960 report, the University of Florida chapter stated: "Arab students are welcoming the opportunity to enroll American friends as club members." It also mentioned it had held a reception in honor of the prophet Muhammad's birthday. At least one other chapter that year hosted an Islamic event, with the Purdue University OAS throwing a party celebrating the Muslim holiday Eid al-Fitr.[16]

Meanwhile, the Muslim Student Association of the United States and Canada (MSA) formed at colleges and universities in 1963, with membership dominated by Arab students affiliated with the Muslim Brotherhood. Heavily influenced by Wahhabism, a conservative sect of Sunni Islam dominant in Saudi Arabia, the MSA rejected the political Arab nationalism that was embraced by the OAS. Much more than did OAS members, MSA members withdrew from American culture and society in their endeavor to practice strict Islam. The organization did, however, occasionally interact with African American Muslims and sought to spread their Islamist ideas to the African American sects.[17]

The Radicalizing Impact of the 1967 War

Although the OAS already had a fifteen-year history of political activism on behalf of Palestinian and Arab nationalism in the United States, the Arab-Israeli War of 1967 proved a defining moment for its members, as it did for most Arabs throughout the diaspora. As Evelyn Shakir points out, for Arabs and Arab Americans who were college students in the 1960s, the war "coincided more or less with their coming of age," when many of them were formulating political views on American policies and international affairs. According to Hatem Hussaini, who was a member of OAS at that time, the organization reacted to the Arabs' defeat not with demoralization but with increasing political radicalism. In the immediate aftermath of the war, the OAS took the lead among Arab American organizations whose "main interest was to strengthen the revolutionary and popular movements in the Arab world and to assist them in mobilizing the masses to defeat Israeli aggression," Hussaini recalls. Organization members met for three intensive days in July 1967 and emerged with a set of "detailed proposals for Arab political and economic action," which they dispatched to leaders of many Arab states.[18]

Especially influential in the students' radicalization was the Palestinian resistance movement; support for the resistance was at the center of the OAS's activism after 1967, and it closely associated with the largest Palestinian fedayeen group, Fatah. At its convention held at MIT in August 1967, the organization resolved that "restoration of Palestine to the Arab homeland is the foremost goal of the Arab Nation" and called for "Arab Unity" in support of "Liberation War." In 1968, Fatah issued an official message to the OAS convention, held in Ann Arbor, Michigan. After expounding the necessity for revolutionary armed struggle and touting the fedayeen as the vanguards of the progressive forces in the Arab world, the message called on the Arab students in the United States to support the Palestinian revolution by ensuring Arab unity for the cause. "Brothers," the message proclaimed, "your responsibility here is no less than that of your brothers who bear arms on the field of battle in the occupied land. The revolution is a complexity of complementary efforts . . . . You bear a responsibility that your brothers back home cannot bear and vice versa."[19] Fatah leaders sent frequent communications to OAS members, some of which were disseminated in OAS literature handed out on American college campuses.[20]

The identification with the Palestinian resistance continued to solidify with the arrival at U.S. universities of more Palestinian students who had been living in the environment of the struggle and who brought a nationalist political consciousness and heightened criticism of Western powers. Abraham describes the years 1968–70 as the "Palestinization of the OAS," and in 1970 the national OAS instituted a new constitution that consolidated the power of the Palestinian resistance movement's supporters and drove out the "reactionary holdouts" from the earlier "establishment OAS."[21]

Not surprisingly, the links between Palestinian resistance groups and the OAS attracted the attention of U.S. government officials and the suspicion of some American Zionists. In their preoccupation with the Arab point of view infiltrating the United States, these Zionists and their government supporters zeroed in on Arab students as constituting the most apparent threat. The prominent American Jewish organization the Anti-Defamation League (ADL) sent members to infiltrate OAS's 1969 convention at Ohio State University. League members pretended to be local media journalists during the convention and used the code names Buckeye, Adam, and Eve in their intelligence reports to the ADL. They reported with alarm that "the political activity of the Arab students in the United States will increase significantly in the coming school year (1969–70) with increasing effectiveness. They are beginning to display a much greater understanding of how to present their arguments to the various levels of the American public (church groups, new left, lower middle class, etc.); and any successes are certain to increase their confidence and, hence, their activity. The situation, however, is by no means hopeless if the proper action is taken immediately. One thing is certain, the threat on the campuses and in the churches can no longer be ignored but must be confronted directly. Otherwise, we will lose by default because the Arabs are making rapid gains in several areas." According to the report by ADL spies, convention participants discussed strategies for bonding with the American Left and persuading non-Arab activists of the Palestinian position.[22]

The same year, Congressman Gerald Ford (R-MI) delivered a speech to the American Israel Public Affairs Committee (AIPAC) in which he branded Arab students as radical agitators and potential terrorists, prompting Arnold Forster, general counsel of the Anti-Defamation League, to write a letter to the editor of the *New York Times* supporting Ford's allegations. Charging that the OAS functioned as "the PLO's transmission belt," Forster declared that the OAS "has been the source of a constant stream of anti-Israel and thinly-veiled anti-Semitic propaganda and . . . has participated in extremist revolutionary activities here with financial aid from Arab governments." The pro-Zionist *Near East Report*, published by AIPAC and based in Washington, D.C., issued warnings about Arab propaganda on American college campuses and claimed that fedayeen were operating here in the United States, hidden among Arab students.[23]

Responding to tips from Zionist groups, both the FBI and the CIA looked into associations between Arab students and Palestinian guerrillas. The CIA did trace money from Arab states to Arab students in the United States, but the agency found no illegal activities and reported to the Nixon White House that the threat was negligible.[24] The FBI had been conducting surveillance of the OAS since at least 1968 and issued a classified report in June 1970 detailing the interactions between the student organization and Palestinian revolutionary groups, especially Fatah. According to the FBI's intelligence gathering, OAS members had traveled to the Middle East to meet with Fatah representatives, and Fatah leaders visited the United States on OAS-sponsored fund-raising and propaganda tours. Information included in the report revealed that the FBI had agents or informants present at the OAS's annual conventions, teach-ins, and fund-raising events, and the agents provided detailed accounts of internal dissension among OAS leaders. The bureau also investigated the funding that OAS received from the League of Arab States. Although the federal government was clearly keeping a watchful eye on the organization's communications with groups the FBI deemed terrorist, the report did state: "There has been no information developed . . . which would establish that terrorist acts have been committed here by any of the Fedayeen groups," and like the CIA, the FBI found no evidence of actionable lawbreaking. However, the report's authors predicted that the fedayeen would continue to cultivate support among Arabs in the United States through its ties to the OAS, which they implied could escalate into a more threatening situation.[25]

Also troubling to federal officials were the OAS's emphatic commitment to socialism and its statements of support for Third World communist regimes, which also put the organization on the administration's watch list. In the resolutions endorsed at its August 1967 convention, the entire first set declared the OAS's solidarity with African Americans, the National Liberation Front in Vietnam, and liberation movements in Africa, before they turned to the resolutions about Palestinian independence and Arab unity. Further resolutions called on Arab states to recognize the People's Republic of China and the People's Republic of Korea and expressed gratitude to the Soviet Union "and other friendly Socialist states which supported the Arab position and resolutely denounced the conspiracies of imperialism and Zionism against revolutionary Arab governments." The convention's opening statement pronounced the students' mode of analysis: "Our battle is an inseparable part of the imperialistic design being executed against the dynamic revolutionary forces in the Third World."[26]

According to Nabeel Abraham, a member of OAS at Wayne State University in Detroit in the late 1960s, the increasingly radical positions of the organization alienated some Arab students who were more conservative or who feared jeopardizing their goal of material success upon their return to the Arab world. Further, OAS students soon found it difficult to promote Arab unity in the face of emerging conflicts among Arab states and between Palestinian factions, which translated into factionalism among the students at American universities. Abraham recalls that "the goal of Arab unity, which was what OAS preached, which was the nationalist tenor of the second half of the fifties and early sixties . . . lost its raison d'etre by the late sixties to early seventies as people started getting into really nit-picky politics, and different governments were trying to play everybody." When leaders of countries such as Jordan and Lebanon withdrew support from the Palestinian resistance movement and attacked PLO camps, the OAS took critical positions against those Arab states, including Egypt, it viewed as conceding to "the Israeli militarists" and not sufficiently supportive of Palestinian liberation. At one point, the Egyptian embassy ordered Egyptian students to leave the OAS. . As Arab unity increasingly broke down and exclusivist nationalisms arose, Palestinian, Lebanese, Egyptian, Iraqi, Libyan, and Gulf (Saudi Arabian, Kuwaiti) students were often at odds with one another.[27] According to Khairy

Abudayyeh, a leader of the Greater Chicago chapter in the 1960s and 1970s, the OAS split between those who advocated that all Arabs unify to liberate Palestine along with the entire Arab world and those who argued that only Palestinians could liberate Palestine. In contrast, Nadine Naber found that Arab Americans who had been members of the OAS-affiliated organization at San Francisco State in that period felt that the organization continued to foster "a collective 'Arab identity'" among its members who hailed from many different Arab countries.[28]

Campus Activism as Part of the Third World Left

Organization of Arab Students campus activities promoting Palestine intensified after 1967. Over the next few years the OAS sponsored teach-ins and staged rallies at universities across the country and mobilized demonstrations at Arab embassies and venues hosting Israeli leaders. For example, Arab students at the State University of New York Oswego held a demonstration on their campus in 1968 on the anniversary of the Balfour Declaration and joined with the OAS chapter at Syracuse University to raise funds "for the widows and orphans of the Palestinian freedom fighters." The Chicago OAS organized a sizable protest march at an Israel fund-raising event at the Chicago Civic Opera House in 1969.[29] The newspaper *Free Palestine* reported on an Arab student sit-in at the Lebanese Mission to the United States in 1969 that was "intended as a firm expression of support for the Palestinian commando movements."[30] Demonstrating the ties between the OAS and the AAUG, the featured speakers at the teach-ins were usually Arab American scholars associated with the AAUG, such as Ibrahim Abu-Lughod, who in early 1969 participated in teach-ins on the Arab-Israeli conflict held at the University of Chicago, Columbia University, the University of Michigan, and Wayne State University.[31]

Collections of flyers distributed by the OAS chapters on the University of Michigan, University of Kansas, and University of California-Berkeley campuses in the late 1960s and early 1970s demonstrate the forms of pro-Palestinian activities the organization undertook and the literature it disseminated. On the second anniversary of the June War, the Michigan OAS advertised a "March & a Ralley [sic] in Support of the Palestinian People" at the Diag, a campus gathering place, and throughout the year additional flyers publicizing teach-ins, speakers, and films were produced at Michigan. The leaflets occasionally reproduced Fatah and PLO statements, such as one handed out on the University of Michigan's campus titled "The Position of

University of Michigan's chapter of the Organization of Arab Students distributed this flyer on the campus "Diag" (a gathering place in the center of campus) in 1969. (Wystan Stevens Papers, Bentley Historical Library, University of Michigan)

Al-Fateh" and another, "The Struggle Goes On," which was adapted from a publication of the Beirut-based PLO Research Center. The University of Kansas and Berkeley's OAS affiliates handed out similar literature, including PLO fact sheets and the Fatah newsletter, during the Palestine Week they commemorated annually in this period. At one point, the *Palestine Resistance Bulletin,* aligned with the Democratic Front for the Liberation of Palestine, was handed out on Berkeley's campus, though it is unclear by whom.

Some literature used both rhetoric and imagery to promote the armed liberation struggle. For example, a flyer from 1969, featuring a sketch of hands holding rifles with bayonets, invited the Michigan campus to a screening of a film about Palestinian commandos. Another, from the University of Kansas's Palestine Week in 1972, was titled "A National Liberation Struggle against Zionism and Imperialism in the Middle East" and depicted a Palestinian guerrilla holding a rifle. Berkeley's Arab student group handed out a flyer in 1969 emblazoned with the catchphrase "The Time of the Gun," and featuring images of guerrilla fighters.[32]

This is an example of another OAS flyer distributed on the University of Michigan campus in 1969. (Wystan Stevens Papers, Bentley Historical Library, University of Michigan)

This celebration of militant anti-imperialist struggle was characteristic of the activist style of the global and American New Left in the late 1960s to the early 1970s. Numerous groups on American campuses were simultaneously producing literature idealizing Vietnamese, Latin American, and African guerrillas with similar iconography of the AK-47 rifle as the symbol for insurgency. Tapping into this discourse, Arab student literature often posed parallels between the Palestinian freedom fighters and other Third World revolutionaries in a strategy to gain broader support from non-Arab leftists. For example, one leaflet handed out at Berkeley declared: "Southeast Asians Struggle for Independence, Palestinians Struggle for Freedom, G.I.'s Struggle for Liberty," and another handbill proclaimed: "People of America: Do Not Allow Another Cambodia in Jordan." Invoking the antiwar movement's disgust with American intervention in Vietnam to the detriment of reform initiatives at home, the Arab Student Association's "Speak Out Now" leaflet from 1973 asked: "Wouldn't the American tax-payer prefer to support projects to combat poverty, environmental pollution and other similar projects with his money than allow Nixon and the Israel-run Congress to force him to pay taxes for Israel's war machinery? Speak out now, support the Arab cause, support the self-determination of the Palestinian people. Stop the murderous 'advisors' in the Middle East. Donate to: Arab Relief Fund."[33]

Creating solidarity out of their shared dedication to anti-imperialist revolution, OAS chapters often partnered with campus organizations that represented Third World students and oppositional politics. The Arab student group at Berkeley regularly formed these coalitions as a major feature of its activist approach. Right after the June War, Berkeley's Arab Student Association convened a press conference (which was mainly ignored by local press outlets) jointly with the university's Tricontinental Progressive Students at which students from Rhodesia, Cuba, Egypt, and Lebanon denounced Zionism, announced a campaign to raise funds for Palestinian refugees, and invited sympathizers to join them at the campus's Iran House. In 1970, the Arab student organization at Berkeley cosponsored a film festival with the leftist group Liberation Support Movement that screened films about "people's wars" in Angola, Vietnam, and Palestine, along with a film about the Black Panthers; later that fall, the Arab students showed *The Battle of Algiers* followed by a film about the Palestinian revolution. Their publicity material announced: "Algiers, Vietnam, Palestine, Angola! Dig! Come and Relive the Battle!" Berkeley's Palestine Week teach-ins and rallies that year featured speakers from the Black Students Union, the Young Socialist Alliance, the Progressive Labor Party, and the Iranian Students Association. The relationship between the Iranian students and the Arab students was especially close. Internationally, the leftist Confederation of Iranian Students National Union (CISNU) was a strong supporter of Palestinians, especially of the General Union of Palestinian Students (GUPS), which had a stronger presence in the Middle East and Europe than it did in the United States at this time. The alliance translated into solidarity among radical Arab and Iranian students at American universities as well.[34]

Pro-Israel students were also organizing and demonstrating at Berkeley in these years. The Hillel organization distributed copies on campus of the periodical *Jewish Radical*, which defended Zionism from a New Left perspective. These activists advocated peace and socialism and evinced concern for Palestinian refugees while strongly advocating Israel's right to exist and Jews' right to self-determination. Rallies for Israel were held on campus, along with a conference at Hillel House by a coalition of Jewish groups calling itself Youth Committee for Peace and Democracy in the Middle East. One of its leaflets presented Arab nations, not Israel, as collaborators with American imperialism and implied that Israel was under threat. It charged: "The Arab states have the oil. Israel's major export is oranges. If you were an American capitalist, which would you support? Right. That's why corporate America through its flunkies in the State Department is trying to twist U.S. foreign policy to abandon Israel. IS A FULL TANK OF GAS WORTH MURDER?" Another pamphlet from the period, which does not identify the sponsoring organization, specifically attacked the Arab Student Association and warned that Arab propaganda was "trying to wash your brain" and "mislead you."[35]

The OAS and Alliances with Radicals at Wayne State

One of the most active OAS chapters during this period was at Wayne State University in Detroit. Representing the activist style of many other OAS chapters, the chapter at Wayne showcased the alliances that the organization cultivated with other leftist groups on college campuses. Like other chapters, Wayne State's OAS was "Palestinized" and stepped up its rallies and teach-ins on campus and in the city in the few years following the 1967 war.[36] Moreover, radical Arab students at Wayne State worked off campus to participate in organizing the large Arab American community in the Detroit area, particularly in the Southend neighborhood of Dearborn.

One of the main activists in Wayne's OAS chapter in the late 1960s was Palestinian American Nabeel Abraham, later a professor of anthropology at Henry Ford Community College in Dearborn. Abraham was born in the United States to parents who had immigrated separately from Palestine and met in America. The family moved to Detroit in 1955 when Nabeel was very young, and he attended Detroit public schools, graduating from Detroit's well-known Cass Tech High School. As he was growing up, his family attended a mosque in the Southend of Dearborn, and he and his siblings also went to an Arabic-language class at the mosque. His family was not very politically active, but he does remember being caught up in the Detroit-area Arab community's enthusiasm for Nasser in the 1960s and his father attending several meetings of the Arab American Congress for Palestine. When the June War of 1967 occurred, he did not become politicized; instead, he recalls that the war "left us rather devastated . . . our ethnic identity took a beating." At the time, he gave up on the Arabs and felt they were "like losers."[37]

Abraham's senior year of high school, the fall of 1967 through the spring of 1968, coincided with a very tumultuous time in the United States. In this year, Abraham experienced a political coming-of-age—but not on Arab

Wayne State University student and OAS leader Nabeel Abraham joins his brother and fellow Wayne State student Sameer Abraham and others in picketing an appearance by Israeli leader Yitzhak Rabin in a Detroit suburb in 1969. (Nabeel Abraham Papers, Bentley Historical Library, University of Michigan, Ann Arbor)

issues. Through his associations with non-Arab friends in Detroit, he was increasingly cognizant of the war in Vietnam and the oppression of African Americans, and he became drawn to the antiwar and civil rights movements. After he enrolled at Wayne State in the fall of 1968, an Arab student activist named Hasan Nawash met Abraham's mother when he was collecting donations for Palestinian relief. She expressed her concern that Nabeel was disconnected from Arab culture and politics, and Nawash told her about Wayne State's chapter of the Organization of Arab Students, of which he was president. She pressed her son to contact Nawash and join the OAS, which he eventually did. It was not long before Abraham became wholeheartedly dedicated to advocacy for Palestine during his college years as a member of the OAS at Wayne State. He remembers shifting from disenchantment to enthusiasm for Arab people; he felt a desire to embrace his Arab identity through mastering the language, specializing in the study of Arab culture, and socializing with Arabs. He remembers, "I saw myself as part of a wider movement to build a new Arab society."[38]

Hasan Nawash's background was a little different from Abraham's. He too came from a Muslim family in Palestine, but he had been born there and lived in East Jerusalem until he was nineteen. He came to the United States on his own in 1960 to attend college and remained in Michigan after graduating. Growing up in occupied Palestine made him feel alienated, like "nothing," "an outcast," he later told Janice Terry in an interview. In his youth Nawash developed a political consciousness that blended Arab and Palestinian nationalism, although by 1960 he and his community had become resentful of the Jordanian regime for its harsh treatment of Palestinians. As a college student in the Detroit area (first at Port Huron Junior College and then at Wayne State), he was passionate about the anti–Vietnam War movement. Although Nawash was already politically active and an officer of the OAS chapter, he experienced the June War as a transformative event, "the wakeful kind of alarm," that caused him to focus even more fervently on the question: "How do I get to make a significant contribution to my own people's struggle?"[39]

Another student who became active in Wayne State's OAS in the late 1960s was George Khoury, born in Palestine to a Christian family. Like Nawash, he came to the United States in the early 1960s to attend college; his parents and two of his siblings joined him in the United States shortly after the war in 1967, and he still resides in the Detroit area. Earlier in the 1960s, Khoury had what he calls a "typical teenage commitment" to Arab nationalism and Nasser. Like so many other Arabs, he identifies the June War as a watershed event, but it did not demoralize him; instead, he states, "something in the soul went in and said regroup and find a new way. Don't give up." He disassociated from his social life and nonpolitical friends and started to spend time with activists who were similarly committed to Palestine. He acquired every publication about Palestine that he could get his hands on with a mission to educate himself about the political stances emanating from various factions in the Arab world. He joined the Arab American Congress for Palestine in Detroit, but he found it too traditional in its approach.[40]

At this point, Khoury was taking graduate courses in bioengineering at Wayne State and became involved with the OAS. He was instrumental in finding and fixing up a building on Cass Avenue near campus to rent for the organization's meeting place, often referred to as the Arab Club. It was also where the organization printed its newsletter. (The Arab students who congregated there sometimes interacted with the staff of the *Fifth Estate*, an anarchist underground newspaper whose office was nearby.) Soon after, the club purchased a shortwave radio to more readily access news from the Arab world, supplementing the Arabic publications they imported. The first OAS meeting Nabeel Abraham attended his freshman year at Wayne State was at the Arab Club on Cass; Hasan Nawash was also in attendance, along with a woman from Saudi Arabia, Soraya Obaid, who was running the meeting and served as president of Wayne's OAS in 1968–69. Abraham recalls that most Arab students at Wayne State in this period came from Lebanon, Jordan, and the West Bank. The few Egyptian students on campus avoided the OAS due to the organization's political stance on Egypt and other Arab regimes.[41]

Similar to OAS chapters throughout the country, the students ramped up their activism at Wayne State in the late 1960s through early 1970s. They held demonstrations, teach-ins, and scholarly seminars, some of which included leftist Israelis as guest speakers. They even staged dramatic plays. Khoury remembers one play put on by the OAS titled *Palestine on the Cross*, which compared Jesus Christ's suffering to that of the Palestinians; it drew a sizable audience and caused considerable controversy. They promoted the Palestinian cause in different venues on campus, including placing literature and exhibits in showcases in the library and student center building. The chapter continued to host its traditional Arabian Night, featuring Arab music and "exotic Arab food," for the purpose of raising funds for Palestinian charities. Members of the organization also participated in demonstrations held in Detroit to protest U.S. support for Israel, such as one in June 1968 when Menachem Begin visited Detroit, and again in January 1969 when General Yitzhak Rabin visited the city to raise funds for Israel. Additionally, OAS members at Wayne State interacted with the national network of Arab student activists, for example, by occasionally attending the national OAS conferences held in different cities. Abraham emphasizes that it was only a select group of radical Arab students, among which he counts himself, who were at the center of these activities.[42]

Perhaps even more than other Arab groups that closely followed Arab world politics, the OAS at Wayne State replicated the divisive factions of the Palestinian resistance movement—chiefly Fatah, the Popular Front for the Liberation of Palestine, and the Democratic Front for the Liberation of Palestine. While the newsletter printed in the OAS's building on Cass Avenue was ostensibly put out by OAS, it was actually taken over by students aligned with one Palestinian faction or another at various times. The newsletter was typically printed in Arabic and featured clippings of publications from Palestinian and other Arab world organizations. Sometimes it included reprints of English-language articles, such as from the *Christian Science Monitor*. According to Khoury, the supporters of Fatah were always the most numerous among the students in OAS. (He emphasizes that he and the other activist Arab students were not actually members of the Palestinian groups; instead, they were sympathizers who operated in solidarity with one faction or another.) The factionalism could be debilitating at times. Organization students quarreled with each other over elections of officers, which speakers would be invited to their functions, and what materials to place in the library showcase. Barbara Aswad, a professor of anthropology at Wayne State, eventually left her position as faculty adviser to the OAS because she "got tired of their fighting, quite honestly."[43]

Though the students had difficulty achieving consensus among themselves, they were able to create coalitions with other leftist organizations on campus, especially with the radicals associated with the League of Revolutionary Black Workers (LRBW). Wayne State was a hotbed of political activism in that period; progressive groups mobilizing around a wide array of causes were active on the urban campus marked by a constant swirl of demonstrations, pamphleting, and marches that often intersected with activism in the larger Detroit community. One organization that bridged campus and community was the LRBW, which formed in 1969 to serve as a central organization for the Revolutionary Union Movements (RUMs) that had formed in many of the city's auto plants after the Detroit Riot/Rebellion of 1967. The first RUM emerged at the Dodge Main plant after a group of workers, white and black, undertook a wildcat strike to protest a speedup on the production line, and the company retaliated against the black participants more harshly than against the white strikers. In response, workers who had become increasingly frustrated with treatment of black workers by both the company and the United Auto Workers joined with a few black activists in the community, namely, John Watson, who published the underground protest newspaper *Inner City Voice*, to organize the Dodge Revolutionary Union Movement (DRUM) to promote Marxist-Leninist black nationalism in the auto industry. Revolutionary Union Movements soon materialized at other workplaces in the city, and in 1969 RUM leaders decided to form the LRBW as a coordinating body that would also promote its revolutionary organizing strategies in the black community.

Also in this period, John Watson, who was taking classes at Wayne State, was selected as editor of the student newspaper, the *South End*. Soon, Mike Hamlin and Luke Tripp, who were active in the League and staff members of the *Inner City Voice*, also joined the staff of the *South End* in 1968, with Hamlin serving as general manager. As editor, Watson transformed the student newspaper into a medium to promote the agenda of the League as well as a whole host of revolutionary causes pressed by other leftist groups on campus, including Palestinian nationalism. As a member of the student publication board, Sameer Abraham (Nabeel Abraham's brother) advised Watson and helped guide the paper in this direction.[44]

Between the fall of 1967 and early 1969, the *South End* published several letters to the editor from OAS leaders as well as articles about the Palestinian movement.[45] In May 1968, the paper ran a long interview with Hasan Nawash in which he called Israel "an alien imperialistic force following classical western colonialism, though under a different banner," and outlined the Palestinian strategy of mobilization of the masses and the deployment of prolonged guerrilla warfare to liberate its territory. It will be a "nibbling campaign against Israel," Nawash stated, which would "proceed in the same fashion as the Chinese and Algerian revolutions at their initial stages." The goal, he declared, was to establish a multinational state that practiced "one-man-one-vote" citizenship. Nabeel Abraham wrote a guest editorial for the paper in January 1969 about the links between Fatah and liberation struggles throughout the Third World, in which he concluded: "Al-Fatah recognizes and identifies with all liberation movements throughout the world. With all the revolutions blooming throughout the world, Fatah has a sweet smell of success. Power to the people! Revolution to the end!"[46]

Demonstrating even more firmly the paper's advocacy of the Palestinian resistance movement, the *South End* helped promote some of OAS's demonstrations and events. For instance, the newspaper cosponsored and publicized the protest at Menachem Begin's speech at Cobo Hall in Detroit. According to the paper, many other campus groups also participated in the demonstration, including a few radical black organizations and leftist groups such as DRUM, the Young Socialist Alliance, and the Anti-Draft Union. The *South End* also cosponsored the demonstration against General Yitzhak Rabin's appearance at the Sheraton-Cadillac Hotel.[47]

Contacts between the OAS and other radicals extended beyond the *South End*. OAS leaders occasionally gave talks at LRBW meetings on Linwood Avenue and sometimes took activists who were visiting from the Arab world, such as representatives of Fatah, to meet with the League. Khoury remembers LRBW activist and attorney Ken Cockrel interacting with the OAS in the late 1960s. For their part, a handful of the OAS activists assisted the League in a few of its organizing activities; for instance, Nabeel Abraham distributed DRUM leaflets at the Dodge Main plant. On occasion the OAS allowed other leftist organizations on campus, including African American, women's liberation, and Greek student groups, use of its mimeograph machine at the Arab Club to reproduce their leaflets. Additionally, a few Arab students participated in antiwar rallies, particularly in protest of the U.S. ground invasion of Cambodia in 1970, that were organized by coalitions of anti-imperialist groups associated with Wayne State, such as the *Fifth Estate*.[48] Detroit attorney Abdeen Jabara, a Wayne State alumnus, was pivotal in connecting the OAS to leftist organizations in the city, such as the National Lawyers Guild and the Socialist Workers Party, as well as to the national pro-Palestinian left, including the AAUG and *MERIP Reports*. [49]

While the OAS maintained links with non-Arab activist organizations on campus and even received support from the student government (which approved the OAS's funding requests to bring in speakers), the alliances were not usually solid or reliable. Abraham remembers planning events with other political groups on campus, to signal solidarity and reach a broader audience, but found that students were frequently "hard to work with," largely because they were focused on their own pet causes. They promised they would come to a demonstration or to hear a speaker but often did not attend. The same phenomenon of pledging support yet not following through also applied to Arab student activists' behavior toward other groups. Moreover, not all members of OAS were supportive of the organizations that comprised the leftist network at Wayne State. Abraham recalls that some Arab students were resistant to forming connections with the women's liberation and gay liberation groups on campus, and some were even hesitant about working with African American groups. According to Khoury, some Arab activists were reluctant about visibly interacting with black radicals because blacks were "always harassed by the whites and the FBI. And if we had done it, we would have been targeted. So we said, let's be friends with them outside of certain areas so we won't be targeted." On the other hand, other political groups on campus were not always welcoming to the Arab activists; Arab students sometimes encountered leftist students in groups such as the SDS who supported Zionism and spurned the OAS.[50]

Although Wayne State's campus newspaper the *South End* clearly communicated a pro-Palestinian position as part of its commitment to Third World revolutionary nationalism, it is important to note that the paper also published numerous letters to the editor from Jewish students and alumni who were upset by the newspaper's stance. Some of the letters criticized the OAS letter writers for presenting distorted information and sought to offer a corrective. Many of the Jewish letters also condemned the newspaper, complaining that it had become a vehicle for Arab propaganda and did not seek balance in its reporting. One letter, by Amos Traub, who identified himself as an "Israeli Student," scoffed at the black radicals on campus who were "rushing to help the 'poor Arabs'" and underlined the crimes committed by Arabs against not only Israelis but also Africans. Another student, Nancy Stein, accused John Watson and the *South End* of anti-Semitism. She wrote, "You've been duped by the white man once again. The white man's old time scapegoat the Jew you've adopted as the cause of all your trouble." Alumnus Leonard Simons told the newspaper it should allow the "local Jewish community an opportunity to present their side of the story. Or, aren't you interested? This is still America, remember?" A member of the local Arab American community, Karen Amin, responded to these charges by acknowledging the paper's pro-Arab bias but reminded readers that they have been "hearing the Zionist side exclusively for the past 20 years" and only needed to consult most major media outlets, such as the *Detroit News*, to find it. She argued that it was very difficult to get the Palestinian viewpoint published in American media, so "at least the *South End* has the courtesy to publish an opposing opinion."[51]

In addition to the Palestinian-Israeli conflict, the *South End* was publishing provocative pieces on a range of political issues, from the war in Vietnam to black power in the nation's cities, workplaces, and unions. The student newspaper was making an impact and unnerving the establishment. Conservative and liberal leaders in business, politics, and labor unions pressed the university's administration to shut down the paper or at least dismiss its editorial staff. In the 1968–69 school year, Wayne State's president William Keast had already unsuccessfully tried to remove Watson as editor by challenging his status as a student. When the *South End* ran a feature article extolling Fatah in early January 1969, which caused further unrest among Jews and their supporters at the university and in the community, Keast and the university's Board of Governors saw their chance. The article was written by the *South End's* news editor Nick Medvecky, a white former paratrooper and member of the Young Socialist Alliance. Abdeen Jabara, who was active in the same leftist circles as Medvecky, invited him on a trip to Jordan, where they met with members of Fatah. In the article, Medvecky sought to "clarify" the position of "perhaps the most misunderstood organization in the world today" and sympathetically reported on Fatah's ideology and objectives. The *South End* reinforced the message a few weeks later when it featured a reprint of a lengthy Fatah statement submitted by Wayne State's OAS. Around the same time, the paper reported on the Arab protest against Rabin's appearance in Detroit and stated that the *South End* had been a cosponsor of the demonstration.[52]

Under considerable pressure from the Board of Governors, alumni, and other community members to shut down the paper, President Keast wrote a strongly worded letter to the editorial staff in which he chastised the paper for "inaccurate and slanted" articles that showed a "looseness of statement far below any standard of responsible journalism." The editorials, Keast wrote, were "mean and spiteful propaganda attacks" featuring "doctrinaire endorsements of the paper's pet view and prejudices." The only example he provided of this objectionable journalism was the paper's coverage of the Arab-Israeli conflict, which he called "highly irresponsible and inflammatory." The paper, he claimed, was alienating students and faculty and "costing the University dearly in the good opinion of the community." The paper must change its reporting, or, he implied, the administration would be forced to take punitive action.[53]

The controversy earned the attention of local and even national media.[54] A flurry of letters supporting or condemning the paper appeared in subsequent issues of the *South End*, all concentrating on the paper's presentation of the Arab viewpoint, not its other provocative political positions. Mike Hamlin, the paper's general manager, claims that he and the staff were unfazed by the administration's rebuke. But in their account, Dan Georgakas and Marvin Surkin state: "Similar articles on African guerrilla organizations had never generated such a reaction, and the editors were genuinely surprised at the storm brought down on them by the Al Fatah piece." Watson and coeditor Harry W. Clark defended the paper, arguing that it was "not anti-Semitic or anti-Jewish" and that it chose to speak for many minority communities in the Detroit area, including the large Arab American population. Hamlin's editorial accused Chrysler, the UAW, the mainstream media, and a powerful Jewish businessman in Detroit of conspiring to use the Palestinian issue to shut down the paper because of the threat it posed to the power structure.[55] In further response to the controversy, the paper hosted a panel discussion on the Arab-Israeli conflict, cosponsored with a local organization of clergy, titled "Racism/anti-Semitism/Nationalism" and announced it would include "speakers from all sides." In its announcement of the panel, the *South End* lamented that it had "become the villain" when all it was trying to do was "open the channels of dialogue" by facilitating discussion and debate on the Israeli-Arab conflict.[56]

The university administration maintained its pressure on the newspaper's editorial staff, and a power struggle ensued between the staff of student writers and the editorial group led by Watson. Eventually, Watson left his post. Nevertheless, the paper remained leftist in orientation, and although it toned down its militant advocacy of some issues, it continued to publish articles supportive of the Palestinian guerrillas and to participate in forums supporting Arab students. For example, in May of 1969, when it seemed that the controversy with the administration had blown over, the *South End* published the "Commemorative Issue on the Arab Struggle," which once again presented the Fatah position and invited readers to attend a march in Detroit to support Palestinians. Later that year, a second article by Nick Medvecky about Al Fatah appeared in the paper, this one recounting his meeting with Yasser Arafat when Medvecky and Jabara had visited Jordan. A couple of years later, the *South End* cosponsored and publicized a campus forum to raise consciousness of the federal government's violations of Arab students' rights. Thus, summarizing the denouement of the flap over the newspaper's promotion of Palestinian nationalism, Georgakas and Surkin conclude: "The radicals had won."[57]

From Campus to Community

While still maintaining an active presence on campus in the early 1970s, some of Wayne State's key OAS leaders shifted to organizing in the Arab American community, focusing on the immigrant neighborhood in Dearborn that, coincidentally, was also called the Southend. By the early 1970s, Arab immigrants, mainly from Lebanon, Palestine, and increasingly from Yemen, comprised the majority of the residents of this historically immigrant, working-class neighborhood adjacent to the Ford Rouge auto plant. Hasan Nawash, who was the OAS student most committed to community organizing, stated, "At the time the Arab student organization saw its mission not just among the students. It really saw its mission to also connect with their community." Abraham echoes this observation, stating, "Increasingly the activists drifted from campus to community." George Khoury also turned his focus to the Southend, but he emphasizes that the community organizing there was undertaken by individuals like himself who had been active in the OAS at Wayne State, not by the OAS as an organization.[58]

Khoury, Nawash, Abraham, and a few other Wayne State students began to interact regularly with the Arab residents of the Southend, mainly by sitting and talking with them at the numerous ethnic-based coffeehouses in the neighborhood, with the goal of organizing support and raising funds for the Palestinian resistance movement. They spent hours arguing over the most effective tactics to resist Israel and the proper role of the Palestinian masses in the revolution. The students sold literature put out by the Palestinian revolutionary groups, such as publications by the Popular Front for the Liberation of Palestine. They also sold posters and buttons with slogans such as "Palestine 'Til Victory," normally written in Arabic. Nawash felt that the recent immigrants in the Southend were "more open to political work" and that the neighborhood provided "a fertile ground" for the students' promotion of Palestinian revolutionary politics. In contrast, they rarely reached out to older generations of Arab Americans (whom Nawash referred to as "the Americans") in Dearborn.[59] The recent immigrants' closer ties with the Arab world, it seemed, made them more receptive to the transnational political work and in particular to the advocacy of armed revolutionary struggle and Marxist ideology that the students promulgated in their visits to the neighborhood.

Despite the students' focus on new immigrants, Nabeel Abraham did influence the political consciousness of at least one third-generation Arab American, albeit one who was already highly politicized on the Left. Abraham encountered Ismael Ahmed at a radical political collective called the People's Exchange that Ahmed and a few other non-Arab leftists had established in a storefront across the street from Dearborn City Hall. Ahmed was organizing around black nationalism and anti-imperialism, but at this point the Palestinian question was not part of his revolutionary consciousness. According to Ahmed, Abraham said to him, "You know, I saw you putting out an underground paper. You talk about all this other stuff, what about the struggles of Arab people?" Abraham gave him the Palestinian literature he had been distributing in the Southend, which inspired Ahmed to incorporate Arab world justice in his political advocacy.[60]

Besides engaging in lengthy discussions of the Palestinian resistance and disseminating fedayeen literature, the students occasionally showed films in the Southend. Abraham had a part-time job at Wayne State as a film projectionist, and he sometimes borrowed the projection equipment from the university and took it into the neighborhood. The students would obtain films about Palestine and the Arab world, usually from the leftist film group Newsreel, and show them on campus and in the Southend to raise money. Abraham specifically remembers showing *The Battle of Algiers* in the community and being pleased that many Yemenis attended. Yemenis who supported the Omani rebels against the British held political events in the Southend, mainly *haflas* (parties) that incorporated lectures and poetry about the rebellion, and the OAS students became involved in supporting those activities as well. This small group of student activists thus established themselves as fixtures in the political life of the Southend. They became part of the nucleus of community activists who established an Arab community center in the neighborhood, which developed into the Arab Community Center for Economic and Social Services (ACCESS) in 1972. And over the next several years, Arab students from Wayne State were part of the volunteer crew at ACCESS.[61] Although the OAS visibly promoted the Palestinian resistance movement both on Wayne State's campus and in the wider community, at least two of the activists question whether the organization accomplished anything consequential. Abraham believes that the squabbling among students aligned with various Palestinian factions was futile and debilitating. Sometimes their revolutionary bravado was "really a means for certain individuals to promote themselves" rather than an effort to construct a workable strategy to advance justice for Arabs. To Khoury, the students, including himself, were "immature" and "spinning their wheels" by engaging in a lot of talk about the Palestinian cause but failing to translate their passion into meaningful action.[62]

While Wayne State's OAS could not point to concrete achievements on the Palestine question, the activist students did raise the consciousness of Arab Americans as well as the visibility of Palestinian and Arab nationalist causes among others in the Detroit area, especially fellow leftists. In doing so, they created bridges between a politicized Arab American community and non-Arab activist groups, which eventually led to coalitions in the city that supported Arab and Arab American rights. Furthermore, the small group of student activists helped foster a political climate in the Southend that led to the formation of ACCESS, a significant accomplishment that held meaningful consequences for Arab Americans in that community.

In Chicago, some OAS members were also instrumental in establishing an Arab community center in the 1970s. Unlike the experience of Wayne State students, in the Chicago center's early years the OAS activists were searching for the Arab community. They started out by renting a building on the north side of the city, where the Arab American population was sparse and scattered. Over the next few years the center migrated to other temporary rental spaces, moving closer to the south side of the city where new Arab immigrants, especially Palestinians, were concentrating. Finally, the activists purchased a building in 1982, and according to founder Khairy Abudayyeh, that move marked the formal establishment of the Arab Community Center. Chicago's center was almost exclusively focused on promoting Arab culture and nationalist politics among the Arab immigrants, in contrast to the social services aspect emphasized by ACCESS in Dearborn.[63]

Arab Student Organizing in the 1970s

Although its activism peaked between the late 1960s and early 1970s, the OAS maintained chapters on some campuses through the 1970s, and pro-Arab student activism manifested in other organizations as well. Arabs in the United States on student visas were a chief target of the federal government's Operation Boulder, a crackdown on Arab activities in the United States initiated shortly after Palestinian guerrillas murdered Israeli athletes at the 1972 Olympics in Munich. Under the surveillance program, which lasted until 1975, the Immigration and Naturalization Service and the Federal Bureau of Investigation jointly monitored students from Arab countries. The government's monitoring operation involved inspecting the students' visa status much more strictly than in the past and often interrogating them about their political views and their associations with various organizations. A few OAS chapters, such as at Wayne State and the University of Kansas, mobilized in opposition to the government's harassment of students, but the organization's activities on this front were limited, likely because students were afraid of the repercussions—including deportation—of speaking out.[64]

Nevertheless, many Arab students came out into the streets in the fall of 1973 to join tens of thousands of Arab Americans across the country in about sixty major demonstrations and over one hundred smaller rallies during the October War. At these protests, which were spontaneous and uncoordinated, demonstrators voiced their support for Arab nations and their strong opposition to U.S. support for Israel. Editors of the *AAUG Newsletter* viewed the outpouring of activism as evidence of an "unprecedented, historical ethnic Arab awakening in America" and estimated that over 70 U.S. cities and 120 college campuses were the sites of pro-Arab demonstrations involving around 150,000 people, including many non-Arabs who opposed U.S. policy in the Middle East. The newsletter's coverage included photographs of Arab students protesting that month at Ohio State University, Ohio University, the University of Colorado-Boulder, and the University of Texas in Austin, as well as of demonstrations in Dearborn; Cincinnati; Denver; Allentown, Pennsylvania; and Jacksonville, Florida.[65]

As the 1970s progressed, OAS chapters continued to respond to conflicts in the Arab world. In 1976, its newsletter and annual convention concentrated on the conflict in Lebanon, with the organization taking a strong stance against the Syrian invasion. The national OAS's main activity was a campaign to support Lebanese leftists and the PLO, and chapters participated in demonstrations against Syria's leader, Hafez al-Assad, at Arab League offices

Pro-Arab rallies erupted at universities and cities around the United States during the October War in 1973. Pictured are students from various campus groups, including the Black Student Alliance and the Young Socialist Alliance, protesting against Israel at the University of Colorado–Boulder. (*AAUG Newsletter*, December 1973, AAUG Papers, Eastern Michigan University, Special Collections Library)

and in New York City, Washington, D.C., Detroit, Seattle, San Francisco, and Los Angeles. The organization continued to express its support for "the anti-imperialist struggle in the Arab world," which included the revolution in Oman and, of course, the Palestinian resistance movement, with which it maintained close ties.[66] A collection of flyers from the University of California-Santa Barbara shows that the OAS was active on that campus in the mid-1970s, screening films about the Palestinian resistance, such as *Revolution until Victory* and *The Day of the Land*; sponsoring Palestinian speakers, such as prominent writer and activist Fawaz Turki; and handing out leaflets featuring such slogans as "Shalom—Yes, Occupation—No. Viva Palestine! Resistance—Yes, Surrender—Never." The OAS also maintained a presence at the University of Michigan in the mid-1970s, holding a teach-in on Lebanon and a symposium titled "Zionism and Racism" in collaboration with other student groups, and drawing media attention when activists, joined by community members from Dearborn's Southend, disrupted Israel president Ephraim Katzir's appearance at the university when he received an honorary degree from the law school in 1975. A similar but much larger protest was staged at Northwestern University three years later by organized Arab students, who were joined by faculty, students, and community members representing a variety of ethnic groups, when Menachem Begin received an honorary law degree.[67]

The OAS's entire focus was on developments in the Arab world, but it sometimes had to confront conflicts on U.S. campuses when its activism provoked Jewish antipathy. At the University of Washington in 1977, the president of the student Jewish Information Society was also editor of the student newspaper and used his position to press for exclusion of the OAS from the university's consortium of student organizations representing racial and ethnic minority groups. The OAS protested the move, arguing that it had "a long history of activist solidarity with local American minority struggles" and "deliberately chose" to define itself as an American ethnic or racial minority group, even if it also included foreign national students among its membership. The Arab students' conception of themselves as members of a marginalized minority that struggled in alliance with other nonwhite Americans for rights and dignity demonstrated the enduring Third World solidarity framework that shaped Arab American student activism and the Arab American Left as a whole. Members of the OAS at the University of Washington reported they had been monitored, harassed, and disrupted, and they pointed to Jewish interests on campus as the culprits. An OAS letter to the University of Washington's newspaper tellingly reached out to "the Progressive Individuals and Organizations," asking them to write letters to the administration to protest "the harassment of OAS and other minority groups."[68]

Campus activism around Palestinian liberation and Arab world issues also expanded to new organizations whose memberships included both Arab and non-Arab students. A main catalyst for new forms of activism was the case of Sami Esmail, an engineering student at Michigan State University. In 1977 Esmail, a U.S. citizen whose family was from Palestine, flew to Ramallah to visit his ailing father and, upon his arrival at the airport in Tel Aviv, was arrested by Israeli authorities and charged with membership in the Popular Front for the Liberation of Palestine. After six days of interrogation without a lawyer present, Esmail signed a confession, and an Israeli court consisting of a three-judge panel convicted and sentenced him to fifteen months in prison. Arab American activists as well as human rights groups throughout the world publicized the case and expressed their outrage at Israel's treatment of Esmail. At Michigan State, activists Barbara Thibeault and John Masterson formed the National Committee to Defend the Human Rights of Sami Esmail, and chapters were established at other universities.

The Esmail case also became a major cause of the newly established Palestine Human Rights Campaign (PHRC), led by James Zogby.[69]

At Ohio State University, the PHRC began by publicizing the Sami Esmail case but soon broadened its scope and mobilized around other cases of violations of Palestinians' human rights as well as against U.S. policy toward the Israeli-Palestinian conflict more generally.[70] The organization created and distributed literature on campus and in the city of Columbus, staged teach-ins and street protests, and held haflas and fund-raisers to promote its agenda. One of its signature events was a three-day conference on Palestinian human rights attended by Abdeen Jabara and Jim Zogby, along with Israeli human rights attorney Lea Tsemel. About half of Ohio State's PHRC members were students of Arab origin, and half were non-Arab students and faculty, including a few progressive Israelis. The president of the chapter in the late 1970s was Mike O'Laughlin, a graduate student studying Middle Eastern politics. His wife, Janice Murphy, was also an active member of the organization, although she was not a student at Ohio State at the time; while residing in Columbus, Murphy was very involved in a feminist organization called Women against Rape (WAR), and a few other members of WAR also joined the PHRC. Another officer of Ohio State's PHRC was Peggy McKee, who was dating Elias Ayoub, an Ohio State student who, like Esmail, was accused by Israeli authorities of being a member of the Popular Front for the Liberation of Palestine; because the Immigration and Naturalization Service refused to extend Ayoub's student visa, he faced deportation.[71]

Murphy and O'Laughlin say they were drawn to the Palestinian rights cause because their education, both at Ohio State and when they were undergraduate political science students at the University of Pittsburgh, "showed us the moral injustice" of the Palestine question. They recall that they had "an intellectual understanding of injustice, but we had nowhere to take it politically. So when the opportunity offered itself through these particular [human rights] cases . . . we brought an intellectual and social movement analysis [and realized] we can mobilize around these cases." Another reason they, as non–Arab Americans, became politically active on Palestine was the wider political climate of the late 1970s: "The whole language of human rights had begun to emerge, with the Carter Administration. That language was part of the political atmosphere and created an opportunity." Although they credit President Carter with fostering greater consciousness of human rights, they protested his facilitation of the Camp David Accords during a theatrical demonstration in front of the state office building in Columbus. O'Laughlin remembers: "Someone wore a mask of Jimmy Carter, two others represented Begin and Sadat, wearing masks, with war toys—plastic airplanes and tanks—and a cake. Off on the side, an Arab representing Arafat had nothing—crumbs. The demonstration got enormous media coverage—television and the *Columbus Dispatch*. It was our most successful protest."[72]

The Palestine Human Rights Campaign also established a chapter at the University of Michigan that involved a mix of Arab Americans and non–Arab Americans, including Israelis. Joel Beinin, a graduate student at Michigan of Jewish background who had been active on the Left, joined the PHRC there in 1978. According to Beinin, the relationships among the diverse individuals associated with the group were very harmonious, and it had a fun social dynamic. As part of the PHRC, he gave talks about Arab world issues on and off campus, and some of the members ran a short-lived weekly Middle East news program on public access television in Ann Arbor. He was still involved in the group in 1982 during the Israeli invasion of Lebanon and participated in PHRC demonstrations opposing Israeli and U.S. actions. Many Israelis on campus, Beinin recalls, "flipped out completely" in response to the protests, which had attracted the support of progressives at the university who were not normally vocally critical of Israel.[73] The progressive coalition in advocacy of justice for Palestinians seemed to be expanding.

The Organization of Arab Students still had some active chapters in the early 1980s, and members of those groups also participated in public protests of the Israeli invasion of Lebanon in 1982.[74] On the whole, though, secular, pan-Arab student organizations were flagging in the United States. As with New Left organizations such as the SDS, the OAS was riven by factionalism and doctrinal disputes. Following the pattern of the "crash-and-burn" radical sixties, the unity and energy to which OAS aspired was difficult to sustain.[75] Arab and Arab American students were gravitating toward organizations identified with particular nationalities and religious sects. By the 1980s, the Muslim Student Association had superseded the OAS as the premier organization appealing to U.S. students of Arab origin, who by then were increasingly Muslim in faith regardless of nationality.[76]

ALTHOUGH SUPPORT FOR THE Palestinian resistance was foremost for OAS activists, they were keenly aware of and invested in other revolutionary movements which were reaching a fever pitch in the late 1960s, and the Arab students strategically situated their political cause among them. The politically active students in the OAS borrowed discourse and tactics from American black and New Left activists at the same time as the American black and New Left movements anchored on many American campuses were becoming progressively oriented toward Third World struggles. This convergence created a fertile space for Arab American pro-Palestinian advocacy in American activist networks in the late 1960s. The intersections among these leftist groups also provoked increased surveillance and repression by American authorities. Nevertheless, the relationships among Arab American activists and other leftist groups continued to grow over the next decade, and by the mid-1980s these relationships had become one factor that contributed to the support shown by more liberal (as opposed to militantly leftist) Americans, especially liberal African American leaders, for the Palestinian position.

3 Intersections

Palestine, Arab Americans, and the Movements of the Sixties

By the early 1970s, Palestinian advocacy spearheaded by the Association of Arab American University Graduates (AAUG) and Organization of Arab Students (OAS) was beginning to raise consciousness and draw attention, especially on campuses and in academia. Although small and marginal, an incipient Arab American movement was moving forward with ambitions to gain global support for Palestinian liberation and Arab transformation. The transnational activism of these organizations was enabled by the increasing ideological affinity felt by many elements of the African American civil rights movement, along with the broader American Left, with the Palestinian resistance movement.[1] For many American activists, an evolving understanding of the Palestinian question emerged from their heightened commitment to Third World solidarity during the period that coincided with Israel's displacement of hundreds of thousands of Palestinians as an outcome of the Arab-Israeli War of 1967. On the whole, nationalist African Americans and (largely white) New Leftists who were at the forefront of antiracist and anti-imperialist activism came to view Palestinians as an oppressed people engaged in anticolonial resistance to Zionist Israel and its American backers.

This perspective was characteristic of the increasing affiliation of the Palestinian resistance movement with the global Third World Left in this period. As Paul Thomas Chamberlin has detailed, Palestinian fedayeen consciously modeled themselves on and cultivated alliances with guerrilla insurgent groups around the world to gain support from the growing Third World revolutionary movement. For example, Chamberlin reports that by 1968, "Fatah had borrowed elements of the politico-military struggle from other revolutionary movements with which it was in contact, as well as sending representatives to the cultural congress of Havana, voicing a strong identification with the experiences of African Americans, and embracing the concept of black power." Soon, nations ranging from Pakistan to China to France declared their support for Palestinian liberation.²

These solidarities spilled over into the American arena and facilitated the intersections among many American civil rights and leftist groups and the expanding Arab American Left. Admittedly, Arab Americans' personal interactions with African Americans and other non-Arab activists tended to be limited. Furthermore, some white leftists and most black moderates heartily defended Israel in this period and viewed the Palestinian revolutionary movement as threatening and anti-Semitic. Nonetheless, in general the American Left formed an ideological alliance with Palestinian nationalism and by extension with Arab American organizations that championed Palestine.

African American Perspectives on Palestine before 1967

Over the course of the twentieth century, mainstream African Americans' attitudes toward Israel and their relationships with Jewish Americans have shifted, in some cases considerably, from mutually supportive interactions and enthusiasm for Zionism to chillier relations and heightened criticism of Israel (and support for Palestinians) by the 1980s. In the early to mid-twentieth century, American Jews and African American civil rights advocates forged a strong alliance around their shared experience of persecution, and Jewish Americans were important supporters of the early black civil rights movement, dating back to the involvement of Jews in the founding of the NAACP in 1909. Their relationship solidified in the decade after World War II as Jewish activists played key roles in civil rights organizations such as the NAACP, the Urban League, the Congress on Racial Equality (CORE), and the Student Nonviolent Coordinating Committee (SNCC). The alliance was particularly strong between Jews and moderate African American activists who prioritized integration and individual legal and political rights.³

Most African Americans generally, and some of them ardently, supported the creation of Israel after World War II. Even some black leaders who promoted a more radical nationalist consciousness, such as W. E. B. DuBois and Marcus Garvey, had earlier admired the Zionist project for its dogged pursuit of nationalism for its people. They did not, at this point, envision Zionism's potential for imperialism.⁴ African American leader Jack O'Dell had supported Israel before the 1960s, when he was ignorant of the Palestinians and their displacement. He recalled, "Those of us who were present at the birth of Israel, and who went to rallies supporting it, knew nothing of the Palestinians. We thought that, given the great human rights traditions of the Jewish people, an answer to the Holocaust that took the form of a state in the Middle East would certainly play a positive role in the region." Later, in the 1970s and 1980s, O'Dell traveled several times to the Middle East and witnessed the plight of Palestinians. Working with Arab American leaders, he and his organization, Operation PUSH, became strong advocates for the rights of Palestinians.[5]

While African Americans' sympathy toward Israel was widespread in the 1940s and 1950s, a minority of radical African Americans who cultivated a transnational consciousness became aware of Palestinians' oppression and felt solidarity with them. Anticolonial struggles not only in Africa but also throughout Asia and the Middle East deeply inspired many African American activists as they increasingly identified black liberation in the United States with anticolonial movements by Third World peoples. Attended by a few African American intellectuals such as James Baldwin and Richard Wright, the Afro-Asian Conference in Bandung, Indonesia, in 1955 brought together figures from over two dozen African and Asian nations to promote their independence from the Cold War superpowers, an endeavor that would eventually emerge as the Non-Aligned Movement. The conference's critique of colonialism was crucial in fostering black internationalists' sense of solidarity with the Third World and helped nurture an analysis of black people's oppression in the United States through the lens of colonialism.[6]

Though the Bandung conference did not specifically address the displacement of Palestinians resulting from the 1948 war, it did promote greater understanding of the Arab world among some African Americans, which would develop into support for Palestinians. African American sympathy with Arab nationalism was further enhanced when Egypt's Gamal Abdel Nasser stood up to Israel and Western powers in the Suez Crisis in 1956. Historian Melani McAlister argues, "Observers would later look back on Suez as something of a turning point in African American perceptions of the Middle East—the moment in which Arab anticolonialism came home to black Americans. It was the beginning of a larger transformation which by the late 1960s would bring black Islam, Arab nationalism, and African American radicalism into a powerful historical alliance." In radical black circles, Nasser had become "an anticolonial hero."[7]

The Algerian revolution against French colonial rule also captured black radicals' imagination in this period and further cemented their identification of the black freedom movement with anticolonial revolution in the Third World. Extensively covered in the African American press, especially in the

Nation of Islam's newspaper *Muhammad Speaks*, Algeria was pictured as a "model of revolutionary struggle." Even moderate leader Martin Luther King Jr. recognized the parallels between the two struggles, an observation he made after meeting with Ahmed Ben Bella, the head of Algeria's National Liberation Front (FLN), in New York City in the early 1960s. Bella also met twice with Malcolm X to discuss the similarities in African American and Algerian battles for dignity and independence, and in a 1964 speech Malcolm X called Algerians "blood brothers." The black intellectual Frantz Fanon's seminal work *The Wretched of the Earth* about the Algerian revolution, published in 1961 and translated into English in 1963, promulgated the necessity of violent anticolonial revolution. Fanon's analysis was exceptionally influential among black and other Third World radicals during the 1960s and 1970s. Screenings of the 1966 film *The Battle of Algiers*, which one black intellectual described as the "movie counterpart" to Fanon's *Wretched of the Earth*, later became instrumental in fostering alliances among Palestinian activists and radical activists who represented black and other Third World communities in the United States.[8]

Among African Americans, Black Muslims in particular were supportive of Palestinians and critical of Zionists during the 1950s and 1960s. Some Black Muslim groups practiced a form of Sunni Islam that hewed closely to Islamic practices in much of the Muslim world, but even sects such as the Nation of Islam (NOI) that diverged significantly from orthodox Islam felt a close connection to Arab Muslim peoples and places. Conjuring the figure of the "Afro-Asiatic black man," NOI leader Elijah Muhammad proposed a racial linkage between African and "Asian" peoples who originated in the Arabian peninsula and Nile Valley. Many African Americans were drawn to Islam because they conceived of it as an "authentically black religion" that was more attuned to the revolutionary nationalism burgeoning in the African diaspora.[9]

The Nation of Islam began condemning Israel in the mid-1950s, and *Muhammad Speaks* frequently addressed the Arab-Israeli conflict. Nation of Islam spokesman Malcolm X cast Israel as a colonial power that had become even "more firmly entrenched" in the Third World than the European powers had been before World War II. He critiqued Zionism as a Western strategy to divide and subjugate Africans and Asians, and he expressed solidarity with "our Muslim brothers" who had been driven out of their homeland by Jews with support from Christians in the United States and Europe. Such arguments from Black Muslim nationalists challenged black Christians' support for Israel.[10]

Their embrace of the Arab world in constructing a transnational identity was, for some Black Muslims, reinforced by interactions with Arab Muslims living in the United States. Links between Muslims from abroad and African American Muslims extend back to the Moorish Science Temple in Chicago in the 1920s where the temple's African American leader Noble Drew Ali interacted with and learned from Muslim scholars who came from across the Islamic world. In the mid-twentieth century, black followers of Shaikh Daoud Ahmed Faisel at State Street Mosque in Brooklyn, as well as the African Americans who worshipped at the Al-Mu'mineen Mosque in Detroit, welcomed Arab and South Asian Muslims into their congregations and hosted Muslim missionaries from abroad. Aliya Hassen, a Lebanese Muslim who later moved to Detroit and became director of the Arab Community Center for Economic and Social Services (ACCESS), was on close terms with Malcolm X while she lived in New York City, helping him make arrangements for his hajj in 1964 as well as assisting in the preparation of his body after his death. One of the African American leaders of the Al-Mu'mineen Mosque established a warm relationship with the Arab American Imam of a Sunni mosque in Dearborn, a bond that, according to historian Sally Howell, "created an important bridge between Arab American and black (Sunni) Muslim communities in the 1960s and 70s, and, in effect, a bridge between the histories of these populations as well." In contrast, despite Elijah Muhammad's evocations of an Afro-Asian Islamic alliance, members of the Nation of Islam generally maintained distance from Arab Americans before the 1970s, owing to the NOI's racial separatism and its deep doctrinal differences with immigrant Muslims. There were instances, however, when Elijah Muhammad did pursue relationships with foreign Muslims and sought to use those interactions to demonstrate that the NOI was authentically Islamic.[11] But outside of the contacts between some black and immigrant Muslims, interactions between African American and Arab American communities were rare.

Black Radicals Embrace Palestine, late 1960s–early 1970s

In a striking convergence, the Arab-Israeli War of June 1967 and the consequent escalation of the Palestinian resistance movement occurred during a period when several black civil rights organizations were undergoing substantial radicalization. Existing organizations such as SNCC and CORE and new organizations such as the Black Panther Party (BPP) represented a trajectory in the mid- to late 1960s toward a more militant conception of black nationalism and rejection of white liberal influence in the black liberation movement. Responding to America's war in Vietnam, along with ongoing anticolonial struggles in Africa and Latin America, these black organizations were prioritizing a transnational anti-imperialist consciousness that connected them to nationalist movements throughout the Third World. Building on the teachings of Malcolm X and Frantz Fanon, they used a colonial analogy to explain blacks' historical oppression in the United States.[12]

The Black Panther Party regularly celebrated revolutionary African struggles in its newspaper, which began circulation in 1967, the year of the Arab-Israeli War. Just one month before the war, SNCC's new chairman, H. Rap Brown, declared that SNCC should position itself as an internationally conscious "human rights organization," instead of a domestically oriented civil rights organization, and should "support liberation struggles" throughout the Third World. Also marking SNCC's emerging Third Worldism, in 1967 the organization established the International Affairs Commission, chaired by James Forman.[13]

For black radicals who had long possessed a radical transnational consciousness, Israel's defeat of the Arab forces and its expanded occupation of Palestinian territory augmented their existing perception of Israel as an imperialist state. For black civil rights groups that were just beginning to develop a Third World nationalist ideology, the June War directed their attention to the Arab world and ignited their consciousness of the Palestinian plight. When the war erupted, James Forman was traveling in Africa and wrote letters to SNCC executive secretary Stanley Wise in which he suggested that SNCC should take a position in support of Arab nationalism. Israel's treatment of Arabs, Forman maintained, was predicated on both racism and economic exploitation. Nations supporting the Arabs and Palestinians were socialist or socialist supporters, he observed, thereby indicating to SNCC which side it should take if it truly sought to engage in the struggle to build "a new society" and "have meaningful relations with forces in Africa, Asia, and Latin America." However, he acknowledged that pronouncing a firm pro-Arab stance would stir controversy and alienate some civil rights supporters. Forman asked Wise to wait until his return to the United States when they could meet with the SNCC's leadership to discuss how the organization should articulate its position on this "delicate question."[14]

But before Forman returned, and without discussion or official authorization by the Executive Committee, SNCC's newsletter published an article in its June–July issue that piercingly condemned Israel. The newsletter announced that the article was the first in a series called "Third World Round

Up" intended to examine global developments because "we African Americans are an integral part of the Third World" and therefore should seek to "understand what our brothers are doing in their homelands" and how "it relates to our struggle here." Employing what scholar Keith Feldman terms "an imaginative geography," Palestine had become a site for black nationalists to explore and analyze their own oppression as a colonized people in the United States. Titled "The Palestinian Problem: Test Your Knowledge," the SNCC newsletter article depicted the Arab-Israeli conflict as part of the global pattern of white imperialist forces subjugating people of color.[15]

Though her name did not appear in the newsletter, the piece was chiefly written by Ethel Minor, a former member of the Nation of Islam who had befriended Palestinian students while she was in college and had been leading a SNCC study group on Palestine for many months before the June War. Closely resembling a pamphlet by Arab League representative Fayez Sayegh titled "Do You Know? Twenty Basic Facts about the Palestine Problem," Minor's article asked "Do you know?" and listed thirty-two "facts" about Israel and Zionism, such as "15. That the Zionists conquered the Arab homes and land through terror, force, and massacres? That they wiped out over 30 Arab villages before and after they took control of the area they now call 'Israel.'" Other points emphasized America's support for Israel, depicting the relationship as another powerful example of American imperialism. Along with photographs of Palestinian victims of Israeli violence taken in the 1950s, the article featured a striking drawing of a double lynching: two men, one Arab (resembling Nasser) and one black (resembling Muhammad Ali), wearing nooses around their necks were seized by a white hand bearing the Star of David. Primed to sever the men from the grip of their Jewish captor, a dark-skinned arm labeled "Third World" clutched a scimitar engraved with the words "Liberation Movement." Other imagery appearing in the SNCC article arguably carried anti-Semitic overtones, principally a cartoonish drawing of Israeli leader Moshe Dayan with dollar signs on his epaulets.[16]

SNCC's "Palestinian Problem" article immediately generated a firestorm of comment and controversy. Leaders of many Jewish organizations charged SNCC with anti-Semitism, such as a spokesman for the Anti-Defamation League who declared that the article "follows the pro-Arab, Soviet, and racist lines and smacks very heavily of anti-Semitism." Prominent media outlets reported these Jewish responses to SNCC and also sought comment from liberal civil rights organizations. According to the *New York Times*, such African American leaders as Whitney Young, A. Philip Randolph, and Bayard Rustin condemned SNCC's position on Israel, characterizing it as anti-Semitic, and portrayed SNCC as an extremist group inconsistent with most African Americans' views. Martin Luther King Jr. refused to comment on SNCC's article, but he assured the *New York Times* reporter that he "strongly opposed" anti-Semitism. Tellingly, mainstream media coverage did not involve an analysis of whether the article's content was justified, nor did it explore Israel's treatment of Palestinians; instead, the American media conveyed the impression that SNCC's charges were groundless and the organization was irrationally anti-Semitic.[17]

Trying to put out the fire, the director of SNCC's central office issued a statement declaring that the newsletter article did not represent the official position of the organization; however, SNCC leaders Ralph Featherstone and Stanley Wise, along with Ethel Minor, held a press conference at which they reiterated their censure of Zionism while denying that their position was anti-Semitic. Their purpose, they stated, was to expose the realities of the Israeli-Arab conflict because the American media had "completely hushed up" the truth.[18]

James Forman felt disappointed that the article had been published without his participation in an Executive Committee discussion, nor was he entirely happy with its indelicate presentation. Nevertheless, he thought the organization needed to stand behind it, arguing that "no formulation of our position would have satisfied the Zionists and many Jews." He believed that taking this position in support of "justice to the Palestinian people" was crucial to the demonstration of SNCC's commitment to an anticolonial ideology. Forman later wrote, "Our position against Israel, as I saw it, took us one step further along the road to revolution." In his memoir, former SNCC chairman Stokely Carmichael concurred with Forman's assessment of the controversy, asserting that any SNCC statement critical of Israel, no matter how it was worded, would have been perceived as vicious. Reflecting upon the castigation SNCC endured, Carmichael wrote, "What this 'overkill' offensive launched immediately by organized Zionist forces demonstrated was that to raise any questions, however legitimate, about Zionist policies and actions was seen as a declaration of war. Unthinkable, verboten, in U.S. political discourse at the time. . . . So war was declared on SNCC."[19]

Outside of fellow black nationalists, a supportive response came from the Organization of Arab Students. At its national convention later that summer, the organization declared that SNCC was being unfairly accused of anti-Semitism. Employing language consonant with SNCC's formulation of the connection between the African American and Palestinian struggles, the OAS convention passed a resolution that identified "the underlying similarities between the continuing struggle of the Palestinian Arabs in Occupied Palestine against Zionist invasion and exploitation, and the ever-increasing resistance of the Afro-Americans in the United States to a power structure of inequality." As reported in the NOI's *Muhammad Speaks,* the OAS president offered his support to SNCC; moreover, he contended that other black groups had refrained from speaking out against Israel due to their fear of losing Jewish support and funding. Many black radicals agreed that civil rights organizations' reliance on Jewish support influenced their hesitancy to take a clear pro-Palestinian stance. They viewed this predicament as representative of a larger pattern of African Americans' shameful dependence on white liberals.[20]

The OAS's cultivation of an alliance with SNCC continued when it invited Carmichael to speak at its next national convention. During the fall of 1967, Carmichael had been traveling throughout the Middle East, issuing public statements pledging African American support for Arabs' armed resistance. Appearing at the 1968 OAS convention in Ann Arbor, he reiterated his vow that, in their fight against imperialism, black militants would "help the struggle of the Arabs in any way we can, not only financially and morally, but with our very lives." He reasoned that because Africa was the motherland of African Americans and because Egypt was in Africa, black people's struggle must extend to combating imperialist threats to Egypt. But the most important contribution blacks could make to the Arab cause, Carmichael declared, was "to spread the propaganda against Zionism and begin to enlighten and educate the masses of our people."[21]

As such black activists as Forman had predicted, the pronouncements on Israel of Carmichael and SNCC offended many Jews who had been supporters of the organization.[22] (However, some Jewish members of SNCC, such as Dorothy Zellner, supported Palestine and remained active on behalf of Palestinian rights for decades.[23]) It must be noted that friction between many Jewish progressives and black radicals had been festering for at least a year before the storm ignited by SNCC's response to the June War, and it was shaped by growing distance between white liberals and SNCC, seen especially in the controversy surrounding the organization's decision to pursue black separatism by excluding white members from its staff. Although Jews and African Americans had historically formed alliances to support a civil rights agenda, relations were frequently tense, especially as the economic disparity between the two communities became more apparent in the mid-twentieth century. The trajectory of SNCC away from a nonviolent, integrationist orientation toward a more militant black nationalism had already alienated many whites, including some Jews, in the movement. Other conflicts in this period, such as a dispute in the Ocean Hill–Brownsville schools in Brooklyn, New York, between the mainly Jewish teachers and the black community, exacerbated the strain between African Americans and Jewish Americans. According to historian Clayborne Carson, "For many Jews the pro-Palestine article was simply another of the accumulating signs that black militancy would be turned against them." As for most SNCC activists' interpretation of the clash, their perception of white racism was reinforced by Jewish withdrawal of support. To Forman, Jewish opposition to SNCC was inevitable because "leading Jewish organizations had [already] joined others in the liberal-labor syndrome to attack us as too radical back in the days when the subject was not the Middle East but Mississippi."[24]

At the same time as SNCC was developing its pro-Palestinian position, the Black Panther Party's emerging theory of "intercommunalism," which posited relationships among African Americans and colonized peoples around the world, also led that organization to powerfully advocate for Palestinian freedom. Panthers interpreted Zionism as "an extension of U.S. imperialism and racial capitalism," the same processes that oppressed blacks in America. Scholar Alex Lubin observes, "Surprisingly little has been written about how the Palestinian question served as a generative location for Panther intercommunalism."[25] Yet the organization's newspaper regularly ran articles, including Fatah statements, which attacked Zionism and expressed solidarity with Arabs and Palestinians. For example, an article that appeared in the *Black Panther* in August 1969 was titled "Zionism (Kosher Nationalism) + Imperialism = Fascism." The same month, the newspaper reported on BPP leader Eldridge Cleaver's appearance before a crowd in Algeria in which he shared the platform with a Fatah leader and proclaimed support for "the Arab commando movement." Cleaver told the crowd: "The United States uses the Zionist regime that usurped the land of the Palestinian people as a puppet and pawn."[26]

Like SNCC, the Black Panthers were widely accused of anti-Semitism by Jewish organizations and their allies, prompting BPP leader Huey Newton to refute the charge. Newton declared, "We are not anti-Semitic . . . we are against the government that will persecute the Palestinian people." He also made sure to affirm the party's support for revolutionaries in Israel who were striving to transform the nation into a "secular peoples' state," as well as the party's disapproval of conservative Arab states that were subverting the struggle to create "truly a peoples' republic" in the Arab world.[27]

The League of Revolutionary Black Workers (LRBW), based in Detroit, represented another radical black organization expressing solidarity with the Palestinian cause in the late 1960s and early 1970s. As detailed in chapter 2, in his position as editor of Wayne State University's newspaper the *South End*, LRBW leader John Watson supported the Organization of Arab Students and its promotion of Fatah. The relationship between LRBW leadership and the fedayeen went even deeper: Watson traveled to the Middle East and met with Fatah leaders, and when representatives of the Popular Front for the Liberation of Palestine visited Detroit, they met with members of the LRBW. Watson established a film company, Black Star Productions, which, among other films about American and Third World revolutionary movements, distributed a film produced by an Italian company titled *Al Fatah—The Palestinians*. Watson intended to donate half the film's proceeds to fedayeen in the Arab world.[28]

Tensions between some Jewish New Leftists and black radicals worsened during the National Conference for New Politics, a convention that brought together many groups of progressive and leftist activists in Chicago in September 1967. Although the white New Left was also forming an anti-imperialist consciousness in this period as it protested U.S. intervention in Vietnam and across the Third World, white radicals generally responded to the June War with more ambivalence than did black radicals. (However, as will be discussed below, by the early 1970s many organizations in the New Left came to share black radicals' condemnation of Zionism.) As the New Politics conference commenced, a caucus of radical black organizations presented thirteen resolutions that it insisted be endorsed if its members were to participate. Most of the resolutions demanded white support for black self-determination and political power, along with support for "liberation wars" throughout the Third World. They also called for 50 percent representation of African Americans on all conference committees and the establishment of a "white civilizing committee." Most white activists in attendance, keen to show solidarity with black nationalism, accepted these stipulations without much discussion.[29]

But controversy and debate greeted the one black caucus resolution that dealt with Palestine. The resolution commanded: "Condemn the imperialistic Zionist war," and added: "This condemnation does not imply anti-Semitism." Stokely Carmichael explained that the purpose of the resolution was, in a sense, to test the revolutionary credibility of white New Leftists: "If white people who call themselves revolutionary or radical want our support, they have to condemn Zionism." One New Left activist, Robert Scheer, attempted to propose an amendment that recognized Israel's existence but demanded its return to prewar borders. But the black caucus representatives refused to accept amendments and insisted that all the resolutions had to be adopted as written. As some Jewish attendees walked out in disgust, conference participants endorsed the set of resolutions by a three-to-one margin.[30]

Subsequently, New Left and progressive publications such as the *Berkeley Barb* and the *New Republic* printed accounts of the New Politics conference that portrayed the black caucus's demands as an outlandish power play and ridiculed the white New Left's acquiescence. According to Justin Vaisse in his study of the rise of the neoconservative movement, "Many young Jewish radicals were traumatized by this turn of events [at the conference] and quit the movement." Arab American activist Abdeen Jabara interpreted the episode differently, praising the conference for exhibiting a "new radicalism" that "refused to compromise the struggle against imperialism in order to mollify the Jewish section of the American left."[31] Jewish leaders called upon civil rights leaders to repudiate the conference's resolution on Israel, prompting leaders of the Urban League and the NAACP to issue denunciations of the conference. Martin Luther King Jr. assured Jewish organizations that the conference participants who represented his organization (the Southern Christian Leadership Conference) had voted against the resolution. King further reiterated his support for Israel, which he had expressed during the June War by signing a paid advertisement in the *New York Times* that pressed the Lyndon Johnson administration to support Israel's security.[32]

The division between moderate and radical African Americans over Israel and Palestine was showcased again in competing advertisements placed in the *New York Times* in 1970. Over two dozen black leaders, such as A. Philip Randolph, Whitney Young, and John Conyers, signed the ad titled "An Appeal by Black Americans for United States Support for Israel," which contrasted Israeli democracy and economic equality with "dictatorial one-party" systems that persecuted minorities in many Arab states. Though expressing concern for refugees, the ad argued that the best way for Arab people to improve their lives was to cease hostilities against Israel. It urged the U.S. government to use its power and aid to "guarantee Israel's right to exist as a nation."[33]

In response, an advertisement titled "An Appeal by Black Americans against United States Support of the Zionist Government of Israel" condemned Zionism as a "reactionary, racist ideology that justifies the expulsion of the Palestinian people from their homes and lands" and expressed "complete solidarity with our Palestinian brothers and sisters, who like us are struggling for self-determination and an end to racist oppression." This ad drew parallels between "the exploitation experienced by Afro-Americans,

Native Americans (Indians), Puerto Ricans, and Chicanos (Mexican Americans)" and "the exploitation of Palestinian Arabs and Oriental Jews by the Zionist state of Israel." Fifty-four activists, ranging from Grace and James Boggs, Frances Beal of the Third World Women's Alliance, and members of the Black Student Union at California State College cosponsored the anti-Zionist statement under the banner of an organization called the Committee of Black Americans for Truth about the Middle East.[34]

The black radicals' advertisement also indicted Israel for its relationship with South Africa, arguing that the two "white settler states" had been supporting each other. In the mid-twentieth century, Israel had opposed the apartheid regime in South Africa and provided assistance to developing African nations, but as the 1970s progressed and Israel found itself increasingly isolated in the Third World arena, it fortified ties to South Africa. Exposure of these ties increasingly became an integral component of African Americans' criticism of Israel. For example, at the National Black Political Convention in Gary, Indiana, in 1972, delegates declared that Israel was "working hand in hand with other militaristic interests in Africa, for example, South Africa" and called for the United States to end its support for Israel.[35]

Arab and Arab American organizations were instrumental in educating black activists about Israel's relationship with South Africa. For instance, at the 1969 Pan-African Cultural Festival held in Algeria, a festival attended by many leading African American radicals, Fatah leaders delivered a statement emphasizing the "racist similarity" which "brought Israel and South Africa together." In 1972, members of the AAUG gave presentations on Israeli–South African relations at the African American National Conference on Africa, held by the Congressional Black Caucus (CBC), and co-organized with many black organizations a symposium on Israel and South Africa at Ohio State University. In a specific instance, an AAUG member in Madison, Wisconsin, began attending meetings of the Madison Area Committee on Southern Africa and discovered that its members were unaware of Israel's policies toward Palestine and Israel's ties to South Africa. She informed the organization of these policies, prompting its members to form a study group on Israel which culminated in a position paper critical of Zionism.[36] Similarly, the OAS highlighted Israeli–South African relations when it interacted with African American activists. In 1978, the OAS joined with the All African People's Revolutionary Party, at the time led by Stokely Carmichael, to stage a major demonstration in Washington, D.C., in support of the PLO and African liberation. Speakers from both groups emphasized links between apartheid and Zionism and promoted Arab and African unity.[37]

Abdeen Jabara (left) and Shirley Chisholm appear together at an AAUG convention in 1972. At the podium is journalist George Hishmeh. (*AAUG Newsletter*, July 1972, AAUG Papers, Eastern Michigan University, Special Collections Library)

The AAUG's role in promoting African American–Arab American solidarity on Arab world politics was also evident in its cultivation of a relationship with U.S. presidential candidate Shirley Chisholm in the early 1970s. Chisholm, a black Democratic Party leader from New York City, attempted to bridge the gap between the moderate African American political leadership that supported Israel and the more radical elements of the black community who viewed Palestinians as fellow victims of white imperialism. As a representative to Congress in 1970, she had been one of the signatories to the *New York Times* ad calling for American support for Israel. But by 1972, while still supporting Israel's existence, Chisholm had grown more critical of Israel's treatment of Palestinians. During her presidential campaign, she issued a lengthy statement on the Israeli-Palestinian conflict that concentrated on the plight of the Palestinians and chastised U.S. policy in the Middle East for "completely ignor[ing] the desperate problems of human beings." Her statement compared the struggles of African Americans and Palestinians: "A generation has grown up in the Palestinian ghetto, and like the young who have survived their early years in our ghettos, the Palestinians have made it clear that they will no longer tolerate the injustice of their condition."[38]

Encountering considerable disapproval for her position, Chisholm backed off, and her name subsequently appeared on a pro-Israel statement issued by the Congressional Black Caucus. Abdeen Jabara, president of the AAUG, sent a telegram to the members of the CBC, including Chisholm, expressing "shock ... that you should consent to affix your name to the Zionist inspired statement which ignores rights of Palestinians." Chisholm responded by assuring Jabara she had not supported the CBC's position on Israel and claimed that a vote on the statement had not been taken. She subsequently accepted an invitation to speak at the annual banquet of AAUG's Washington, D.C., chapter, delivering a speech that evaded direct criticism of Israel but reiterated her sympathy for the Palestinians' struggle. Significantly, she represented Arabs' movements for justice as equivalent to movements of other oppressed peoples: "It is just and inevitable that Arab and Black Americans and other minority groups should be tired of being governed by laws they have little or no part in making and by officials in whose choice they have no voice.... There is now a social revolution in progress in this country. Black Power, Red Power, La Causa, and La Huelga; and yes, *Arab Power*—these are a few of the slogans of that revolution" (emphasis added). Chisholm thus asserted what most members of her AAUG audience likely believed: Arab and Arab American activism was intertwined with the constellation of "the movements" of the 1960s and 1970s.[39]

The New Left's Complicated Position on Palestine

As with many African American organizations, most white liberals and leftists evinced a pro-Zionist consensus in the mid-twentieth century, with some American leftists embracing the Israeli kibbutz movement. Compared with black nationalists, the white Left possessed minimal ideological bonds with Arab anticolonial movements before 1967. Indeed, discussion of the Israeli-Arab conflict was nearly absent from leftist writings prior to the June War. Although Israel's stunning victory caused some white leftists to appraise the Zionist state more critically, it increased the admiration of many others who viewed the country as a dynamic, democratic force heroically fending off reactionary powers.[40] But by the early 1970s, as anti-imperialist, Third World consciousness intensified and developments in the Middle East more clearly demonstrated the Palestinians' plight, most American leftist groups developed a pro-Palestinian, anti-Zionist position.

Nevertheless, on the whole, the American Left's commitment to the Palestinian revolution was soft and somewhat perfunctory; in general, the activists' understanding of the Arab-Israeli conflict was superficial, and their position was rooted in an idealized image of Third World guerrillas. Advocacy for Palestine was relegated to a minor place in the New Left's agenda, even when its organizations were concentrating on Third World causes. A few white American New Left activists, however, were well informed about the Middle East conflict and passionate about Palestinian liberation; some of them even led Palestinian solidarity organizations in the United States. No matter their level of awareness and commitment, New Leftists' expressions of sympathy for Palestinians and critiques of Israel offended and aggravated Zionists attached to the New Left, provoking most of them to leave the movement, as seen in the aftermath of the New Politics Convention.

Unlike radical black organizations such as SNCC and the Black Panthers, New Left groups did not immediately respond to the June War's outcome with unequivocal condemnation of Israel. For example, the alternative paper the *Berkeley Barb* published articles shortly after the war that praised Israel as "a bastion of liberal democracy" and favorably compared the Israeli military to the defiant underdog Viet Cong while likening the futile and corrupt Arab armies to the U.S. military.[41] One Jewish New Left activist observed in 1968 that most young people in the New Left were uninformed about and unconcerned by the Arab-Israeli conflict because they were so focused on domestic social conflicts and America's role in Vietnam. Of those who had formed some opinion, a few were ardently anti-Israel, but according to this activist, most of the "rank and file of the New Left, especially of the Jews within it, are sympathetic" and some were even "enthusiastic supporters of Israel." But he did think that, given the New Left's concerns about inequality and oppression, it was understandable that the movement would be asking critical questions of Israel's recent actions.[42]

The New Left magazine *Ramparts*, whose staff and financial backers included several Jewish activists, devoted its July 1967 issue to a measured discussion of the Arab-Israeli conflict. One contributor was I. F. Stone, the Jewish left-leaning journalist who had been a stalwart proponent of Zionism in the early twentieth century. After Israel's creation, Stone had grown concerned about the state's mistreatment of Palestinians, and he increasingly challenged Zionist thought. His essay in the *Ramparts* issue was generally evenhanded, expressing sympathy for the predicaments faced by both Israelis and Palestinians, but he put the onus upon Israel to find a way to compromise with Arabs. Placing the conflict in the context of 1960s anticolonialism, Stone wrote: "She [Israel] cannot remain a Western outpost in an Afro-Asian world casting off Western domination . . . . She must join the Third World if she is to survive . . . . [I]n the long run she cannot defeat the Arabs. She must join them."[43]

In contrast, Michael Walzer and Martin Peretz's joint contribution to the *Ramparts* forum was solidly supportive of Israel. Over the next three years the magazine continued to print articles by such leftist Jewish writers as Maurice Zeitlin, Michael P. Lerner, and Sol Stern that defended Israel as an embodiment of progressive democratic values and criticized Arab nations as backward and autocratic and thus unworthy of New Left support.[44] But *Ramparts* editor Robert Scheer, also Jewish, had become increasingly disenchanted with Israel and balanced his critique of antidemocratic Arab states with a critique of Israel's expansionism and the military's influence in the Israeli government. In 1972, after many Zionist Jews had parted ways with the magazine—and with the New Left as a whole—the magazine's book imprint, Ramparts Press, published a celebratory anthology of writings by Palestinian resistance groups.[45]

Other periodicals aligned with the New Left also published occasional pieces supportive of Palestinian nationalism. Like *Ramparts*, the leftist newspaper the *Guardian* shifted from a largely pro-Israel stance to a position in solidarity with the Palestinian resistance, in accordance with the paper's trajectory toward a Maoist, Third World orientation, and consequently antagonized its Zionist followers.[46] Though Students for a Democratic Society (SDS) was ambivalent about Israel, its propaganda arm, the Radical Education Project, included at least three anti-Zionist pamphlets in its catalog of literature on a wide assortment of leftist issues. Furthermore, a special issue of SDS's *New Left Notes* devoted to the stories of revolutionary women throughout the world included a piece about Palestinian women guerrillas.[47]

The New Left's underground press burgeoned in the 1960s and early 1970s, and just as the mainstream media acquired many of their reports from wire services such as the Associated Press, most of the alternative papers ran articles supplied by the Liberation News Service (LNS). Included in the collective of journalists that produced the LNS were Sheila Ryan and George Cavalletto, two New Leftists who had been involved in the civil rights and antiwar movements and had little prior knowledge of the Middle East. In 1969 they were traveling in Europe on their honeymoon and met French pro-Palestinian activist Ania Franco, who advised them to go to Cairo and meet with Fatah representatives. The Fatah members in turn suggested they proceed to Jordan, where Ryan and Cavalletto witnessed the appalling conditions experienced by Palestinian refugees. The following year, the LNS decided it should enhance its reporting about Third World liberation movements and stationed its reporters in Latin America, Asia, Africa, and the Middle East. Ryan and Cavalletto volunteered to serve as the LNS's Middle

East correspondents during which time they developed contacts not only with Fatah but also with the Democratic Front for the Liberation of Palestine and the Popular Front for the Liberation of Palestine, becoming passionate advocates of Palestinian liberation.[48]

When Ryan and Cavalletto returned to the United States, they conveyed what they had learned to their colleagues and discovered, in their words, that "there was minimal knowledge of the Palestinian issue in the anti-war, alternative movement that LNS was part of." They also encountered some resistance to the pro-Palestinian position within LNS and other underground papers. In response, they embarked on a project to educate LNS staffers and other New Leftists about the situation in Palestine. Ryan remembers that they held "sessions talking about Palestine because these papers were tending to stay away from the articles we were writing in LNS. We felt pretty successful. There was resistance but not intransigence. Most often I think they were won over. LNS was a very collective organization, so if there had been real resistance we wouldn't have gotten our articles published." Subsequently, their articles about Palestinians, along with reports about the Middle East by other LNS journalists, were occasionally picked up by leftist newspapers throughout the country.[49]

Organizations whose principal thrust was protesting the Vietnam War, however, seldom incorporated the Palestinian question in their agendas. Occasionally, activists who were informed about the Palestinian resistance tried to inject the issue into the antiwar movement's demonstrations. For example, a coalition of leftist antiwar activists who sought to address the Arab-Israeli conflict formed an organization after the June War called the Ad Hoc Committee on the Middle East. It led a protest at the Israeli Mission to the United Nations and charged that Israeli military leaders, chiefly Moshe Dayan, had received training from U.S. military commanders in Vietnam. The Committee on New Alternatives in the Middle East, which existed from 1970 to 1974, was formed by activists in the anti–Vietnam War movement, such as Noam Chomsky, Eric Fromm, and I. F. Stone, and embraced a socialist position.[50] The Committee to Support Middle East Liberation, based in New York City, disseminated literature critical of Israel on college campuses, and in early 1969 it cosponsored a demonstration with the leftist groups Youth against War and Fascism and the Coalition for an Anti-Imperialist Movement at the U.S. Mission to the United Nations calling for solidarity with the Arab people against U.S. imperialism.[51] Some leftist peace activists who by the late 1960s had radicalized their agenda and formed anti-imperialist organizations included Palestine among the Third

World liberation movements they championed, just as the Liberation News Service did in this period. At the University of California-Berkeley, the Tri-Continental Progressive Student Committee distributed leaflets with themes such as "Vietnam-Palestine One Struggle," and the campus's Liberation Support Movement showed "films of liberation" about Vietnam, Angola, the Black Panther Party, and Fatah. The Anti-Imperialist Movement at Columbia University concentrated primarily on Vietnam, with a secondary emphasis on Latin America, but it also sponsored talks by Sheila Ryan and George Cavalletto about the Palestinian resistance.[52]

At times the effort to blend Palestine with Vietnam proved contentious. For example, at an organizing committee meeting for the Mobilization to End the War in Vietnam in June 1967, one revolutionary organization tried to put the simultaneously occurring June War on the agenda but was voted down because the issue was deemed "divisive" and "antidemocratic." Similarly, when Arab and Iranian students at San Jose State brought up Palestinian and Iranian revolutionary movements during an antiwar protest, Jewish students at the demonstration asserted that participants should focus only on Vietnam.[53]

The late 1960s and early 1970s saw prominent peace activists Noam Chomsky and Daniel Berrigan address the plight of Palestinians as they protested threats to human rights around the world. Chomsky, the Jewish linguist and major figure on the left, was becoming well known not only for his challenge to America's role in Vietnam but also for his sympathetic consideration of Palestinian rights, a position that stopped short of support for armed resistance. Invited to speak at AAUG's convention in 1970, Chomsky advocated the establishment of a Palestinian state encompassing both Arabs and Jews, but he warned that a military approach to statehood would be self-destructive.[54] Berrigan, the Catholic priest and radical pacifist, also criticized Israel as an obstacle to peace in the Middle East, and he also spoke at an AAUG convention in this period. Calling for the protection of both Jewish and Arab human rights in the Middle East, Berrigan was much more evenhanded in his talk than was the stance held by most leftist supporters of Palestinian liberation; nevertheless, his appearance in front of the AAUG prompted damaging accusations by Jewish groups that he was anti-Semitic.[55]

The famed American counterculturalist Timothy Leary also exhibited support for the Palestinian resistance in the early 1970s, comparing "the holy fanaticism of the Palestinians" to "the rage of the blacks, the fierceness of the browns, . . . the righteous mania of the Weathermen, and the pervasive resentment of the young" as they joined in resistance to "genocidal war" conducted by the American war machine. Broken out of a California prison by members of the radical group the Weather Underground (WU), Leary hid out with several members of the WU and the Black Panthers in Algeria in 1970. During this period of exile, in what fellow activist Stew Albert recalls as an effort to "build up Tim's Third World credentials" to transform him from an acid proponent to a political heavy, Leary and a few members of the BPP and WU traveled to Lebanon and attempted to enter Jordan to meet with leaders of Fatah. Their plan was foiled when the American media discovered their presence in Beirut.[56] It is doubtful that Leary or the Weather Underground possessed an in-depth understanding of the Palestinian cause, but support for the fedayeen became a part of their romantic revolutionary rhetoric, as demonstrated in this "communiqué" from the WU in 1970: "With the NLF [National Liberation Front] and the North Vietnamese, with the Democratic Front for the Liberation of Palestine and Al Fatah, with Rap Brown and Angela Davis, with all black and brown revolutionaries, the Soledad brothers and all prisoners of war in Amerikan concentration camps we know that peace is only possible with the destruction of U.S. imperialism. Our organization commits itself to the task of freeing these prisoners of war."[57]

The American organizations most unequivocally supportive of the Palestinian resistance movement were revolutionary Marxist groups, such as the Socialist Workers Party, Youth against War and Fascism (an affiliate of the Workers World Party), and the Progressive Labor Party. Their advocacy extended to encouragement of the Arab people's armed revolution against both Israel and conservative Arab states in pursuit of an international proletarian revolution. Members of these organizations joined with Arab and Arab American students at various American universities in pro-Palestinian demonstrations and interacted with representatives of Palestinian fedayeen groups who were visiting the United States. For example, in Detroit the Socialist Workers Party, which included progressive Jews such as Peter Buch, was instrumental in working with the League of Revolutionary Black Workers and other leftist groups to stage a screening of *The Battle of Algiers* to promote understanding of the Palestinian resistance.[58]

In contrast, the Communist Party USA (CPUSA) took a more moderate position due to its alignment with the Soviet Union, whose contradictory policy on the Israeli-Arab conflict supported both Israel's existence and Arabs' military resistance. Although it saw Israeli leaders as "agents of U.S. imperialism" who were bent on oppressing Arab people, the CPUSA supported a political, not military, solution that would restore Israel's pre-1967 borders. Maoist groups in the United States tried to maintain the Chinese position on the Middle East, which was most concerned with ending both U.S. and Soviet influence in the region while promoting Third World liberation movements and condemning Zionism as imperialist.[59]

Revolutionary organizations operating in Detroit auto plants promoted the Palestinian cause as a strategy to appeal to Arab workers and encourage unity among all Third World workers, including African Americans. In its publication distributed to workers at one of Chrysler's factories, the radical labor organization Wildcat featured articles that condemned Israeli and U.S. imperialism and encouraged socialist revolution in the Middle East. The Maoist Revolutionary Communist Party stationed Arabic-speaking organizers, including Joel Beinin, in Detroit auto plants. Beinin worked with Arab Americans in the city who were sympathetic to the Popular Front for the Liberation of Palestine to blend appeals to liberation of Palestinians and workers' rights in America.[60]

A few activists in the American New Left who possessed a keen consciousness of Palestinian oppression devoted their energies to organizations established expressly to promote Americans' solidarity with Palestine. Representative of this effort was the Middle East Research and Information Project (MERIP), a collective of activist journalists and scholars, most of whom were not Arab, founded in 1971. Many of the MERIP staffers had prior experience in the Arab world, such as through service in the Peace Corps or as children of missionaries in the Middle East.[61] The group put out a monthly publication, *MERIP Reports*, to present examinations of Middle East issues from the Arab Left's perspective. In addition to producing its own reporting, MERIP distributed the publications of the Beirut-based Institute for Palestine Studies and the PLO's Research Center. Like the LNS, MERIP intended to operate as a news service whose articles would be picked up by other media outlets. Not surprisingly, *MERIP Reports* occasionally ran articles about the Palestinian resistance written by LNS's Sheila Ryan, who operated in the same New Left network.[62]

Soon, Ryan, who had a background of civil disobedience activism on civil rights and antiwar causes, was motivated to engage in more grassroots advocacy on behalf of Palestinian liberation. Along with George Cavalletto, she headed up the Palestine Solidarity Committee (PSC) in New York City, which by the mid-1970s was staging major demonstrations in support of Palestine. (Palestine Solidarity Committees were also established in other American cities.) Other members of New York City's PSC, such as Marion Feinberg, Milt Taam and Lou Shafer, were young, radical Jews who had been involved in a number of New Left causes in the late 1960s and early 1970s, including antiwar activities and the American Indian Movement. The PSC worked closely with Palestinian community organizations and Arab American organizations and tried to create bridges between them and other groups associated with the American New Left. As a solidarity organization, its emphasis was on raising the consciousness of non–Arab Americans, particularly those already active in leftist causes, through frequent speaking engagements and teach-ins around the country, protest actions, and its newspaper, *Palestine!* Ryan gave hundreds of talks at both American universities and Arab American fund-raising events. She also used connections she had made with Fatah when she had visited the Middle East to set up meetings between Fatah and PLO representatives and New Left activists in New York City.[63]

The PSC's "Salute to Palestine" march in June 1976 was planned as a counterdemonstration to a simultaneous "Salute to Israel" parade in New York City. The pro-Palestine demonstration was cosponsored by a coalition of over twenty anti-imperialist organizations, including the Black Panther Party, the International Indian Treaty Council, the Puerto Rican Socialist Party, the Union of Democratic Filipinos, and the Venceremos Brigade. It also included a contingent of anti-Zionist Jews. The PSC's *Palestine!* reported that demonstrators marched through midtown Manhattan "carrying Palestinian flags and banners in English, Spanish, and Arabic." Speakers included a representative of Columbia University's Arab Student Association, a PLO observer to the United Nations, and Jimmy Durham of the American Indian Movement, who compared his people's circumstances to those of Palestinian refugees.[64]

In a more recent interview, Ryan and Cavalletto stated they found "immediate openness" from "the Third World parts of the New Left" and observed that "African Americans and Hispanic Americans had less resistance" to the Palestinian cause than some constituencies of the white New Left. Nevertheless, as with their earlier experience in the LNS, they encountered some resistance to the PSC's work within progressive circles. For example, they failed to gain representation at a large demonstration in Philadelphia in 1976 held to advocate Puerto Rican independence. The Puerto Rican Day organizers, who cultivated an impressive coalition of progressive and Third World groups, decided that the involvement of the Palestine Solidarity Committee would have, in Ryan's recollection, "dissuaded more mainstream organizations from participating." As another example, PSC activists tried to reach out to New York City elected officials to support their stances (such as opposition to the City Council's attempts to close PLO offices in the city) but found that even progressive African American and Puerto Rican American council members were reluctant to take public positions that could be deemed "pro-PLO." According to Ryan, "It was already clear that we had narrower groups that we could draw on than groups who were concerned about, say, Chile. Even people who could agree with us had to have some caution about how the positions they espoused on Palestinian issues would affect their ability to work with broader constituencies on anything else.... So we need to nuance what we're saying about the acceptability of this issue. It was acceptable to people who were very much of the Left. But once you move beyond that, there were a lot of sensitivities." Still, Ryan and Cavalletto believe their work did positively influence the New Left's, and even the wider American public's, assessment of the Palestinian position. Before 1969, they argue, most Americans, including progressives, had little cognizance of critiques of Zionism or the plight of Palestinians. But by the end of the 1970s, support for, or at least awareness of, the case for Palestinian independence had markedly increased, in part due to consciousness-raising by groups like the PSC.[65]

While the advocacy of Palestinian rights certainly became more acceptable in progressive circles over the course of the 1970s, the issue remained on the margins of American leftist activism. Arabs and their revolutionary struggles were often omitted even from American organizations devoted to Third World activism. The Third World Liberation Front, which took hold in the Bay Area in the late 1960s, spoke expansively about Third World coalitions among African, Latin American, Asian, and indigenous American peoples, but in its imagining of "Asians" (and in its development of ethnic studies programs in Californian universities) it ignored Arabs, Iranians, and other Middle Easterners. Similarly, Columbia University's Third World Coalition only addressed Vietnamese, Latin Americans, Africans, and African Americans in their demonstrations, omitting Arab world issues. Joel Beinin recalls that the Revolutionary Communist Party in the 1970s essentially ignored the Palestinian cause except when the party organized in the Detroit area, where it recognized it needed to appeal to the substantial number of Arab American workers in the auto plants. Even Abdeen Jabara, who interacted with many leftist organizations that supported Palestine, acknowledged that maintaining sustained commitment to Palestinian advocacy from sympathetic non-Arab groups was difficult when they were consumed by their own issues and struggles. While Jabara was convinced that most elements of the American Left accepted that Israel was imperialist, he recognized that leftists faced two main obstacles that tested their support for the Arab position: first, Jewish charges that critics of Zionism wanted to annihilate

Israel, and second, the conservative nature of most Arab states.[66] These concerns caused some leftists' uncertainty or avoidance of the Arab-Israeli conflict in their Third World activism.

Taking a pessimistic view of the New Left's commitment to Arab positions, Joe Stork, a leftist journalist on the MERIP staff who often worked with Sheila Ryan, argued in 1972 that the New Left's interest in and commentary on Palestine had been conspicuously limited. One reason for the movement's lack of attention to Palestine, he noted, was the "belief that such activity would be diversionary and hinder the primary goal of the movement—that is, to stop the war in Indochina." Further, Stork pointed to overall confusion and ambivalence about Arab world issues on the part of the New Left. In general, when American activists did incorporate Palestinian liberation into their advocacy, they possessed an "unsophisticated position" deriving from their "uncritical romanticism" about "guerrilla movements in general," instead of careful understanding and close study of the Israeli-Arab conflict. Thus, according to Stork, when Jewish Americans expressed distress over the New Left's anti-Zionism—and, by extension, anti-Semitism—their alarm was overblown because the New Left's commitment to the position was often ambivalent and largely superficial.[67]

In a similar piece, "Israel and the New Left," Noam Chomsky also denied that there was a "New Left doctrine on the Middle East." In response to Jews who charged that the New Left pushed an anti-Zionist agenda, Chomsky contended that most anthologies of New Left writing omitted discussion of Middle East problems, and those publications that did address Israel and Palestine, such as *Ramparts*, usually presented a diversity of views and rarely, if ever, called for the destruction of Israel. He charged that many of his Jewish colleagues had been exaggerating the Left's (including his own) antipathy toward Israel because their real aim was to discredit the New Left and all the positions it stood for, especially its determination to end the war in Vietnam.[68]

Indeed, Chomsky was defending himself against charges of anti-Semitism and treachery launched by many Jewish activists against Jewish intellectuals who were critical of Israel. During and after the June War, most Jews in America had adopted a resolute devotion to Israel, and this fervent embrace—a turning point which historian Judith Klinghoffer calls an "epiphany"—extended to many progressive Jews who had been skeptical of Zionism and previously felt distant from Israel. Suddenly, their Jewish identity was bound up in the survival of Israel, and they could not accept fellow Jews who questioned Israel's justification for defeating its Arab enemies or who interpreted Israel in an imperialist framework.[69]

Some leftist Jews struggled to reconcile their ideological commitment to the Left with their unwavering support for Israel. For instance, two students at Wayne State University who identified themselves as members of the leftist Israeli organization Hashomer Hatzair wrote a letter to the editor of the student newspaper the *South End* to express their distress at the paper's promotion of the Palestinian cause. They wrote, "As socialists, we find it difficult to align ourselves with a nation [Israel] who, in order to survive, must pay lip service to imperialist powers. As Jews, however, we find it impossible to align ourselves with revolutionaries whose Third World will be at the expense of the state of Israel, and thus at the expense of the Jewish people." This political tension was also experienced by Sol Stern, a New Left writer whose essay in *Ramparts* entitled "My Jewish Problem—and Ours" explored the dilemma of being Jewish and a leftist. He felt caught between his commitment to Israel, whose rightward drift and closer ties to U.S. power troubled him, and his participation in the New Left, which he castigated for its "crude and infantile approach to the complex moral and political issues underlying the Arab-Israeli dispute."[70]

In that 1971 essay, Stern remained hopeful that pro-Israel leftists could still find a place in the American New Left. But many other Jewish leftists who shared Stern's disgust at what they perceived as the New Left's "knee jerk approach to the Middle East" were abandoning the movement, particularly after episodes such as the anti-Zionist resolution at the Conference for New Politics. Shifting sharply to the right, these erstwhile leftists soon helped formulate a new movement, neoconservatism, comprised of diverse individuals, Christian and Jewish, who took conservative positions on a number of political and economic issues, including promotion of American strength on the world stage. One neoconservative principle was advocating staunch U.S. support for Israel. While support for Palestine by the New Left and, especially, black radicals triggered the rightward swing for most of the Jewish neoconservatives, many Jews rejected the Left as a result of more fundamental transformations in the civil rights and New Left movements that they found alienating. Many Jews in such movements were already feeling disaffected from the growing militancy and antiwhite ideas embraced by certain groups of activists. Believing that the movements were tending toward both communism and anti-Semitism, many Jews could no longer envision a place for themselves in the New Left.[71]

Still, Jewish neoconservatives grappled with why activists on the American Left were taking a position critical of Israel. Dismissing the substance of the leftists' criticism of Israel, scholars such as Nathan Glazer and Mordecai Chertoff attributed what they saw as the New Left's anti-Zionist doctrine to the movement's immature urge to rebel against success and rationality. Seymour Martin Lipset argued that the New Leftists would reflexively support any underdog, whether or not the underdog was principled and justified; while the New Leftists had formerly viewed Israel as the underdog and worthy of support, they now believed the Arabs had earned that sympathetic position. Further, Lipset stated, in the New Left's use of "guilt by association," the movement would impulsively oppose any state that was supported by the U.S. government. As for the black radicals, Lipset thought their anti-Zionism (which he considered anti-Semitism) was a symptom of their desire to cut ties with white liberals as well as an expression of their resentment of Jewish prosperity in America, rather than a principled objection to Israel's policies. Yet, even though these Jewish intellectuals found the movements' "anti-Jewish foolishness" to be puerile and illogical, they considered the anti-Zionist rhetoric dangerous and warned Jews and American policymakers to be vigilant against American-led threats to Israel's existence.[72]

Some Jewish groups extended this vigilance to keeping an eye on the interactions between American leftist groups and Arab and Arab American groups. It seems clear that some Jewish activists were urging U.S. authorities to monitor the American Left's relationship with Arab groups and that Israeli intelligence sources passed information to the federal government about these groups' activities in the United States and abroad. In the late 1960s and early 1970s, the FBI augmented its existing investigations of American leftist organizations under COINTELPRO (a portmanteau derived from counterintelligence program) by also monitoring the organizations' contacts with Palestinian groups and the Organization of Arab Students. A classified FBI report issued in June 1970 included sections titled "Arab-Black Extremist Relations" and "Support for Arabs among Subversive Groups and Radicals." Other U.S. officials similarly pegged these interactions as threatening to American interests. This climate of suspicion soon led to a crackdown on Arab Americans' political activities and violations of their civil liberties in a federal government program called Operation Boulder, detailed in chapter 5.[73]

Arab Americans' Interactions with the Movements

As has been demonstrated, connections between Arab American organizations and American black and leftist organizations during the late 1960s and 1970s existed, but the links were often tenuous. Usually they existed more in the realm of ideology—specifically, anti-imperialist ideology—than in sustained face-to-face interactions among members of the various groups. Other times the linkages hinged on the personal relationships a few Arab American individuals maintained with a few African American or white leftist activists, rather than widespread and mutually supportive interactions between most members of these communities. These patterns—both the interactions among individual activists representing different racial and ethnic groups as well as the obstacles to such crossover interactions among the rank and file—were also experienced by other activist communities of color in this period.

Despite the difficulties of constructing solid alliances with non-Arab groups, the key leftist Arab American organizations and their leaders recognized that, as a marginalized minority whose political concerns and diasporic position were little understood by other Americans, they needed to attract broader support from Americans who were engaged in oppositional politics. Michael Suleiman has observed that "in advancing their views, [Arab American] organizations often use leftist rhetoric and project themselves as anti-imperialist rather than simply nationalist."[74] This anti-imperialist framing by Arab American leftists was both a genuine ideological conviction and a strategy to legitimize their issues and gain representation in the American public sphere. Their emphasis on antiracism and anti-imperialism, as well as their opposition to U.S. government violations of their civil liberties, tapped into the common threads that united and intertwined the panoply of oppositional movements on the left into "The Movement."

Several Arab American activists in the Detroit area serve as prime examples of individuals who, through their participation in other leftist movements, formed personal relationships with non-Arab activists, relationships that translated into institutional linkages. Ismael Ahmed, a third-generation Arab American from Dearborn, became deeply involved with the network of white leftist and black radical activists in the Detroit area and worked on antiwar, civil rights, and labor issues in the late 1960s. Meanwhile, he was barely cognizant of Arab American organizing. Ahmed spent a lot of time at a coffeehouse in Dearborn called the People's Exchange, described by him as "a hothouse of leftist recruiting." As a part of the collective that gathered there, he multiplied his contacts with members of radical groups such as the Black Panthers and the White Panthers. For a time, he lived in a house in Detroit with SDS members from Ann Arbor who wanted to organize in the city. Through these contacts, he was invited by the leftist Venceremos Brigade to join its trip to Cuba to cut sugar cane and learn about the revolution. Upon his return to Detroit, Ahmed moved to a different house where he hung a big poster of Che Guevara on the front door and often hosted community activist meetings. Eventually he started his own underground newspaper, the *Stillborn Press*, which featured commentary on issues ranging from Third World liberation struggles to racial oppression in Detroit.[75]

By this time, the early 1970s, Ahmed had grown more politically aware of Arab world conflicts and Arab American activism, largely owing to his contacts with activists Nabeel Abraham and Hasan Nawash, members of Wayne State University's Organization of Arab Students. As discussed in chapter 2, Abraham and Nawash frequently visited the Southend neighborhood of Dearborn to promote Palestinian fedayeen groups. In their encounters with Ahmed, they persuaded him that given his commitment to anti-imperialism and minority rights, he should be politically active on causes dear to the Arab diaspora. Ahmed soon became deeply involved in Arab American community organizing in the Southend and combined his dedication to antiwar and civil rights agendas with his emerging politicization on Arab and Arab American issues. For instance, alongside articles about South Vietnamese guerrillas and the trial of Black Panther leader Bobby Seale, the February 1971 issue of the *Stillborn Press* featured a story on the Southend's fight against a city plan to destroy the largely Arab immigrant neighborhood.[76]

During the 1970s, when Ahmed organized Arab American autoworkers in the Arab Workers Caucus (discussed in chapter 6), he drew upon his contacts with the League of Revolutionary Black Workers. When he helped create the Arab American community center ACCESS in the Southend, he borrowed from models he was familiar with in community programs created by the Black Panthers and Latin Americans for Social Development (LA SED). And when he contributed to organizing Palestine Day demonstrations in Dearborn, he was able to mobilize supporters from non-Arab activist groups to participate. He remembers, "I began challenging other people on the left on these questions" of Arab and Arab American justice. As a well-known figure in Detroit's leftist community, Ahmed represented the transference of ideas, tactics, and personnel from the wider American Left to Arab American organizing.[77]

The American-born Nabeel Abraham also began his activism in the civil rights and antiwar movements before embracing Arab diasporic politics. While in high school at Detroit's Cass Tech, he dated a young non-Arab woman whose family members were prominent progressive activists. By accompanying her to demonstrations and being introduced to activists, Abraham's leftist consciousness began to form. Even as he devoted most of his energy to activism on Arab issues while a member of the OAS at Wayne State, he still participated in rallies against the Vietnam War and demonstrations in support of African American rights, along with helping the Dodge Revolutionary Union Movement (DRUM) with organizing activities. Abraham remembers participating in one antiwar sit-in at the university president's office during which he spent most of the time arguing with a Zionist SDS member over the Arab-Israeli conflict.[78]

Other students in OAS made connections between their activist focus, Palestinian liberation, and the New Left's protest movements. OAS members Hasan Nawash and George Khoury were strongly opposed to American intervention in Vietnam and were active in demonstrations against the war. In a later interview, Nawash remembers "feeling like I'm a Vietnamese myself.... I would feel their pain... just like if these people were Palestinians." Khoury, a graduate student at Wayne State who was also employed by Chevrolet, was fired from his job because his boss had seen him on television making a speech at an anti–Vietnam War rally in Detroit and accused Khoury of being anti-American and thus unemployable at Chevrolet.[79]

Probably the most notable Arab American leader to traverse the Arab American and American activist communities, both in Detroit and nationally, was attorney Abdeen Jabara. Even growing up in the remote northern Michigan town of Mancelona, Jabara developed a keen interest in Arab world affairs from an early age, largely due to his extended family's enthusiasm for Arab politics, especially their admiration for Gamal Abdel Nasser's pan-Arab nationalism. During his undergraduate years at the University of Michigan, Jabara had the opportunity to take language classes in Arabic and travel in Egypt, Lebanon, and Syria. His awareness of Third World nationalism was further sparked by his participation in the Institute of World Affairs, an institute in Connecticut that studies international conflicts, the summer after he graduated from the University of Michigan. He learned about the Non-aligned Movement and the Bandung Conference and became intensely interested in the Algerian Revolution. Later, while attending law school at Wayne State University in the early 1960s, he began relating developments in American politics to developments worldwide. Jabara told interviewer Janice Terry: "In law school the civil rights movement and the war in Vietnam . . .

had a very profound impact on my consciousness" in terms of making connections between American politics and global conflicts. "I related the social struggles in the Middle East and the social struggles and the political struggles that were happening in the U.S., and I related the American prosecution of the war in Vietnam to the ... colonial involvement in the Middle East." His early commitment to pursuing civil and human rights law was evident when he established a chapter of the Law Students Civil Rights Research Council while he was a student at Wayne State.[80]

After spending a year following law school in Beirut working for the PLO Palestine Research Center, Jabara returned to the Detroit area and became increasingly dedicated to advocacy of both the Palestinian resistance and socialist causes in the United States. Before opening his own practice, he worked for Ernest Goodman's law firm in Detroit, which was well known for its work on social and political causes as well as its racial integration; the firm's involvement in the southern civil rights movement, in particular, made a significant impact on Jabara. While working there he moved to a poor, rundown neighborhood in Detroit. According to Jabara, living in that destitute inner-city environment, "coupled with what was happening nationally and internationally," radicalized him even further. In the late 1960s and early 1970s, he developed connections to a number of radical organizations active in Detroit, including the Socialist Workers Party and the Youth against War and Fascism, along with national left-leaning organizations such as the National Lawyers Guild and the National Peace Action Coalition, and he soon became a significant figure in Detroit's antiwar network. As a participant in these organizations, he urged non-Arab leftists to take positions in support of Palestinian and Arab revolutionary movements by impressing upon them the consistency of such a stance with their commitment to Third World self-determination and human rights.[81]

ONLY A MINORITY OF Arab American activists practiced the kind of sustained transmovement involvement that such individuals as Abdeen Jabara and Ismael Ahmed did. But their individual associations and personal relationships (what Nabeel Abraham described as his activist "freelancing") carried over in significant ways to the organizational level. As a leader of the AAUG, Jabara pursued alliances with non-Arab organizations that represented American minorities and subscribed to anti-imperialism. He, Ibrahim Abu-Lughod, and other AAUG leaders consistently positioned the association in support of liberation movements throughout the Third World and the United States, and they cultivated relationships with American antiwar and black activists.

On university campuses, OAS chapters sought support from other student activist organizations and often shaped their literature and demonstrations in such a way as to appeal to antiwar and pro–Third World students. At Wayne State, the personal connections between a few Arab student activists and black radicals on campus facilitated black organizations' cosponsorship of anti-Israel protests. Ismael Ahmed was able to attract outside support for the Arab American community center in Dearborn through his personal contacts with activists in other movements and institutions. When Arab American activists such as Jabara and Ahmed were illegally monitored and harassed by the FBI and other law enforcement agencies, they reached out for support from activists in other organizations who had experienced that form of political persecution, further enhancing the bonds between American racial minorities, American leftists, and Arab Americans who were often treated as "enemies" by the American state.

The predication of cross-ethnic organizational bonds on the networks created by individual activists was not unique to Arab American organizing in the 1960s and 1970s. For example, black activist Denise Oliver was a pivotal figure in fostering alliances between the Puerto Rican revolutionary group the Young Lords and communities of African American activists, even when exclusivist nationalist impulses were driving them apart. Similarly, Japanese American activists Yuri Kochiyama and Richard Aoki reached out to activists in other racial and ethnic minority groups to create solidarities among Third World liberation movements.[82] In her study of the American Indian activist movement, historian Sherry Smith documents the significant support provided to "Red Power" by a whole host of American activist movements. The support often surfaced when prominent movement figures such as Dick Gregory, Angela Davis, or Corky Gonzalez appeared at Indian protests as a way to demonstrate cross-group solidarity.[83] Often, then, it was the agency of individual activist "entrepreneurs" that brought movements together, at least at the level of leadership.

As Jabara and other Arab American leaders understood, the coalition-building strategy was imperative for Arab Americans—a marginalized, largely invisible minority—to claim legitimacy, augment their clout, and promote their transnational politics in the American public sphere. In his AAUG presidential address in 1972, Jabara asserted that it was only when Arab Americans "act[ed] in concert with their natural allies that they can make a difference." Sherry Smith argues that a similar priority operated for the American Indian movement. A crucial part of the American Indian movement's strategy was to "consciously and purposefully [seek] partnerships" with activists in other movements. In doing so, the Indians "intended to strengthen their own power through loose coalitions with them."[84]

In building coalitions, the AAUG could have sought allies among white Americans in the power elite, but leaders such as Abu-Lughod, Jabara, and Naseer Aruri did not view powerful whites as Arab Americans' "natural" allies. The orientation of these Arab American activist leaders was influenced by the inhospitable political climate in the United States. The major American political parties were so sympathetic to Israel and averse to Arab, particularly Palestinian, interests that most left-leaning Arab Americans believed they would encounter intractable repudiation from the political establishment. Instead, for political and ideological reasons, they oriented the AAUG toward alliances with victimized people of color around the world and their supporters. This strategy was a way to gain access to, in Louise Cainkar's words, "mainstream vehicles of dissent." [85]

The Action Committee on American-Arab Relations (ACAAR), a small organization founded and run by Dr. Mohammad T. Mehdi, also nurtured these alliances and employed this framing of Arab issues in the American protest arena. Based in New York City, ACAAR picketed events at which Israeli bonds were sold; brought antidiscrimination suits against businesses, organizations, and the state of New York; and filed complaints with media outlets to demand equal time for presenting the Palestinian point of view. One example of the connection ACAAR sought to draw among the movements is its newsletter article about government repression of the Black Panthers and the trial of the "Chicago Eight" (eight antiwar activists accused by the government of conspiring to incite a riot at the 1968 Democratic National Convention in Chicago). The article declared: "The Panthers are the natural allies of the Palestinians, and the Conspiracy 8 are the allies of the Panthers. The links grow stronger every day, for all are engaged in the same struggle against a common enemy. Repression, no matter what its face, is repression: be it the genocidal attacks on the Panthers, the counterrevolutionary war in Vietnam, or the expansionist aggressions by Israel."[86] This rhetoric, patterned on the analysis used by the American New Left to weave together numerous oppositional movements, was common among Arab American leftist activists and their organizations.

Formulating bonds with other racial and ethnic minority groups in a spacious Third World coalition required positioning Arab Americans as a parallel nonwhite minority. In her study of interactions among minority group activists in Los Angeles in the 1960s, Laura Pulido shows how Japanese American leftists believed they had to reach out to other racial minorities because their group was small and often ignored in activist circles, a concern less experienced by the relatively larger communities of African Americans and Mexican Americans, which, she states, "felt more empowered to act alone." Blacks and Mexicans generally did not view Asian Americans as fellow victims of American racism, a view that contrasted with Japanese American activists' self-perception as an oppressed minority. Thus, to foster solidarity with African American and Mexican American activist groups and participate in the network of oppositional politics, Japanese American activists in Los Angeles actively claimed a nonwhite identity so they could be accepted in an alliance as Third World "people of color."[87]

This process of "racialization" was fraught with tension among Arab Americans, a people whose racial identity had long traversed the boundary between white and nonwhite. As Sarah Gualtieri has shown in her book *Between Arab and White*, which concentrates on Syrian Americans, their relationship with whiteness has been "uneven and contested" since the early twentieth century. Gualtieri argues, "In certain instances Syrians participated in white supremacy, but in others they resisted it and forged alliances with people of color." On the whole, though, most Arabs in the United States, particularly before the 1960s, claimed a white racial identity, just as most ethnic groups coming to the United States from Europe had done. Whiteness, of course, conferred overwhelming political and social privileges and protections in America.[88]

This dominant association with whiteness began to shift in the 1960s and 1970s owing to a convergence of factors both internal and external to Americans of Arab ethnic origin. First, the demographics of Arab immigrants shifted, particularly after a change in American immigration policy in 1965 that expanded immigration opportunities for people living in the Arab world. Arab immigrants in this period came from several countries, including Palestine, Yemen, Lebanon, and Iraq, and more of them were Muslim than in previous waves of Arab immigration to the United States. Their class backgrounds varied, but many were poor and from peasant origins. Due to their social status and to the recent histories of the countries from which they came, Arab immigrants in this period tended to have an identity grounded in anticolonial movements of people of color.[89]

Second, Arab Americans were influenced by the atmosphere of civil rights and antiwar activism taking hold in the United States in this period. More specifically, many were inspired by the Black Power model which challenged assimilation and promoted the political assertion of minority group identity and cultural pride in racial and ethnic differences—an attitude that was also energizing the consciousness of white ethnic groups. Third, Arabs in America increasingly were subject to more stereotyping and discrimination, especially after the 1967 war and subsequent Israeli-Arab clashes. The "racism" experienced by Arab Americans was variable; in some cases it emanated from Americans' political animosity toward Arabs in the Middle East, sometimes it stemmed from xenophobic bigotry, and often it was a combination of political, nativist, and jingoist antagonism. Whatever the nature or source of the prejudice, Arab Americans were marked as "others" and have encountered widespread hostility and suspicion in the ensuing decades.[90]

In the 1970s, the experience of Arab immigrants in their homelands thus combined with the paradoxical pro–civil rights and anti-Arab environment they encountered in the United States to produce a community more apt to identify as nonwhite and to critique white power and western "Orientalism." Development of this minority consciousness also involved, more than ever before, the construction of a collective identity as Arab Americans. Although assertion of an Arab American identity was not entirely new in this period, multiple generations of immigrants with origins in various Arab nations, villages, and sects were increasingly united as they found themselves grouped together, stigmatized, and even attacked in the United States. While this "ethnopolitical awakening," as political scientist Yossi Shain has termed it, was most keenly felt by the recent immigrants, it was also experienced by many American-born Arabs, especially those whose political sympathies tended to the left. Even assimilated Arab Americans who had always considered themselves a white ethnic group comparable to Americans of European heritage increasingly felt the sting of negative stigma, which served to heighten their sense of "Arabness."[91]

Although Arab American organizing in the few years after the 1967 war focused on addressing Arabs' oppression in the Arab world, activists in groups such as the AAUG and ACCESS increasingly recognized and contested the discrimination faced by people of Arab origin in America. In the early 1970s, AAUG conferences were incorporating discussions of the federal government's violations of Arab Americans' civil liberties, discrimination against Arab Americans in communities such as Dearborn, and harmful stereotypes of Arabs in American school textbooks. While the analysis of the Arab American experience was still secondary to their promotion of Palestinian liberation and Arab nationalism, Arab American activists' consciousness of minority group discrimination in the United States was heightened in the 1970s, and many of them used the term "racism" to characterize the prejudice.[92]

Some non-Arab leftists also conceived of Arabs as people of color who suffered from racism in the United States. Often, these activists characterized Arabs as one of the groups comprising "Third World" people, a designation used to indicate colonized people of color. For example, Greek American leftist Dan Georgakas viewed Arab immigrant autoworkers as occupying the same "Third World worker" position as Caribbean and South Americans, Mexicans, and Asians. He predicted that an alliance between Arab workers and militant black workers would develop out of common experiences and grievances. In their book *Detroit: I Do Mind Dying*, Georgakas and Marvin Surkin argued that blacks in the revolutionary labor movement saw Arab Americans as a "racial minority" that, like other racial minority groups, could organize in solidarity with African Americans.[93]

This categorization of Arabs as a nonwhite people can also be seen in Ismael Ahmed's participation in the Venceremos Brigade. During a Brigade meeting to prepare for the trip to Cuba, the leader directed the participants to split into caucuses of "white people" and "third world people." Ahmed remembers, "I looked both ways and I said, where should I go, I'm not really white, but I don't know if Arabs fit into this group or not. So I decided that I was closer to the other group than I was to the white people." When he joined the Third World group, the members asked him: "Brother, what third world community are you from?" Ahmed felt "very much afraid that I'd be cast out," but he replied: "I'm an Arab." The Third World group was delighted to include him, and Ahmed considers that episode to be indicative of "a period of real recognition that we had a place in those communities." He adds: "In the Arab world you had a developing affinity based in the struggles for Nationalism, and more and more there was clarity for us here where we fit in."[94]

Although some third-generation Arab Americans such as Ahmed were embracing a racialized Third World identity in the late 1960s and early 1970s, this consciousness was resisted by many, if not most, second- and third-generation immigrants who had always conceived of themselves as racially white. Even Abdeen Jabara is resistant to conceiving of Arab Americans as a racial minority, preferring the term "ethnic" minority.[95] Accordingly, many African Americans did not perceive Arab Americans as fellow people of color, instead seeing them as many Arab Americans saw themselves—as white people. While in some circumstances sympathetic associations developed between Arab Americans and African Americans, just as often, if not more frequently, distance and tension existed between the two groups. Some members of both communities held prejudiced assumptions about the other.

Tension was especially manifest in conflicts between Arab owners of gas station and convenience stores and their customers in African American neighborhoods in cities such as Chicago and Detroit.[96] In 1980, after a Chaldean (Iraqi Christian) store owner in Detroit killed a black man, followed shortly by the killing of a Chaldean man during a robbery of his store by black men, Abdeen Jabara wrote and distributed a pamphlet arguing that the economic system placed the two communities in conflict. Arab and African American leaders participated in task forces and community forums in an effort to assuage mistrust and build bridges. Jabara concludes, however, that "we did not make much headway." The "progressives" in the Arab American community "got it," he recalls, but many Arab Americans, including Arab American leaders, were not progressive. Many were racist yet were victims of racism at the same time.[97]

African American activist Gloria House, a proponent of Palestinian rights who has lived in Detroit since 1967, believes that most Arab Americans identified as white during the 1960s and 1970s and appeared to be guided by racist attitudes toward African Americans similar to those of other Americans. She encountered condescending attitudes from Palestinian intellectuals in the United States and among those whom she met during her trips to Palestine. However, she remembers being received quite warmly by working-class Palestinians and students. According to House, while African American activists in SNCC and in other radical organizations supported the Palestinian cause, Arab Americans in the United States did not extend solidarity to African Americans in their ongoing civil rights and self-determination struggles of the period. She was on the faculty at Wayne State University in the 1970s but does not recall any political organizing efforts mounted by Arab American students, and certainly not actions carried out in unity with African Americans. House points out that the solidarity that African American activists expressed toward the Palestinians was rooted in their recognition of Palestinians as a colonized, Third World nation. However, she suggests that Arab Americans did not begin to represent *themselves* as Third World people in the United States until after the racial profiling and antagonism that followed the 9/11 disaster. As she was part of Detroit's activist network, House knew Ismael Ahmed and Abdeen Jabara. She saw their progressive political orientation and associations with African Americans as exceptional among Arab Americans.[98]

African American activist Mike Hamlin, who was involved with the Detroit-based League of Revolutionary Black Workers and Wayne State's *South End* newspaper, similarly describes black sympathy for the Palestinian resistance yet remembers limited interaction between black activists and Arab Americans. Arab Americans in the Detroit area "seemed kind of insular," he recalls, "and I can understand why—it's a hostile country." In his view, the distance between Arabs and blacks stemmed from the "rulers in this country" who promoted antipathy and separation between racial and ethnic minorities in order to thwart their potential for solidarity. Hamlin, too, knew Ahmed and Jabara as well as Hasan Nawash, and he considered them "comrades." But those individual contacts seemed to be the extent of his personal associations with Arab Americans in the late 1960s and early 1970s.[99]

Considering his centrality in these networks, Ismael Ahmed views the relationships between Arab Americans and African Americans in the Detroit area as more substantive. But Nabeel Abraham tends to validate House's and Hamlin's perceptions of limited interactions among the two groups. Although activists in the communities reached out to one another, the rank and file remained aloof. Many Arab Americans held racist assumptions about black people that the activist leaders were trying to dispel. Both Abraham and George Khoury recall that some Arab students involved in the OAS at Wayne State were reticent about partnering with black students (and Abraham recalls particular resistance to working with feminist and gay liberation groups on campus). Nevertheless, OAS leaders persisted in promoting coalitions with black and leftist organizations.[100]

In some situations the distance between Arab Americans and African Americans (and between Arab Americans and other minority groups and organizations) was not attributable to purposeful antagonism but was a function of finite time and energy. Barbara Aswad, on the faculty at Wayne State in the late 1960s and 1970s, sensed that other minority faculty members at the university generally supported Arab Americans' positions, but because they themselves were enormously beleaguered and focused on their own battles, active coalitions were not sustained among "Third World" faculty.[101]

Coalitions among other Third World groups, such as between Chicanos and African Americans and between Puerto Ricans and African Americans, encountered similar difficulties in maintaining alliances, even when broad goals and ideological underpinnings united them. While all the groups fought racism and oppression, they each had experienced racism and oppression differently in their histories in the United States and therefore developed differing issues and priorities, as well as distinctive cultures of resistance. In her study of racial and ethnic activist groups in the Los Angeles area, Laura Pulido observes that "although activists developed elaborate class ideologies and were anticapitalist, their frame of reference was always their racial/ethnic position."[102] Sometimes mutual cooperation among minority groups foundered when the groups occupied different economic positions in a particular community's hierarchy, and this friction was exacerbated when the groups had to compete for limited political and economic resources from the state.[103]

In some cases distance between the minority groups, even when they lived in close proximity to one another, stemmed from the prejudice many of its rank-and-file members held against outsider groups, even when the communities' leaders counseled understanding and solidarity. In his study of Puerto Rican activism in the United States, Lorrin Thomas notes the paradoxical situation in some cities where tensions and even "open hostility" existed between Puerto Ricans and African Americans in the 1960s, yet among the radical activist leaders of both groups, the bonds had strengthened.[104]

Sherry Smith acknowledges that support of non-Indian activists for the American Indian Movement proved "short-lived and episodic" in the late 1960s and early 1970s. Like other scholars who have studied cross-group interactions, she recognizes that "the shared experiences of oppression and racism went only so far. Distinctive historical experiences, interests, and goals worked against consistent or permanent alliances. Racial or ethnic nationalism encouraged separation over integration. And individuals in these groups carried their own reservations and even racist disinclinations about engaging with one another."[105]

Though she admits these limitations, Smith joins scholars such as Johanna Fernández in emphasizing the force and significance of the coalitions, however transitory, that were formed among various oppressed groups in America and throughout the world, at least at the level of activist leadership. The "intercultural and interracial" nature of the movements deserves more attention, Smith argues. "The tendency of historians and others, in retrospect, to separate them from one another . . . does a disservice to the tenuous and temporary but powerful intersections which took place. It ignores the collaborations that occurred in a constellation of overlapping interests and issues."[106]

Both at the national level, best represented by the efforts of AAUG and OAS leaders, and in some localities, especially Detroit, activist Arab Americans joined in these collaborations. Radical African Americans were most likely to embrace Palestinian revolutionary nationalism and endorse leftist Arab Americans' activism on behalf of that cause. Other radicals of color also welcomed activist Arab Americans into the Third World liberation fold, on the occasions when they came into contact. White New Leftists, however, tended to be more ambivalent about criticizing Israel and championing Palestine, and the Palestine question caused some strains within the movement. On the whole, though, the New Left shifted toward support of Palestinian liberation, and a few anti-imperialist activists even formed solidarity organizations that allied with Arab American communities. Increasingly seeing themselves as people of color joined with these other groups in anticolonial struggle, Arab American activists participated in the intersections that invigorated the anti-imperialist and antiracist movements on the left.

PART TWO
A HOSTILE CLIMATE FOR ACTIVISM

4 "A Disturbed Individual, not a Martyr"
Sirhan Sirhan's Impact on Arab American Activism

In the months after the Arab-Israeli War of June 1967, organizations such as the Association of Arab American University Graduates (AAUG) and the Organization of Arab Students (OAS) had begun to engage in promising organizing work on behalf of Palestine. But just as pro-Palestinian activism was getting off the ground in the United States, a terrible tragedy cast a shadow on the work of these Arab American organizations. In the middle of 1968—a tumultuous year characterized by a contentious presidential contest, escalating protest against the Vietnam War, and the assassination of Dr. Martin Luther King Jr.—the Palestinian question was thrust into the national spotlight. Exactly one year after the start of the Arab-Israeli War, on 5 June 1968, Palestinian American Sirhan Bishara Sirhan shot and killed presidential candidate Robert F. Kennedy in a Los Angeles hotel. Sirhan's crime did not destroy the incipient Arab American movement but did make it more difficult for political Arab Americans to gain a sympathetic hearing and to disassociate from stereotypes of terrorists.

Twenty-four years old at the time and a resident of the Los Angeles area, Sirhan had become increasingly upset by U.S. support of Israel and particularly disturbed by Robert Kennedy's vocal advocacy on the campaign trail. Sirhan also seems to have been psychologically troubled as well as drawn to the occult. His defense attorneys, who included Arab American activist Abdeen Jabara, argued that the trauma Sirhan had experienced as a child in Palestine, combined with mental illness, resulted in a diminished capacity that absolved him of criminal responsibility for the murder. The jury was unpersuaded: tried in a Los Angeles district court in 1969, Sirhan was convicted of first-degree murder and sentenced to death.

Arguably, Sirhan's assassination of this popular American political figure reinforced many Americans' association of Arabs with extremism and terrorism and made Palestinian organizing even less acceptable in mainstream American society. His lone, isolated act of political violence put Arab

American activists in a bind. An Arab American who proclaimed Palestinian liberation and denounced Zionism had become a household name, in the worst possible way. It became very difficult for commentators to separate Sirhan the individual from Sirhan the symbol. Realizing the potential of the assassination to poison any sympathy for Arab perspectives, the vast majority of Arab Americans, including the major organizations, ignored and completely disassociated from Sirhan. However, a few activists seized on the opportunity to explain Sirhan's political passion to the public, at the risk of alienating Americans even further from the Palestinian cause.

Several theories, ranging from the credible to the ridiculous, have been advanced to explain Sirhan's motives for assassinating Bobby Kennedy, with some even alleging a larger conspiracy in which Sirhan served as a tool for Kennedy's enemies. What is clear is that Sirhan's experiences as a displaced Palestinian, along with his anger at Americans who supported Israel, played at least some role in his crime. But there is debate about whether the murder constituted a political assassination, putting it in the category of terrorism, or an act of violence committed by a psychologically ill individual and therefore irrational and apolitical. Robert Kaiser, a journalist and defense team investigator who conducted many interviews with Sirhan, interprets the assassination in the latter vein. While acknowledging the political aspect of Sirhan's act, Kaiser argues that Sirhan and his attorneys developed the Palestinian political rationale after the fact. Kaiser maintains: "I did not believe that Sirhan killed Kennedy in order to strike a blow for his side in the Arab-Israeli conflict. . . . Instead, he worked out his role as Arab hero little by little, as the months rolled by after the assassination." Another journalist, Mel Ayton, who has published a book with the provocative title *The Forgotten Terrorist,* counters that Sirhan's animosity toward Zionism and his fury over Kennedy's support for Israel guided his hand from the beginning. Ayton portrays the act as a political assassination that, as evident from his book's title, qualifies as terrorism. In "First Shot in Terror War Killed RFK," historian Michael Fischbach makes a similar argument but with a slightly different message, declaring that Sirhan's murder of Kennedy offered a "lesson that the nation completely failed to absorb, a lesson about Palestinian anger," which should have been heeded if America were to understand and head off future conflicts and terrorist acts by "Arabs motivated by anger at American foreign policy toward the Middle East."[1]

Whether Sirhan's political motive was fully developed before he shot Kennedy or constructed subsequently as he was preparing a defense, at least some Americans and Arabs politicized the assassination in the ensuing months and used it as a vehicle to discuss the Israel-Palestinian conflict and how it impacted the United States. While the assassination did allow for an airing of the Palestinian predicament in the American media, it does not appear that sympathy for Palestinians increased as a result of the press coverage on Palestine that often accompanied reports on Sirhan. Instead, Sirhan's crime contributed to the growing climate in America of suspicion and hostility toward Arabs and Arab Americans in the years immediately following the June 1967 war.

Many Americans then (and now) claimed to have no cognizance of the Arab political connection to Bobby Kennedy's assassination. Certainly, most Arab Americans who know Sirhan's personal history have distanced themselves from him and have screened him out of Arab American history. This reaction is understandable—Sirhan's crime was reprehensible; moreover, most Arab Americans admired the Kennedys. That Sirhan was Palestinian and that he claimed a nationalist motive for the crime proved deeply embarrassing to most Arab Americans. They recognized that Sirhan would not only discredit the Palestinian cause but bring suspicion and censure upon Arab Americans who sympathized with Palestine. Remarkably, even though Sirhan is often the only Arab American individual cited in national history texts of the United States in the 1960s, he merits nary a mention in Arab American historical literature about this period. Sirhan needed to be disowned.

Nevertheless, despite Americans', including Arab Americans', forgetting of Sirhan as a passionately political Palestinian, both the prosecution and the defense argued that Sirhan was driven by political motives, and most American media outlets discussed this aspect of the case in some detail, especially when reporting on the trial proceedings. The jurors who found Sirhan guilty of first-degree murder accepted the prosecution's argument that he was a cold-blooded political assassin who targeted Bobby Kennedy because of his support for Israel on the campaign trail. While most Americans may not have fully absorbed the details of the political argument, for those who were paying attention to the fairly abundant media reports that discussed his Palestinian background, the figure of Sirhan provided a rare, concrete illustration of an Arab American and likely reinforced existing stereotypes of Arabs as fanatical and vicious.

Sirhan, Kennedy, and the Assassination

In 1948, when he was four years old, Sirhan Sirhan and his family were forced to flee their home in Jerusalem when Zionists overran the western part of the city, and for the next few years the Palestinian Christian family lived as refugees amid violence and instability. Mary Sirhan, her husband, Bishara, and their children were living in a comfortable five-room apartment in the New City of Jerusalem when the Zionists occupied that area of the city and drove the Sirhans, like thousands of other Palestinians, from their homes. Leaving almost everything behind, the Sirhans escaped to a Greek Orthodox convent in the Old City and huddled there with dozens of other refugees for over two weeks. Mary and Bishara found a tiny, rundown apartment in the Old City to rent and crammed into the building with many other refugee families.[2] Over the next several years of living in war-torn Jerusalem, young Sirhan Sirhan witnessed several atrocities and became increasingly traumatized. Family members and acquaintances recalled that as a boy he was exceedingly sensitive to violence and disruption and often went pale and shook with fear. Sirhan's father became acquainted with an American missionary in Jerusalem and asked him for assistance in relocating the family to the United States. The missionary found members of a Nazarene church in Pasadena who offered to sponsor the Sirhans and helped secure visas for them.[3] In 1957, when Sirhan was twelve, the family arrived in New York City and soon made their way across the country to Pasadena. Not long afterward, Bishara, who was having trouble adapting to American culture and increasingly clashed with his wife and children, returned to Palestine. Mary was determined to stay in her new country and bought a small house in Pasadena, where she lived with Sirhan and two other sons.[4]

Sirhan graduated from Pasadena's public high school in 1964 and attended Pasadena City College for a short time, but he was not a committed student. He found work as a horse walker at a local racetrack, and in an incident that became part of his defense, suffered a serious fall that resulted in a head injury. His mother and brothers claimed that Sirhan changed after the accident, becoming "withdrawn and irritable." Although the record is unclear, some accounts depict him as a politically engaged young man who maintained an interest in international events, particularly developments in the Arab world, and claim he also sympathized with the New Left and Black Power movements in America. Furthermore, Sirhan later maintained that he had been an admirer of John F. Kennedy and for a time favored Robert Kennedy as well.[5]

Like many Arab Americans, Sirhan was greatly distressed by the Arabs' defeat in the 1967 war, and over the ensuing months he became increasingly agitated by the support of American political figures for Israel. Also in this period he dabbled in mysticism and kept notebooks in which he engaged in "free writing," a technique he had apparently learned from a book on mysticism. In his notebooks, which were introduced as evidence in his trial, he registered his anguish about the Israeli victory in the war, writing: "A Declaration of war against American Humanity when in the course of human events it has become necessary for me to equalize and seek revenge for all the inhuman treatments committed against me by the American people." At one point, he jotted, "Long Live Nasser . . . Long Live the Arab Dream." Months later he wrote: "I advocate the overthrow of the current president of the fucken [sic] United States of America, I have no absolute plans yet but soon will compose some[.] I am poor—This country's propaganda says that she is the best country in the world—I have not experienced this yet—the US says that life in Russia is bad—Why," along with statements supporting communism and anarchy.[6]

Meanwhile, the 1968 presidential contest was in full swing and Democratic senator Robert Kennedy had thrown his hat in the ring. Along with his positions supporting civil rights and social justice and advocating American withdrawal from Vietnam, Kennedy made campaign statements supportive of Israel, as did all the other candidates. But Kennedy, according to Democratic Party consultant Stuart Gerry Brown, was "tougher and more specific" in communicating his support for Israel than his rivals.[7] As Kennedy campaigned for the Oregon and California primaries in May 1968, he included visits to temples and sometimes wore a yarmulke while proclaiming that the United States should provide increased military support for Israel. During a speech at the Neveh Shalom Temple in Portland, Oregon, he pledged that the United States "must defend Israel against aggression from whatever source. Our obligations to Israel, unlike our obligations towards other countries, are clear and imperative. . . . The U.S. should without delay sell Israel the fifty Phantom jets she has so long been promised." An article about this appearance, accompanied by a photograph of Kennedy wearing a yarmulke, ran in the Pasadena newspaper, to which the Sirhan family subscribed.[8] Also that month, the local CBS station broadcast a documentary about Kennedy that featured a brief segment about his support for Israel, going back to his stint as a foreign affairs reporter for a Boston newspaper in 1948. During his trial testimony, Sirhan recalled watching the program and becoming extremely upset when he learned this aspect of Kennedy's background. He testified: "But when I saw, heard, he was supporting Israel, sir, not in 1968, but he was supporting it all the way from its inception in 1948, sir. And he was doing a lot of things behind my back that I didn't know about . . . it burned me up sir." It was around this time that Sirhan began writing about Kennedy in his notebook. On one page he wrote over and over: "RFK must die," "RFK must be killed," "RFK must be assassinated before 5 June 68," and in another entry, "Robert F. Kennedy must be sacrificed for the cause of the poor exploited people."[9]

On 4 June 1968, Kennedy won the Democratic primary contest in California and held his victory celebration at the Ambassador Hotel in Los Angeles. Sirhan had spent part of the day shooting at a gun range in a suburb of Los Angeles. That evening, Sirhan made his way to the Ambassador Hotel with his gun tucked in his pants and somehow managed to enter the kitchen where Kennedy was escorted after he made his victory speech around midnight. Sirhan pulled his gun and fired several shots, hitting Kennedy twice, along with five other people in the crowded kitchen. He was quickly tackled to the ground. According to some reports, Sirhan declared "I did it for my country" not long after he was apprehended.[10] When police searched him, they found in his pocket a clipping of an article that had appeared recently in the Pasadena newspaper. The article, titled "Paradoxical Bob," identified a contradiction between Kennedy's positions advocating U.S. support for militarism in Israel and U.S. withdrawal from Vietnam—he was a "hawk" on Israel and a "dove" on Vietnam.[11]

The Trial and Defense Strategy

Importantly, both the prosecution and the defense depicted Sirhan's motive as politically related; however, they presented the political motive in slightly different ways and for divergent purposes. The prosecution opened the trial by recounting Sirhan's alleged statement after he shot Kennedy: "I did it for my country." The *Washington Post*'s headline summation of the prosecution's argument proclaimed: "Sirhan Motive Called Political." Although the prosecutors did not want to portray Sirhan as insane, they used Sirhan's Arab heritage and anti-Zionist fervor to present him as unsympathetic and unhinged. They counted on tapping into the widespread American attitude that the Palestinian position was in itself confused and even deranged. In closing arguments, prosecutor David Fitts tried to associate Sirhan in the jury's mind with Fatah guerrillas. As *Newsweek* put it, the prosecution's strategy was to portray him "as a self-appointed Arab soldier committing an act not of lunacy but of war." (Interestingly, in an aside the *Newsweek* writer remarked that such a claim likely met with Sirhan's approval.) Thus, the prosecution's depiction of Sirhan as a calculating anti-Zionist zealot who acted with premeditation evoked a foreign, depraved figure who was deserving of the death penalty.[12]

The defense, too, used Sirhan's Palestinian background and politics to paint him as ipso facto disturbed, but Sirhan's attorneys employed that portrait to argue that his experiences as a Palestinian caused him to be mentally incapacitated and incapable of rational planning or premeditation, thereby justifying a lighter sentence. Defense attorney Grant B. Cooper asked the court: "Though the motive was political, was it a healthy motive? Obviously the motive in killing any human being is not healthy, but was it a mature motive?" Cooper proceeded to argue that Sirhan's political motive was not, in fact, "mature." Cooper also warned the jury members that if they found in the prosecution's favor and granted a verdict of first-degree murder, they would, ironically, give Sirhan what "he desires, [to be] a hero in the Arab world."[13]

Clearly, the defense was walking a fine line in incorporating the political motive—the centerpiece of the prosecution's case—while trying to obtain leniency for Sirhan based on the mental incapacitation argument. Moreover, different members of the defense team preferred different strategies in making this argument, and thus some inconsistency afflicted the presentation of Sirhan's case. Defense attorney Russell Parsons wanted to highlight Palestinian grievances and brought Abdeen Jabara onto the defense team for that reason.[14] According to Jabara, "Parsons told me that he needed assistance developing Sirhan's defense with respect to how the Palestine-Zionist conflict had affected Sirhan." Jabara spent months trying to find experts who would testify about the history of Palestine and sent Parsons many memos and relevant materials. In his research, Jabara keyed in on studies of psychological alienation experienced by oppressed peoples, including a sociological study of African Americans in the Watts district of Los Angeles and the chapter "Colonial War and Mental Disorders" in Frantz Fanon's book about the Algerian liberation struggle, *The Wretched of the Earth*.[15]

To Jabara's dismay, when he arrived in Los Angeles in December to help prepare for the impending trial, two other members of Sirhan's defense team, famed attorneys Cooper and Emile Zola Berman, declared that they wanted to soft-pedal the political angle and declined to call any of the expert witnesses or introduce any of the evidence suggested by Jabara. As they tried to prove that Sirhan was not capable of planning the assassination, the lead defense attorneys emphasized Sirhan's traumatic experiences as a child of war as well as his "rage" at the Arab defeat in the June War, but they avoided a specific presentation of the Israeli-Palestinian conflict.[16] Instead, they sought to emphasize his mental instability and susceptibility to trances and claimed that he had no recollection of his crime. Likely, Cooper and Berman expected that oblique reference to Sirhan's ardent anti-Zionism would accomplish their goal of persuading the jury that he was disturbed. In contrast, Jabara wanted to link Sirhan's trauma as a Palestinian to his mental imbalance in a more sympathetic way, for Jabara assumed that a thorough explanation of the *Nakba* using expert testimony would show the jury Sirhan had been victimized and was not fully in control of his actions. However, the danger of Jabara's approach was that closer attention to the Palestinian question could backfire and serve to reinforce the prosecution's argument that Sirhan's act was politically rational yet abhorrent. Whether because the lead defense attorneys did not want to present Palestinian politics sympathetically or because they decided that attention to the politics might help support the prosecution's case, Jabara's strategy was rejected.

Nevertheless, when Sirhan took the stand he provided a lucid, detailed account of Palestine's plight reaching back to the late nineteenth century. His testimony added to the inconsistency of the defense's case. When he began, Sirhan stated that he could not recall the assassination or remember writing statements in his journal expressing his hatred of particular American leaders, including Bobby Kennedy, for their support of Israel. Then he proceeded to explain the terrible things Zionists had done to his family and Palestinians as a people and how those experiences caused him to despise American leaders who supported Israeli policies.[17] He relayed his angry reaction after recently reading a Zionist book: "Where is the justice involved, sir? Where is the love, sir, for fighting for the underdog? Israel is no underdog in the Middle East, sir. It's those refugees that are underdogs. And because they have no way of fighting back, sir, the Jews, sir, the Zionists, just keep beating away at them. That burned the hell out of me." He discussed his distress at the Arab defeat in 1967 and at America's support for Israel. Claiming that he had once been appreciative of the United States for providing refuge and opportunity to his family, he conveyed that his attitude had decidedly darkened after the war. "From 1967, from June of that year on," Sirhan testified, "I was very resentful toward the United States for their foreign policy, sir, in the Middle East, for their one-sided support, sir, for Israel against the Arab people." In addition to Kennedy, Sirhan also expressed anger at Lyndon Johnson and U.S. ambassador to the United Nations Arthur Goldberg for their stances on Israel. Still, he testified that he did not remember his actions leading up to the assassination or the shooting itself.[18]

But at another point in the trial, when listening to his attorneys and psychiatrists portray him as unintelligent and incapable of planning or rational thought, Sirhan grew infuriated and blurted that he had plotted and carried out the murder of Kennedy—an outburst that must have delighted the prosecution.[19] Commenting on the confusing figure of Sirhan, the *Washington Post* opined: "Thus we have the picture of a man who admits killing Robert Kennedy, shouts one day that he is ready to die for it, protests any revelation of his private thoughts that might raise doubts about his mental stability, and announces on a later day that he cannot be proud of the deed for he does not remember doing it, although he is not sorry it was done."[20]

Finally, fifteen weeks after the trial began, with most of the last month taken up by psychiatrists' testimony, the jury delivered a guilty verdict and recommended the death penalty. (In 1972, when the state of California overturned the death penalty, Sirhan's sentence was converted to life imprisonment.) The first-degree murder conviction meant that the jury accepted the prosecution's case that Sirhan was a political assassin who had acted intentionally and with forethought, thus rejecting the defense's argument that his political passions were symptomatic of mental illness.

Proponents of Palestine Defend Sirhan

Jabara was one of just a handful of Arab Americans who took pains to explain Sirhan's crime. Disappointed by the outcome of the trial, he contended that the jury must not have comprehended Sirhan's political motive because if they had, then they would have viewed it as a mitigating factor and understood that the trauma of the *Nakba* and ensuing Zionist violence had diminished Sirhan's mental capacity. Operating under the assumption that sustained political oppression could cause psychological damage, Jabara was convinced that the defense could have persuaded the jury to spare Sirhan's life if his attorneys had more effectively presented and highlighted the injustice in Palestine and how it had affected Sirhan's mind. Sirhan's own testimony was successful in this regard, but Jabara thought Sirhan's story became "obfuscated" by the ensuing weeks of confusing testimony by psychiatrists who concentrated on hypnotism and trances and conflicting definitions of paranoid schizophrenia. A year later, Jabara wrote, "By refusing to offer testimony on the Palestine-Zionist conflict and the intense Arab nationalism it engendered, possibly out of their own political considerations, Sirhan's attorneys may have gambled away his only chance of avoiding a death sentence. The diminished capacity defense required a foundation of information making Sirhan's condition credible to some members of the jury who, like Sirhan, may have experienced discrimination and oppression." Sirhan's motives, Jabara believed, were steeped in his experiences as a Palestinian: "Sirhan wanted the world to understand his behavior as the undeniable protest of a fervently patriotic man whose country, homelife, and aspirations were crushed by imperialism and racism." In a more recent interview, Jabara stated that it is unreasonable to paint Sirhan as a guerrilla fighter, as some Arabs tried to do, but that he should be viewed as a "disturbed individual" because he was "a victim of what happened over there." He continued: "He was a victim, just like Robert Kennedy was a victim. They were both victims." Sirhan's personal tragedy, which represented the personal tragedies of two million Palestinians, was, in Jabara's view, withheld from the court and from the American people.[21]

In an attempt to rectify what he viewed as purposeful suppression of Palestinian nationalism in the trial and in the media, Jabara provided the foreword to a 1969 pamphlet sponsored by the OAS at the University of Southern California (USC), titled "The Lost Significance of Sirhan's Case." Along with Jabara's essay, the pamphlet consisted of a transcript of Sirhan's trial testimony. In the belief that if more people knew Sirhan's story and comprehended his people's travails it would make an impact and change minds, USC's OAS chapter and Jabara sought to disseminate Sirhan's words, although the specific audience for the pamphlet is unclear. In his foreword, Jabara explained what he most hoped people reading Sirhan's testimony would understand: "The tragedy of Robert Kennedy was preceded by the tragedy of Sirhan Bishara Sirhan. The trauma experienced by Sirhan throughout the course of his life made him identify Robert F. Kennedy with a moral contradiction of such enormous proportions that it made Sirhan burn with anger, a rage, a sense of deep personal desperation."[22] Presumably, he hoped that Americans would develop a more sympathetic understanding of the root of Sirhan's rage and the suffering of Palestinians more generally. Perhaps the assassination would serve to pierce the veil of ignorance surrounding the Palestinian question in American society.

Two other writers published books advancing arguments similar to Jabara's interpretation of the assassination, arguments that underlined Sirhan's political motives and were thus ironically similar to the claim advanced by the prosecution and used to convict him of first-degree murder. Jabara also

This is the cover of "The Lost Significance of Sirhan's Case," a pamphlet by the University of Southern California chapter of the Organization of Arab Students, issued in 1968. (Abdeen Jabara Papers, Bentley Historical Library, University of Michigan)

supplied the foreword to a book by Godfrey Jansen, an East Indian journalist whose career had concentrated on the Middle East. Titled *Why Robert Kennedy Was Killed: The Story of Two Victims* and published by the Third Press in New York City in 1970, Jansen's book presented Sirhan's violent act as "one of political protest . . . the projection of a liberation struggle across the width of a sea. . . . It took the passions aroused by Palestine to produce the killing by an Asian of an American, deeply involved in the Palestine problem, and on American soil." After carefully tracing Sirhan's Palestinian nationalism and Robert Kennedy's support for Israel, Jansen, like Jabara, argued that this information had been suppressed by the American media and government. To Sirhan's defense attorneys, Jansen claimed, the Palestinian cause was "incidental." Regrettably, the defense's strategy to instead emphasize the psychiatrists' testimony made Sirhan appear as "a pathetic nut case." Jansen maintained he did not want to excuse Sirhan's crime, but he did want his book to convey another side of the story. He wrote, "Perhaps the end does not always justify the means, and if this can be said of Sirhan's assault on his victim, RFK, it can also be said of the assault of the Zionist and pro-Zionist forces on the homeland and the psyche of their victim, Sirhan Sirhan. . . . Perhaps if the American media had been more sensitive, the American Middle East policy more equitable, and the American people less ignorant of the sensibilities of the rest of the world, RFK might yet have been alive today."[23] In a differing assessment, J. Anthony Lukas critiqued Jansen's book in the *New York Times Book Review*. Lukas admitted that despite what he identified as Jansen's pro-Arab bias, "much of what he writes has the ring of truth." Yet Lukas concluded that trying to "turn Sirhan's act into an object lesson in Middle East politics . . . makes a bad book."[24] Nevertheless, the appearance of the review in the *Times* provided wider dissemination of the pro-Palestinian political perspective on the Kennedy assassination.

In 1968, Arab American activist Dr. Mohammad T. Mehdi imparted this perspective in an even more obscure book, titled *Kennedy and Sirhan: Why?*, before Sirhan's trial had even begun. Mehdi, who possessed a Ph.D. in political science from University of California–Berkeley, had been an outspoken proponent of Palestinian nationalism since the early 1960s, especially through his organization the Action Committee on American-Arab Relations, based in New York City. His stated purpose for writing the book was to explain Palestinian suffering so that the jury, and all Americans, would be "impartial"–and, he implies, more lenient—toward Sirhan. He wanted Americans to know that Sirhan was "a survivor of an act of genocide committed against his people with the implied and actual Kennedy support."

The book is essentially an argument against Zionism, and in some sections Mehdi invents Sirhan's words in an imagined dialogue between Sirhan and Israeli politician Abba Eban. The assassination, Mehdi argued, "was not the haphazard act of a murderer . . . Sirhan's act was a political decision."[25]

Although their stances and outspokenness were not representative of Arab Americans, the efforts of Mehdi, Jabara, and Jansen to explain, if not defend, Sirhan's act illustrate the difficult position in which pro-Palestinian activists found themselves. They felt they must challenge the pro-Israel bias in American culture and educate people about Palestine, but they ran the risk of validating the prosecution's portrayal of the assassination as a calculated political act.

American Press Coverage

Some who have recognized the political aspects of Sirhan's crime have argued that the American media, and even the U.S. government, suppressed the assassination's connection to Arab world politics, resulting in Americans' ignorance about its relevance to Palestinian nationalism. As we have seen, Abdeen Jabara and Godfrey Jansen made this claim. Jansen argued that Zionists participated in this conspiracy of silence, keeping quiet about Sirhan's Palestinian connection because they wanted it to seem like the assassination "had nothing to do with them." More recently, journalist Mel Ayton has argued that in its reporting on the assassination, "the U.S. media not only downplayed the reality of Arab-Israeli tension but it also was enjoined by the American government." United States government officials, Ayton claims, did not want to fan the flames of the Arab-Israeli conflict or provide an outlet for discussion of U.S. leaders' support for Israel, fearing that it might call America's Middle East policies into question.[26] These claims about active U.S. government and Zionist intent to suppress information, however, are not supported by concrete evidence and remain speculative.

True, many media reports were silent on these issues, sometimes stating that Sirhan's family was from Jordan and providing no mention of Palestine or Israel. In those reports, the assassination was presented as the random act of a mentally ill man, and the bizarre aspects of the crime, such as Sirhan's hypnosis, were accentuated. The reasons for the crime, this coverage suggested, were unknowable and absurd.[27] Other commentaries framed the murder as just another symptom of America's culture of violence and chaos—part of the pattern that had produced John Kennedy's and Martin Luther King's assassinations as well as street violence in the 1960s—and said nothing about either the particularities of Sirhan's motivation or the Arab-Israeli conflict. At the time of the assassination, an anticrime bill was being considered by Congress, and President Johnson invoked the shooting of Robert Kennedy when pressing Congress to include stronger gun control measures in the legislation. Another explanation for the assassination was proclaimed by Los Angeles mayor Sam Yorty when, in a speech widely reported in the national news, Yorty declared that Sirhan must be a communist.[28]

But my review of national newspaper coverage of the assassination and trial reveals that, contrary to claims that the media ignored or actively concealed the Palestinian context, significant attention was paid to Sirhan's Palestinian background.[29] Moreover, many news articles described Kennedy's support for Israel and represented his position as a motive for Sirhan, thus associating the assassination in some way with the Arab-Israeli conflict. To be sure, much of the media coverage, particularly the initial reporting, was patently derogatory in its depiction of Sirhan's Arab identity, tapping into enduring Orientalist stereotypes of Arabs as exotic, emotional, fanatical, and pernicious.[30] For example, in one of its earliest reports on the assassination, *Time* magazine depicted Sirhan's motives as distinct from other American assassins due to his Arab heritage: "[Bobby] Kennedy was not shot by a white racist angry with his defense of the Negro, or a Negro militant incensed with his white liberalism, or a high-school dropout like Lee Harvey Oswald who felt himself rejected by a capitalist society. The man charged with his murder is a virulent Arab nationalist, whose hatreds stem from the land where he spent the early part of his life, and where political assassination is commonplace and violence as accepted as the desert wind." *Life* magazine also used the term "political assassin" to describe Sirhan, portraying him as "small, proud, polite, repressed and aboil with a secret, almost religious sense of cause: Arab nationalism." To *Life*, these characteristics and his larger political motive markedly differentiated Sirhan from Martin Luther King Jr.'s assassin James Earl Ray, whom the magazine described in the same article as "cynical, alley-shrewd, and money-hungry"—in short, more along the lines of a common criminal. A *Newsweek* journalist attributed Sirhan's act to his "blind Arab rage at his victim's oft-expressed sympathy for Israel."[31]

In a long piece on Sirhan that ran four days after the assassination, the *Washington Post* investigated Sirhan's family history, portrayed him as a fanatical anti-Semite, and implied that his anti-Semitism had increased once living as a troubled young man in the United States. "In America—in a world where Arabs keep their heads above the black ghetto with difficulty, while Jews are among the wealthiest communities in the world—any Arab with the faintest tendency to paranoia might have a feeling that the enemy was closing in," the article claimed. The *Post* also reported that Israeli security forces were investigating Sirhan's family in Jerusalem to hunt for connections to Arab political groups and evidence of a wider political conspiracy, but so far had come up empty.[32] These media portrayals used the familiar image of the depraved Arab to imbue in the American public's mind a portrait of a foreign zealot. At the same time, they conveyed that the assassination was connected in some way to a political purpose, even if the politics—Arab nationalism—were represented as irrational and bizarre.

A few media reports were more sympathetic in their treatment of Sirhan. A lengthy profile that ran in the *Los Angeles Times*, titled "Sirhan—The Wanderer—Never Found His Way," presented him as a pathetic figure. The journalists, Robert Toth and Dave Smith, described the Sirhans as "an upright, Christian family, among the best educated of their class, once accustomed to financial security but uncomplaining and industrious in hard times." Sirhan's mother, Mary, was "a tight-lipped, proud, strong woman," while Sirhan was "serious-minded, religious, polite, devoted to his mother, absorbed in books." Somewhere along the way, he became "troubled" and "confused." Though it acknowledged Sirhan's political position on Palestine, the piece placed his increasing "instability" in the realm of the personal.[33]

Other articles presented a fairly objective analysis of the role of Palestinian politics in the assassination. *The Economist* linked the Palestinian-Israeli conflict to the Kennedy assassination in an 8 June article titled "A Year Nearer the Next War": "The man charged with killing Senator Kennedy is a Palestine Arab. When are we all going to tackle the root of the refugee problem?" The Associated Press's Harry F. Rosenthal led off one piece by quoting what Sirhan allegedly proclaimed after he shot Kennedy: "I did it for my country." Subsequently Rosenthal stated that Sirhan "has been pictured as an ardent Arab nationalist."[34] Though it may not have been carefully rendered, Sirhan's political identity as a Palestinian was not concealed or ignored in most media outlets.

Once the trial began, major newspapers reported Sirhan's testimony about his youthful experiences in Palestine. For instance, Seymour Korman's report in the *Chicago Tribune*, which referred to Sirhan as a "Palestinian Arab," quoted at length Sirhan's testimony about Zionist crimes against Palestinians and what had happened to his family. Korman followed the recitation of Sirhan's story by stating, "Kennedy, in campaigning for the Democratic Presidential nomination, had urged American aid to Israel against the Arab nations," thus implying that Kennedy's position had triggered Sirhan's crime.

An Associated Press article on Sirhan's trial testimony claimed that even though nine months had passed since the shooting, "Sirhan still was provoked to seething anger by Kennedy's support of Israel." "The defense," the article continued, "contends that childhood scenes of war between Zionists and Arabs crippled Sirhan's mind to the point he could not form a meaningful plot against Kennedy."[35] Many press reports on Sirhan's trial also mentioned Kennedy's campaign statement supporting the sale of fifty Phantom jets to Israel, suggesting it had inflamed Sirhan and thus served as a motive for the assassination.[36]

The *Washington Post* reported that when the Los Angeles District Attorney was considering a plea deal to avert a trial and save Sirhan from the death penalty, he met with Secretary of State William Rogers to discuss how Sirhan's fate might affect U.S. relations with the Arab world. According to the *Post*, Rogers made it known that the State Department preferred that no trial take place, to avoid "inflammatory" testimony about the Arab-Israeli conflict, and that Sirhan be granted life imprisonment, to avoid inflaming Arab animosity. Whether or not Rogers actually communicated these messages, which is questionable, the newspaper's reporting was playing up the connection between the trial and U.S.-Arab world relations.[37]

Further media coverage of Sirhan's Palestinian association came through in press interviews with Abdeen Jabara and with Sirhan himself. When Jabara gave interviews about the Sirhan case, he stressed his interpretation: that past and present events in the Middle East were pivotal to understanding, though not excusing, the assassination. A *New York Times* interview with Jabara that ran during the trial quoted him as stating that he hoped "an understanding of the Arab cause" would result from Sirhan's trial. In a televised interview NBC conducted with Sirhan shortly after the trial, he spoke several times of the connection between killing Kennedy and his desire to publicize the Palestinian plight. When the interviewer asked Sirhan if he felt he had accomplished anything, Sirhan responded, "I think that the world, sir, should know that 20 years of suffering deprivation, of injustice for the Palestinian Arab people, sir, is enough." He also expressed regret for having killed Kennedy and at one point in the interview said he wished Kennedy were still alive.[38]

The impact of the media coverage on Americans' attitudes toward Sirhan specifically or toward Middle East politics more generally is difficult to ascertain. Almost certainly, it did not generate greater understanding, or even cognizance, of Palestinian nationalism. One could argue that even though many prominent press reports highlighted the Arab-Israeli connection to the assassination, the Middle East context did not penetrate Americans' consciousness, and certainly not enough to generate widespread sympathy. Preoccupied by Vietnam and racial strife in 1968 and 1969, most Americans probably did not understand or care about political conflicts in the Middle East; moreover, most Americans were not apt to view those conflicts from the Arab point of view. Instead, media coverage of the assassination likely reinforced perceptions of Arabs as alien and threatening, and despite some instances of careful reporting, the portrait of Sirhan that came through most viscerally was of an unhinged Arab.

Supporters of Sirhan

Just a few isolated organizations and individuals in the United States expressed sympathy for Sirhan, and some went to great lengths to assist his defense. A group calling itself the Organizing Committee for Clemency for Sirhan, based in New York City and led by John M. Lawrence, an erratic radical, referred to Sirhan as a "Palestinian Arab refugee" and asked in its 26 June press release: "If death is to be the penalty for Sirhan's misguided political act, then what penalty shall world justice and military might deal out for the genocidal massacres and exiling of Palestinian Arabs from their native land?" Besides Lawrence, eleven members of the committee were listed, most of whom were Arab American, including Abdeen Jabara. However, Jabara consulted with Elaine Hagopian, his colleague in the Association of Arab American University Graduates, and together they decided that Lawrence's reputation was suspect and that Jabara should ask to be removed from membership.[39]

Not only did Mohammad T. Mehdi write his book politicizing Sirhan's case but he also attempted to exert pressure on the judge to commute Sirhan's sentence to life imprisonment. In May 1969, after the trial had ended and Judge Herbert Walker was preparing to issue a sentence, the Arabic newspaper *Al-Islaah*, published in New York City, printed a copy of a telegram Mehdi had sent to Walker, imploring him to save Sirhan from the death penalty. Beneath this telegram (which was also printed in Arabic) appeared a petition for readers to clip and mail to the judge: "We appeal to you to commute Sirhan's sentence to life imprisonment." The reproduced telegram and petition also appeared in a subsequent issue of *Al-Islaah*.[40]

Another organization, the Beirut-based Americans for Justice in the Middle East (AJME), published pieces in its *Middle East Newsletter* that, while condemning Sirhan's action, placed the assassination in a political framework and mused, "If only the American people, through Sirhan Sirhan, will realize their responsibilities toward the Arabs and in particular the Palestinians who have been driven from their homes and from their native land." In its coverage of Sirhan's case, the AJME made a political point by reminding readers that Israeli leaders such as Menachem Begin should be looked upon as terrorists and assassins. Sirhan, the newsletter continued, is among millions of Arabs who "are still wondering how to assert their rights," but Arabs do not choose the violent method that Sirhan used. Turning the Orientalist depiction of naturally violent Arabs on its head, the AJME insinuated that violence was part of American culture, not Arab society. Sirhan must have been "influenced by the climate of violence in which America lives."[41]

In the Arab world, some factions celebrated Sirhan's act and featured him in their pro-Palestinian propaganda. According to one report, newspapers and radio stations across the Middle East devoted prominent coverage to Sirhan's trial. The PLO even produced a poster of Sirhan, with his image placed next to the figure of a guerrilla soldier, under the words, "I Have Done It for the Sake of My Country." The American press wrote about the poster—again, cementing the association between Sirhan and Palestine, at least to those readers paying attention—and *Newsweek* magazine reprinted the poster with the caption: "Arab nationalists have been distributing posters throughout the Middle East portraying Sirhan as a freedom fighter."[42] (A few years later, when Palestinian commandos associated with Black September kidnapped diplomats in Khartoum, Sudan, they demanded the release of Palestinian prisoners around the world and specifically named Sirhan Sirhan.[43]) The existence of such propaganda frustrated Jabara, and likely other Arab American activists, who recognized the damage that celebration of Sirhan would do to the Palestinian cause in the United States. Jabara lamented the poster, asserting: "I told people there don't put his face on [the posters]" because he is not a martyr, he is a "disturbed individual."[44] Arab world propagandizing about Sirhan made the political work of leftist Arab Americans more difficult.

In interviews he conducted with Jordanians (in Jordan), Arab American journalist Aziz Shihab found a mixture of disbelief and support for Sirhan, as well as a tendency to comprehend the assassination in the context of U.S. support for Israel. Shihab reported, "They did not seem to believe that Sirhan was capable of it, but they accepted it and sympathized with Sirhan saying that they understood how he felt. Then, almost every one of them expressed his own bitterness against American politicians who support Israel 'to get the Jewish vote.'"[45]

But another journalist, stationed in Egypt, observed little Arab sympathy for Sirhan and the assassination. Mahmoud Abdel-Hadi, a correspondent for the newspaper *Akhbar Elyoum* in Cairo, argued that Sirhan "is deeply committed to making his trial a public and political forum for the Arab position" and expected Arabs to treat him as a hero. However, Abdel-Hadi asserted, "except for some Palestinian extremists, his act has been universally repudiated by the Arab world." Abdel-Hadi also claimed to have interviewed members of the Arab Student Association, apparently in California, who condemned the assassination and called it "a terrible mistake."[46]

New Left Reaction

As for the American New Left, discussion of Sirhan and his relationship to the Palestinian cause was nearly absent. Although leftists in this period increasingly employed rhetoric celebrating guerrilla warfare and violent revolution, they did not embrace Sirhan as a revolutionary figure or engage with his politics. And while the radicals, suspicious of most politicians, did not necessarily embrace Kennedy, to most of the New Left, the liberal and antiwar Bobby Kennedy did not fall into the "enemy" category. Many antiwar and civil rights activists who bridged the Left and liberal camps supported him as the best hope for the presidency and would not offer any sympathy or comprehension to his assassin. An exception was Jerry Rubin, the provocative Yippie activist notorious for smashing all sacred cows, who in his 1970 book *Do It: Scenarios of the Revolution* included the passage: "When he assassinated Robert Kennedy, Sirhan Sirhan consciously saw himself as an Arab patriot, representing oppressed peoples as he fired a pistol bullet, shattering the myth of rich, white, Amerikan power. Amerika drives the exploited people of the world to become Lee Oswalds, Sirhan Sirhans, Viet Kong. What dedication and fanaticism is inspired by Amerikan greed! The Amerikan people dismiss Sirhan as a crazy, fucked-up, irrational extremist. But it is the extremism of Amerikan power and Kennedy power which drives her powerless people to such 'extremism.'" Then Rubin quoted Eldridge Cleaver: "What seems irrational from the viewpoint of the Mother Country may be rational from the viewpoint of the colony."[47] Though Rubin painted Sirhan in the vein of the colonized victim inevitably and understandably driven to violent reaction against his oppressors, among whom he included the Kennedys, the vast majority of the New Left responded to Sirhan with silence, probably because they, like most Americans, found him and his crime incomprehensible. A common refrain was, "Why Kennedy?"

Arab American Attitudes

Many Arab Americans felt this way too. Detroit activist Ismael Ahmed remembers that the "Kennedys were heroes for Arab Americans, generally," and he did not know anyone who politicized the assassination or "embraced [Sirhan] in any way." In fact, Arab Americans were "horrified" to find that Sirhan was Palestinian, and they hoped they would not be associated with him. In Ahmed's recollection, Arab Americans just "didn't know what to make of" Sirhan and his crime. Likewise, Barbara and Adnan Aswad recall Arab Americans condemning the assassination, and except for knowing Jabara was on his defense team, they never heard of anyone sympathizing with Sirhan. In a report shortly after the killing, the *Washington Post* claimed that the majority of Arab Americans "seem to have a sense of shame that one of them had been implicated in such an act."[48] Ron Amen, a Muslim Arab American who lived in Dearborn, does not recall much attention to the assassination, but those in his community who did discuss Sirhan dismissed him as "a mental case" or emphasized that he was Christian. As another example of Arab Americans disassociating themselves from Sirhan, Amen recalls a shop in Dearborn named "Sirhan's Market" that hung a sign in the window announcing that Sirhan Sirhan was not a relation.[49]

Except for the pamphlet about Sirhan produced by the USC chapter of OAS, mention of Sirhan is absent from the documentary evidence I have unearthed from the OAS and, for that matter, from any major Arab American organization of the period, even the AAUG in which Abdeen Jabara was so heavily involved. Jabara expressed frustration that he was unable to persuade the AAUG to join his effort in explaining Sirhan's desperation.[50] Unlike some groupings in the Arab world, these Arab American organizations did not seek to make a political point out of Sirhan.

A main reason for disassociating themselves from Sirhan was Arab Americans' fear of repercussions for their civil liberties in the United States. Though the backlash against Arab Americans was not extreme, perhaps because American officials downplayed the connection between the assassination and Palestinian politics, a few U.S. leaders did make inflammatory statements linking Arabs and Arab Americans to terrorism in connection with Sirhan. Most notably, in his speech on Capitol Hill shortly after Sirhan's trial, Congressman Gerald Ford declared: "We are painfully aware of how the Middle East conflict has already spilled over our shores in the case of the convicted murderer Sirhan Sirhan. This nation will not tolerate assassination and terrorism."[51] Other commentators also linked Sirhan to the alleged threat of Arab terrorism in the United States. For example, in a *Los Angeles Times* piece about a Palestinian militant group's attack on an airplane in Zurich in February 1969, journalist Max Lerner proclaimed, "If Americans think they will be immune, they have the example of Sirhan B. Sirhan to reflect on . . . . But what Americans must see in the killing of Robert Kennedy is that the terrorist mentality reached all the way from Jordan to Los Angeles."[52]

Arab American activist George Khoury believed that the media portrayed Sirhan as fanatically committed to Arab nationalism in order to discredit and persecute Arab Americans. The situation was "not as big as 9-11," he reflected in a more recent interview, "but it was similar" in the way the media used an act of violence committed by an Arab to promote a stereotype of all Arabs as violent and as potential terrorists. Barbara and Adnan Aswad agree that the assassination "put a bad mark" on Palestinians and their supporters in the United States. In 1973, when confronting intensified U.S. government violations of Arab Americans' civil liberties, the AAUG argued that the government had been "using the killing of Senator Robert Kennedy as a pretext" for harassing Arab Americans since 1968.[53]

THE TIMING OF Sirhan Sirhan's heinous act—one year after the 1967 war and in the midst of increasing pro-Palestinian activism in the newly formed AAUG and on American college campuses—meant that the discussion about the Palestinian-Israeli conflict that accompanied the assassination and trial influenced the context in which Americans viewed Arab Americans' advocacy of Palestine and criticism of Israel. Although concrete policy ramifications are not apparent, Sirhan's assassination of Kennedy and his avowal of a Palestinian political motive arguably made the climate for Palestinian activism in America much less hospitable. Some media representations resurfaced long-standing Orientalist tropes which reinforced many Americans' existing stereotypes of Arabs as violent, irrational, and threatening. To many, Sirhan likely became representative of all Arabs and Arab Americans. Furthermore, the Palestinian political connection, whether treated objectively or pejoratively, was communicated in many U.S. media outlets, especially during the trial. Thus Sirhan Sirhan and the ways in which his crime was represented in the media and other discourse shaped the environment in which Arab Americans practiced pro-Palestinian advocacy in the late 1960s.

The assassination created a dilemma for Arab American activists, forcing them to grapple with the predicament of how to make progress on Palestine in the American political arena in the face of Sirhan's deplorable act, a crime that they did not condone and a major public relations setback that they could not control. While the main organizations, chiefly the AAUG and OAS (except for the USC chapter), responded by completely ignoring Sirhan, hoping to suppress any discussion of him in the context of the Palestinian-Israeli conflict, a handful of activists sought to use the crime as a teaching moment to educate the American public about Palestinian grievances. In so doing, however, they risked further alienating American public opinion. The few who dared, such as Jabara and Mehdi, had to walk a fine line between their stated support for armed struggle in Palestine and appearing to justify terrorism and assassination on American soil. In the end, Americans' widespread antipathy to Arabs, intensified by the violent instability of Sirhan, overrode any objective appraisal of the Israel-Palestine conflict and arguably served to impede, not advance, the Palestinian cause in the United States.

5 "Enemies Within"
Operation Boulder and Infringements of Civil Liberties

Like other politically active racial and ethnic minority groups in this era, many Americans of Arabic heritage were targeted for harassment and surveillance by federal, state, and local government authorities. But the government's persecution of Arab Americans was unique in its aim to link their activism to foreign terrorism. Derided as primitive and irrational or stigmatized as violent and threatening, most Arabs and Arab Americans endured a type of racism that derived not from their phenotypic characteristics but rather from negative political impressions many Americans held of the Arab world in general and of Palestinian nationalism in particular.

These impressions drew on long-standing derogatory stereotypes of Arabs, but they heightened after the late 1960s. Helen Hatab Samhan has termed this phenomenon "political racism," and Amaney Jamal argues that "the racialization of Muslim and Arab Americans as the enemy 'Other'" has facilitated violations of their civil liberties, namely, by justifying "policies that target them as a distinct group of people and criminalize them without evidence of criminal activity." In her study of Arab American activism in the San Francisco area since the 1960s, Nadine Naber explains that all activists understood that speaking out on behalf of Palestine could create the perception that they were "enemies within" and render them vulnerable to U.S. government harassment; this realization, Naber argues, made Arab Americans feel "the impact of U.S. empire in their own lives in the United States."[1]

The federal government's treatment of Arab American activists as suspicious can be traced back to 1967, when the Arab-Israeli War galvanized many Arab Americans' and Arab students' political activism on behalf of the Palestinian cause. The harassment intensified in the early 1970s when the government, reacting to Palestinian terrorist acts overseas, launched a program called Operation Boulder to scrutinize and restrict the visas of Arab nonresidents. The program was overseen by a new federal government body, the Cabinet Committee to Combat Terrorism, that used additional methods to investigate Arabs and Arab Americans for possible terrorist connections. Arab Americans and their allies came to refer to the U.S. government's entire system of harassment in this period as Operation Boulder. The investigative sweeps and surveillance endured by Arab students and Arab American activists subsided when the Operation Boulder visa restrictions ended in 1975, but through the rest of the century federal government agencies continued to monitor Arab Americans and pro-Palestinian organizations it deemed politically subversive.

A central figure in resisting the government's violations of Arab Americans' civil liberties was attorney and activist Abdeen Jabara. After the June 1967 war, Jabara was among the group of professionals who formed the Association of Arab American University Graduates (AAUG). In 1967 federal government agents began tracking Jabara's activities, along with the activities of several other prominent Arab American leaders, many of whom were associated with the AAUG.[2] Over the next several years, the Michigan State Police and Detroit police joined the federal government in monitoring him. In 1972, after the Palestinian terrorist group Black September murdered Israeli athletes at the Munich Olympics, the federal government significantly stepped up its surveillance and investigations of Arab Americans, including Jabara, as well as of Arab immigrants in the United States. This harassment became formalized as Operation Boulder, which the Nixon administration justified for national security reasons.

The government's widespread violations of Arab Americans' civil liberties—before, during, and after the Operation Boulder regime—constituted another link between Arab Americans and other outsider American groups, such as black liberation and antiwar activists, who were also being illegally monitored and harassed by the government to intimidate them and stifle their political expression. Many Arab Americans protested their treatment, and some, such as Jabara, sought to build coalitions with members of other targeted groups to create strength through numbers. Despite some bonds with other persecuted groups, Arab Americans felt singularly vulnerable to government intimidation. As the government painted them with a broad brush as "dangerous terrorists," they felt marginalized from the support and sympathy of other Americans in these years.

The marginalization of Arab Americans in the broader discourse about civil rights has been reinforced by their invisibility in the literature on the federal government's infringements of Americans' civil liberties. With the exception of brief discussions in Tim Weiner's *Enemies: A History of the FBI* and Timothy Naftali's *Blind Spot: A Secret History of American Counterterrorism,* scholars and journalists have not picked up on media reports during the 1970s that exposed the government's illegal surveillance of Arab Americans, although these researchers have used some of the same sources to discuss violations of the rights of other activists and minority groups.[3] The recognition that Arab Americans were also targeted by agencies such as the Federal Bureau of Investigation, the Central Intelligence Agency, and the National Security Agency during the Lyndon Johnson and Richard Nixon administrations demonstrates that they, too, were victims of this unfortunate episode of federal government overreach. Furthermore, uncovering the national security state's harassment of Arab Americans in the 1960s and 1970s reveals that the government's violations of Arab Americans' civil liberties since 11 September 2001 has a longer history in the United States and stems from enduring strains of stereotyping, paranoia, and bigotry.

Early Monitoring

Suspicion of Arab supporters of Palestine, especially directed at Arab students in the United States, heightened after Sirhan Sirhan assassinated Bobby Kennedy in 1968. As mentioned in the previous chapter, Gerald Ford fanned these flames in an incendiary speech to the American Israel Public Affairs Committee (AIPAC) in 1969. Associating Kennedy's assassination with "Peking-trained agitators from the Middle East" on America's college campuses, Ford demanded that the government monitor all Arab students in the United States.[4] Within days of Sirhan's sentencing, leaders of the Anti-Defamation League (ADL) of B'nai B'rith made similar charges and demands. Arnold Forster, ADL's general counsel, publicized his accusation that the Organization of Arab Students (OAS) was a subversive tool of Arab governments, and he played up the OAS's connections to "extremist revolutionary" groups in the United States, such as the Socialist Workers Party and the Black Panther Party, as well as with revolutionaries in China, Algeria, Cuba, and Vietnam. Forster echoed Ford's call for an "official inquiry."[5] Also in 1969 AIPAC's pro-Zionist newsletter the *Near East Report,* circulated to policymakers in Washington, D.C., warned about the threat of Arabs and their propaganda at American universities and expressed the suspicion that Palestinian fedayeen were circulating among them.[6]

Heeding these warnings about potential Arab terrorists infiltrating American campuses, in 1969 and 1970 the CIA investigated connections between fedayeen groups abroad and Arab students in the United States. According to reporting by Seymour Hersh published in the *New York Times* a few years later, the CIA found "no significant connection." One of Hersh's sources told him that the agency did find some money being funneled from Middle East embassies to Arab students groups in the United States, but "there were no illegal activities by those students—no recruiting American spies and no bomb-throwing."[7] Although the CIA informed the White House of the lack of evidence for Arab-sponsored espionage and subversion in the United States, the Nixon administration directed the FBI to include "potential Arab saboteurs" in its wide-ranging counterintelligence program against black radical and other leftist groups.[8]

The FBI's investigation resulted in two classified reports, "The Fedayeen Terrorist—A Profile" and "Fedayeen Impact—Middle East and United States," both issued in 1970. While the reports admitted that the agents could find no evidence of existing Arab terrorist activities or threats in the United States, the bureau documented the interactions between the Organization of Arab Students and Fatah, emphasizing that the strategy of the fedayeen was to cultivate support among Arab students in the United States. The FBI concluded there was a very real possibility that the students might collaborate in terroristic activities, particularly against Israeli targets in the United States. One of its reports stated, "If the Fedayeen do carry out terrorist acts in the United States, they will probably rely on the large segment of sympathetic Arab students residing here for at least the planning stages of the operation."[9]

Thus, the federal government's intelligence gathering on supporters of Palestine in the United States dated back to at least 1969, but the CIA and FBI investigations were not publicly revealed until Hersh's articles in 1973. Government investigations of Arabs in the United States were carried out secretly, and the surveillance was generally discreet.[10] This circumspection began to change in the spring of 1972 when Jabara by chance discovered that the FBI had been monitoring his activities. He learned from an employee of a Detroit bank that in February 1972 a third party—eventually revealed in court to be the FBI—had requested information about his bank account. Complying with the request, the bank sent an interoffice memo to its branches asking for reports of Jabara's transactions with certain Arab organizations and individuals and disclosed the information to the FBI. Because the bank had provided his private information without his authorization or a warrant, Jabara sued.[11] During the lawsuit's discovery process, Jabara began to learn the extent of the federal government's intelligence gathering on him since 1967. Just a few months later, the federal government's harassment not only of Jabara but also of dozens of other Arab American activists and thousands of Arab students became more open and intrusive when the Nixon Administration launched its antiterrorism initiative in September 1972.

The Cabinet Committee to Combat Terrorism and Operation Boulder

In early September 1972, in what is often referred to as the Munich massacre, members of the radical Palestinian group Black September murdered eleven Israeli athletes at the summer Olympics in Munich, Germany. In the days following, President Nixon and his national security adviser Henry Kissinger discussed their concern that the Israeli government would overreact in retaliation against Arabs, thereby igniting a broader conflict. Seeking a way to placate Israelis and their American Jewish supporters, Nixon and Kissinger decided to establish the Cabinet Committee to Combat Terrorism (CCCT), which directed the FBI, the State Department, and the Immigration and Naturalization Service (INS) to enact "special measures" to monitor both noncitizen residents of Arab origin along with Arab American citizens.[12] Essentially, all ethnic Arabs in the United States could be subjected to scrutiny. Nixon announced the formation of the Cabinet Committee on 25 September 1972, the day before he was to meet with a group of American Jewish leaders to cultivate their support for his reelection. In a conversation with Nixon that day, Kissinger told him "the reason why we do it [establish the committee] is it's good for your meeting with the Jewish leaders tomorrow. The Israelis want it."[13]

Although Nixon and Kissinger's main purpose in establishing the Cabinet Committee appears to have been appeasing Israel, and Kissinger in particular did not seem to expect the committee to endure or make a significant impact, the committee took on a life of its own, and its "working group" met every two weeks for several years to coordinate the federal government's counterterrorism activities and intelligence gathering.[14] Its member agencies drew on other motives entrenched both in the Nixon administration and in American society at large, chiefly a misplaced fear of Arabs and antipathy to Arab political positions, to expand their investigations and surveillance of Arab Americans.

The Cabinet Committee was charged with oversight of the government's visa screening program, Operation Boulder, which the State Department had already initiated in the preceding two weeks. A committee official later declared that even if the visa checks on Arabs only produced a few visa "stops," the resources devoted to it were worthwhile because the operation's intent was "to build up a good body of evidence"—presumably evidence of Arab political activities, both domestic and abroad.[15] The Operation Boulder visa program thus became entwined with a multipronged federal government initiative aimed at identifying pro-Palestinian activity and catching "terrorists," an effort that ensnared activist Arab Americans. On 18 September, Nixon received a memo from Secretary of State William Rogers outlining the steps that State had taken since the murders at the Olympics, including "screen more closely visa applications of potential terrorists"; "tighten controls" over groups that have connections with "movements advocating or practicing political terrorism, e.g. . . . groups of Arab and Iranian students in this country"; and increase protections for Israelis in the United States.[16] Soon after, the CIA shared with the Cabinet Committee lists it had compiled of Arab American organizations and leaders, along with a recent chronology of Arab terrorist activities. The committee set about creating its own list of "potential targets for terrorists" in the United States and formulated plans to protect "Jewish organizations and prominent Jewish persons in the U.S."[17] Over the next few years the FBI reported to the Committee and the U.S. Attorney General that it was surveilling Fatah, Black September, and Popular Front for the Liberation of Palestine operatives in the United States; agents were especially concerned about their infiltration of "legitimate Arab [American] organizations."[18]

The federal government's effort to thwart Palestinian terrorism by screening Arabs in the United States was announced on the front page of the *New York Times* on 5 October 1972 with the headline: "U.S. Checks Arabs to Block Terror." The article quoted a tight-lipped INS official conceding that the operation was "a touchy one." *Newsweek*'s revelation of the counterterrorism committee stated: "The concern centers on the safety of Israeli officials" in the United States. Throughout October, several other prominent media outlets, such as *NBC Nightly News*, reported on the new initiative to investigate Arabs and Arab Americans.[19] In their statements to the media, federal government officials represented this wide-ranging investigative sweep as a "precautionary measure." A few months into the program, officials told the media that the Cabinet Committee received tips almost every day about suspicious Arab activities in the United States, and some of those tips came from intelligence provided by foreign governments—governments that the officials declined to identify.[20]

Lasting about two years, Operation Boulder checked the status of all Arabs in the country on student visas. Other policies initiated by the operation consisted of more stringent requirements and clearance for Arabs seeking to enter the United States, as well as the termination of travel visas for people from Arab countries who wanted to briefly visit the United States. In what were called "Boulder checks," the State Department used new technology (a teletype system) to screen Arab visa applicants against the records of the INS, FBI, CIA, and U.S. Secret Service. As of January 1973, when Operation Boulder had been in effect less than four months, government officials reported they had screened about 28,000 visa applications originating in the Arab world, had rejected only four, and were still reviewing fifteen, owing to the connection they discerned between the applicants and certain Arab political groups. (Within a few months, the government eased the restrictions on travel visas, granting them to "special cases," usually Arab diplomats and businessmen who had close ties with American interests.)[21]

Immigration and Naturalization Service agents set out to track down and question every Arab student in the United States with the expressed purpose of verifying their visa status but with the unstated goal of investigating the students' political views. As has been demonstrated, since at least 1969 the federal government had suspected that Arab students were serving as tools of the Palestinian fedayeen in the United States. To Jabara, it was clear that among all Arabs in the country, students had become top targets for government harassment because they so visibly promoted the Palestinian struggle on American campuses. Closely scrutinizing Arab students' visa status, INS agents enforced penalties, including deportation, for visa violations that the agency normally overlooked, such as an immigrant being temporarily employed while a student.[22]

But when conducting the visa screening process, the agents regularly questioned the students on their political views and activities—interrogation that significantly departed from permissible INS procedure. If a student responded in a way that an INS agent found suspect, then in some cases the INS would call in the FBI to further investigate the student. The partnership between these two agencies was evident in a memo from Secretary of State Rogers to President Nixon on 21 September 1972, explaining that the State Department had asked the INS to provide the FBI with "the names and locations of all Arab students currently in the United States."[23] By January 1973, according to the INS, it had screened 3,500 Arab students and Arabs in the country on visitor visas and found 282 with "deportable violations." Deportation proceedings had been filed against 68 of them, while 41 had left the country voluntarily. The most common reason for deportation was employment without permission.[24] The agency jailed one Arab immigrant, Essam El-Kotob, a former student who the INS charged was in the country illegally and had declared to an INS agent that he wanted to return to Jordan and join Fatah.[25]

The federal government's investigations of Arab students occurred at universities all over the country, but agents especially concentrated on students in the Los Angeles region.[26] Joe Stork and René Theberge termed the investigations of nearly 200 Arab students around Los Angeles in the fall of 1972 a "blitz."[27] The agents' visits began with standard inquiries about visa status but often proceeded to questions such as whether the students supported Fatah, if they knew anyone who did, what the students thought about Israel, and what organizations they belonged to. For example, when INS officials visited the apartment of David Aldamalani, a graduate student at California State–Long Beach, they looked through his books and other personal property and, upon finding a pro-Palestinian poster, took him to their office and interrogated him about involvement with Fatah.[28]

In Detroit, an INS official met with a group of international student advisers from local universities to inform them that the agency was commencing Operation Boulder investigations of their Arab students. The official began the meeting by declaring that "all ethnic Arabs are being routinely screened to determine their purpose in the U.S." so as to carry out President Nixon's goal of providing security for Israelis in the United States. He told the advisers that government officials would be visiting their campuses to check on the immigrant status of all Arab students and assured them that if any students were found to be in violation of their visa but not determined to be involved in "terrorist organizations," then they would be treated "regularly."[29]

A couple of weeks later, the Organization of Arab Students chapter at Wayne State University in Detroit sent a letter to Arab students informing them of the INS's ongoing investigations, which the OAS called a "program of harassment and intimidation." The letter declared, "Many students have been asked questions by the Immigration Department which are not pertinent and do not have to be answered." Appended to the letter was a memo from Abdeen Jabara informing the students of their rights when questioned by government officials and advising how to protect themselves from harassment.[30]

While occasionally called in to follow up on INS screenings of Arab students, the FBI was simultaneously conducting its own investigative sweeps of Arab Americans who had some affiliation with the Palestinian cause or with Arab American political organizations. For example, agents visited Pierre Alwan, a Lebanese immigrant living near Los Angeles who had become a U.S. citizen in 1961 and belonged to a humanitarian organization that aided Palestinian refugees. According to Alwan, the agents told him, "We are checking on you Arabs because we don't want a repeat of Munich." They asked him questions about his associations with Palestinian political groups and about the activities of other Arab Americans.[31] In another instance, a senior design engineer for the Missouri State Highway Department, Jamil Azzah, was visited in his apartment by an FBI agent who claimed to have evidence that Azzah was a member of a terrorist organization and demanded to fingerprint him. Azzah denied the agent's charges, which were never filed, and later complained to the FBI about his treatment. The agent's supervisor subsequently apologized to Azzah for the interrogation.[32]

When an FBI agent asked him about his support for Fatah, Ihsan Diab, a professor of pharmacology at the University of Chicago who had emigrated from Palestine when he was twelve years old, responded: "90 per cent of the 15,000 Arabs in the Chicago area sympathize with Al Fatah!" Reflecting on such situations, Arab American attorney and activist M. Cherif Bassiouni observed that U.S. government officials were so ill-informed about Arab perspectives that any expressed support for Palestine and opposition to Israel seemed threatening and subversive to them. Journalist Lawrence Mosher likewise described a situation in which government investigators did not understand distinctions among various Palestinian organizations and perceived any sympathy with Fatah as terroristic.[33]

Abdeen Jabara made an effort to document these investigations, and his files are full of affidavits by Arab immigrants from across the country who had been interrogated by INS or FBI agents. He also kept notes on the investigative activities of the FBI in Detroit and Dearborn, listing names of thirty-one individuals who reported being approached. They include most of the prominent Arab American activists of the Dearborn community. For example, Don Unis, an activist in Dearborn's Southend neighborhood, told Jabara the FBI agents had asked him, "What is ACCESS, AACC, Arab Center? Do Red Crescent and UHLF send money to fedayeen? Do you donate? . . . What kind of meetings do you go to and where? Will you cooperate and give information if you know of some terror activities? Do you think the above names are capable of doing terror?" Then they showed him pictures of Arab American individuals and asked if they had any connection with fedayeen organizations. Ismael Ahmed and his grandmother Aliya Hassen, director of ACCESS, were also caught up in the sweep and asked about their knowledge of terrorist activities. Jabara's evidence demonstrates that agents were monitoring several Dearborn activists' activities on a daily basis in this period.[34]

The AAUG also became a specific target of federal government harassment. Many years later, M. Cherif Bassiouni revealed that in the early 1970s the FBI began investigating him and many other AAUG leaders, entailing surveillance that in some cases lasted for years.[35] Related to the Cabinet Committee to Combat Terrorism's crackdown but emanating from another federal government agency with punitive power, the Internal Revenue Service (IRS) audited the AAUG in 1973 and recommended revoking the organization's tax-exempt status, offering the rationale that the AAUG was engaged in political activities. Calling the IRS's proposal "another form of political harassment," Jabara vigorously refuted the IRS's claims, and the AAUG was ultimately able to keep its tax-exempt status. Jabara understood that the IRS's action against the Arab American organization was part of a larger Nixon administration agenda to use the IRS to punish individuals and organizations it considered political enemies.[36]

Also representative of Nixon-era tactics, in 1972 the FBI burglarized the Dallas offices of the Arab Information Center in an attempt to gain intelligence on Palestinian guerrillas with American connections. The break-in was characteristic of the illegal "black-bag jobs" perpetrated by both the FBI and the Nixon White House's "plumbers" against individuals and organizations in the early 1970s, a practice that was later investigated and condemned by congressional investigative committees.[37]

In 1973, in response to terrorism abroad, such as Black September's murder of American hostages in Sudan, and attempted terrorist acts in the United States, officials in the Cabinet Committee to Combat Terrorism concluded that Arab terrorism was worsening. They warned that U.S. intelligence and law enforcement agencies needed to be ever more vigilant.[38] The federal government's monitoring of Arab and Arab American activists intensified that summer after two incidents targeted Israeli officials on American soil. First, preceding Israeli premier Golda Meir's visit to New York City, the National Security Agency (NSA), working with the New York City Police Department, used Israeli-supplied intelligence plus an intercepted message to Baghdad to locate three bombs placed in cars around the city. Fortunately, the bombs were faulty and did not detonate. A few months later, Israeli colonel Yosef Alon, the naval attaché at Israel's embassy in Washington, D.C., was assassinated at his Maryland home. In the wake of these incidents, the federal government implemented an antiterrorist plan that had been devised months earlier by the Cabinet Committee to Combat Terrorism, shortly after the Munich massacre. The plan involved tracking the locations of Arabs and Arab Americans whom the government had placed on a watch list and in some cases subjecting the individuals to direct surveillance.[39] For example, the day after Alon's assassination, federal agents approached Abdeen Jabara's family members and associates to ask about his whereabouts at the time of the murder. (The answer: he had been working at his Detroit law office.) Although the federal government spent resources investigating Arab Americans such as Jabara, the NSA had immediately received reliable information that Iraqis who were affiliated with Black September and who had no connection to the United States were responsible for both crimes.[40]

Arab Americans Challenge the Government

Many Arab Americans and their allies continually spoke out against their treatment by the government under Operation Boulder and associated measures. Because the Cabinet Committee to Combat Terrorism's investigations singled out members of one ethnic group, they charged, the measures constituted discriminatory harassment. Activists argued that the ensuing violations of civil liberties—arbitrary enforcement of immigration laws, political interrogations of immigrant students, burglaries, warrantless wiretapping—were not justified by claims of national security. Further, because the Arab visa checks and investigations of Arab Americans were publicized in the American media as constituting the U.S. government's reaction to the Munich massacre, the government had in effect stigmatized all Arabs as suspect in the public's mind.[41]

Many Arab American leaders asserted that the real purpose of Operation Boulder and associated measures was not to protect national security—and indeed, the investigations never detected a single case of terrorist or espionage activity among Arabs living in the United States—but to suppress Arab Americans' legal political expression, particularly their pro-Palestinian activism. Essentially, it was a program of political intimidation.[42] Not only did it intend to suppress Arabs' political activism in America, particularly on college campuses, but it also sought to "divide and conquer" Arab American communities by making them suspicious of one another. Stork and Theberge charged that the "most important aspect of this Operation is the clear intention of the US [government] to drive a wedge between the relatively small number of politically active Arabs and Arab Americans, and the majority of 'ethnic Arab' communities who might be otherwise inclined to support them."[43]

Several critics compared the program to the government's internment of Japanese Americans during World War II, a case when another stigmatized ethnic group was singled out and its civil liberties violated for purported associations with America's foreign enemies, in the name of national security.⁴⁴ Other opponents noted the program's parallels with the federal government's tactics during the Second Red Scare. In their investigations FBI agents pressured Arabs and Arab Americans to "name names" of others who were politically active or were members of certain organizations and used the information to compile lists of Arab and Arab American activists and organizations in what was essentially an "intelligence dossier."⁴⁵

At Long Beach State University, where several Arab students had been investigated by INS officials, Dr. Alan Johnson, the associate director of International Student Affairs, spoke out against the government's harassment, calling it a "heavy handed overreaction," and emphasized that the students had not participated in any illegal activities. Arab students at Long Beach State, he reported, reacted to the government's repressive techniques with resentment and fear. The director of the nearby Islamic Foundation of South California agreed that Operation Boulder investigations of the students in the area constituted discriminatory harassment and charged that the government's true purpose was to bully students into leaving the country.⁴⁶

Equally troubling to many Arab American activists was the suspected collaboration of Israeli intelligence forces and American Zionist groups with the U.S. agencies investigating Arab students and Arab Americans. In their *MERIP Reports* article, Stork and Theberge highlighted an October 1972 report in the *Washington Post* about the cooperation between Mossad, the Israeli intelligence and special operations agency, and the CIA and FBI in tracking suspected Palestinian terrorists. Stork and Theberge declared, "Israeli collaboration in Operation Boulder is all but bragged about, although the details are hard to come by." More details emerged in an article in the *Chicago Tribune* two years later which reported that Israeli officials, U.S. officials, and the Anti-Defamation League had continually exchanged information about suspected Arab subversives residing in the United States, including American citizens. The reporter cited as sources both a former Israeli security official and an Anti-Defamation League spokesman who, according to the article, "keeps files on the more active Arabs living here and routinely passes them on to the FBI." The former Israeli official declared that Israeli intelligence agents did not in fact believe that Arabs' main purpose in the United States was terrorist in nature. Instead, Israelis considered Palestinian representatives in the United States to be "agents of influence, not terrorists," suggesting it was their political influence that caused Israeli officials most concern.⁴⁷

Abdeen Jabara protested Israeli and American Zionist influence on the Nixon administration, emphasizing that both sources had been providing the federal government information about Arabs in the United States since at least 1970. Jabara argued that the Nixon administration's establishment of Operation Boulder and associated measures could "only be understood against the background of the definite pressure that [has] been brought to bear by Israel and its supporters in the U.S.," who saw the aftermath of the Munich massacre as an opportunity to curtail the "political and information work" by individuals and organizations promoting the Palestinian side of the Middle East crisis.[48]

Shortly after the federal government's establishment of the Cabinet Committee to Combat Terrorism and Operation Boulder in September 1972, the AAUG sprang to action. Its leaders instituted a public protest campaign that included publishing an advertisement in the *New York Times*, forming a civil liberties committee, and writing letters to government officials, media outlets, and potential allies.[49] Jabara, who was serving as AAUG's president in 1972, realized that as a nonprofit, mainly educational organization, the AAUG had to be careful about its level of political and legal involvement in resisting the government's actions, especially because the IRS had the AAUG in its sights. Moreover, a few AAUG board members expressed hesitancy about mobilizing on this issue, and at least one member implied that the organization's reaction to the government's investigations could become "overblown" and warned his colleagues not to become paranoid. But with the support of several other AAUG leaders, Jabara was convinced that the association had to spearhead a publicity campaign to create pressure on the federal government and help protect Arabs in America threatened by government harassment.[50]

Over the next month, Jabara sent telegrams to several federal government officials, including Secretary of State Rogers, complaining of government harassment of Arabs and Arab Americans. His AAUG colleague M. Cherif Bassiouni joined the letter-writing campaign and dispatched protests to President Nixon and FBI acting director L. Patrick Gray, among others. Gray responded by denying that the screenings were "based upon any ethnic factor" and avowed that "the investigations are based solely upon membership or activity in organizations which have been reliably reported to threaten" national security. In reply, Bassiouni asserted that as an activist in the Arab American community for the past ten years, he was unaware of any Arab organizations that "threaten the internal security of the United States," and he charged that the FBI was making false assumptions about Arab American political activity.[51]

When Jabara wrote a letter of complaint to James Greene of the INS,

Greene responded by echoing Gray's denial of violations of due process or equal protection rights. Yet when more voices protested the INS's illegal procedures, Greene admitted that "some zealous officials overstepped their authority by looking into political activities" and assured those who had expressed concerns that the agents had subsequently been disciplined and trained in permissible interviewing techniques.[52]

Jabara and Bassiouni also enlisted the aid of Senators Philip Hart of Michigan and James Abourezk of South Dakota, an Arab American. Hart agreed to inquire into Department of Justice and INS methods and pressure the agencies to cease any harassment. He wrote to Raymond Farrell, commissioner of the INS, asking him to explain his assertion that the INS was not investigating aliens based on their Arab nationality in light of the numerous reports that INS officials were inquiring about the immigrants' political beliefs, to which Farrell offered a weak reply.[53] Abourezk intervened on behalf of Hassan Husseini, a journalist for the *Columbus Dispatch* newspaper who was under investigation by the FBI. Jabara also asked Abourezk to check into cases of Arab immigrants whose applications for U.S. citizenship had been forwarded to the FBI and inexplicably delayed.[54]

Meanwhile, AAUG leaders were communicating with their members as well as with other Arab American and civil liberties organizations about proper responses if victimized by government harassment. In his career as a civil rights attorney and activist, Jabara had formed close associations with the American Civil Liberties Union (ACLU) and the National Lawyers Guild (NLG) and naturally reached out to them for assistance and advice.[55] A couple of weeks after the government launched its antiterrorist operation, Jabara wrote to his colleague in the ACLU asking the organization to speak out against the government's violations of civil liberties and equal protection principles. Within a week, Mel Wolfe, executive director of the ACLU, wrote to the U.S. attorney general charging that Operation Boulder and associated measures comprised "dragnet investigations based solely upon an individual's national origin" and went "beyond fair and respectful inquiries by Law enforcement." The government's "interrogation and surveillance of members of a specific national group . . . has the effect of harassing and intimidating them," the ACLU director continued, and the program should be "condemned as constitutionally impermissible."[56]

Jabara also maintained contact with attorneys in the NLG who provided legal representation to Arabs, especially Arab students on the West Coast who experienced government harassment. The NLG's newsletter announced, "The panel has undertaken the responsibility to provide defense at deportation hearings for persons victimized in what appears to be a national campaign to terrorize Arab people in the United States." The NLG had already been working on immigrant deportation problems, mainly concentrating on Mexican and Iranian immigrants, and readily incorporated the violations associated with Operation Boulder into its existing initiatives.[57]

At the end of October 1972, the AAUG published an ad in the Sunday *New York Times* with the headline: "Is the Nixon Administration Playing Politics with Civil Liberties?" The ad enumerated several objections to the Cabinet Committee to Combat Terrorism's measures, emphasizing the discriminatory and stigmatizing effect of the government's program and the fact that Arabs in the United States were innocent of terrorism. "Anti-Arab racism in the U.S. has been on the increase. Is it now being accorded official sanction?" the ad demanded. It also claimed the government's crackdown on people of Arab background in the United States was harming the country's relations with Arab nations. Quoting the ACLU's letter of protest to the attorney general, the ad emphasized the government's violations of individuals' civil liberties, charging that the administration was relying on the insidious concept of "collective guilt by ethnic association." To make the crisis relevant to non-Arabs and stir up wider alarm, it declared: "Undermining the civil liberties of one ethnic group is the first stage in a process of steady erosion which can eventually extend to all groups." Demonstrating a network of support, several other Arab American organizations cosponsored the protest ad, including the Antiochian Orthodox Archdiocese in Toledo, Ohio; the Detroit Yemeni Association; the Committee for Better Relations in the Middle East of Birmingham, Alabama; and the Federation of Islamic Associations in the United States and Canada. Many organizations that cosponsored the ad had generally been nonpolitical and isolated from one another, but the Cabinet Committee to Combat Terrorism's measures, ironically, raised their political consciousness and boosted the mobilization of the Arab American community.[58]

Other Arab American activist organizations vocally protested the government's harassment during the Operation Boulder years. Dr. Mohammad T. Mehdi, the New York City–based director of the Action Committee on American-Arab Relations (ACAAR) and longtime critic of Zionism as well as American treatment of Arabs in the United States, predictably spoke out against Operation Boulder investigations. The *New York Times* quoted Mehdi denouncing the operation as "witch-hunting" and "defamation" and declaring that "Zionist terrorism against the Arabs is a greater menace to American society and its Arab community than any possible Palestinian terrorism." Not surprisingly, Mehdi attracted considerable hostility, and the ACAAR constantly received threats. In 1974, ACAAR's office in New York City was burned down, and Mehdi suspected arson by a Zionist organization.[59] The Arab American Congress for Palestine, at the time based in Chicago, wrote a letter of complaint to the U.S. attorney general about intimidation of Arab Americans in the Chicago area. The AACP threatened, "Unless such harassment ceases at once, we will be forced to file suit against your agency and send a representative delegations [sic] on the national level to the Arab Governments demanding appropriate and immediate actions," and sent copies to several Middle East embassies in Washington, D.C., as well as to a few members of Congress.[60]

The Organization of Arab Students also mobilized in opposition to the government's investigations, sending out a press release protesting Operation Boulder and organizing a forum at Wayne State University on 7 December 1972. The forum featured as speakers a member of the ACLU, a professor in Wayne State's urban affairs program, a national officer of the OAS, and Abdeen Jabara. The leftist student newspaper *South End* cosponsored the event and declared its purpose was to "expose the government campaign presently being waged against people of Arab extraction" and to provide information about the "overt violation of constitutional liberties by Federal authorities" that the "establishment media" was ignoring.[61] A few American leftist groups joined the protest against Operation Boulder, including the Socialist Workers Party (SWP), which issued a press release attacking the Nixon administration's "racist" policy of screening Arabs in the United States. At its national convention in 1972 the Young Socialists included a program titled "Imperialism's Anti-Arab Witch Hunt."[62]

Legal Challenges and Efforts at Common Cause

Besides applying public and political pressure, Abdeen Jabara fought the federal government's methods in the legal arena. As discussed earlier, when he discovered in mid-1972 that the government had been monitoring his financial transactions at a bank in Detroit, he brought suit, charging that he had been subject to illegal surveillance. When Operation Boulder began later that year, Jabara initiated another lawsuit and was eventually joined by the ACLU in a legal battle against the government that would last thirteen years. In discovery proceedings, U.S. District Court judge Ralph Freeman required the FBI to reveal records of its surveillance, and the FBI disclosed that it had repeatedly received electronic surveillance information on Jabara from the

NSA.⁶³ According to Jabara's attorney, the ACLU's John Shattuck, the ruling marked the first time the NSA was compelled by the justice system to reveal subjects of its electronic surveillance. Both agencies' files revealed that the government's surveillance of Jabara dated back to 1967 and had continued through the time of court-mandated disclosure, 1974. The files included lists of Jabara's organizational affiliations, reports of his travels across the country and overseas, transcripts of at least forty wiretapped conversations (including his overseas phone calls), interviews with over one hundred people, contacts with five Detroit-area banks, and summaries of his speeches and activities at scores of public and private meetings, which indicated that the agencies were using informants close to Jabara. The NSA and the FBI had exchanged information about Jabara with three foreign governments and a Zionist organization. Yet, throughout the proceedings the FBI admitted that Jabara was not the subject of criminal investigation.⁶⁴

Judge Freeman decided that the NSA's interception of Jabara's communications with people outside the United States constituted unconstitutional search and seizure. Jabara argued that his constitutional rights of free speech and assembly also had been violated. Not a single element of the government investigation, he declared, was "a legitimate law enforcement surveillance issue. [It] was pure intimidation."⁶⁵ In an interview with the *Washington Post* shortly after the government released these files, Jabara announced that the reason the government monitored him was improper concern about his leadership of the AAUG and his political position on Israel. Furthermore, he charged, the agents attempted to intimidate his friends and colleagues and deter them from associating with him. The FBI countered that its actions were legal and necessary and constituted "lawful national security electronic surveillance conducted to obtain foreign intelligence."⁶⁶

In the course of the lawsuit and the FBI's revelations, Jabara discovered that the Michigan State and Detroit police had been working with the bureau to monitor his political activities and affiliations. The records indicated that Jabara was not the only political activist about whom the Michigan State Police was collecting information, and he soon joined a class action suit, *Benkert et al. v. Michigan State Police*, with several other leftist figures in the Detroit area. Of the plaintiffs in the Benkert suit, Jabara was the only Arab American. He realized, of course, that the government's harassment of him was part of a wider pattern of assault on the civil liberties of Americans during the Johnson and Nixon years that principally targeted activists on the political left.

The FBI's counterintelligence program, COINTELPRO, established in the mid-1950s, pursued groups the government deemed subversive, such as the Southern Christian Leadership Conference, the American Indian movement, and Students for a Democratic Society, using harassment techniques that included infiltration, surveillance, burglary, and other covert operations without warrants or other judicial sanction. The program's illegal tactics were exposed and terminated in 1971, but the Nixon White House, in conjunction with FBI agent Bill Sullivan (who had long championed COINTELPRO), was developing a similar plan to harass groups and individuals it considered political enemies, such as antiwar activists and the Black Panthers. Though the program—dubbed the "Huston Plan" after its main author, White House aide Tom Charles Huston—was never officially approved, elements of it were secretly implemented, and the federal government's illegal surveillance of leftist organizations persisted in the early 1970s. These repressive methods were uncovered during inquiries into Nixon's Watergate activities in 1973, and more details were revealed when a Senate committee chaired by Senator Frank Church investigated federal government intelligence practices in 1975.[67]

As he prepared his cases against the federal and state governments, Jabara researched many cases from across the country involving illegal investigation and harassment of leftist groups and activists in the early 1970s, some of which resulted in lawsuits similar to the suits he was bringing. He joined Philip Berrigan, brother of the antiwar activist Daniel Berrigan, at a rally held at Wayne State University in May 1974 to support the Socialist Workers Party's Political Rights Defense Fund, which raised money for legal challenges to the government's use of illegal surveillance and other forms of harassment.[68]

In a speech to AAUG members in Chicago in 1975, titled "Investigating the FBI/CIA Apparatus: Will It Include the Arab-Americans?," Jabara made the connection between the Cabinet Committee to Combat Terrorism's measures and other Nixon administration schemes. He explained that the federal agencies' harassment of Arab Americans had been facilitated by the investigative practices encouraged by the Huston Plan. Indeed, as already mentioned, White House documents from 1970 reveal that the main targets for investigation and repression were black activists, antiwar radicals, Soviet spies, and "potential Arab saboteurs."[69] Bassiouni also viewed the government's repression of Arab Americans and non-Arab leftists as coordinated and intertwined, arguing that the Nixon administration's "thrust was thus two-fold: to strike at administration opponents in respect to pro-Israeli policies and simultaneously at those Blacks, leftists, radicals and intellectuals who opposed the administration's internal policies and who also support Arab and Palestinian claims."⁷⁰

Jabara saw the persecution as an opportunity for Arab Americans to open a new avenue for political mobilization, chiefly by building coalitions with other groups who similarly had endured harassment by law enforcement. He did not think that Arab Americans would get very far if they remained isolated in their struggle against the government's misconduct. Informing potential allies in the liberal-left community, such as the ACLU and the NLG, about Operation Boulder and associated measures, and asking for their support, were primary ways to educate politically active Americans about the Arab American community and thereby build common cause. Jabara tapped into a network of non-Arab leftists in Detroit to construct a struggle against local, state, and federal government surveillance tactics and to emphasize Arab Americans as part of the larger community on the left. These alliances were necessary both for moral and political support and for legal potency when challenging the government's authority in court. Another example of his efforts at outreach was when Arab Americans in Lawrence, Kansas, sponsored a forum to publicize the federal government's harassment of Arab immigrants. Jabara advised them to include in their presentation the experiences of other groups of immigrants who suffered persecution in the United States, such as Iranians, Mexicans, and Vietnamese, as a way to widen the audience and relate the Arab American experience to a broader struggle for justice.⁷¹

Nevertheless, gaining sympathy from other persecuted ethnic minority and leftist groups proved difficult, a divide that some activists attributed to lingering distrust of Arabs and, especially, the Palestinian cause. Jabara, for instance, recalls meeting with initial resistance when he approached the ACLU about supporting his lawsuit. Although the organization agreed to represent him, its leaders hesitated about publicizing the case among its members because, as he understood it, they feared its support of an Arab American might hamper fund-raising.⁷² According to Bassiouni, although the federal government was using repressive tactics against many other activist groups in the United States, Arab Americans stood alone. At least the other groups, no matter how far outside the American mainstream, could count on some pockets of sympathy in American society, whereas "there wasn't too much support for the pro-Palestinian movement," he recalls. Jabara similarly doubted Arab Americans would gain support of other Americans trying to restrain the federal government intelligence apparatus in the Watergate era.

As the Church Senate committee was undertaking its investigations of the FBI and CIA, Jabara predicted that the committee as well as public opinion would condemn the government's illegal tactics used against American antiwar groups but would ignore the violations of Arab immigrants' and Arab Americans' rights. Jabara mused, "Here the division is us Americans and them foreigners, even though some of us Americans may be them foreigners."[73] Even among leftists agitating against the government's persecution of political expression, Arabs and the Palestinian cause were widely viewed as suspect and threatening, and Arab Americans remained fairly isolated and vulnerable.[74]

Moreover, although many Arab Americans protested the government's investigations and asserted their Arab identity and right to hold and express pro-Palestinian political views, some Arabs in the United States were intimidated by the government's crackdown. An Arab American professor at the University of Chicago claimed that other Arabs he knew feared "that if their names are on membership lists they will be deported. Many are not yet citizens, do not know their rights, and are frightened of authorities." Shrinking back from affiliations that might make them suspect in the eyes of the federal government's growing antiterrorism surveillance apparatus, some Arab Americans refrained from travel to the Arab world, stopped attending Arab community centers, or ceased their donations to Palestinian-affiliated organizations, such as the United Holy Land Fund, which saw contributions decline steeply in the years 1973 to 1975.[75]

The End of Operation Boulder

By the spring of 1974, Operation Boulder investigations were still in effect, but federal government agencies were debating whether to continue the program. Immigration and Naturalization Service officials claimed that the screenings of Arab immigrants demanded too many resources, and they questioned its efficacy. Supported by the CIA and some offices of the State Department, the INS recommended either reducing or ending the operation. The FBI, on the other hand, reiterated the existence of a terrorist threat and demanded the program's continuation. At that point, the U.S. State Department's coordinator for combating terrorism decided that Operation Boulder should continue without modification.[76] But a year later, in April 1975, the State Department finally decided to terminate the operation because, according to a *New York Times* interview with John Gatch, a State Department antiterrorist official, "it was not worth the manpower that went into it. From the standpoint of cost effectiveness, it was not worth it." While Gatch acknowledged that he and other government officials thought there was some risk in stopping the checks, the State Department believed that "other screening measures that involve less paper work will be effective." Thus, at least according to its public statements, the federal government dropped the program not because of ethical or constitutional considerations but because they deemed it inefficient. Gatch depicted the operation as a success, emphasizing that during its existence the government had "processed" 150,000 individuals and as a result prevented a few suspicious people from entering or remaining in the country.[77]

Although Operation Boulder officially ended in 1975, government monitoring of politically active Arab Americans persisted for years. Various chapters of the Organization of Arab Students endured sustained harassment, and the National Lawyers Guild continued to assist the student organization through the late 1970s. In 1980, Jabara, who chaired the AAUG's Civil Rights Committee, sent "Action Alert: FBI Surveillance and Harassment" to all AAUG members, informing them that reports from Arab Americans across the country "suggest an FBI campaign similar to that launched . . . in 1972." He suspected the government was trying to clamp down on pro-Palestinian activity, such as that generated by the newly established Palestine Human Rights Campaign, and he urged his colleagues to be vigilant about their rights.[78] Over the next decade, the American-Arab Anti-Discrimination Committee (ADC) reported continual harassment by the FBI at its offices around the country. The Detroit area attracted the particular attention of federal law enforcement. In 1982 the *Detroit Free Press* reported: "The FBI keeps close tabs on the Palestinian community in Detroit. Those who participate in any kind of organized Palestinian activity say they are almost certain to be visited by an agent. Agents even write the letters FBI in Arabic on calling cards left with Palestinians." And, still, the federal government had never charged an Arab American political activist with a crime.[79]

Persecution of Arab Americans extended beyond the law enforcement community, and organizations such as ACCESS in Dearborn experienced increased prank phone calls and bomb threats along with other expressions of hostility from the general populace. Most serious, in 1985, the Boston office of the ADC was bombed, injuring two people, and later that year, the Palestinian American leader Alex Odeh was assassinated by a bomb attack at the ADC office in southern California. The FBI classified the bombings as terrorist acts and suspected Jewish Defense League members as the perpetrators; however, no one has ever been convicted of the crimes.[80]

THE WORSENING MISTREATMENT OF Arab Americans in these years can be attributed to a noxious combination of ethnic discrimination and "political racism," the latter stemming from widespread American antagonism toward the pro-Palestinian political stance held by most ethnic Arabs. While all Arabs in the diaspora might be subject to stereotyping and possibly harassment, it was primarily politically active Arab Americans who experienced persecution. Although some Arabs in America, particularly noncitizens, responded to the atmosphere of repression by retreating from activities and commitments associated with the Arab world, for other Arab Americans the political persecution produced the opposite effect. Indeed, in the face of widespread violations of their civil liberties, many Arab Americans developed a deeper sense of their Arab identity and community consciousness. In some respects Operation Boulder and associated measures helped politicize Arab Americans who previously had been fairly apathetic. Once the federal government began treating anyone with Arab heritage as suspect, more Arab Americans realized, as Hagopian remarks, "they were somehow involved." Likewise, in his book about the Nixon administration's "special measures," Bassiouni observed that "what was intended to drive the Arab-Americans underground and silence their opposition to US foreign policy caused them to become more united and vocal. This time, however, it was not only in opposition to US foreign policy but also to a facet of its internal policy."[81] This shift to an intermingling of Arab world and Arab American political issues heralded an incipient Arab American civil rights movement. Arguably, the antagonism encountered by Arab Americans enhanced their activism on behalf of their own rights in the United States and tied it to their activism on behalf of the Palestinian cause, thus creating a wider space for transnational political expression. Furthermore, their protest against overzealous government surveillance afforded another opportunity, though limited, to create common cause with other Americans who were challenging similar civil liberties violations. As we shall see, Arab American organizing that tied together local grievances, global issues, and inspiration from American protest groups was unfolding in Dearborn, Michigan, in the early 1970s.

PART THREE
AMERICANIZATION OF ACTIVISM
Local Organizing and National Integration

6 Traversing Arab and American Spaces
Community and Labor Organizing in the Southend

Nestled against Ford Motor Company's mammoth River Rouge factory in Dearborn, Michigan, the immigrant enclave dubbed the "Southend" became a major site of Arab American activism in the 1960s and 1970s, with a climate that one activist described as "electric."[1] The Southend demonstrates on a local level the national trajectory of Arab American community building and identity assertion in these years. The neighborhood functioned as a crucible for the growing numbers of Arab immigrants who settled there, a space that galvanized different generations of Arab Americans into activism and facilitated ethnic solidarity. Diverse contingents in the neighborhood, sometimes joined by outside allies, mobilized to challenge injustice from multiple centers of power: the local government, local and national corporations, and, transnationally, the U.S. government, Israel, and conservative Arab regimes.

The Southend's activism manifested in several arenas that were linked together by a network of Arab American activists connected to the working-class neighborhood. The class position of the Southend shaped its leftist politics and underdog pride. First, residents representing diverse ethnic groups joined together to protest plans by the city of Dearborn to destroy houses in the neighborhood during the late 1960s and early 1970s. Meanwhile, Arab Americans increasingly practiced diasporic political activism in the Southend, especially during and after the October War of 1973, connecting their Arab politics to the local struggle to save their neighborhood. Then, out of the ferment generated by both their fight against the city and their growing assertion of Arab political identity, activists in the Southend established a neighborhood center, the Arab Community Center for Economic and Social Services (ACCESS). The center concentrated on providing social services to new immigrants, as it does now, but it in its early years it was also a hotbed of secular, leftist Arab political organizing.

Finally, some of the Southend leaders involved in the fight against urban removal and the formation of ACCESS extended their activism into the workplace and founded the Arab Workers Caucus (AWC), a dissident workers' organization based in southeast Michigan. Modeled on Detroit's black Revolutionary Union Movement and the League of Revolutionary Black Workers, the AWC was part of a broader movement of leftist labor agitation in the United States in the late 1960s through the 1970s. Consisting almost entirely of autoworkers, the AWC challenged the auto companies and the United Automobile Workers (UAW) for their unfair treatment of Arab American workers and blasted the UAW for its pro-Israeli position. By closely integrating its support of Palestine with its advocacy of Arab workers' interests in the United States, the AWC provided another representation of Arab Americans' transnational political consciousness.

Arab Americans' experience of injustice in the Southend, and the community's grassroots organizing to resist it, parallels the histories of other racial minorities and newer immigrant populations in American cities in this era. In her study of the Puerto Rican revolutionary organization the Young Lords, Johanna Fernández argues that such radical grassroots groups as the Young Lords and the Black Panthers were emerging in a context of "new structures of capitalism" that exacerbated the economic struggles and social isolation borne by the urban working class, particularly by poor people of color. In the 1960s and 1970s, Puerto Ricans in several American cities formed community organizations to resist urban renewal plans, preserve their neighborhoods, provide social services, and assert their cultural and political identities as members of the diaspora by advocating Puerto Rican independence alongside claims for economic justice and civil rights in the United States.[2] Arab American activists in the Southend drew on the discourse and practices of other dispossessed groups' struggles in urban America and endeavored to connect their movement to the larger narrative of civil and human rights struggles. Together, the Southend struggle against urban removal, the grassroots movement to establish ACCESS, and the workers' challenge to the UAW illustrate the larger trajectory of Arab American activism linking the local and the transnational. By the 1980s, Arab workers' radicalism subsided as they established friendlier relations with the UAW and ACCESS moved away from its oppositional position, eventually becoming a key institution in the state and federal nexus of government and nonprofit social service agencies.

The Fight against Urban Removal in the Southend

The polluted industrial area occupied by the Southend neighborhood is physically separated from the rest of Dearborn by factories and railroads, a large cemetery, and, on the other side, the city of Detroit. Since the early twentieth century, the Southend has been a working-class, largely immigrant neighborhood. Early on its residents came mainly from southern and eastern Europe, with a few hailing from the Middle East. The neighborhood also included a substantial number of whites who had migrated from the American South, looking for work at Ford. Most residents worked in the adjacent Ford Rouge plant or for a nearby industrial enterprise, and many had been involved in the critical unionization battles at Ford in the 1930s and 1940s. Important to the neighborhood's identity is its rich history of leftist labor activism, practiced by the diverse groups of workers who made their homes there.[3]

Starting in the 1940s, more immigrants from Arab countries, mainly Palestine and Lebanon, joined the mix, and in the 1960s Yemenis also began settling in the Southend. By the 1960s people of Arab origin constituted about half of the neighborhood's roughly five thousand inhabitants, and whereas the vast majority of Arab Americans in the Detroit metropolitan area were Christian, most Arab Americans residing in the Southend were Muslim. Moreover, the Arab Americans in the Southend were poorer and less educated than most Arab Americans in the Detroit area, and they were mainly employed as industrial workers instead of as independent entrepreneurs.[4]

While some Arab American residents of the Southend in the 1960s were second- or third-generation Americans, the majority had been born in the Arab world and maintained close cultural ties with their homelands along with intense political identification with Arab nationalism. In the 1950s and 1960s, widespread support for Egypt's Gamal Abdel Nasser was evident among Arab Americans in the neighborhood, a political sentiment that had shifted in favor of the Palestinian fedayeen by the late 1960s (particularly after the Palestinian resistance's strong showing in the Battle of Karameh in 1968). Many of the immigrants had recently left their countries because of the turmoil generated by nationalist struggles. Sociologists Laurel Wigle and Sameer Abraham designate the neighborhood as a "primary community," one in which "migrants have not assimilated into the mainstream of American society but have retained their traditional social structural arrangements, as well as their language and cultural heritage." By the mid-twentieth century, markers of Arab culture were increasingly apparent in the Southend, especially in the numerous Arab coffeehouses and the prominent mosque on Dix Avenue, the main road through the neighborhood.[5]

In the 1950s, Dearborn city leaders, led by Mayor Orville Hubbard, developed a city plan that included rezoning the Southend from residential to industrial use. The "urban renewal" conversion would ultimately require destroying the neighborhood's homes, shops, and places of worship to allow Ford Motor Company and other industries to expand their operations into the area, thereby increasing its tax revenue. The city began razing homes in the northern part of the neighborhood in the early 1960s, and by 1968 nearly 200 families had been displaced. The cleared land was sold to industries, including a brick company and an asphalt company, which resulted in huge piles of slag and heavy truck traffic through the Southend. Subsequently, city planners deemed the remaining residential neighborhood inhabitable because of the increased industry and resulting pollution, which the city's scheme had, of course, produced.[6]

Although the city publicized its plan to demolish the neighborhood and convert it to industry, for the most part it did not declare eminent domain and take the homes, nor did it offer homeowners fair value compensation or develop an adequate relocation plan for displaced residents. Instead, it used a number of methods to undermine the value of residents' homes, such as encouraging encroaching industry, preventing homeowners from making improvements to their homes, and allowing deteriorating vacant homes to remain standing to promote blight. The city then bought the homes at rock-bottom prices and destroyed them. As activist Barbara Aswad explained to a reporter, the residents faced a Catch-22: "You can't sell a house in Dearborn unless it comes up to one of the country's strictest housing codes. And to improve your house . . . you have to have a permit. And you have to get a permit from City Hall which tells you you can't unless you agree to do everything your house needs done at once. But if you want, you can sell to the city at any time, whether or not your home meets code standards."[7]

In treating the Southend as marginal and its residents as disposable, city leaders were operating out of both class and ethnic bias; they did not see any value in the working-class immigrant enclave and could not understand why anyone would want to live there. According to some residents, Mayor Hubbard and other Dearborn leaders were also motivated by racism. Some have speculated that in the aftermath of the Detroit race riot of 1967, Hubbard, a notorious racist, grew determined to create a "buffer zone" between Dearborn and Detroit by turning the Southend, which bordered Detroit, into an industrial park. Others pointed to the Southend's increasing population of Yemenis, who tended to be darker skinned than other Arab groups, and suggested that Hubbard and like-minded city leaders applied their racial prejudice against African Americans to Yemenis. Don Unis, a Southend resident and third-generation Lebanese immigrant, thought the city's true aim was removal of Yemenis. He recalled, "They wanted us out because you know what was coming after those Lebanese Arabs? Those Desert-Nigger Yemeni Arabs. I mean, they would tell me, 'Donny, you're okay, it's those Yemenis.'"[8]

As the city demolished homes, Southend residents mobilized, using the neighborhood's Southeast Dearborn Community Council (SEDCC) as a vehicle for resisting the city's underhanded methods. The most recent immigrants, especially Yemenis, lived in the southern part of the neighborhood and were scarcely involved in the struggle against the city's project. But over time, as the demolitions moved from the north to the middle of the area, and Arab immigration to the Southend swelled in the wake of upheavals in Palestine and Yemen, more Arab Americans participated in the demonstrations.[9]

Earlier in the 1960s, the Community Council had protested the pollution and slag trucks in the area and tried to call the city government's attention to the health risks it created for Southend residents. By 1970 the SEDCC was channeling its considerable energies and meager resources into a movement to preserve its unique neighborhood. It organized campaigns to resist the city's plans to close the neighborhood library branch as well as the neighborhood school, which by then had a largely Arab student population and a staff who was sensitive to the immigrants' needs.[10]

The Community Council's main focus, though, was halting the further devaluation and destruction of homes. Don Unis's sister, Katherine Amen, also lived in the Southend with her family; when the city made an offer on her family's home, she grew determined to push back against the city's bullying and became involved in the SEDCC's activities. Her son Alan Amen soon joined her effort to save their neighborhood, becoming president of the SEDCC in 1970. Another key leader in the SEDCC's resistance movement was Helen Atwell, a mother of eight whose parents had immigrated to Dearborn from Lebanon. In 1971, with assistance from the Center for Urban Law and Housing, a division of Wayne County Neighborhood Legal Services and an affiliate of the federal government's Office of Economic Opportunity, the SEDCC filed a class-action suit against the city, with Katherine Amen as the named plaintiff.[11]

In their campaign to mobilize the neighborhood, SEDCC leaders distributed a steady stream of newsletters and flyers, some printed in Arabic and many of which urged residents to sign petitions and attend SEDCC's frequent community meetings and rallies. For instance, one flyer declared:

> Warning!!! To all of you concerned about your homes and community! The City Hall is attacking you again. First, with the Urban Removal, now called Community Development, the city has attempted to clear out the Southend—that means to kick you out! The Mayor has always said the people ought to get out of here because our homes and neighborhood are not fit for human beings to live in. When we say we don't agree, that *most* of us want to stay in the Southend and Dearborn, that we like our homes and neighborhood, he calls us fools and liars, refuses to make it possible to rebuild and improve the area! They are sending around a petition he wants you to sign—don't. Don't be misled . . . this is the worst doublecross yet! On the city petition it says that the SEDCC and officers you helped elect do not represent you "in the matter of Amen et al versus the City"—this is the name of the court case that is fighting your battle and has begun to make them change their plans . . . . Sign only a petition headed in big letters "A Petition for the People of Southeast Dearborn."

Another flyer appealed to pride in the distinctive ethnic diversity of the neighborhood, announcing:

> We are Italians, Greeks, Roumanians [sic], Armenians, Syrians, Lebanese, Yemeni, Southern, Northern, In-Between, and Many More! We are Catholic! Protestant! Moslems! Hindu, or what have you! But we're all Americans and human beings who want the right to be sure of renting or owning our own homes, have help in fighting pollution, and be treated like adults, not children! Right? Right!! Then come out fighting! And over to City Hall! Don't be Put *Down*! It's the *In* Thing to have guts enough to speak *Out*! Be American! No more Rezoning until the master plan is changed to protect the people.[12]

The Community Council's entreaty to "Be American!" by "hav[ing] guts enough to speak out" sought to overcome immigrants' reticence to express public dissent and assimilate them into American civic engagement. With these rallying cries, the SEDCC organized pickets around homes being torn down, at one point forming a human chain to halt the wrecking crew. They also demonstrated at City Hall, carrying picket signs proclaiming: "Save the South End," "Poor People Have Rights," and "Don't Tear Down Good Homes." One SEDCC letter to the Dearborn City Council charged the city

In 1971 residents of the Southend in Dearborn, Michigan, protest at City Hall against the city's plan to demolish homes in the heavily working-class, immigrant neighborhood. (Courtesy of the *Dearborn Press and Guide*)

government with "the removal of a group of people who are as much a part of this city as the people living in other areas of the city but whose homes *and cultures* have been determined to be detrimental to the city [emphasis added]." The class and ethnic identity of the neighborhood informed the protesters' sense of injustice and persecution.[13]

Southend activists also reached out to activists and organizations outside the neighborhood for assistance. Crucial in this regard was the intervention provided by Barbara Aswad, a professor of anthropology at Wayne State University in Detroit who studied peasant culture in the Middle East. Aswad was persuaded to get involved by Iris Becker, a veteran teacher at the Salina school located in the Southend. Becker cared deeply about the neighborhood and became active in the SEDCC's fight to save it. She was also politically active in a number of social justice causes in Detroit and Michigan, through which she had become acquainted with Aswad. Aswad recalls Becker saying to her, "Quit working in the Middle East, we've got people here. . . . Why don't you come down, why don't you do something here?" Subsequently, Aswad designed a survey to administer to Southend residents, aimed at discerning their ethnic and class identities and exploring how they related to their neighborhood. Several Wayne State students, including Arabic-speaking student activists Nabeel Abraham and George Khoury, helped her go door to door and interview residents for the survey. As she grew both professionally and personally invested in the neighborhood, Aswad became a proponent of combining scholarship with activism. During this period she gave a lecture at a college in Dearborn attended by another young Southend activist, Ismael Ahmed, who asked her how professors could contribute to grassroots organizations. She replied that academic professionals could provide credentials and legitimacy to a grassroots social movement. Aswad remembers that Ahmed's eyes lit up, and from then on they formed a close bond around their shared activism in the community.[14]

The main finding of Aswad's survey, which she shared as an expert witness when the SEDCC's case against the city went to trial, was that a significant majority of the residents preferred to remain in the Southend and were culturally attached to their neighborhood. As she claimed in an academic paper published shortly after the trial, her survey showed that "the people identify strongly with the community and most do not want to leave or see its destruction, they would like to see it renewed." Aswad interpreted the conflict as a class and ethnic struggle, arguing: "The groups that will benefit from the community's destruction are big business and the more affluent Dearborn residents. It is obviously a case of class dominance and exploitation and it simultaneously appears to have the overtones of ethnic discrimination." She drew a parallel between the city's removal plan and imperialism as it manifested within the United States and globally against marginalized peoples, stating: "In many ways [the city's plan] is analogous to the methods of dominance and exploitation of a colonized or imperialized region by outside powers, and can be likened to the treatment of the Black ghettos in the United States."[15]

Aswad also reflected on the neighborhood's significance to first-generation immigrants, especially those coming from peasant backgrounds, as had many of the Southend residents who migrated from Yemen, Palestine, and Lebanon. A peasant's adjustment from the "close family and social ties of a village" to an "industrial foreign city" was usually "tremendously difficult, both psychologically and materially." According to Aswad, the Southend's "coffee houses, mosques, and ethnic restaurants" provided the newcomers "a sense of the familiar and sense of security." Moreover, many of the recent immigrants had experienced violent upheaval in their homelands, principally the civil war in Yemen and the Israeli occupation of Palestinian lands after the June War. Being expelled from their new homes would compound their trauma. Thus, on top of economic hardship, destroying the neighborhood would cause undue social and psychological distress to immigrants assimilating to their new country in the accommodating environment of this "primary community."¹⁶

The SEDCC also attracted support from Detroit activist and attorney Abdeen Jabara, who became acquainted with the neighborhood's predicament through his associations with the Arab activist students at Wayne State who were organizing in the Southend. Jabara was instrumental in soliciting legal assistance for the council as well as publicizing the struggle to Arab Americans across the country. As president of the Association of Arab American University Graduates (AAUG) in 1972, Jabara wanted to see the organization, which had been focused on Arab world issues and national-level politics, become more immersed in local issues affecting Arabs in America. In his presidential address to the AAUG that year, he cited the Southend struggle as an example of the "the immediate problems and needs of the Arab American community" in which the AAUG should become involved. In the period 1971 to 1974, the AAUG's newsletter published several articles about the movement against urban removal in the Southend, and at the association's 1972 national conference in Berkeley, California, Barbara Aswad and Alan Amen presented papers about the struggle. Nevertheless, except for the crucial support provided by individual members of the AAUG such as Jabara, the AAUG as an organization did not devote substantial resources to the movement in the Southend, nor did it become the kind of grassroots-oriented organization that Jabara had envisioned.¹⁷

According to Ismael Ahmed, some liberal organizations in the Detroit area, especially churches and the teacher's union, backed the Southend residents in their fight against the city. In contrast, Barbara Aswad's perception was that before 1973 few institutions or people outside the Southend were cognizant of or involved in the struggle, not even Arab Americans who lived elsewhere in the Detroit metro area. The few outside, non-Arab activists who did come to the neighborhood to help, Aswad recalls, were personally connected to Jabara or Ahmed.¹⁸

The Activist Origins of ACCESS

Ismael Ahmed—known to most as "Ish"—could draw on outside supporters for the Southend cause because he had been deeply involved in a number of leftist causes and closely connected to a network of radical activists in the Detroit area years before he became active in Arab American issues and the neighborhood's movement. Son of an Egyptian father and a third-generation Lebanese mother, Ahmed grew up in the Southend and socialized with an ethnically diverse group of peers in the neighborhood. He recalls the Dearborn police using heavy-handed tactics against Southend youths and reflects that he had been learning "a political lesson . . . about being a working-class kid." As a teenager he spent some time living in New York City with his grandmother, Aliya Hassen, a Muslim activist with close ties to Black Muslims in the city, including Malcolm X. Then he served a stint in the Merchant Marine, which took him to ports throughout Africa and Asia and opened his eyes to colonial powers' subjugation of Third World peoples. An army tour in Korea further contributed to his consciousness of American power abroad. Upon his return to Detroit, he continued his education and worked in auto plants to pay for it, but in his free time he became active in the civil rights, labor, and antiwar movements, developing relationships with the Black Panthers, the White Panthers, and several radical organizations aligned with the American Left.[19]

But in the late 1960s, Ahmed was not yet politicized on Arab world issues. The Arab loss in the 1967 war had not constituted a turning point for him, as it had for so many Arab American activists. He remembers feeling upset but powerless, reflecting that "there was nothing we could do," and "it wasn't until the 1970s that it had its effect." While Ahmed maintained his bonds with American leftist groups, in the early 1970s his consciousness shifted to both the Southend struggle and Arab nationalism. The homes of some of his relatives who lived in the Southend were being threatened, and their fight against the city grabbed his attention. Around the same time, as discussed in previous chapters, he encountered some of the student activists from Wayne State who were in the Southend trying to organize political support for Palestinian resistance groups. They pressed him to apply his anti-imperialist principles to the cause of Palestine and educated him on the Palestinian resistance movement. Consequently, Ahmed began spending more time in his old neighborhood, attending SEDCC meetings and associating with recently arrived Arab immigrants as well as with second- and third-generation Arab American community activists.[20]

Ahmed then became part of a diverse coalition of Arab American activists working in the Southend who, through their organizing around the housing removal issue, came to realize that a nonsectarian community center was essential to serve the economic and social needs of Arab immigrants. This neighborhood center, which eventually became ACCESS, was initiated by a nexus of four main groups of activists: the mainly second- and third-generation Arab Americans in the SEDCC who had been fighting the city's removal plan, the Palestinian political activists from Wayne State who thus far had been tangentially connected to the Southend's struggle against the city, leftist Yemenis who lived in the Southend, and AAUG leaders and academics, such as Abdeen Jabara and Barbara Aswad, who lived outside the Southend but supported the residents' battle. The genesis of the center thus represented a fusion of the Southend's focus on working-class Arab American concerns with Arab transnationalist politics. It was also undergirded by the overall atmosphere of grassroots activism nurtured by the civil rights and antiwar movements in the United States and more locally in Detroit.[21]

In 1971, a few of the activists came together to open a community center on Dix Avenue in the Southend, but within a couple of weeks it was burned down. Though the arsonists were never caught, some suspect that they were conservative Arabs who resisted the kind of leftist, secular activism that many of the center's organizers represented.[22] But the activists regrouped and expanded their sources of support—most crucially by obtaining $1,000 in funding from the AAUG—and opened ACCESS in a building on Vernor Avenue in southwest Detroit, right across the Dearborn border. In its first few years, ACCESS's resources were very limited; although it had only a small, all-volunteer staff, it managed to provide language services and legal aid to Arab immigrants in the area. George Khoury offered a class intended for male Arabic-speaking workers, teaching them the English names for tools. The center combined these basic social services with Arab political activism and, according to Ahmed, became a "meeting place for activist workers, Yemeni workers in particular."[23]

The political activities associated with ACCESS in the early 1970s gained the notice of law enforcement authorities and made the activists targets of the federal government's surveillance program of Arabs in the United States, as discussed in chapter 5. Many Arab Americans active in ACCESS told Abdeen Jabara, who was compiling evidence in order to sue the government, that they had been interrogated and harassed by FBI agents during a sweep of the Southend in the fall of 1972 and intermittently through the next year.[24] Nonetheless, the activists were not intimidated by the government's crackdown, and the political momentum created by the founding of ACCESS soon received a major boost from two events in 1973, one in the neighborhood and one in the Middle East.

The Southend and the October War

First, the SEDCC's case against the city of Dearborn finally went to trial in February 1973, and the presiding U.S. District Court judge, Ralph Freeman, ruled in favor of the Southend residents. After a seven-week trial, which featured the expert testimony of Barbara Aswad and a psychologist at Eastern Michigan University as to the detrimental cultural and psychological consequences of destroying the neighborhood, Judge Freeman ordered the city to halt the tactics it was using to undermine housing values and to cease further demolition of Southend homes. He agreed with the plaintiffs that the residents had been unfairly pressured into selling their homes to the city and that the city did not offer fair value for those homes.[25] The SEDCC's credibility was considerably advanced by the ruling, and some Arab immigrant residents who had kept their distance from the Council's protests, because their homes were not immediately threatened and because they were reticent about challenging the government's authority, now gained confidence in the activists' leadership. The SEDCC's court victory also won the admiration of Palestinian and Yemeni political activists in the Southend who had previously discounted the efficacy of domestic activism.[26]

The battle was not yet over, however: after the ruling, the city government filed an appeal. The SEDCC continued its mobilization of the community, now with even more support from recent immigrant residents, and secured outside assistance from church groups and civic associations for its ongoing campaign to save the neighborhood. Later that year, the SEDCC decided that one of its main Arab American leaders, Helen Atwell, should run for a seat on the Dearborn City Council, and members organized a voter registration drive in the Southend. Although she did not win, Atwell's candidacy and campaign, managed by Alan Amen, demonstrated the heightened visibility and activism of Arab Americans in city politics.[27]

The second major event of 1973 to impact Southend activism was the outbreak of the October War between Israel and a coalition of Arab nations led by Egypt and Syria. The war produced an outpouring of Arab nationalist activism in the neighborhood that, like ACCESS, brought together diverse groups in a pan-Arab coalition. Ismael Ahmed views this war as even more momentous than the June 1967 War in heightening Arab American transnational political consciousness. Similarly, in her account of Alan Amen's activism in the Southend, Alia Malek writes, "Neither Alan nor any of the others were going to sit this one out, like they had six years ago when they had been stunned, confused, and shamed by the defeat, the American official reaction to the war, and the portrayal of the Arabs." The relationships formed in the interceding few years between second- and third-generation Arab Americans such as Amen and the recently arrived immigrants in the Southend fostered the politicization of the more Americanized immigrants

Southend Dearborn Community Council members celebrate their victory in halting the city's plan to demolish homes as well as name a city street after one of their leaders, Iris Becker. Helen Atwell appears in the center of the photograph, wearing glasses, and Ismael Ahmed is kneeling on the bottom right. (Courtesy of the Arab American National Museum, Dearborn, Michigan, and the City of Dearborn)

on Arab world issues. From the new immigrants, Amen and other Arab Americans gleaned information about Middle East conflicts that they never encountered in the American media, which strengthened their critical response to Israeli and American actions in the October War.[28]

Yemeni immigrants in the Detroit area were pivotal to the activism sparked by the war. Their numbers had been growing in the Southend, reaching at least two thousand by the mid-1970s, while another contingent of Yemenis was migrating to a neighborhood in Detroit near a Dodge auto plant where many of them worked. Yemeni immigrants normally refrained from political or workplace activism in the United States. Most were single men who intended to stay in the country for only a short time to earn the maximum amount of money they could in a low-skilled industrial job and return to Yemen to purchase land and support their families. Nabeel Abraham characterizes the Yemeni immigrants in that period as transient, or nonsettler, communities. They maintained detachment from political and labor issues affecting them in the United States, first because they did not desire a future in the country, and second because they sought to avoid any "troublemaking" activities that might jeopardize their ability to earn money and return to their homeland. They did, however, remain engaged in the political conflicts brewing in Yemen, especially the conflict between royalists and republicans in North Yemen and the leftist insurgency against British rule in South Yemen, and some of them were intensely active on Yemeni political issues through their involvement in the Southend-based Yemeni Arab Association and Yemeni Benevolent Society.[29]

In the early 1970s, a few leftist students who had been active in the Organization of Arab Students at Wayne State began to reach out to the Yemeni leftists in the Southend. Previously, the students had been narrowly focused on soliciting support among Southend Palestinians for the Marxist-Leninist factions of the Palestinian resistance movement, but by 1972 the students broadened their political organizing to encompass all Arab revolutionary movements, including those in the Arab Gulf. Together, the Yemeni and Palestinian leftists in the Southend formed the Committee to Support the Omani Revolution (CSOR), which not only sought to rally support for the leftist rebellion in Oman but also aimed to organize Arab workers around labor grievances they faced in Detroit and Dearborn. The CSOR folded after a few months, but when many of the participating Yemeni and Palestinian activists subsequently became involved in the creation of ACCESS, they maintained both their commitment to leftist Arab revolutions and to organizing Arab workers.[30]

In the months before the October War, increasing activism among the Detroit Yemeni community was evident when sizable crowds publicly protested the recent murders of two Yemeni immigrants. Yemenis staged a protest march in Dearborn in honor of Nagi Daifullah, a Yemeni agricultural laborer who was murdered while participating in a United Farm Workers organizing drive in California that August. Around the same time, responding to the robbery and murder of Yemeni immigrant Ahmed Ali Almulaiki in Detroit, groups such as the Detroit Yemen Society organized hundreds of Yemenis in a demonstration in front of the Detroit police headquarters to demand improved police protection.[31] These incidents likely facilitated the capacity of Yemenis for major political and labor activity in the fall of 1973.

When the October War started, Arab Americans in the Southend immediately mobilized. Several groups came together to form the American Arab Coordinating Committee (AACC), through which they would harness

Arab Americans in the Southend of Dearborn, Michigan, rally in support of Arab forces during the October War in 1973. (*AAUG Newsletter*, December 1973, AAUG Papers, Eastern Michigan University, Special Collections Library)

and channel their political sentiment. Activists from ACCESS were key players in the AACC, and they came to dominate the AACC's most important subcommittee, the Arab Mobilization Committee (AMC). The AMC, which constituted the hub of the community's political organizing in response to the war, established its meeting place at the Hashemite Hall (often called Hashmi Hall), a Shia mosque in the Southend. Nabeel Abraham points out that because ACCESS was the only "pan-community institution in existence at the time," it had the ability to "capture the leadership of the Dearborn [Arab American] community in the event of a major crisis," as was presented in that moment by the October War. It took a sweeping Middle East crisis to bridge all the national, ethnic, religious, and generational divisions among Arab Americans in the Southend.³²

The AMC's first action was to hold a press conference at which activists denounced American support for Israel, along with the American media's characterizations of Arabs, and afterward it staged a teach-in at Wayne State University. The AMC's biggest demonstration occurred on 14 October, when it assembled about two thousand Arab autoworkers and community members at the UAW Local 600 headquarters (the Ford Rouge union hall) in the Southend. In addition to their condemnation of Israeli and U.S. policy in the Middle East, demonstrators expressed outrage that their own union was supporting Israel. Arab American activists had recently discovered that their UAW local, without seeking approval from rank-and-file members, had used union dues to purchase $330,000 of Israeli bonds in 1967, while the national UAW owned Israeli bonds worth about $750,000. Holding signs declaring in English and Arabic "No Vietnam in the Mideast" and "Stop U.S.-Israeli Terror against Arab People," they marched from the UAW hall through the Southend to the American Moslem Society mosque. The rally raised over $20,000 for relief efforts. According to Ali Baleed Almaklani, many Yemenis in attendance signed their meager and precious paychecks over to the relief fund because, in an expression of pan-Arab solidarity, they were so moved by the suffering experienced by Arabs in the war.[33]

The demonstration linked the crisis in the Middle East to American practices and policies at home. Such speakers as Alan Amen supported the Arab nations' armed struggle to reclaim territory occupied by Israel, and they demanded that the United States maintain neutrality and cease supplying arms to Israel. Ismael Ahmed observed that the October demonstration "emphasize[d] the protest against UAW bond holdings as much as American involvement in the war." Most notably, Abdeen Jabara encouraged workers in the crowd to sign a petition insisting that the UAW divest its Israeli bonds. The circulation of the petition was the genesis of what would in a few weeks' time become the Arab Workers Caucus. [34]

The Arab Workers Caucus

Arab American worker activism drew on the Southend's deep community history of labor agitation. In fact, Arab immigrants in the neighborhood had been involved in the initial efforts to organize Ford back in the 1930s. After the mid-1960s, Arabs leaving countries embroiled in nationalist uprisings and migrating to the United States increasingly possessed a consciousness as colonized subjects, exploited both economically and politically by imperialist powers. Ahmed, one of the lead organizers of Arab American industrial workers, argued that they saw themselves in solidarity with other workers of color. In his view, Arab autoworkers experienced the same "intense exploitation" as did African American and new immigrant workers from other parts of the Third World. In a similar vein, leftist scholar and activist Dan Georgakas interpreted the conditions of Arab American workers in the same context as workers migrating from other non-Western countries. "On the West Coast, the cheap labor was primarily of Mexican and Asian ancestry," Georgakas stated. "In Detroit the new labor pool was Arab." Presenting the Arab workers as alienated, "confused," and "fearful," Georgakas argued that they were probably even more exploited than black workers in the Detroit auto factories.[35]

Leftist labor organizations had already been reaching out to Arab workers in the Detroit area in recent years. Radical groups such as the Revolutionary Union, a Maoist organization, were active in Detroit plants, trying to promote class-based solidarity among distinct groups. Labor activists understood that employers often recruited immigrant workers as part of their strategy of pitting groups of workers against one another to suppress worker militancy. Thus, dissident labor organizations tried to counter that strategy by striving to integrate Arab workers, an effort that included educating native-born workers about the immigrants' circumstances in order to cultivate acceptance and understanding.[36]

African Americans who spearheaded the Dodge Revolutionary Union Movement (DRUM) also recognized the importance of organizing Arab immigrant workers in their drive to challenge both the company's and the UAW's racist and exploitative practices. The black radicals' labor activism was informed by a commitment to Third World solidarity, and they tended to see Arab immigrants, especially Yemenis, as fellow workers of color. Arab Americans constituted almost two thousand out of the ten thousand total workers, the majority of whom were black, at the Dodge Main plant in Detroit, and Arab workers were also substantially represented at Chrysler's Jefferson Assembly, Eldon Avenue, and Mound Road plants in Detroit. Dodge Revolutionary Union Movement organizers attempted to gain Arab workers' support, as can be seen in DRUM's leaflets, some of which featured sections translated into Arabic. In their documentation of the Revolutionary Union Movement and the League of Revolutionary Black Workers, Dan Georgakas and Marvin Surkin explained that substantial common ground existed between black and Arab workers. Arab workers "had many of the same on-the-job problems as blacks," and like many black workers, "the new Arab immigrant workers . . . felt that the UAW, like most American institutions, was hostile to them."[37]

Despite these gestures at solidarity, the bond between Arab immigrant and black workers was precarious. One reason was that managers usually grouped together the Arab workers to keep them isolated from other workers in the plants. Language differences could also present a barrier. Moreover, the willingness of many Arab immigrants to work substantial overtime hours and their reluctance to press for higher wages or join the blacks' labor actions sometimes caused tension between the two groups. While a few Arab workers supported DRUM's wildcat strikes in the late 1960s (including a noted case at the Jefferson plant, when Arab workers helped protect two black workers who had stopped the assembly line), most crossed the picket lines in fear of losing their jobs. Mike Hamlin, DRUM organizer, recalls limited interaction between the rank-and-file black and Arab workers. Upon invitation, Hamlin spoke through an interpreter to a group of Yemeni autoworkers, but these contacts were rare. According to Hamlin, DRUM organizers did not ask Arab immigrant workers to join them on wildcats because they did not want to put these immigrant workers, who they feared would be punished with deportation, at risk. But Hamlin affirmed that DRUM did strive to dampen conflict among these workers of color.[38]

Though Arab immigrant workers had been largely reticent to participate in labor agitation alongside black and other leftist organizers, by 1973 Arab worker militancy had escalated. Out of the momentum created by the October War protest, Arab American labor activists such as Ahmed and Amen determined "they needed their own workers' caucus—like blacks—to facilitate their own organizing and advocacy in the factories as well as to be able to take their issues to the other workers." They convened a meeting attended by Arab workers representing most auto plants in the Detroit area and formed the Arab Workers Caucus. As a mobilizing issue, the organizers decided to keep pursuing the indignation over the UAW's investment in Israeli bonds.[39]

Confronting the UAW

Working with the American Arab Coordinating Committee that had come to fruition in the October War protests, the AWC planned a demonstration at a fund-raising dinner for Israel to be held at Cobo Hall in Detroit on 28 November 1973. To the Arab labor activists, this dinner was especially offensive because the Jewish organization B'nai B'rith was honoring UAW president Leonard Woodcock, a stalwart supporter of Israel, with its Humanitarian Award. In Ahmed's view, staging a protest at this event would provide AWC members the perfect opportunity "to point out the hypocrisy of this leader who would force his constituency to finance the murder of their brothers and sisters back home with their union dues." The AACC also planned an adjoining memorial service in Dearborn for victims of the October War. The organizing groups distributed tens of thousands of leaflets in both English and Arabic to convince Arab American autoworkers to leave their jobs that day to attend the memorial service and the protest rally. The AWC also tried to mobilize non-Arab UAW members, using the occasion to educate the workforce about both Palestinian nationalism and the conditions of Arab immigrant workers. Alan Amen counseled the workers to make their case to non-Arab workers by focusing on the UAW's use of members' dues to help foreign countries instead of American workers. In particular, Arab American labor activists tried to appeal to black autoworkers for support, asking them "how they would feel if the UAW had bought the national bonds of . . . South Africa or Rhodesia."[40]

In the days before the demonstration, the American Arab Coordinating Committee ran an advertisement in Detroit newspapers, including Detroit's leading black newspaper, the *Michigan Chronicle*, that broadcast its denunciation of UAW's ownership of the Israeli bonds. Headlined "Is the UAW Leadership Acting in the Interests of Its Members?," the ad employed two arguments. First, to raise the point of UAW inconsistency and to play on Americans' increasing tendency toward isolationism at the end of the Vietnam War, it juxtaposed the UAW's investment of funds in a foreign government with an assertion that Leonard Woodcock had recently made to Congress regarding the Vietnam War, that the country needs to "turn our eyes homeward to the necessities of our own people." Second, the ad appealed to African American sympathy by posing a hypothetical parallel between the workers' relationships with their respective diasporas: that "purchase of Israeli bonds is regarded by these [Arab] workers similarly as a UAW investment in racist South Africa would be regarded by black workers." The ad also informed readers that Israel maintained diplomatic ties with South Africa. It invited all rank-and-file union members and anyone opposing the Israeli bond purchase to join the demonstration at Cobo Hall.[41]

Hundreds of Arab Americans, especially Yemeni autoworkers, missed work that day and flocked to the demonstration. So many workers left their jobs that they were successful in shutting down one of the assembly lines at the Dodge Main plant and slowing down the other line. Alan Amen recounts that they were aided by non-Arab workers who "walked off in solidarity with them." On ACCESS letterhead, letters from the American Arab Coordinating Committee, cosigned by eight Christian and Muslim clerics, were sent to nearby UAW locals requesting their endorsement and protection of the Arab workers' absence from work on the "day of remembrance." About one thousand protesters, almost all Arab Americans, gathered around the front doors of Cobo Hall carrying protest signs reading "Bonds Murder Black Brothers in

IS THE UAW LEADERSHIP ACTING IN THE INTERESTS OF ITS MEMBERS?

The UAW International Union has purchased over ¾ million dollars in Israel bonds which yield 5½ per cent interest and mature in 1986. Pressures for additional purchase of Israel bonds by many American institutions are increasing.

ANOTHER RIPOFF

UAW President Leonard Woodcock testified on March 12, 1973, before the U.S. Congress Ways and Means Committee that: "The problem of our domestic needs is one which can no longer be pushed aside. For nearly a decade now, almost every aspect of our public well-being has suffered neglect from the concentration of our money, energies and goods on prosecuting the war in Indo-China. Now that our involvement in this unhappy war is apparently coming to an end, it is a major responsibility for us to turn our eyes homeward to the necessities of our own people."

Can the purchase of noneconomical, low-interest, foreign bonds be justified in view of Woodcock's position in this statement?

The UAW has an estimated 15,000 Arab members. Purchase of Israeli bonds is regarded by these workers similarly as would a UAW investment in racist South Africa would be regarded by black workers. While 26 black African countries have severed political relations with Israel in the last two months, Israel and South Africa maintain diplomatic ties.

Tens of thousands of Arab Palestinian workers in Israel from Arab territories militarily occupied by Israel in 1967 are not protected by even minimal labor union guarantee.

A CALL TO ACTION

Rank and file union members and their supporters are called on to participate in a peaceful assembly to protest this arbitrary purchase by the UAW of Israeli bonds on the occasion of an award ceremony for UAW President Leonard Woodcock.

PEACEFUL ASSEMBLY WILL BE HELD IN FRONT OF COBO HALL, WEDNESDAY, NOVEMBER 28, 1973, AT 6:00 P.M.

Sponsored by the American Arab Coordinating Committee

This advertisement calling for protest against the UAW's Israeli bond investments ran in the *Detroit Free Press* in November 1973. A similar ad ran in the *Michigan Chronicle*, Detroit's African American newspaper, the same day.

South Africa" and "Jewish People Yes, Zionism No" and chanting "no more bombs, no more bonds." While some non-Arab workers may have walked off the line with them, there is little evidence that non-Arabs participated in the Cobo Hall demonstration. Mike Hamlin knew that Arab workers were agitating over this issue and holding the protest, but he does not remember that he or other black labor activists attended.[42]

To the demonstrators' chagrin, Woodcock entered the hall through the back door so they could not confront him. At the dinner Woodcock addressed the controversy by announcing that the UAW was attempting to work with both Israeli and Egyptian labor unions in hopes of bringing them together to reach peaceful resolutions. Emil Mazey, the UAW's secretary-treasurer, defended the union's purchases of Israeli bonds, calling them a "good investment." He continued: "We made the investment because we believe the state of Israel has a right to live. It is the only democracy in the Middle East" as well as the only country in the Middle East "with a free trade-union movement." Afterward, Mazey stated that the Arab protesters were aligned with communists and accused them of telling "outright lies."[43] Nevertheless, the leader of the UAW Local 600 in Dearborn, Walter Dorosh, agreed to meet with representatives of the Arab Workers Caucus and acquiesced to the activists' demands that the local divest the bonds, support Arab workers, and inform workers how their dues were being used. However, Dorosh issued a strong warning to the AWC that they should never again practice that kind of public dissent against the union.[44]

The Yemeni workers who had left their posts at the Dodge Main plant to attend the demonstration faced more severe repercussions than did other demonstrators and consequently felt resentful. Over five hundred of the workers received disciplinary notices, and those who had worked there only a short time were laid off. The UAW leadership did not intervene to protect them and in fact attempted to make the Yemeni workers sign a paper stating they had been absent from work without a valid excuse.[45] According to Nabeel Abraham's study of Detroit's Yemeni community in this period, the Yemeni workers believed they had borne the brunt of the company's and union's punishment, and they thought the AWC had "exploited them to achieve certain parochial political ends." Caucus leaders had appealed to Arab nationalism to mobilize the immigrant workers with the aim of transferring Arab politics to workplace organization, dovetailing the two issues. The activists used the October War, combined with the UAW Israeli bonds controversy, to "whip people up," Abraham states, and recruit to the AWC. Had the demonstration against Woodcock and the bonds occurred at any other time, Abraham contends, it would have lacked the mass participation inspired by the war. After the fallout at Dodge Main, most Yemeni workers withdrew from participation in the AWC and further political activities. Abraham argues that the activists had "mistaken the Arab nationalist sentiment of the Yemenis for genuine support for their anti-union, anti–auto company position."[46]

The Arab Workers Caucus's Challenge

Although the enthusiasm experienced in the fall of 1973 had dissipated somewhat and most Yemeni workers were averse to participation, AWC activists (who included some Yemeni leftists) persisted in their efforts to organize the Arab workforce and confront the UAW leadership. Ahmed credited the influence of the black revolutionary union movement and the network of Arab American community organizations as factors that "facilitated in-plant worker organizing" in 1974 and 1975.[47] In addition to protesting the UAW's Israeli bonds, the AWC stressed a range of Arab immigrant workers' problems and demands. In a recruitment pamphlet, the AWC presented three main problems faced by Arab workers: communication hurdles causing them to misunderstand and run afoul of company and union rules; unsafe conditions in the plants; and "prejudice . . . in the employment offices." The AWC also pointed to the high cost of living and excessive overtime hours as grievances. Besides advocating Arab worker solidarity and empowerment to improve their treatment and opportunities, the caucus demanded that the union and company find better ways to overcome the language barrier, including the provision of interpreters. The pamphlet challenged, "WHY HAVE OUR UNIONS FAILED US IN THESE AREAS?" and called for the rejection of their UAW local's contract with the company. Using language similar to materials put out by the League of Revolutionary Black Workers and other leftist workers' caucuses in the plants, it concluded: "SO WE THE WORKERS SHOULD GET TOGETHER TO DEMAND THAT THE UNION TAKE A STRONGER STAND FOR THESE RIGHTS AND INSIST THAT OUR UNION LEADERSHIP TAKE OUR PROBLEMS INTO CONSIDERATION. . . . NO TO LENARD [sic] WOODCOCK AND HIS TEAM."[48]

Another AWC statement, "The Basis for Unity: Our General Call," placed more emphasis on the Zionist takeover of Palestine and on U.S. corporations' exploitation of the Arab world. It drew a parallel between those "attack(s) against our people" abroad and the Arab workers' experience in the United States, where they are "subject to the humiliation and degradation of racism and exploitation by these same big companies." Continuing the transnational framing, the manifesto called on Arab workers to organize and fight back against their U.S. oppressors ("big Auto companies and sell-out union officials") just as Palestinians were fighting both the Zionists and the Arab leaders who cooperated with imperialists. The statement also held up the example of Arab farmworkers in California and their struggle against police and farmers, praising "our fallen martyr" Nagi Daifullah. Knitting together all aspects of the oppression they experienced in the Arab world and the United States, the AWC authors asserted that their "ethnic and racial and cultural being and our homeland and communities" were under attack and called on "all Arabs" to persist in "our national and class struggle" in the tradition of proud Arab fighters. They represented their struggles as in concert with "liberation movements throughout the world," as well as with movements by other "national minorities in the U.S.," and called on their members to educate the American working class about these connections. Demonstrating Marxist influence, the AWC's "General Call" identified the need to "analyze our role with the American working class and our mission within that class." Rejecting assimilation into an ethnicity-blind working class, the AWC aimed to preserve its Arab identity at the same time that it sought to "consolidate our caucus as an inseparable part of the workers movement in the U.S."[49]

While dedicated to organizing at the local level in Detroit, the AWC also developed a strategy to accrue more power in the national UAW. Caucus leaders set their sights on winning support for a set of resolutions and candidates at the UAW constitutional convention in California in 1974. The resolutions included demands for full minority representation in direct voting for union leadership, provisions for language translators and training programs for ethnic groups, longer leaves of absence for workers visiting families outside the United States, and stronger repercussions for company supervisors and union officials who practiced racial and ethnic discrimination. Its final resolution concentrated on the Israeli-Palestine conflict. The AWC called not only for UAW divestment of Israeli bonds but also for the UAW to cut all ties with the Israeli labor organization Histadrut. Most striking, the final resolution connected the Palestinian struggle with liberation struggles around the world by declaring that the "UAW should stand firmly in support of all workers and people struggling in Africa, Asia, and Latin America. In the Middle East, the UAW should support the principle of establishing a secular, nontheocratic, democratic state in Palestine for all people, Jews and Arabs, and stand against any outside intervention."[50]

Though Arab workers made up a substantial portion of some metro Detroit UAW locals, the AWC realized that its concentrated presence in Detroit would not translate into national power. Organizers knew that the traditional leadership of the UAW, whom they considered to be distant from the rank and file, would have firm control of the convention through their hold on committee positions. The AWC would need to form a coalition with other UAW dissident groups in order to have any national influence, so it set about establishing contacts with a national network of those groups, including the militant United National Caucus, which organized black and white autoworkers in Detroit. The two caucuses joined for a press conference in Detroit at which they presented several demands, including the divestment of Israeli bonds and breaking ties with Histadrut, and called for a demonstration at the upcoming UAW convention.[51]

In preparation for the national convention in California, the AWC also sent organizers to UAW plants throughout that state, trying to inform workers about Zionist injustice and the role of Zionists in the UAW and to mobilize their support for the AWC's resolutions. Also joining their forces were Arab and Iranian students in California who helped publicize the planned demonstration. About one hundred workers picketed the convention, protesting Israel's occupation of Palestinian territories and the union's holdings of Israeli bonds. Despite the mobilization, the UAW Resolutions Committee rejected the AWC's proposed resolutions and instead passed a resolution, approved by the convention, declaring support for America's current Middle East policy as well as for the UAW's continuing cooperation with Histadrut.[52]

In the wake of this defeat at the national level, the AWC continued its organizing efforts in Detroit-area plants, including participation in a four-day wildcat strike with many non-Arab workers at a Dodge truck plant, but the organization dissolved over the next couple of years. Writing in 1975, Ahmed saw encouraging results from the Arab workers' organizing efforts and pointed to Chrysler's and Ford's establishment of English and other training classes, the UAW's divestiture of a portion of its Israeli bonds, and Ford's "interest" in ACCESS. But he considered the most significant consequence of the AWC's work to be ideological: "the integration of anti-imperialist ideas among rank and file workers."[53] Making the connection between the corporate structures that exploited workers, especially minority workers, in the United States and the imperialist structures that subjugated people of color globally was a key organizing breakthrough for the Arab Workers Caucus as it was for many other leftist labor and political organizations of the 1970s.

Leftist Labor Groups and Arab American Workers

In the mid- to late 1970s, after the AWC had declined, leftist groups organizing in Detroit auto plants continued to pay attention to Arab American workers. For example, a radical labor organization called Wildcat which operated at Chrysler's Eldon Avenue plant distributed its publication *Spark*, which covered a whole host of national and international events from a leftist perspective, and prominently included coverage of Arab issues that defended the Palestinian revolutionaries and pilloried Western and Israeli imperialism.[54] Some *Spark* articles were printed in both English and Arabic. An article that appeared in a 1975 issue titled "Workers of All Lands, Unite!" tried to correct workers' misconceptions about and resentment of Arab workers by explaining why they were forced to come to the United States to find work: American corporations' imperialistic exploitation of the Arab world. It went on to describe the particular disadvantages faced by these immigrant workers. The companies, it claimed, were purposely creating resentment against Arab workers, in effect using them to divide and weaken their workforce.[55]

In an era of heightened consciousness of Detroit police brutality against African Americans, *Spark* drew workers' attention to the murder of two Yemeni autoworkers in 1975, accusing two white off-duty policemen of the crime. In an article that was also translated into Arabic, *Spark* labeled the cops "racist thugs" and reminded readers that "racism is not just applied to Black people in this country . . . . These terrorist attacks are an attack on us all. We must defend our Arabian comrades." And in 1976, when two more Yemeni workers were murdered in Dearborn, *Spark* again blamed "racist scum" who were "terrorizing the Arabian community" and made an appeal to "all workers, especially white workers [to] speak out against racist brutality."[56] Similarly, in 1977 a dissident labor organization at the Dodge Main plant issued a leaflet rallying support for a Yemeni worker who had been beaten by a foreman and then fired in what the Dodge Main Workers Committee labeled a pattern of "racist abuse and attacks" that the UAW leadership refused to confront. The leaflet charged: "Capitalists promote insulting words like 'Camel Jockey' and 'Ay-rab' to split the unity between Arab workers and all other workers."[57]

Another radical organization promoting cross-ethnic unity in Detroit auto plants was the Revolutionary Communist Party (RCP). In the mid-1970s, the RCP sent Joel Beinin from Boston to Detroit to organize Arab workers in solidarity with other workers at Chrysler plants. Beinin, who had been raised in a Jewish family and spent some time living on an Israeli kibbutz, was chosen for the assignment because he could speak Arabic. According to Beinin, the RCP's strategy was to combine workers into a multiethnic revolutionary force, instead of forming caucuses based on ethnicity as the AWC had done, a method that the RCP viewed as divisive.[58]

At the time, Beinin was convinced of the potential for labor militancy of Arab, particularly Yemeni, workers, which he communicated in response to an article about Yemeni workers by Nabeel Abraham that appeared in *MERIP Reports* in 1977. Abraham emphasized Yemeni workers' reluctance to participate in the labor union movement, especially after the 1973 protest against the UAW's Israeli bonds. "Ironically," Abraham wrote, "this attitude of passivity towards employers emerged out of the most militant period of Yemeni worker actions to date in Detroit." He noted that Yemenis were unwilling to join strikes attempted at Ford and Chrysler in 1976. Beinin responded by arguing that Yemenis were active in labor struggles and gave two examples, first of a Yemeni worker who helped organize a petition drive in support of a black worker who had been harassed by a white foreman at the Ford Rouge plant, and second of a group of about forty Yemenis who had met to discuss and reject the Ford-UAW contract and support the Ford strike. Abraham in turn replied by discounting the examples Beinin had provided, claiming that the workers cited by Beinin were exceptions that proved the rule. Abraham reaffirmed his initial observation of little potential for worker militancy among Yemenis, calling most of them "apathetic" toward the issues that unions raised because they were so focused on returning to Yemen and chose to isolate themselves from American society.[59]

Thus, while activists associated with Arab American and non–Arab American leftist organizations had endeavored to organize Arab immigrant workers in Detroit around both their class and their ethnic-national interests for most of the 1970s, the results of those efforts are uncertain. Beinin recognizes that, overall, in-plant organizing by groups such as the Revolutionary Communist Party was ineffective, largely because the radical organizations did not understand how the deleterious economic climate of the 1970s was diminishing worker radicalism. He also acknowledges that organizing Arab immigrants had its particular challenges because, as Abraham had emphasized, many of them believed they were in the United States only temporarily. Beinin and fellow organizers knew that, historically, the odds were that most of the immigrants would remain in the country, but "we couldn't convince people of that." Furthermore, the activists were confronted by the hostile attitude of other groups of Arab Americans, chiefly Lebanese and Chaldeans, who were more prosperous and lived outside the Southend in affluent suburban neighborhoods. Beinin remembers, "Insofar as they had racist attitudes and distanced themselves from the working class, they were a problem for us, and we didn't have much to do with them." Presenting a contrary explanation, George Khoury believes that radical organizing of Arab immigrants failed in these years because the immigrants were averse to the communist ideology promoted by most of the revolutionary groups in the plants. But while the Arab Workers Caucus faded away and Arab American workers were not mobilized in any consequential way by other dissident organizations, Ismael Ahmed emphasizes that over time Arab American autoworkers developed a positive relationship with the UAW. In his view, the union came to genuinely support and understand the needs of Arab American workers as well as of the broader Arab American community in the Detroit area.[60]

The Rise of ACCESS

Growing out of the activism spurred by the October War, the AWC's organizing work contributed to Arab American political consciousness by linking local concerns with transnational issues. While that war served to galvanize labor activism only briefly, it had a more lasting effect on ACCESS, providing momentum and energy that would ultimately transform the Southend's community center into an institutional success. After its tentative establishment on Vernor Avenue, ACCESS began to thrive after the October War demonstrations in 1973. As Ahmed sees it, ACCESS "inherited" the intensity created by the war and the accompanying protests against the UAW's Israeli bonds. Employing a diasporic framing that linked engagement with the Arab world to the local lives of Arab immigrants in Dearborn, an ACCESS pamphlet from the mid-1970s claimed that the war "aroused the nationalistic feelings of the masses of Arab people and their enthusiasm for the Arab Center." To Don Unis, this was when ACCESS really launched—a moment marked by the center's move from Vernor Avenue in Southwest Detroit to a temporary site in the Hashemite Hall (where the Arab Mobilization Committee had been operating) and then to a building on Salina Street in the center of the Southend in 1974. Also during this period, Aliya Hassen came to Dearborn from New York City and, even though she had intended to retire, was persuaded to become director of ACCESS, a position in which she served for ten years. Over the next few years, ACCESS expanded upon the limited services it had provided at its Vernor Avenue location, providing language classes and other training, translation services, legal aid, employment services, health services and counseling, and recreational and social programs, all the while expanding its staff and funding sources.[61]

The Arab Community Center originated with an authentic grassroots ethic and a commitment to providing "community-determined services," as Barbara Aswad and Nancy Adadow Gray have described its philosophy. Upholding these values also meant that, in the early years, ACCESS leaders were resistant to outside funding and direction. As much as possible, the organization tried to encourage community participation in decision making, which involved monthly sessions that Ahmed compares to Boston town meetings in which hundreds of residents discussed ACCESS's activities and plans. "The community built ACCESS, and ACCESS defended the community," declares George Khoury, remembering how working-class Arab American residents of the Southend contributed their meager funds to the center. This dedication to self-determination and participatory democracy at the local level was indicative of community organizing efforts among other marginalized groups across the country in this period. Benefiting from Ahmed's connections with activist networks throughout Detroit and the United States, ACCESS leaders visited the community service programs run by Latin Americans for Social Development (LA SED) and the Black Panthers to learn from their initiatives.[62]

Wedded to the center's purpose of providing social services was the activists' political objective of using the center to, in Ahmed's words, "challenge policy and to build progressive ideas in the community." Don Unis acknowledges that ACCESS in the early 1970s "had a leftist base to it.... By the very nature of working in the community you have a leftist nature."[63] The 1975 statement "Who We Are" in ACCESS's newsletter *Arab Center* demonstrates this leftist orientation: "We are dissatisfied with the conditions prevailing in our community and in this country, such as unemployment and the low standard of living caused by big corporations against the interests of the overwhelming majority of the people. We stand for the liberation of our people in the Middle East and other peoples of the world from social oppression, and we think that by relying on ourselves, mobilizing our people and uniting with other community organizations and people upholding similar aspirations, we can best serve our people and bring progress to our community." Covering diverse political and societal issues, both domestic and international, that affected Arab residents of the Southend, the *Arab Center* featured articles on ACCESS services, such as karate classes and a Christmas party; on union and auto company maneuvering, such as the UAW contract negotiations with Ford; on state and national politics, such as unemployment benefits under attack in the Michigan legislature; on the activities of other Arab American organizations, such as the local Beit Hanina Club; and Arab world developments, such as the Lebanese Civil War.[64]

George Khoury concurs that "what built ACCESS was political activism—it was not just social services activism. It was political commitment to the poor people, the oppressed people by the system, by economics." But he is even more specific when identifying the political purpose of ACCESS. Palestinian activists, he claims, were the real impetus behind ACCESS, and they envisioned the center as a place, more effective than the Southend coffee shops, to mobilize Arab Americans' support for the Palestinian resistance movement. Khoury articulates the activists' mindset: "I cannot go to the Arab community and ask for their support for the Palestinian revolution unless I provide to them something local to relate to, and that is ACCESS."[65]

One of the founders of ACCESS who had been promoting the Palestinian fedayeen in the Southend, Hasan Nawash, recalls that some radical Arab activists thought "to hell with the needs of the community." However, Nawash believed that Arab American community issues were important because one must be "connected materially to the people" who will be recruited to the cause of Palestinian liberation. Nabeel Abraham echoes this perspective on ACCESS's origins, stating that some of the activists who created ACCESS were more interested in Arab world, mainly Palestinian, matters than in the living conditions of Arabs in America. They imagined the center as a means to "radicalize [immigrant] workers with the ultimate aim of changing the Arab world," but over time, as it became more apparent that the immigrants were permanent settlers who needed immediate assistance, the activists "evolved ... a more domestic" focus. While ACCESS shifted away from visible advocacy of leftist Arab politics over the years, throughout the 1970s it remained a center for progressive activism on Arab world issues and was a key organizer of annual Palestine Day demonstrations in Dearborn.[66]

The commitment by ACCESS to serving "the Arab community" encompassed two goals: to aid economically disadvantaged Arab Americans (usually new immigrants in the Southend) with their daily needs, and to assist all Arab Americans by improving their image in the eyes of Americans and fighting against generalized discrimination. In a letter to the ACCESS Advisory Board in 1979, Khoury outlined the organization's main objectives: "ACCESS is a grassroots organization, established and run by a group of Arab Americans who aim to alleviate the hardship on the poor segment of our community, obtain our rights from the local institutions and governments, fight racism and slanderous propaganda against Arabs, and establish a positive link between the Arab-American community and the Arabic history and culture." Thus, ACCESS combined social service and civil rights pursuits; as described by Ahmed, it was a civil rights organization for Arab Americans that was influenced by the African American civil rights movement. One way that ACCESS sought to improve the Arab image and foster positive associations with Arab culture was its significant participation in annual Arab World Festivals held in Detroit. Nawash, an organizer of the first Arab World Festival, saw it as an important component of ACCESS's mission because it reached out to both the wider Arab American community and to non-Arabs so as to develop appreciation and respect for Arab culture.[67]

The commitment to serving multiple constituencies of Arab Americans brought a sense of pragmatism to the organization and required compromise. Activists operating with a leftist ideology worked alongside community members who were not particularly ideological but were intent on solving problems and serving people. According to Ismael Ahmed, many women active in ACCESS, such as Helen Atwell, Aliya Hassen, and Katherine Amen, "were pivotal to grounding [the activists], to making their battle for justice a true battle . . . for people, not ideas."[68] This type of action-oriented commitment was characteristic of women's participation in diverse community organizing efforts in twentieth-century America, as seen, for example, in the tenacious activism of African American women in local civil rights campaigns in the South. In an observation that can also be applied to the Southend, historian Jennifer Frost explains the importance of women's participation in her study of New Left community organizing in the 1960s: "In the course of fulfilling their caretaking duties, [neighborhood] women struggled daily with community conditions and, indeed, identified problems as part of their domestic responsibilities. They also generally established the friendships and networks that tied the neighborhood together."[69] Because of the Southend movement's emphasis on lived experience and action over theory, organizations of the American Left with which Ahmed had been associated eventually discounted ACCESS as being insufficiently radical. Originally, the organizations had been supportive of Ahmed's work in ACCESS, expecting it to become a "vehicle of the Left," but when they realized that ACCESS represented "reform, not revolution," they parted ways with him and his community work.[70]

Ahmed and Barbara Aswad, who was also a key participant in ACCESS in the 1970s, agree that what made the organization effective and enduring, instead of plagued by ideological battles and debilitating factionalism, were the working relationships forged among various groups of Arab Americans, from second- and third-generation Arab Americans who were better acquainted with American society and politics to recently arrived Arab workers, to Arab-born professionals, to leftist Palestinian and Yemeni activists. After Ahmed left his position as an Arab Workers Caucus organizer in the auto plants and became director of ACCESS in the late 1970s, his leadership philosophy prioritized inclusion, and he ensured that the many national and political groups that constitute the diverse Arab American community were represented on ACCESS's board.[71]

Throughout the late 1970s and early 1980s, Arab Americans in the Southend continued to fight for fair treatment. Over the course of the seventies, the neighborhood experienced the influx of even more immigrants from the Arab world, many of whom were fleeing political strife and oppression in their homelands (with now an even greater influx from Lebanon because of turmoil from civil war), and thus the Southend was populated by increasing numbers of struggling new immigrants who possessed a nationalist consciousness. In a *Detroit News* article from 1977 titled "How Arab Throngs Vie for New Mecca in Dearborn Homes," Abdeen Jabara was interviewed about the Southend's continuing problems, which he identified as inadequate police protection, job insecurity, and lack of accessible health care. Tensions between Arab Americans and non-Arabs in the city heightened in these years, and Don Unis spoke out against the rest of Dearborn's hostility toward the Arab immigrants living in the Southend. One article in the local press reported that many Dearborn residents outside the Southend perceived the Arab immigrants as "clannish and unwilling to adapt" and accused them of shoddy upkeep of their homes as well as household overcrowding.[72]

On the front lines of these disputes, in 1977, in reaction to the city's decision to cease funding teachers and social workers who served the center's clients, ACCESS leaders staged a demonstration at City Hall and equated the survival of the center with the survival of the Southend Arab American community. In a leaflet (printed in both English and Arabic) mobilizing community support for the demonstration, ACCESS organizers invoked the neighborhood's history of conflict with the city government, declaring, "The truth is the city of Dearborn . . . [does not] want a community-run center in the Southend that stands up for the people's interest. This doesn't come as an isolated attack. For years they have been trying to tear down our homes and turn our community into an industrial area. *This attack on ACCESS is really an attack on our whole community* [emphasis added]." Then the leaflet accused the city of fostering racial prejudice among and against Arab Americans in order to weaken the community: "The racist policy of certain Dearborn City officials to divide white against Black is well known. Their attempts to divide Arab against Arab and Arab against American are not so well known. But that's exactly what they're trying to do, and it will not work. We must stand up and fight these attacks." Around the same time, Alan Amen pressured the city to hire Arab Americans on the police force, charging that the hiring process was discriminatory and that Arab Americans were sorely underrepresented in the community's law enforcement ranks.[73]

Thus, community activism advocating Arab Americans' rights as citizens of the city was carrying into the 1980s the earlier struggle against the city's urban removal plan and the political activism fostered by the October War. By the mid-1980s, that activism became increasingly funneled into local electoral politics, as seen in voter registration campaigns, Arab American candidates for City Council, and pressure to require bilingual ballot instructions. Veteran community activist Joseph Borrajo, director of the Arab-American Voter Registration and Education Committee in Dearborn, told the *Detroit News*, "We have come to the realization that if we don't get involved in the political structure, we are not going to satisfy our needs. The people here are really stirred."[74]

The Arab Community Center was also part of the project to integrate the Dearborn Arab American community into the larger political structure. During the 1980s, ACCESS began to apply for and receive grants from city and state government agencies, nonprofit organizations, and corporations, using the funds to enlarge its staff and operations, thereby allowing it to serve even more Arab Americans. As ACCESS was on the brink of deciding to pursue outside funding and shift away from its community-determined, grassroots genesis, its leaders sent a letter to members stating: "This is a crucial time for our center and a time of decision for you as a member. The possibilities of governmental and other kinds of funding are now presenting themselves, with certain conditions. We feel that the structural and organizational changes that these conditions consist of hold great dangers for the center and would remove much of the decision making process out of the hands of the membership. Yet on the other hand if we refuse these resources we will be turning a great opportunity for money and resources down. What do we do, the choice is yours."[75]

Presented with this dilemma, ACCESS members deliberated and ultimately determined that the benefits of expanding services and increasing influence in the political system outweighed possible compromises to its independence and progressive political agenda. The center heightened its visibility and reach by cultivating relationships with social service agencies throughout Michigan and the country as well as by forming coalitions with organizations representing multiple ethnic and racial groups in the United States. It developed a positive relationship with the UAW and was allowed free use of the UAW Local 600 hall in the Southend for fund-raising events. Eventually ACCESS members served on the board of directors of many major corporations and nonprofit institutions in the Detroit area.[76] In a 1996 interview, Ismael Ahmed stated, "ACCESS has become a city wide player.... [A]ll the big systems come to us as the representative of the Arab community." Perhaps reflecting on the irony of that situation, given ACCESS's antiestablishment origins, Ahmed added: "That's a little weird." [77]

With its enlarged scope and reliance on establishment funding sources came diminished attention to Arab world political advocacy and, some contended, a detachment "from its community base." Some critics came to think that "ACCESS used to be an organization of the people; now it's all corporate." Abdeen Jabara, however, believes that ACCESS has experienced "a natural progression" of an organization that has become part of the mainstream, and he declares, "I'm not critical of that." Barbara Aswad and Nancy Adadow Gray note that while ACCESS has been transformed by accepting millions of dollars from granting agencies that "ignore the social and economic causes" of Arab Americans' problems, the center remains closely connected to the community it originally sought to serve because of its location in the Southend and its ongoing responses to "client-sponsored needs." It can be argued, as Karen Rignall does in her study of ACCESS, that the community organization's new direction has "given Arab Americans a more public political presence" and that such presence "has helped Dearborn residents begin to challenge the structural problems that affect the most disadvantaged and marginalized sectors of Arab Detroit." Now nationally and even internationally recognized for its innovation and effectiveness in providing social services, ACCESS has become a highly influential and well-connected community organization with a budget of around $20 million. Another reason for the expansion of its role in the larger urban community is that, as a condition of receiving substantial government funding as well as its philosophy of outreach, ACCESS serves a diverse range of disadvantaged Americans, not just Americans of Arab heritage.[78]

THE OCTOBER WAR and its repercussions in the Southend show a particular manifestation of the connections between activists' leftist homeland focus and their more local emphasis. As a site where different generations of Arab American workers concentrated and coalesced, the neighborhood served as a space for constructing an Arab American political identity and expressing it in institutional forms, especially ACCESS, the most important community-based Arab American organization in the country. The Southend's status as an immigrant hub and its proximity to both student and labor militancy influenced the particular forms of Arab American activism generated there. The burgeoning transnational activism located in the neighborhood resulted from generative synergies and historical convergences. Emerging in the context of heightened civil rights activism, community organizing, and Third World consciousness throughout the United States, as well as mounting crises and upheavals in the Middle East, ACCESS appealed to the immigrant workers' immediate domestic concerns (employment and social services) so as to promote Arab nationalism. Operating in a different direction, AWC activists tried to tap into Arab nationalism as a way to foster the support of immigrant workers for a domestic issue (labor organizing). The recently arrived immigrants helped maintain the more established Arab Americans' consciousness of Arab world politics and cultural identity, whereas the second- and third-generation Arab Americans in the Southend facilitated acculturation of new immigrants to political organizing and expression in America.

By the end of the 1970s, the AWC and its militant approach had faded away, whereas ACCESS, which adjusted its focus to pragmatic issues faced by Arab American immigrants, had expanded its services and strengthened its ties to the mainstream social welfare system. While facing many obstacles and setbacks, Arab Americans in Dearborn steadily improved their position in the community, including in political representation, over the ensuing decades. However, in many ways the national climate worsened in the 1970s and 1980s as pernicious stereotypes and even violence against Arab Americans intensified across the country. But in their local and national organizations, Arab Americans continued the activism pioneered in the late 1960s and early 1970s, pressing for their civil rights and appealing for the support of an even wider net of progressive Americans.

7 Seeking Integration

Arab American Political Organizing in the 1980s

Connected to increasingly tense relations between Arab nations and the United States, the cultural climate for Arab Americans deteriorated in the 1970s and 1980s. Oil crises, conflicts in Lebanon and Libya, and hijackings and other acts of terrorism abroad all heightened widespread suspicion and denigration of Arabs in America. Most Arab Americans observed a proliferation of derogatory stereotypes and unfair depictions of Arabs in U.S. media and popular discourse, representations that extended to Americans of Arab heritage.[1] A notorious illustration of the increasing acceptability of defaming Arabs was the ABSCAM affair in 1978–80. This fiasco transpired when FBI agents posed as Arab sheiks to entrap U.S. politicians by offering bribes in return for political favors. Furthermore, prominent Arab American activists faced revived FBI harassment in the early 1980s.[2]

Later in the decade, in what scholar and activist Nabeel Abraham considered "the most alarming example of government harassment of Arab Americans to date," the FBI and local police rounded up and arrested several Palestinians living in Los Angeles (dubbed the "L.A. 8") and charged them under a McCarthy-era anticommunist law with belonging to the Popular Front for the Liberation of Palestine, seeking to deport them. (The government was never able to prove the charges, and in 2007 the case was finally dismissed.)[3] Even more disturbing, vigilante violence against Arab Americans escalated, particularly at the hands of the Jewish Defense League, a Jewish extremist organization, and in the most egregious episode, American-Arab Anti-Discrimination Committee (ADC) leader Alex Odeh was murdered in a bombing of his California ADC office in 1985. According to Arab American leaders, intimidation by the Anti-Defamation League (ADL) and the American Israel Public Affairs Committee (AIPAC) also noticeably increased. Even the national media took note, with *Newsweek* running the article "Arab Bashing in America" in 1986.[4] A year later, scholar and activist Helen Hatab Samhan argued that antipathy to Arabs emanated not so much from "generalized societal prejudice" but from the encouragement of "those, including a minority of pro-Israeli organizations and individuals, with the political motive of monopolizing the discussion" about U.S. policy in the Middle East. She charged that these groups, using guilt-by-association tactics reminiscent of the McCarthy era, smeared pro-Palestinian organizations and individuals as anti-Semitic and supportive of terrorism in an attempt to delegitimize, silence, and exclude their perspectives from the American political arena.[5]

Building on the organizing efforts forged in the 1960s and early 1970s, Arab Americans responded to this antagonistic climate by increasing their involvement in politics at all levels of government, founding new organizations, continuing their efforts to develop coalitions, and devoting more attention to the advocacy of Arab American civil rights. These avenues of domestic activism remained linked to Arab homeland politics and to the goal of influencing U.S. policy toward Arab nations. As the major Arab American organizations and their allies expanded their political activities in the late 1970s through the 1980s, they tended to moderate their stances and style in their pursuit of integration into the mainstream political arena. Most organizations and key activists maintained their critique of Israel, support for the PLO, and many of the causes embraced a decade earlier, but—except for the Organization of Arab Students (OAS)[6]—groups ranging from the Association of Arab American University Graduates (AAUG) to the Arab Community Center for Economic and Social Services (ACCESS) generally toned down their previously vocal support for armed resistance and eschewed overtly Marxist or Third World revolutionary rhetoric. Furthermore, most groups came to advocate, or at least signal openness to, a two-state solution to the Arab-Israeli conflict.[7] Newly established organizations such as the Palestine Human Rights Campaign (PHRC) and the ADC similarly adopted this less radical approach, while still pressing insistently for Arab and Arab American rights. Certain Arab American activists, particularly in the National Association of Arab Americans (NAAA) but also in the AAUG and other organizations, had possessed a moderate position for many years, but by the 1980s this approach was ascendant throughout the movement.

This eventual deradicalization was a result of several entwined factors. Probably foremost was a general sense of frustration and even disgust at the futility and factionalism of the Palestinian resistance movement, which, according to Palestinian activist Fawaz Turki, was "directionless" by the early 1980s.[8] Many Arab Americans who had been invigorated by the radical Palestinian resistance felt increasingly dismayed with and detached from the movement. These activists sought more measured approaches to achieving Palestinian rights and statehood. Furthermore, many of these activists had come of political age in the heady atmosphere of America in the 1960s; by the late 1970s they were maturing and preferred a more pragmatic political style, similar to activists in many antiestablishment movements. In general, the heyday of Third Worldism had passed among American movements on the left.[9]

At the same time that events in the Middle East generated widespread anti-Arab sentiment, Middle East conflicts engendered support for Arabs among certain segments of Americans. African Americans in particular tended to react to the Arab states' oil embargo with criticism of Israel, viewing themselves as the victims of the higher gas prices that they understood as resulting from America's support for Israel's intransigence in its relations with the Arab world. This view augmented their rising wariness of Israel owing to its increasingly close relationship with South Africa. While most African American radicals had been strong opponents of Israel going back to the 1960s, by the 1980s, as historian Salim Yaqub argues, "the criticism came out of the African-American mainstream, from figures who supported Israel's existence but believed US policy had become excessively partial to Israel."[10] Israel's invasion of Lebanon in 1982, striking Palestinian refugees and their Lebanese supporters and generating images of civilians assaulted by Israeli forces, was instrumental in producing greater American sympathy for Palestinians and criticism of Israeli aggression, especially by liberals. The invasion created new momentum for solidarity organizing in support of Palestine. Later in the 1980s, a Palestinian uprising against Israeli occupation, the First Intifada, similarly generated support for Palestinians among some Americans while producing renewed backing for the Israeli state among others.[11]

Thus, as they entered the 1980s, Arab American activists encountered the ironic situation of heightened antagonism toward Arabs in American society as a whole, yet greater political opportunities for advancing Arab and Arab American causes among a wider range of left-leaning Americans. Some Arab Americans responded to the hostile climate with defensiveness and fear, and to protect themselves they disengaged from American society, reinforcing their marginality.[12] But many Arab Americans expanded their political engagement as they confronted these challenges. Located between continual resistance and increasing sympathy, their leaders tended to adopt a more politically realistic approach than such organizations as the AAUG had practiced in the past, leading them to seek compromises and pursue concrete advancements on Arab and Arab American issues by participating in mainstream political arenas.[13]

The new crop of Arab American organizations that emerged in the late 1970s through mid-1980s, each filling a distinctive niche but all embodying the characteristics described above, made forming coalitions with progressive minority-rights and peace groups a central component of their organizing strategy. Arab American organizations also made attempts—some productive, some not—to collaborate with one another. As in earlier years, this strategy was envisioned as a way to achieve greater power and influence through greater numbers of supporters, and activists reached out both to one another and to groups they thought were most likely to understand the plight of Arabs and Arab Americans. Isolation, they understood, was disempowering. Arab American organizations continued to attract solidarity from the Left, but in the 1980s they also made more inroads with many liberal groups that had been lukewarm, or even antagonistic, to Arab positions a decade before. Still, politically active Arab Americans often found themselves frozen out of political networks, sometimes even from leftist circles, owing to stalwart support for Israel and persistent suspicion of Arab intent that permeated mainstream American politics.

The Foundational Organizations: The NAAA and the AAUG

Throughout the 1970s the National Association of Arab Americans carried on its role as a moderate lobbyist organization, targeting the highest levels of the U.S. government, but its positions increasingly converged with those of the AAUG, both because the NAAA was growing more aggressive in its criticism of Israel and because the AAUG was moderating its opposition to Israel's existence.[14] Also marking a growing tendency to overlap with the AAUG, some NAAA members thought the organization should put more emphasis on addressing anti-Arab discrimination throughout American society, rather than focusing narrowly on foreign policy matters. Combining these two avenues of activism, in 1978 NAAA president Hisham Sharabi penned a sharply worded letter to President Carter charging that the White House deliberately discriminated against and excluded Arab Americans and demanding "affirmative action to engage qualified Americans of Arab ancestry on the White House staff," as well as appointment of a special liaison to the Arab American community akin to the liaison already established with the Jewish community.[15]

The NAAA was in the forefront of arranging meetings with President Gerald Ford, Henry Kissinger, and President Jimmy Carter, and it usually invited leaders of the AAUG as well as other Arab American organizations, chiefly the Ramallah Federation, to join the meetings and to cosign statements. In 1977, the three organizations launched a concerted effort to collaborate in what Michael Suleiman, outgoing president of AAUG, envisioned as a "loose council" and for which Elaine Hagopian, the incoming president of the AAUG, was appointed Ad Hoc Coordinator for Inter-Arab-American Cooperation.[16] A few national media outlets paid attention to the emerging coalition, such as Nick Thimmesch of the *Saturday Evening Post*, who identified a growing "Arab lobby" intended to counter the "Israel lobby" in Washington. Thimmesch credited the NAAA with exercising more influence on the Carter administration than Arab Americans had ever experienced. (While this may have been the case, relations between the NAAA and the White House were sometimes tense, as demonstrated by Sharabi's letter to Carter, and the association was ultimately dissatisfied with Carter's Middle East policy.) Jewish groups also noted the increasing influence of the Arab American organizational network. For example, the American Jewish Committee (AJC) issued a report in 1978 also warning of an increasingly effective Arab lobby and observed that Arab American organizations were coalescing "to bridge old religious [and] national divisions and create a sense of Arab American solidarity." Most concerning to the AJC, the NAAA and conservative Lebanese Americans were becoming more vocal in criticizing Israel because, according to the report, such criticism was becoming more "respectable" in mainstream institutions such as Congress.[17]

Despite these advances toward inter–Arab American coalition, however, important differences continued to divide the AAUG and the NAAA, most important the NAAA's openness to Carter's peace efforts at Camp David (a position that the NAAA later came to regret). Another divergence was that, unlike the AAUG and the organizations it would spawn, the NAAA did not view the strategy of cultivating alliances with American minority and leftist groups as politically advantageous and tended to be closer to the Republican Party.[18] In any case, a political controversy in 1978, in which some NAAA and AAUG members charged certain NAAA figures with being too cozy with the CIA, dashed the attempt at formal collaboration between the groups.[19]

Through the 1980s the AAUG continued to assert positions on foreign and domestic issues of interest to Arab Americans, such as human rights violations of Palestinians, and it sponsored delegations of Americans to visit occupied Palestine.[20] Probably its greatest contribution in this period remained its initial core mission: disseminating scholarly information on the Arab world. The association's journal, *Arab Studies Quarterly,* as well as its information papers and monographs, sustained this tradition. However, internal dissent often proved debilitating, including turmoil over whether to abandon the organization's inflexible opposition to Israel's existence. Although some AAUG members held to this uncompromising position and the organization never formally declared support for a two-state solution, other members favored a pragmatic position on the question of Palestine more in line with the emerging international consensus as well as with new stances in the Palestine National Council. Abdeen Jabara recalls, "It was not an easy transition from the rhetoric of 'revolution until victory' to the slogan 'shiber, shiber' ('liberate two hand widths now, the rest later')."[21] But eventually many, and perhaps most, AAUG members made the transition. Its convention resolutions replaced earlier unequivocal declarations of support for "a secular and democratic Palestine in all of Palestine" with statements advocating "the right of the Palestinian people to self-determination and national independence." By the early 1990s, observers such as political scientist Yossi Shain sensed that the AAUG was moving to a more moderate, centrist position.[22]

A New Wave of Activism: The PHRC

As the established Arab American political organizations persisted in their political work, the first of the next generation of Arab American activist organizations emerged. The Palestine Human Rights Campaign began as a committee of the AAUG in 1977 before splitting off to become its own entity in 1978. Its strategy was to employ organizing techniques learned from the anti–Vietnam War movement to incite political agitation among a broader segment of Americans against Israeli violations of Palestinians' rights. As one of its organizers, Abdeen Jabara claimed the PHRC "brought a new style to the activity which was kind of oriented around mounting campaigns and protest and involving... a large number of people." Jabara and the campaign's other principal leader, Jim Zogby, decided that to engage in broader outreach and to practice the political organizing techniques they envisioned, they needed to separate this initiative from the AAUG. Nonetheless, the AAUG was strongly supportive of the PHRC's work, and considerable overlap existed in the two organizations' memberships.[23]

Unlike the AAUG, the PHRC was not intended to be an expressly Arab American organization. It concentrated on alerting a targeted group of Americans active in other peace and human rights causes to specific cases of mistreatment of Palestinians. Many of the incidents publicized by the PHRC involved Palestinians residing in the United States, often as college students, who were extradited and imprisoned by Israel. A key case that sparked the formation of the PHRC was that of Sami Esmail, discussed in chapter 2. Another crucial case to which the PHRC, along with many other Arab American organizations, dedicated itself was the extradition of Ziad Abu Eain, a Palestinian residing in America whom Israel charged with a terrorist act—setting a bomb in Israel that killed two and injured dozens—committed in 1979. Eain's defense team, which included Abdeen Jabara, maintained that his confession to the bombing was falsified, arguing that the U.S. district court was not following proper prosecution procedure for the bombing, which several Arab American groups considered a political, not criminal, offense.[24]

The PHRC's main tactic was raising consciousness through publicity. In this era before the Internet and social media, the group used, in Zogby's words, "postcard campaigns, letter writing or telephone calling, petition signing, [and] bumper stickers to build support and education on the specifics of an individual Palestinian victim." Its bulletins reported on Middle East conflicts and American policymakers' statements and actions and urged readers to contact U.S. officials and advocate interventions or oppose policies. An example of the PHRC's publicity tactics was the advertisement it placed in the *New York Times, Washington Post,* and *Christian Science Monitor* on 20 May 1980, condemning Israel's persecution of Palestinian mayors. The ad had over fifty signers, including prominent liberal-left figures Pete Seeger, I. F. Stone, Jack O'Dell, Rep. Tom Harkin, Rep. John Conyers, Daniel Berrigan, Edward Said, Ralph Abernathy, Ron Walters, Dave Dellinger, and Noam Chomsky. Organizers claimed that their publicity and agitation helped release dozens of people unjustly imprisoned in Israeli jails.[25]

Mobilizing for Civil Rights: The ADC

While the primary purpose of the PHRC was to draw the attention of American activists and policymakers to human rights violations of Palestinians, some of its leaders, including Zogby and Jabara, decided an organization dedicated to Arab American civil rights in the United States was also needed. Founded in 1980, the American-Arab Anti-Discrimination Committee was envisioned as a civil rights organization for Arab Americans. Although its leadership centered around a few key figures who were mainly Lebanese American, it sought a grassroots, national, diverse membership of Arab

Americans. The main leader of the ADC was James Abourezk, the nation's first Arab American U.S. senator, representing the state of South Dakota from 1973 to 1979. As senator, he worked on a range of issues, including American Indian rights, and at times he spoke out on America's Middle East policy and criticized anti-Arab prejudice. In the mid-1970s, the Zionist publication the *Near East Report* regularly assailed Abourezk. He later reflected, "I don't suppose I would have ever become so deeply enmeshed in the Middle East conflict had I not been attacked so unfairly at the onset."[26] Choosing not to run for reelection to the Senate, Abourezk decided to devote his public career to advocacy, and he joined forces with Zogby, Jabara, and others dedicated to Arab American civil rights.

A significant impetus for Abourezk, as it was for others who sought a more assertive organization for Arab Americans, was distress over the FBI's ABSCAM scandal. According to scholar and activist Jack Shaheen, author of the ADC pamphlet "ABSCAM: Arabiaphobia in America," the FBI decided to adopt Arab personas for the sting operation because they were drawing on Americans' misconception, promoted by the popular media, that Arabs were "buying up America." He called it nothing less than "government-sanctioned racism." When the operation was exposed in 1980, twenty-four members of Congress called on the FBI to apologize for its insulting exploitation of Arab stereotypes, but it refused. Jabara remembers the ABSCAM episode as a "turning point for Arab Americans because that was a purely domestic operation by a federal agency that demeaned and defamed and denigrated people of Arabic ethnic background." Abourezk responded to the offensive scheme by calling a meeting of about sixty Arab American leaders to mobilize a new organization to contest these and similar affronts to Arabs and Arab Americans.[27]

Launching the ADC, Abourezk focused attention on these insidious prejudices in his address, "Arabs: The Convenient Scapegoat." After pointing out numerous examples of the American media's biased reporting about Arabs, he refuted charges that he and other Arab Americans were being "too sensitive." He reminded his audience that racism has real consequences that translate into serious violations of civil liberties, and he drew parallels between the prejudice experienced by Arab Americans and the discrimination faced by other outsider groups in America.[28]

Abourezk claimed that the so-called Arab lobby, talked up in the aforementioned *Saturday Evening Post* article and AJC report, was "virtually powerless" because it, unlike the Israeli lobby, lacked a sufficient grassroots base. More than the AAUG and the PHRC, the ADC aimed to reach out and mobilize all Arab Americans to foster their "collective level of consciousness" and educate them about their "rights and privileges" as Americans. Seeking new momentum in community building and heightened visibility as an American ethnic minority, ADC leaders chose "Arab Americans come of age" as the theme of the first convention. On the model of the African American civil rights movement, it employed field organizers to organize local ADC chapters throughout the country, and unlike the AAUG, it did not confine membership to university graduates. This grassroots strategy further developed the work of preceding Arab American organizations to foster an even greater awakening of a "minority consciousness" among Arab Americans.[29]

Yet, as signaled in the organization's decision to make the first words of its title "American-Arab," leaders such as Abourezk intended a moderate (some might say conservative), assimilative approach to civil rights advocacy, one that prioritized American over Arab in the claiming of a hyphenated identity. This emphasis on "American" was probably intended to assuage the ascendant fears and hostility felt by Americans who viewed anyone of Arab heritage as a foreign enemy. Nevertheless, building on the efforts of the AAUG and the PHRC, the ADC sought coalitions with other minority groups and was especially successful at cultivating an alliance with Operation PUSH (People United to Serve Humanity), which in the mid-1980s became the National Rainbow Coalition led by the black civil rights leader and Democratic Party politician Jesse Jackson, whose support of Palestinian rights is discussed in more detail below. As part of the Rainbow Coalition, the ADC played an important role in supporting Jackson's campaigns for U.S. president in 1984 and 1988.[30]

In its work as essentially an antidefamation league for Arab Americans, the ADC spent much of its time and energy monitoring and protesting offensive or inaccurate portrayals of Arabs and Arab Americans in the news media, entertainment, and statements by public officials. Some of the campaigns were national in scope, such as against the Goldie Hawn movie *Protocol* and against the television program *20/20*'s episode on Arab terrorism, whereas others were taken on by ADC chapters which protested insulting coverage in local media outlets as well as defamatory textbooks and other school materials. Often these campaigns produced apologies from the media source or public official, occasionally yielding the offering of space or time to present an Arab perspective. Nevertheless, contesting these stereotypes and biased information was an uphill battle, and it would be difficult to claim that the ADC succeeded in overcoming the widespread prejudice against Arabs in American media.[31]

Though its main emphasis was raising consciousness about stereotypes and discrimination against Arabs in America, the ADC functioned as a diasporic political organization and thus also incorporated Arab world problems in its advocacy efforts. From time to time the ADC participated in the PHRC's publicity campaigns about Palestinian political prisoners and U.S. aid to Israel and sent out its own press releases and publications about injustices and conflicts in the Middle East. In addition to the ABSCAM incident, the conflict in Lebanon in the early 1980s intensified Arab Americans' distress and boosted their motivation to gain a greater voice in American politics and society through the ADC. According to Jabara, the organization "really took off because of the Israeli invasion of Lebanon in 1982." The Detroit chapter was among those particularly active in seeking to correct biased media reports of the war in Lebanon. In 1983, Zogby spun off from the ADC an organization called the Save Lebanon Project to focus efforts on aiding the victims of the violence there. The Save Lebanon Project brought dozens of injured Lebanese children to the United States for medical treatment.[32]

Regrettably, ADC's outspoken activism made it a target for harassment and outright violent attacks. Its headquarters in Washington, D.C., was set on fire; its Boston office was threatened by a pipe bomb on its premises; and, most egregious, at its office in Santa Ana, California, a bomb killed the ADC's West Coast director, Alex Odeh. It was widely suspected that the militant Zionist organization the Jewish Defense League was responsible for these attacks. Numerous Arab American, civil liberties, peace, and minority rights groups sponsored an advertisement in the *New York Times* in early 1986 that condemned the recent violence against the ADC and proclaimed: "Let Us Resolve Together: Don't Let Terrorism Spread into America." Reporting on her interview with Abdeen Jabara, Janet McMahon of the *Washington Report on Middle East Affairs* wrote that he is "convinced that these were more than hate-inspired acts of violence, that they were politically motivated attacks designed to intimidate Arab Americans and discourage them from organizing to demand their political rights."[33] Despite the threats, the ADC pushed on with its mission of advocacy.

Palestinian Americans Organize and Collaborate: The PCNA

Another organization formed in this era for the purpose of Palestinian advocacy was the Palestine Congress of North America (PCNA). At the end of the 1970s, a number of Palestinian activists in the United States believed that a Palestinian-only umbrella organization was necessary to coordinate the multitude of Palestinian American groups and to represent the specific issues and unique identity of Palestinians, instead of subsuming them in pan-Arab organizations such as the AAUG. In late 1978, members of several Palestinian groups met at the All Palestine Congress in New York City and decided to hold a Palestine American Congress Constitutional Convention in Washington, D.C., the following year. At that convention, which was fueled by Palestinian Americans' opposition to the 1978 Camp David Accords—an agreement between Egypt and Israel that affected the future of Palestinians but excluded the PLO from negotiations and reduced Palestinians' autonomy—and a sense of betrayal by other Arabs, they formed the Palestine Congress of North America. Nevertheless, throughout the 1980s the organization frequently worked and cosigned policy statements with the AAUG, NAAA, and PHRC. Furthermore, PCNA leaders such as Jawad George, Naseer Aruri, and Samih Farsoun were also prominent members and leaders of the AAUG and the NAAA. Despite the PCNA's commitment to Palestinian unity, it was constantly challenged by the durability of factions among Palestinians.[34]

Aiming for Political Influence: The AAI

By the mid-1980s, Jim Zogby came to believe that an organizing strategy more focused on achieving a presence for Arab Americans in electoral politics was necessary to achieve progress, with a primary goal of winning wider American support for the Palestinian cause. To embody the electoral approach, in 1985 Zogby broke off from the ADC and founded another organization, the Arab American Institute (AAI).[35] A nonpartisan organization, the AAI identified Arab American candidates for party delegations and political offices and concentrated on building Arab Americans' clout at the ballot box, supporting both Democratic and Republican Party candidates. Zogby, who had delivered a nomination speech for Jesse Jackson at the Democratic National Convention in 1984, again served as a presidential campaign adviser to Jackson in 1988. Zogby believed that even though Arab Americans represented a tiny percentage of the total U.S. electorate, they could carry influence if mobilized strategically. The institute's public affairs spokesperson, Mark Dressler, reasoned, "In New York, if the Jewish constituents don't like a candidate, that candidate will not be elected." Likewise, if Arab Americans made their voices heard, Dressler insisted, their needs and interests would also be addressed in the political arena.[36] Zogby endeavored to work with other Arab American organizations, such as the AAUG, to project a united "pro-Palestinian agenda" with strategic "issues and language ... to focus U.S. attention on Palestinian rights" in a proactive rather than reactive manner. The organization's Vote '88 project was intended to mobilize Arab American voters to "directly challenge the Presidential candidates on their failure to speak out on Palestinian rights."[37]

In the 1980s, Arab Americans were becoming more politically organized and expressive. Reporting on the results of a mid-1980s AAI survey of Arab American political attitudes, Zogby stated, "Although Arab Americans have only recently emerged as a visible organized political constituency, they have already demonstrated political sophistication in their activity and their attitudes." Ismael Ahmed agrees with this assessment, observing that "Arab-American involvement in both Michigan and national party politics became solidified" in the 1980s and 1990s. Arab Americans' involvement in the Rainbow Coalition (represented by both the ADC and the AAI) and Jesse Jackson's campaigns were instrumental in fostering Arab Americans' political visibility. Ahmed notes that "Jesse Jackson was possibly the first national politician to acknowledge the Arab-American community publicly as a potentially valuable constituency," and Arab Americans were pivotal to Jackson's victory in Michigan's Democratic caucus primary contest in 1988. While some community activists were uncomfortable with what they considered a narrow political approach that would likely involve compromises with the established system, Ahmed, who led the Dearborn-based grassroots organization ACCESS, saw merit in AAI tactics. He stated, "For our lobbying work, we were beginning to realize that you couldn't just look away from electoral politics; that was the game and if you weren't at least a part player in it you were a loser." A prime example of an Arab American organization that made the transition from a leftist, outsider organization to a mainstream player, ACCESS connected to corporations, government agencies, and liberal nonprofits over the course of the 1970s and 1980s. Palestinian American activist and scholar Rabab Abdulhadi also views the Jesse Jackson campaign as a critical moment. She argues that before their involvement in the Rainbow Coalition, most Palestinian activists did not see electoral politics "as a vehicle for public claims, which was partly due to Palestinian distrust of U.S. politicians and the tilt toward Israel and partly because the majority of immigrants did not view themselves as Americans, only as Palestinians. All of this began to change during Jesse Jackson's first presidential campaign in 1984, thus marking a significant turning point in activists' strategies."[38] To leaders such as Ahmed and Zogby, these realizations and developments signaled that Arab Americans were becoming integrated into the American political mainstream while maintaining their distinct identity.

Progressive Coalitions

Already an emphasis of the AAUG and the OAS in the late 1960s and early 1970s, Arab Americans' efforts to build coalitions with other activist groups expanded after the mid-1970s. Targeting groups that activists had long conceived of as "natural allies," such as African Americans and white progressives, Arab American organizations had more success achieving support and understanding from moderate or liberal groups than they had in earlier years when their supporters tended to be more radical. The coalitions with liberals resulted both from the softening of "Third World liberation" theoretical stances by most Arab American activists and from the increasing consciousness of—and sympathy for—the Palestinian side of the Palestine-Israel conflict among American progressives, due in large part to the efforts of Arab American organizations but also to growing attention to global human rights issues.

After about a decade of organized activism on behalf of justice for Palestinians and Arab Americans, Abdeen Jabara was one Arab American leader who grew increasingly convinced that, to make progress on these issues, Arab Americans must gain the support of non-Arab organizations. In a 1978 essay published in the *AAUG Newsletter*, Jabara argued that Arab Americans could not achieve much influence on their own because of "the paucity of their resources." They should "ally with groups which are organized to promote interests such as civil rights, disarmament, and opposition to the role of the United States as a weapons supplier." While continuing to pursue coalitions with analogous minority groups, they needed to make a greater effort to convince "Americans from all walks of life," especially people with positions of status and respectability in their communities and institutions, "to endorse our positions publicly" as a step toward "break[ing] down the taboo that has been placed on our concerns generally."[39]

Representative of this effort was Jabara's successful initiative to convince the left-leaning National Lawyers Guild (NLG), of which he had been a member since the mid-1960s, to take a position in favor of Palestinian rights. Like many liberal organizations, the NLG had long been a proponent of Israel, and it took the guild almost ten years of debate to arrive at the pro-Palestine stance. Another guild member who served on the NLG Middle East Subcommittee argued more recently, "In the seventy-five-year history of the Guild, no issue has been more difficult and contentious in our organization than support for or criticism of Israel and Palestine." Jabara's attempt to convince the NLG to recognize Israel's violations of Palestinians' rights dates back to 1969, when, at his urging, the Detroit NLG chapter introduced a resolution condemning Israel's human rights violations. Though the resolution was shelved, the national NLG leadership agreed to publish an article by Jabara about Israel's treatment of Palestinians in its 1970 newsletter.[40]

Five years later, as concern increased within the NLG about the deteriorating situation in the Middle East, the national leadership asked each chapter to deliberate over a set of questions about the conflict and formulate positions. As the ensuing discussions heightened its attention to Palestine, in 1977 the NLG arranged for ten members to visit occupied Palestine and surrounding areas. Led by Jabara, the delegation observed the deplorable conditions under which most Palestinians lived. One Jewish member of the delegation, who remembers feeling "no emotional stake or any real empathy for Palestinians" before the trip, was powerfully moved by the circumstances he witnessed in the Territories and henceforth became committed to activism on behalf of Palestinians. Upon its return, the delegation drafted a report that documented abuses by Israel of Palestinians' rights and also submitted resolutions calling for support of the political and human rights of Palestinians. The report and the resolutions, however, generated considerable discord among guild members, which was finally resolved after mediation and compromise. The NLG ultimately passed a human rights resolution condemning Israeli practices, along with a political resolution that recognized the PLO, supported Palestinians' self-determination and right of return, and favored a two-state solution. In 1978 it issued the delegation's detailed investigative report, *Report of the National Lawyers Guild 1977 Middle East Delegation: The Treatment of Palestinians in the Israeli Occupied West Bank and Gaza*, which, according to Jabara, served as "a tremendous resource for the burgeoning New Left." The transformation of the National Lawyers Guild on the Israel-Palestine issue, after careful study and debate over the course of the 1970s, carried added significance because most of its members were also members of other liberal and leftist advocacy organizations. In a ripple effect, they contributed to shifting positions on the conflict among a wider segment of liberal Americans. They also contributed to a greater willingness to work with organized Arab Americans on these issues.[41]

As a mark of the expansion of support for Arab causes, by the early 1980s more African American moderates who previously had been strong supporters of Israel were advocating for Palestinian rights. In a major milestone for the Palestinian movement, in 1975 the United Nations General Assembly passed a very controversial resolution that equated Zionism with racism. Following similar resolutions passed by the Organization of African Unity and the consortium of nonaligned countries, the UN resolution drew parallels between South African apartheid and Israeli Zionism. In a vote of 72 to 35, most Third World nations and Soviet-aligned states endorsed the resolution, while the United States, nearly all Western nations, and a few African and Latin American countries rejected it.[42] As earlier in the decade, African Americans' response to the condemnation of Zionism divided along moderate and radical lines, with most black moderates conforming to mainstream American public opinion in defense of Israel. Nevertheless, the claims about Israeli and South African relations disconcerted many black leaders associated with moderate liberal groups, such as the Southern Christian Leadership Conference (SCLC), and over the next five years they increasingly diverged from American supporters of Israel. While taking a critical stance toward Israel, most black moderates continued to support Israel's existence but called for a return to its pre-1967 boundaries as well as recognition of the PLO as the representative of the Palestinian people.[43] Meanwhile, black radicals maintained their emphatic anti-Zionist stance, as seen, for example, in a joint demonstration between the All African People's Revolutionary Party and the OAS in 1978.

The creation of the Palestine Human Rights Campaign in 1978 further generated support for Arab interests by African American moderates as well as other American liberals. Though it was established and led by Arab Americans, the PHRC's aim was to cultivate a diverse membership to advocate for Palestinian human rights. As discussed earlier, a main reason its organizers decided to separate the PHRC from the AAUG organizational apparatus was to allow it to more effectively build coalitions with organizations outside of the Arab American community and engage in broader political outreach.[44] Thus, not only did the PHRC foster more American awareness of injustice in the Middle East, but it also enhanced the working relationships between Arab American activists and non-Arab progressives in the United States.

Leaders of the campaign consciously modeled their organization on the activist style that had long been employed by civil rights and peace groups, and they promoted links with those groups on both the tactical grounds of grassroots activism and the moral grounds of human rights.[45] Since at least the mid-1960s, black activists had been expanding the conceptualization of African American civil rights to the universal category of global human rights.

By the late 1970s, during President Jimmy Carter's administration, human rights discourse had become pervasive. Thus, by advancing a human rights agenda, the Palestine Human Rights Campaign was tapping into a powerful organizing framework that encouraged joint actions with other groups dedicated to protecting global human rights. To accentuate the moral position of the Palestinian cause, PHRC leaders especially sought alliances with liberal Christian clergy in both predominantly white and predominantly black denominations. For instance, a conference held by the PHRC in May 1979 titled "Palestinian-Israeli Conflict: Responsibilities for the Christian Church" drew the participation of several noted progressive Christian leaders, such as civil rights activist Rev. Ralph Abernathy of the SCLC, who gave the keynote address; Donald Will from the United Methodist Church; and Don Luce of the peace organization Clergy and Laity Concerned. Also attending were former attorney general and progressive activist Ramsey Clark and African American leaders Jesse Jackson, Joseph Lowery, and Walter Fauntroy. The conference called for Palestinian self-determination and condemned Israel's recent bombing of South Lebanon. Chapters of the PHRC across the country sponsored similar events designed to build alliances with African American and peace groups in their localities. For example, the Detroit PHRC chapter held a conference titled "Palestinian Human Rights and the American People" in 1980 which attracted an audience that was half Arabs and half non-Arabs and featured speakers including African American congressman John Conyers and a top aide to Detroit's African American mayor Coleman Young. The PHRC became integral to another coalition, the Middle East Peace Action Coalition, which involved a range of progressive figures and organizations, including pacifist Dave Dellinger, the Methodist Federation for Social Action, the SCLC, the New American Movement, Raza Unida, *Sojourners Magazine*, and the Black Theology Project, in activism on behalf of Palestinians.[46]

A key figure in the strengthening coalition between African American moderates and Arab American activists was Jack O'Dell, a black activist who had been an important leader of the SCLC in the early 1960s (before the SCLC was red-baited by the FBI and O'Dell was pushed out for his earlier Communist Party affiliation) and of the anti–Vietnam War movement. In the 1970s he was influential as the editor of the progressive journal *Freedomways* and as the international affairs director of Operation PUSH, the aforementioned social justice organization formed by Jesse Jackson in the early 1970s. In the 1980s, O'Dell continued his activist work on international peace and human rights causes through his involvement in Jackson's Rainbow Coalition, which later merged with Operation PUSH. Through the 1970s, O'Dell became increasingly conscious of the Palestinians' plight, and by the end of the decade he was working with both the AAUG and the PHRC to promote American activism on behalf of Palestinians. In a book he coedited with James Zogby titled *Afro-Americans Stand Up for Middle East Peace*, published by the PHRC, O'Dell stated, "The response of Black Americans to the Palestinian appeal for justice is one of sensitive appreciation, for we too know what it is to be dispossessed, exploited, lied about, insulted, and ignored." During a period when he was participating in fact-finding trips to Central America and South Africa, O'Dell organized a delegation of black and Latino civil rights figures to visit Lebanon in June 1979 for an "information gathering mission" sponsored by the AAUG. While in the Middle East, the delegation met with PLO leaders, including Yasser Arafat.[47]

Just when relations between black Christian-affiliated organizations and Arab American organizations were warming, an incident occurred in the summer of 1979 involving Andrew Young, the U.S. ambassador to the United Nations, that bolstered the African American–Arab American alliance. President Carter's appointment of Young, a former SCLC leader and congressman from Georgia, as the first African American U.S. ambassador to the United Nations was widely perceived to signal a novel, progressive direction in U.S. foreign policy. Shortly after the SCLC delegation returned from Lebanon, Young accepted an invitation to meet with O'Dell and its other members, who shared what they had observed and urged him to meet with PLO leaders. Within a few weeks, Young met with a PLO representative, Zehdi Terzi, a Columbia University professor who served as the PLO's observer to the United Nations. The purpose of the meeting was to secure PLO acquiescence in a plan to postpone UN deliberation of a resolution calling for the creation of a Palestinian state because Young felt the timing was wrong and the resolution would embarrass the United States, whose reputation was being battered by several other crises that year. Young chose to conduct the meeting in secret because the United States had vowed in 1975 not to recognize PLO representatives as long as the PLO would not recognize Israel.[48] But when news of the meeting was leaked to the American press by Israeli sources (which presumably had been monitoring Terzi's activities), considerable controversy ensued about Young's breach of protocol and swirling implications that he had negotiated with a "terrorist organization." The Carter administration reprimanded him for violating State Department policy, and under substantial public pressure and official criticism, Young resigned on 15 August 1979.[49]

Most African Americans reacted to this turn of events—the humiliation and resignation of the highest-level African American appointed federal official—with great dismay and anger. Many of them charged that Israel and its Jewish supporters in the United States had used their untoward influence to drive Young out. (In response, Jewish organizations pointed out that only one group, the American Zionist Federation, had publicly called for Young's resignation. Young himself denied Jewish influence in his resignation.) By this time, many moderate black leaders had started to sympathize with Palestinians and criticize Israeli policy, and Andrew Young's resignation took them further down that path. Many questioned whether the U.S. refusal to recognize the PLO was a wise or moral policy and believed that Young had been unfairly punished for what they saw as a reasonable diplomatic move. Some African American leaders, including Coretta Scott King and National Urban League president Vernon Jordan, pointed out that the U.S. ambassador to Austria, Jewish businessman Milton Wolf, had recently met with PLO representatives in Vienna, yet the Carter administration had not reacted with a reprimand.[50]

A week after Young's resignation, the NAACP convened a meeting at its headquarters in New York City that included participation by the National Urban League, the SCLC, and the Congressional Black Caucus, among many other black organizations. Many of the leaders in attendance had been solid supporters of Israel earlier in the decade, and their organizations had contested the anti-Zionist position taken by many radical black activists. But in what black journalist Roger Wilkins described as "a significant coalescing of black thought," African Americans at the meeting issued a statement supportive of Andrew Young and critical of Jewish supporters of Israel. Further, they advocated American meetings with the PLO. As in the past, many of the black leaders were concerned about appearing anti-Semitic and losing Jewish support for their organizations, but after what Wilkins called the "watershed" moment of the Andrew Young affair, their views on Israel-Palestine and their own sense of empowerment on foreign policy issues overrode their caution about criticizing Israel.[51]

The statement, read at a press conference by Georgia state senator and former Student Nonviolent Coordinating Committee activist Julian Bond, discussed the divergence of Jewish and black organizations not only over foreign policy matters but also over recent disputes concerning affirmative action. (Black leaders at the meeting thought that most Jews were insufficiently supportive of affirmative action policies, as demonstrated in ongoing tension over the 1978 *California v. Bakke* Supreme Court case.) The statement also brought up relations between Israel and South Africa and called on American Jews to condemn Israel's support for the apartheid regime. What especially instigated the black leaders' indignant response to the Andrew Young affair was their perception that Americans in power did not respect African Americans' views on U.S. foreign policy. When leaving the meeting, black psychologist Kenneth Clark told the press that the statement constituted African Americans' "declaration of independence" in regards to the positions of black organizations on foreign policy matters.[52]

Also responding to Young's resignation with protest was the AAUG, which issued a strongly worded statement criticizing U.S. foreign policy in the Middle East and calling for U.S. recognition of the PLO as the representative of the Palestinian people. The AAUG passed a resolution condemning President Carter for "submitting to Israeli pressure" in his treatment of Young. Its statement queried: "Was Ambassador Young victimized because of his outspoken and courageous stands against apartheid, racial inequality, tyranny, and oppression? Was he victimized because he chose to question the wisdom of sending millions of dollars in American arms to Israel as an inducement to peace in the Middle East? Was he victimized because he questioned Israeli annexation policies in the occupied West Bank and Gaza Strip?" Association activists joined the chorus of African American voices charging that Young had been unfairly targeted because of his race, combined with his critical views of Israel.[53]

Over the next few months, the relationship of the AAUG and the PHRC with African American organizations further solidified as the SCLC and Operation PUSH became increasingly invested in finding solutions to the Israeli-Palestinian conflict. Leaders of these organizations believed that African Americans should play a significant role in Middle East diplomacy because their history of oppression in the United States gave them a uniquely constructive perspective on Third World conflicts with major powers. The same week as the NAACP-sponsored meeting concerning Andrew Young, Rev. Joseph Lowery, the president of the SCLC, met with the PLO's Terzi in New York City. The SCLC's Lowery and Fauntroy then led a delegation to the Middle East and met with both PLO and Israeli leaders. Seeking to base their diplomacy on nonviolence and Christian values, the SCLC leaders urged the PLO representatives to recognize Israel's existence and cease violent tactics. Nevertheless, they expressed solidarity with the Palestinians, and press reports of the SCLC leaders singing "We Shall Overcome" with their Palestinian hosts caused considerable controversy in the United States.[54]

Two weeks later, Jesse Jackson and other members of Operation PUSH also visited the Middle East intending to meet with both PLO and Israeli leaders, along with leaders of Egypt, Syria, and Jordan. However, Israeli prime minister Menachem Begin refused to allow any Israeli officials to meet with Jackson and his delegation. The snub further bruised Jewish-black relations. The tenor of Jackson's talks with Arafat and other PLO representatives was similar to those of the SCLC delegation, striking a tone of support for the Palestinian cause while counseling restraint. Media coverage of the Jackson delegation's visits to refugee camps and sites destroyed by Israeli firepower reinforced a sympathetic portrayal of the Palestinians' plight. Upon his return to the United States, Jackson frequently pronounced America's "no-talk policy toward the PLO" to be "ridiculous."55

Meanwhile, Arab American organizations continued to reach out to the SCLC, Operation PUSH, and other moderate African American groups. The *New York Times* ran an article on 30 October 1979 titled "Arab Groups in U.S. Seek to Woo Blacks" that described Arab Americans' "new campaign to forge a broad political alliance with blacks" in an effort to "change American policy in the Middle East." Both Jesse Jackson and Joseph Lowery accepted invitations to speak at the PHRC's conference in September 1979. Lowery, Jackson and his wife, Jacqueline, CORE chairman Roy Innis, and Detroit congressman John Conyers were among the black leaders to speak at the AAUG's convention that November.56 Additionally, the AAUG created ties with the civil rights organization Congress on Racial Equality by serving as a conduit for Arab states' investment in black communities.57 On the other hand, as reported in the *New York Times* article, some African American groups refused to accept Arab or Arab American money, and even some of the groups that had participated in the meeting after the Andrew Young affair were reluctant to associate with Arab American organizations.58

Bridges between Arab Americans and African American leaders were also being built on the local level by the early 1980s. In Chicago, Arab Americans mobilized along with other minority groups to support African American politician Harold Washington's successful 1984 campaign for mayor. According to Louise Cainkar, this experience marked Arab Americans' inclusion in the city's "multi-racial, multi-ethnic progressive coalition." African American leaders, including Washington and Jesse Jackson, had been instrumental in calming tensions that had arisen between Arab American merchants and black residents of the city. Following his victory, Washington established an Arab American advisory council in the Chicago Commission on Human Relations.59 In Detroit, Arab American activists such as Abdeen Jabara had developed cooperative relationships with John Conyers and George Crockett, both black congressional members, and Arab Americans worked on Crockett's staff. Though leaders of both communities acknowledged that substantial racial and ethnic antipathies existed between the two groups, they were confident that they were making progress in overcoming conflicts and fostering coalitions.[60]

All of these efforts at black-Arab coalition building really came to fruition with the nexus of the American-Arab Anti-Discrimination Committee and Jesse Jackson's Rainbow Coalition in the 1980s, as discussed earlier in the chapter. Highlighting its commitment to civil rights and emphasizing its conviction that Arab Americans suffered from discrimination and persecution akin to other American minority groups, from the outset the ADC sought coalitions with civil rights groups representing nonwhite races and ethnicities. In his founding address, ADC president James Abourezk drew connections between Arab Americans and other groups of Americans, including African Americans, Polish Americans, and Mexican Americans, who had experienced discrimination and declared, "We must remember that if one group is under attack, we are all under attack." In return, Jackson demonstrated his awareness of Arab Americans' suffering when he proclaimed during his speech at the 1984 Democratic National Convention that, like other minority groups, Arab Americans "know the pain and hurt of racial and religious rejection. They must not continue to be made pariahs."[61]

Building on the relationships the PHRC and the AAUG had already constructed with the SCLC and Operation PUSH, ADC activists became an integral part of Jackson's Rainbow Coalition. As mentioned earlier, Arab American activists (some of whom were affiliated with the Arab American Institute after 1985) also worked on Jackson's presidential campaigns in 1984 and 1988. In addition to hiring Zogby as a chief campaign adviser, Jackson appointed Marisa Tamari to be Arab American liaison for the Jesse Jackson for President Committee, and she promptly launched an "Arab Americans for Jesse Jackson Network" which raised tens of thousands of dollars. Camilia Odeh, an activist at Chicago's Arab community center, served on the Rainbow Coalition's board and was active in Jackson's campaigns. Arab American community centers across the nation played an important role in supporting Jackson by organizing community meetings, fund-raisers, and voter registration drives.[62]

A key initiative endorsed by Jackson was securing resolutions advocating Palestinian statehood in each state's Democratic Party platform, a campaign that met success in several states during the lead-up to the National Democratic Party Convention in 1988. At the national convention, the Jackson delegates led by Zogby introduced the Palestinian statehood plank. Palestinian self-determination was debated on the convention floor, and intense negotiations over the party's position on Middle East peace took place between Jackson's and Michael Dukakis's delegates. Although the plank was not adopted in the party's platform, such debate was unprecedented in a mainstream American political forum and marked a step toward inclusion of Arab American interests in major party politics.[63]

Meanwhile, the AAUG had been forming a relationship with the Congressional Black Caucus, and along with the PCNA it sponsored at least one policy roundtable for African American congressional members and their staffs.[64] These coalitions between mainstream civil rights activists and Arab American activists had not materialized before the late 1970s, as seen, for instance, in the friction between the Congressional Black Caucus and the AAUG when the AAUG cultivated a tentative relationship with Shirley Chisholm in 1972. But the adoption by many Arab American activists of a more moderate, pragmatic position on Israel, corresponding with mainstream black leaders' calls for peaceful coexistence between Palestine and Israel, facilitated the mutual associations between Democratic Party African Americans and Arab American groups by the 1980s.[65]

As Arab Americans were being incorporated into the civil rights organizing framework in a more legitimizing, programmatic way than ever before, some leaders initiated a campaign to gain formal recognition of Arab Americans as a distinct ethnic category in the U.S. Census. In the 1980s, census categories existed for African Americans, American Indians, Alaskan natives, Asians, and Pacific islanders, but people of Arab origin were presumably subsumed in the broad category "non-Hispanic Caucasian."[66] To remedy Arab Americans' invisibility and marginalization in American society and to gain affirmative action benefits accorded to other recognized minority groups, during the mid-1980s these activists lobbied policymakers to assign Arab Americans a protected status as non-Caucasians. While recognizing the assimilating tendencies of earlier generations of Arab Americans, they felt that Arabs' experience in America had been marked more by exclusion and discrimination (even "racism") than by inclusion and tolerance. As a group, activists argued, Arab Americans had more in common with people of color than with white ethnics. But this effort was controversial among Arab Americans, many of whom believed that maintaining a "white" racial categorization was a better strategy for attaining inclusion and acceptance than claiming outsider status. In any case, the federal government shot down the reclassification proposal.[67] In the 1990s, the ADC and the AAI again tried and failed to persuade the federal government to introduce an Arab or Arab American category in the census.[68] However, Arab Americans seeking official minority status did realize a victory in 1987 when the U.S. Supreme Court ruled that ethnic groups considered white—specifically referencing Arabs, Jews, and Hispanics—were protected under existing civil rights legislation.[69]

Despite many Arab Americans' increasing identification as a stigmatized minority group and their organizations' expanding alliances with other minority and oppositional groups, they still encountered considerable rejection by mainstream liberals and protest organizations in the 1980s. Though Jackson embraced Arab Americans, other Democratic Party leaders, such as Walter Mondale, were wary of being associated with them. Jackson's pro-Palestinian stance and incorporation of Arab Americans into his civil rights coalition did become a political liability and caused some white liberals to withdraw their support for him.[70] In other cases, black politicians who even moderately advocated Palestinian rights were charged with anti-Semitism and suffered political consequences. Examples are Grantland Johnson, a Sacramento, California, city councilman, and Faye Williams, a candidate for Congress in Louisiana, who were vilified by Jewish groups for their positions on Middle East issues, and African American politicians, such as Julian Bond in Georgia, who reported being visited and interrogated by Jewish community leaders about their loyalty to Israel. Sizing up the potential for collaboration with the Congressional Black Caucus in 1980, an AAUG leader surmised, "It appears that most members of the Black Caucus have some sympathy for Palestinian rights, but fear sticking their necks out on such a controversial issue when so many other issues are pressing for the Black community and their own political careers."[71] W. Wilson Goode was another African American politician who recognized the damage an association with Arabs or Arab Americans could do to his career. After a local Arab American leader threw a fund-raising event for Goode's candidacy for Philadelphia mayor in 1983, prompting Goode's opponent to question the campaign contribution, Goode returned the money. Other more prominent politicians, including Mondale and Joe Kennedy, returned Arab Americans' donations to their political campaigns after receiving public pressure that implied that such money was somehow tainted by terrorism or anti-Semitism.[72]

Arab American activists were also sometimes frostily received by civil rights and peace group coalitions, as evidenced by the ADC's experience during the twentieth anniversary commemoration of the March on Washington. When the organizers of the 1983 march invited the ADC to participate and included statements about Palestinians' rights in their organizing literature, some Jewish and African American groups threatened to pull out of the march. To mollify these groups, the organizers watered down the statements to merely indicate a desire for peace in the Middle East. The previous year, the ADC had tried to join the Coalition for a New Foreign and Military Policy, described as "the main peace and justice lobby on foreign policy issues," but its membership was blocked by the Union of American Hebrew Congregations and like-minded groups, according to the ADC's Marvin Wingfield. The ADC was allowed to join in 1984, but Wingfield claimed the coalition refused to address Middle East issues. He hoped that the ADC's efforts to "strengthen a network of interconnections between the Arab American community and the communities of activists on other issues" would allow Arab Americans to be as fully represented in as many movements as he said the Jewish community was. "We can begin to establish a presence and have an influence," Wingfield declared, "and perhaps we will come to the point where peace and justice activists will hesitate to support Israeli domination of Palestinians because they 'don't want to offend' their Arab friends. And because their understanding of the Middle East conflict has been shaped through contact with the Arab American community."[73]

In his study of American radicals who advocated Third World revolution, Max Elbaum argues that in the 1980s the American movement for Palestinian independence was "arguably the most vilified peace and solidarity effort in the country." He provides as an example an enormous rally against nuclear arms in New York City in 1982, which took place one week after Israel's invasion of southern Lebanon. Some activists in participating organizations wanted to inject condemnation of Israel's actions, as well as warnings about Israel's nuclear capability, into the nuclear freeze demonstration, but the main organizers barred discussion of the issue from the protest platform. Scholar and activist George Katsiaficas also discusses the exclusion of the Lebanon conflict from this rally, and he concludes that Zionism continued to pervade the Left. (But two years later, the ADC staged a nuclear freeze and anti-intervention rally in Boston that featured Middle East issues among many other social justice and global causes.) Palestinian activists such as Rabab Abdulhadi understood that although they were finding additional allies among liberal-Left groups in America, the support was more limited than other Third World liberation movements, such as those representing Central American peoples, enjoyed.[74]

Arab Americans also experienced friction with the mainstream American feminist movement in the 1980s. Systematic intersections with second-wave feminist organizations had been negligible before the late 1970s. In 1978, activists in the newly formed Women's Caucus of the AAUG recognized the need to connect with the American and international feminist movements in order to further its agenda for Arab and Arab American women's rights. For example, Women's Caucus leader Noha Ismail believed the caucus needed to "link our efforts directly to the [UN-sponsored] International Women's Year" and "integrate some of the goals set by the National Plan of Action which was adopted [at the National Women's Conference] in Houston last year." The following year, Ismail excitedly reported to caucus members that the California Federation of Women's Clubs had invited them to join. She noted, "If we decide to belong, we would be the first Arab American organization to do so," and she encouraged AAUG women to view the invitation as an opportunity for mobilization and outreach. She counseled: "We need to penetrate other women's organizations in the country in order to avoid operating in a vacuum. If we are going to succeed in reaching the American public, we had better concentrate on building bridges." Recognizing that support for the feminist agenda corresponded to its progressive positions on civil liberties and human rights, the AAUG had endorsed the Equal Rights Amendment by the early 1980s.[75]

Nevertheless, many Arab American women were wary of Western second-wave feminism because they felt that the dominant women's organizations and principles not only failed to address their experiences but actually denigrated women of Arab heritage. Some Arab and Arab American feminists and their allies were stunned by the article "Anti-Semitism in the Women's Movement," published in *Ms.* magazine in 1982, about Arab-Israel tensions recently on display at international women's conferences. Author Letty Cottin Pogrebin, a *Ms.* founding editor, opened the piece by announcing her identity as a Jewish feminist. She argued that the PLO had "monopolized" the 1975 women's conference in Mexico City and "drag[ged] Israel through the mud," by popularizing the claim that "Zionism is Racism." She then provided several examples of anti-Semitic slurs she witnessed or was informed about at the women's conference in Copenhagen in 1980. Pogrebin wrote that in most Arab countries, women are disfranchised and treated badly, and she expressed hurt and bafflement that when Arab women were allowed the rare privilege to vote at these conferences, they used their vote to condemn what she considered the one country in the Middle East that empowered women and was a liberal democracy, Israel. She could not believe how many "Third World and Western women . . . sided with the Arabs" at these conferences, even allowing what she called PLO terrorists to be delegates. Asserting that the feminist movement asks Jewish women to "hide their Jewishness," she claimed that the movement had not examined the anti-Semitism within. According to Arab American scholar and feminist Mervat Hatem, several Arab and Arab American women wrote responses to Pogrebin's piece, but *Ms.* declined to acknowledge or print them.[76]

When Azizah Al-Hibri and Carol Haddad attended National Women's Studies Association (NWSA) conferences in the early 1980s, they were dismayed to find that many women in attendance held Orientalist views of Arab women, seeing them as helpless victims and sex slaves of backwardly oppressive regimes and fixating on symbols of oppression, such as the veil and clitoridectomy. Leila Ahmed had similar experiences at academic conferences about women in those years. Ahmed remembers feeling "shocked" at the "combination of hostility and sheer ignorance that the Muslim panelists, myself included, almost invariably encountered. We could not pursue the investigation of our heritage, traditions, and religion in the way that white women were investigating and rethinking theirs." Instead, she felt that "white women, Christian women, and Jewish women" demanded that Arab and Muslim women should abandon their traditions which were deemed hopelessly patriarchal and misogynistic. These Arab American feminists felt that the American women's movement was silencing Arab women, thoughtlessly imposing Western feminist ideas on women in different contexts and producing insensitivity and cultural damage.[77]

At a 1982 NWSA conference held during the Israeli invasion of southern Lebanon, Carol Haddad was part of the NWSA's Third World Caucus that proposed a resolution to denounce the invasion. However, the association effectively rejected the resolution, causing Haddad and other Arab American women to question the American feminist movement's commitment to peace and justice in the Arab world. Despite this disappointment, Haddad found the conference worthwhile because she gave a presentation titled "Arab-Americans: The Forgotten Minority in Feminist Circles" on a panel "featuring some of the most prominent women of color in women's studies circles," she recalls. Her talk contended that the American women's movement was complicit in the same anti-Arab prejudice characteristic of larger American society, and she specifically discussed the Arab-Israeli conflict. Arab women, especially Palestinian women, had been strong and important participants in nationalist movements, Haddad maintained. After pronouncing that "Arab women are lumped together in a single group, and American feminist values are applied without knowledge or regard for the opinions of Arab feminists themselves," she called on American feminists to "seek out and include views of Arab feminists."[78]

Haddad was again disappointed when the feminist journal *off our backs* published a critique of her talk in its summary of the conference. Specifically reacting to Haddad's comments about the irony of Holocaust survivors "participat[ing] in the attempted annihilation of the Palestinian people," *off our backs* editor Jeanne Barkey called Haddad's comparison of the Holocaust with the current Palestinian-Israeli conflict an "appalling distortion which discredited her argument" and declared Haddad's use of the words "annihilation" and "genocide" in her talk "grossly inappropriate." Haddad responded with a letter to the editor demanding an apology and questioning why, of all the conference presentations summarized by *off our backs*, only hers was subjected to editorial comment. She claimed that the journal generally ignored Arab and Arab American women's issues and requested that it print both her entire conference presentation as well as African American poet June Jordan's poem "Apologies to all the People in Lebanon," both of which *off our backs* published in its March 1983 issue, along with the requested apology.[79]

Subsequently, Haddad was motivated to construct a new organization, the Feminist Arab-American Network (FAN), which organized workshops at the next NWSA conference and inserted Arab feminist voices into other events and publications. Due to lack of funding and organizational commitment, FAN was short lived. But by the early 1990s, mainstream feminist groups and publications, including *Ms.*, were more accepting of and sensitive to Arab and Muslim women. Arab American feminists such as Haddad and Hatem also pressed the major Arab American organizations to become more aware of male privilege and the need for gender equality within their groups and communities. More women had taken on leadership positions in the AAUG and the ADC by the early 1990s. As an indication of a growing connection between the feminist and Arab American movements, in 1994 the ADC invited the president of the National Organization for Women, Jill Ireland, to speak at its convention. Nevertheless, many members of the ADC evinced discomfort at Ireland's comments in favor of gay and lesbian rights as well as on abortion and domestic abuse. The relationship, therefore, remained strained.[80]

WHILE A THIRD WORLD liberation stance may have facilitated bonds between the American Left and organizations such as the AAUG in the 1960s and 1970s, it tended to alienate liberals, who were supportive of Israel's existence and uneasy about radical anti-imperialist, pro-guerrilla positions. However, it is doubtful that American liberals would have been supportive of Arab Americans and their advocacy of Palestine even if Arab American activists had toned down their rhetoric and disassociated from the Far Left before the late 1970s. Several other developments had to occur to engender a more favorable reception by mainstream progressives. These included the expanded acceptance of multiculturalism in American society, along with a greater recognition of Arab Americans' place in that patchwork quilt; African Americans' reactions to the economic pain caused by the Arab oil embargo, along with their upset at Andrew Young's resignation and the mounting ties between Israel and South Africa; more pronounced criticism of Israeli aggression as a result of its invasion of Lebanon in 1982 and its persistent expansion of settlements in occupied territories; and the prominent support Arab Americans received from mainstream black leaders, especially Jesse Jackson. Also crucial was the Palestine National Council's growing support of coexistence with Israel. While these external developments were crucial, the increasing tendency of Arab American activists to soft-pedal their revolutionary politics and adopt a more moderate, pragmatic approach to gaining influence in America was also an important factor in opening up a more sympathetic relationship with progressives in the 1980s.

Yet, while Arab Americans continued to make headway among liberals and moved forward in their political mobilization, identity formation, and community solidarity, a growing conservative mood in America lessened the influence of progressive voices, harmed the civil rights agenda, and heightened many Americans' firm backing of Israel and suspicions of Arabs. Terrorist acts, oil embargoes, the Iranian hostage crisis, and conflicts in Lebanon and Libya all fed Americans' negative perceptions of Arabs and Muslims in these years. A 1980 public opinion poll revealed that many Americans held very negative views of Arabs, and particularly of Palestinians, characterizing them as "barbaric, cruel," "treacherous, cunning," "mistreat[ing] women," and "bloodthirsty," whereas respondents tended to associate positive characteristics with Israelis, including "brave," "intelligent," and "competent." The poll showed 72 percent had a "very high" or "fairly high" opinion of Israel, whereas only 34 percent held that opinion of Palestinians.[81] The rise of neoconservatives in the Republican Party, who made unwavering support for Israel a bedrock principle, along with the increasing convergence of Christian evangelicalism and Zionism by the late 1970s, meant that the New Right, represented by the Ronald Reagan administration, vigorously supported Israel's retaliation against its Arab foes. Melani McAlister has shown how Americans' heightened attention to and support for Israel in political and popular culture during the 1970s and 1980s was a way to vicariously combat America's "Vietnam Syndrome" as well as frustrations over the Iranian hostage crisis.[82] Nevertheless, the Republican Party did reach out to an Arab American constituency through the Reagan campaign's Ethnic Voters Division, and the AAI reciprocated by helping to mobilize Arab Republican clubs (along with Arab Democratic clubs). Moreover, at several points during their presidencies, relations between the Reagan and Bush administrations and Israel and its American Jewish supporters proved tense.[83]

The Persian Gulf War in 1991 further exacerbated widespread hostility to Arabs and, by extension, to Arab Americans.[84] At the same time, many Arab American Muslims, corresponding with Muslims around the world, were adopting a more conservative Islamic practice, and in some circles there was a shift from secular nationalism to Islamicism. The increasing emphasis on conservative Islam, both in the Middle East and among Muslims in America, also served to alienate many in the United States from Arab Americans (who were often mistakenly equated with Muslim Americans).[85] Paradoxically, the deteriorating climate coexisted with greater political opportunity and visibility for Arab Americans, a pattern that persisted even after 9-11 in areas such as Detroit that featured a high concentration of Arab Americans.[86] Although some Arab Americans turned inward and exhibited more insularity, and despite internal tensions caused by divisions over positions on Middle East conflicts, the period since the 1980s has seen greater public outreach and political integration by numerous Arab American figures and organizations.

Conclusion

As we approach the third decade of the twenty-first century, the United States continues to wrestle with defining its role in Middle East conflicts and fully accepting and fairly treating Arab and Muslim Americans. In this contentious and often ill-informed climate, it is crucial to appreciate the struggles, priorities, and accomplishments of Arab Americans over the past several decades, both what has set them apart and what has integrated them into the politics and culture of the United States. Arab American organizing in the environment of minority rights movements in the 1960s and 1970s fostered a heightened consciousness of and pride in Arab American identity.[1] This American political-cultural environment coincided with major disruptions in the Middle East, especially the 1967 Arab-Israeli War, and the arrival of increasing numbers of Arab immigrants who possessed an Arab political consciousness critical of Israel, the United States, and conservative Arab regimes. The coalescence of these developments promoted a cross-generational Arab American identity increasingly geared toward political activism.

For Arab American activists on the left, this identity was wrapped up in political positions supporting Palestinian independence, Arab nationalism, and anti-imperialism throughout the Third World. Their commitment to anti-imperialist and antiracist ideology, seen, for example, in the Association of Arab American University Graduates (AAUG), along with the use of militant rhetoric and activist tactics by organizations such as the Arab Workers Caucus and the Organization of Arab Students (OAS), marked their participation in the American New Left and Third World Left of this period. This book reveals the existence of multiple forms of Arab American organizing in that period and also shows that their activism was not as isolated from the American political experience as conventionally thought. Their activist escalation in the years after the 1967 Arab-Israeli War built upon previous periods of Arab American political consciousness—also now being uncovered and studied in a new light—and has continued to expand and evolve into the twenty-first century.[2]

ALTHOUGH INCORPORATED INTO aspects of the American political experience, Arab American activism was distinguished by its transnationalism, evident in the way that activists' political concerns and actions crossed borders and "link[ed] together their country of origin and their country of settlement."[3] Its close connection with geopolitics in the Middle East was a function both of many Arab Americans' continuing cultural and political allegiances to their homelands and, because of many Americans' tendency to associate them with foreign Arab (and sometimes Iranian) "enemies," of their need to constantly explain their relationships with and perspectives on the Middle East. In surveying the field of Arab American studies, Theodore Pulcini remarks, "One must remember that the voice of Arab Americans is muffled or magnified as a result of political developments in the Middle East. Perhaps no other American ethnic group is so affected by political and military events abroad."[4] These events both galvanized and undercut Arab American organizing, often bringing activists from diverse generations, nations, and religions together to promote Arab world justice or Arab American rights, while frequently dividing them over their opposing positions on issues such as the Lebanese Civil War, the Gulf War, and the Oslo Accords.[5] These disagreements have continued to erupt over conflicts such as the Iraq War, the Arab Spring, and the Syrian Civil War.

Furthermore, the overseas orientation of most Arab American activists in the 1960s and 1970s sometimes created tension with those who wanted more emphasis placed on Arab Americans' experiences in American society and politics. Activists who pressed for an "over here" orientation often criticized organizations such as the AAUG for being too insular and detached from American political culture and thus unable to exert meaningful influence on American attitudes and policy.[6] As more Arab American voices raised this contention over time, organizations such as the American-Arab Anti-Discrimination Committee and the Arab American Institute arose in the 1980s to concentrate on the domestic arena and pursue integration in American mainstream and electoral politics.

Although this divergence between Arab Americans focused on the Arab homeland and those more firmly situated in the American environment certainly existed, it has tended to obscure important links between them. Many of the influential activists from this period, for example, Abdeen Jabara, operated along a continuum between these orientations, suggesting that the depiction of such organizations as the AAUG and OAS as entirely dominated by foreign-born Arabs or as completely absorbed with Arab issues and aloof from the American environment requires reevaluation.

True, when compared with the skillful political organizing and integration into the American arena realized by American Zionist organizations (which were the groups that Arab Americans were most often compared to, and compared themselves to), Arab Americans' inroads into American political culture fell short, and they often appeared out of touch. Nevertheless, many Arab American activists in the 1960s and 1970s were making inroads with Americans in one arena: activists in other leftist, oppositional movements. These Arab Americans understood that a coalition strategy in America, even if limited and halting, was important to advancing their causes. Furthermore, the AAUG tried to engage with American policymakers as well as promote their positions in American mainstream discourse, such as advertisements, editorials, and letters to the editor in major media outlets.

The AAUG constituted the most significant Arab American organization in the decade after the 1967 Arab-Israeli War, and its most important legacy remains its emphasis on education with respect to Palestinian rights. The organization's leftist orientation and its pursuit of support from other minority rights and anti-imperialist movements demonstrate the importance of connections between the American Left and Arab American activism in this period. Michael Suleiman has observed that like earlier Arab American organizations, the AAUG was founded out of trauma resulting from an Arab world crisis, and the association followed a trajectory of decline similar to those earlier organizations, caused by divisive events overseas, American policies supporting Israel, and structural weaknesses.[7] Although some of these difficulties were arguably unique to Arab American organizing, it is worth noting that the overall course mirrored that of many other American activist organizations that also experienced debilitating factionalism and flamed out by the late 1970s. For example, the Students for a Democratic Society, which imploded in 1969, was consumed by infighting and was criticized for becoming increasingly insular and disconnected from American progressive views.[8] Plenty of other examples from the black freedom, peace, and feminist movements, among others, could be offered here—and yet these movements adjusted, carried on, and, like the fledgling Arab American movement of the 1960s and 1970s, continue their activism and influence through today. Thus, both the AAUG's anti-imperialist ideology and its internal and structural weaknesses can be seen as factors that brought the association closer to at least one segment of the American political experience, rather than setting it apart.

The even more radical Organization of Arab Students, confined as it was to college campuses and claiming a mostly foreign student membership, was further removed from American political culture than the AAUG. Yet the OAS operated within the milieu of American student radical groups in the 1960s and 1970s, and many of its chapters cultivated alliances with non-Arab organizations, especially those ensconced in the Third World Left. Also spreading the pro-Palestinian cause through consciousness-raising were many Arab American activists in southeast Michigan, principally those involved in the protests against the United Auto Workers and active in the ensuing Arab Workers Caucus, who reached out to non-Arab constituencies for support.

These politically conscious Arab Americans portrayed the Palestinian and other Arab nationalist issues in the language and ideology of the broader New Left, emphasizing anti-imperialism, Third World liberation, and self-determination, as well as the romance of the guerrilla revolutionary. Also drawing them together, many Arab Americans suffered from ethnoracial discrimination and violations of civil liberties similar to the persecution other leftists and minorities were experiencing in the late 1960s to the early 1970s. Simultaneously, a small number of non-Arabs politicized on the Palestinian question became active in the 1970s and founded organizations such as the Palestine Solidarity Committee to advocate for the recognition of Palestinian rights by other American New Left and minority groups.

THE 1967 ARAB-ISRAELI WAR, the resulting Israeli occupation of more Arab territories, and the intensification of the Palestinian refugee crisis were momentous global events, and they occurred precisely when the New Left was moving into a more radical phase characterized by Third World consciousness. As I have demonstrated, Arab American organizing to promote Palestinian rights garnered some support from other American leftist and antiracist movements, and coalitions that included Palestine as part of a broader Third World anti-imperialist agenda materialized. The coalitions usually proved loose and fleeting and rarely produced meaningful results or concrete agendas for change. But a similar dynamic commonly existed in partnerships among other activist communities in this period. Indeed, appraisals of African American–Mexican American coalitions, for example, tend to focus more on disappointments and missed opportunities than on accomplishments.[9] Nonetheless, recognition of intersections among various minority groups seeking local, national, and global change has become an increasing feature of civil rights and activist scholarship, and Arab Americans' history of activism in those years should be included in this narrative.

However, I do not want to overestimate the importance of Arab American activists to leftist movements and Third World coalitions. Palestine and other

Arab American causes never became a focal point of the American New Left, and attention to these issues or acknowledgment of Arab American organizations was seldom included in discourse about American oppositional movements of the 1960s–70s, either at the time or in retrospective studies. Contemporary discussion of the intersections occurred in Arab American organizations and a few publications, such as the *Journal of Palestine Studies* and *MERIP Reports*, that regularly examined the nexus between Arab American/Palestinian activism and other American movements. Black nationalists also visibly incorporated Palestine and Arab nationalism into their political imaginings. But most organizations and publications lacking a specific Arab American connection rarely considered Palestinian or Arab nationalism or recognized the existence of Arab Americans.[10]

The near absence of Arab Americans and their political issues from historical literature on American political activism in the 1960s and 1970s, even literature that closely analyzes minority groups and leftist causes, can in part be attributed to the marginal demographic position of this ethnic group. In his preface to a 1969 AAUG book about Arab American communities, Ibrahim Abu-Lughod observed, "The relatively small number of Arab immigrants to the U.S. and Canada and the dispersion of these peoples across the expanse of the continent together with their tendency to acculturate rapidly and assimilate to the American environment may be important factors accounting for the paucity of hard data and studies on the Arab-American community."[11] In the decade after Abu-Lughod wrote those words, Arab Americans' numbers and visibility grew and their purported assimilative tendencies receded, and yet there was still a palpable reticence among non-Arab scholars to include them in their studies or to acknowledge their political causes, especially Palestine, as part of the discourse on civil and human rights activism increasingly prominent in the 1970s.

The silence has also stemmed from many scholars' and activists' discomfort with, if not outright opposition to, the pro-Palestinian position, as well as widespread American antipathy toward Arabs that has impinged on sections of the academic and activist communities. In the late 1960s–early 1970s, this prejudice against Arabs and the Palestinian cause may have heightened in reaction to Sirhan Sirhan's assassination of Robert F. Kennedy, along with other acts of violence associated with Palestinian solidarity. Attention to Arab Americans and their political perspectives is sometimes unfairly construed as anti-Semitic, and this charge can dampen the willingness of scholars and activists to engage with the subject. The strong support for Zionism found in American progressive circles generally prevented the critical perspective of Arab American activists on the Israeli-Palestinian conflict from making much headway in American social movements, academia, and mainstream politics before the 1990s and constituted a major reason why Arab American activists and institutions were marginalized.[12]

YET OVER THE COURSE of the 1980s Arab American organizing began to have an impact outside of the Left. This occurred both because organizers built upon the activism of previous decades and because they diverged from earlier ideologies and strategies to claim a more moderate ground aimed at greater integration into the American political arena. Even as Arab American activists maintained their passionate advocacy of Palestinian rights, many of them increasingly avoided messages implying support for nationalist revolution or violent struggle, and some conveyed support for compromise with Israel. Further, some Arab American leaders, including James Abourezk, James Zogby, and Abdeen Jabara, gave more concerted focus to influencing mainstream political leaders and parties and participating in the American political process. As Helen Hatab Samhan observes, this integration involved more compromise on the part of Arab American activists, necessitating the capacity both to close the gap between ideology and expectations and to make more modest demands of potential political allies. This developing political pragmatism marked Arab Americans' growing transition from "protesters" to "participants."[13]

These efforts were especially effective in gaining support from moderate African American leaders as well as from other elements of the Democratic Party, and pockets of support were also emerging in the Republican Party. Arab American organizations, principally the American-Arab Anti-Discrimination Committee, assertively contested biased media depictions of Arabs and Arab Americans, and mainstream media coverage exhibited greater balance through the 1980s and 1990s than in previous decades. Moreover, Arab American perspectives began to see more inclusion in feminist, race, and ethnic studies scholarship, as well as Middle East studies, in these years as an "epistemic shift in university knowledge production" exhibited an embrace of activist scholarship that embodied the liberation of previously voiceless and dehumanized peoples.[14]

Arab American leftist activism during the heyday of the New Left and civil rights movements laid the groundwork for the growing—though still contentious and incomplete—visibility and influence of Arab Americans and their political causes by the beginning of the twenty-first century. The Arab American Left followed a trajectory similar to other American leftist movements in the late 1960s and 1970s, many of which adopted increasingly radical ideology and militant rhetoric, participated in a tenuous "Third World" alliance with one another, changed some minds, alienated many other Americans, suffered from factionalism and insularity, and eventually fizzled out (or, in some cases, crashed and burned). Examinations of oppositional movements of that era tend to emphasize mixed legacies of success and failure, diagnoses of external obstacles and internal deficiencies, and recognition of unfulfilled agendas, themes that also apply to Arab American organizing. Some leftists, including some Arab American activists, carried on by moderating their political style and accommodating to the mainstream.

In the early twenty-first century, Arab American activists have often faced an uphill battle as Americans' fear and hatred of Arabs and Muslims has heightened after 11 September 2001, and again after the San Bernardino attack in 2015 and the continuing Syrian refugee crisis. Relations of the United States with various Arab states have deteriorated and in some cases led to war, and relations between Israel and Palestine remain very contentious. At the same time, the activist seeds planted in the 1960s and 1970s have begun to bear fruit, especially in pursuing coalitions with American peace and civil rights groups that were set in motion a generation earlier. Along with the ongoing political mobilization generated by the American-Arab Anti-Discrimination Committee, the Arab American Institute, the Arab American Action Network, and many other Arab American and Islamic American national, regional, and local organizations, today we see new momentum in the US Campaign to End the Israeli Occupation, a solidarity organization composed of dozens of peace and anticolonial groups. The campaign strongly supports African American rights and has recently provided backing for the Black Lives Matter movement and invited comparisons between Ferguson, Missouri, and Gaza.[15] Similarly, Students for Justice in Palestine, founded at the University of California-Berkeley in 1993 and now sustaining chapters at around eighty universities, devotes itself to solidarity work predominantly focused on supporting the Boycott Divestment and Sanctions (BDS) campaign. As the first university student council to pass a resolution supporting Israeli divestment in 2003, pro-Palestine students at Wayne State University in Detroit have continued to be leaders in this activism.[16] Formally founded in Palestine in 2005, BDS builds upon a long history of boycott and divestment appeals, for example, the Arab American call for the United Auto Workers to divest its Israeli bonds back in the early 1970s, and aims to isolate and condemn Israel for its persistent occupation and settlement practices. In the United States, the BDS movement has especially gained ground within academia, maintaining the earlier pattern of the university as a critical site of Arab American and Palestinian organizing. While this movement has garnered significant sympathy from ethnic and racial studies programs, it has also continued to isolate Arab American activists and scholars who have been harassed and mistreated for their outspokenness on this issue.[17] As Arab Americans grow in visibility and the Palestinian movement expands, these continuities with a prior period of activism demonstrate the importance of uncovering and understanding the history of Arab Americans' experiences in the context of American movements for equality and justice.

NOTES

Abbreviations

AAUG	Association of Arab American University Graduates
AAUGP	Association of Arab American University Graduates Papers, Special Collections Library, Eastern Michigan University
AJP	Abdeen Jabara Papers, Bentley Historical Library, University of Michigan
AN	*AAUG Newsletter*
ASAR	Arab Student Association Records 1968–1974, Social Protest Collection, Bancroft Library, University of California–Berkeley
BAP	Barbara Aswad Papers, Bentley Historical Library, University of Michigan
BHL	Bentley Historical Library, University of Michigan
FSP	Fayez Sayegh Papers, Marriott Library, University of Utah
HAP	Helen Atwell Papers, Bentley Historical Library, University of Michigan
IACR	Israeli-Arab Conflict Records 1969–1973, Social Protest Collection, Bancroft Library, University of California–Berkeley
IMJCP	Imam Mohamad Jawad Chirri Papers, Bentley Historical Library, University of Michigan
JTP	Janice Terry Papers, Bentley Historical Library, University of Michigan
LAT	*Los Angeles Times*
NAP	Nabeel Abraham Papers, Bentley Historical Library, University of Michigan
NPL	Nixon Presidential Library
NYT	*New York Times*
OAS	Organization of Arab Students in the United States and Canada
PAAA	Pamphlets about Arab-American Associations, Michigan State University Library
RL	Walter P. Reuther Library, Wayne State University
SCL-UM	Special Collections Library, University of Michigan
SE	*South End*, Wayne State University
SPC	Social Protest Collection, Bancroft Library, University of California–Berkeley
WP	*Washington Post*
WSP	Wystan Stevens Papers, Bentley Historical Library, University of Michigan

Introduction

1. "Is the UAW Leadership Acting in the Interests of Its Members?," *Detroit Free Press*, n.d., in AJP, box 13, folder UAW Arab Workers Caucus Press Clippings, 1973.

2. Suleiman, "The Arab American Left"; also see Naber, *Arab America*, 43–44, 49.

3. Bawardi, *The Making of Arab Americans*.

4. It is difficult to determine how many people of Arab heritage lived in the United States in the 1960s and 1970s. The largest concentration (about 70,000) resided in the Detroit metro area, and other large communities were located in New York, Chicago, and Los Angeles. See Suleiman, "A History of Arab-American Political Participation," 16–17, and Aswad, "The Southeast

Dearborn Arab Community," 53. On the difficulty of determining the Arab American population, see Schopmeyer, "A Demographic Portrait of Arab Detroit."

5. I recognize that a few Arab American organizations in that period, primarily the National Association of Arab Americans, practiced a more traditional form of interest group politics.

6. Haddad, "Inventing and Re-inventing the Arab American Identity,"117–18.

7. Suleiman, "A History of Arab-American Political Participation," 6.

8. Although the extent of ethnic cleansing of Arab populations during the 1948 war remains in dispute, work by the so-called New Historians has demonstrated definitively that it did occur. See an overview of the New Historians in Shlaim, "The War of the Israeli Historians," and Sa'di, "Afterword: Reflections on Representation."

9. Judis, "Zionist Movement."

10. Naber, *Arab America*, 36–37. Suleiman, *The Arabs in the Mind of America*, features analysis of American media coverage and public opinion polls about the Arab-Israeli conflict in the 1940s–1970s and finds significant bias against Arabs and Palestinians and for Israelis. See also Stockton, "Ethnic Archetypes"; Little, *American Orientalism*, 24–41; Judis, *Genesis*; Abu-Lughod and Sa'di, "Introduction: The Claims of Memory"; and McAlister, *Epic Encounters*, 33, 158–85. Christian evangelicals were particularly attracted to Zionism for its millennialist implications. See Shalom Goldman, *Zeal for Zion*.

11. Chamberlin, *The Global Offensive*, 40–42, 258. On the Third World Left in the 1960s and 1970s, see Young, *Soul Power*; Kelley and Esch, "Black Like Mao"; Elbaum, *Revolution in the Air*; Dirlik, "The Third World"; and Rodríguez-Morazzani, "Political Cultures of the Puerto Rican Left."

12. David, "The Creation of 'Arab American,'" 845. For an instructive discussion of the evolving theories on citizenship, see Baker and Shryock, "Citizenship and Crisis," 7–12. Werbner, "Introduction: The Materiality of Diaspora," and Thomas, *Puerto Rican Citizen*, inform my discussion of migrants' diasporic politics.

13. Behnken, "Introduction"; Smith, *Hippies*; Pulido, *Black, Brown*; Mantler, *Power to the Poor*; Williams, *From the Bullet to the Ballot*; Ho and Mullen, *Afro Asia*; Brilliant, *The Color of America*; Lee, *Building a Latino Civil Rights Movement*.

14. Omi and Winant, *Racial Formation in the United States*; HoSang, LaBennett, and Pulido, *Racial Formation in the Twenty-First Century*.

15. Abdulhadi, "Activism and Exile," 239.

16. Gualtieri, *Between Arab and White*, 165–66; Shryock and Lin, "Arab American Identities," 52–57.

17. Suleiman, "A History of Arab-American Political Participation," 4; Terry, "Community and Political Activism," 243.

18. Dawisha, *Arab Nationalism*, 278. Some Muslim Arab Americans and their organizations were also politically active on behalf of Palestine in this era. For example, see the stance of the Federation of Islamic Associations on Palestine in its publication *Muslim Star* in the early 1970s, located in IMJCP, box 8, subseries Zehia Kahil, folder Muslim Star. Also see Howell, *Old Islam in Detroit*, 188, 204–5.

19. Pulido, *Black, Brown*, 56–58. See discussion of "core members" in diasporic politics in Shain and Barth, "Diasporas," 452–53. Gary David argues that this activist element and its formation of an Arab American identity fused with positions favoring Arab and Palestinian nationalism could be exclusionary and alienating to other Arab Americans who did not share these politics. David, "The Creation of 'Arab American,'" 845–46, 850.

20. Abraham, "The Yemeni Immigrant Community"; Friedlander, *Sojourners and Settlers*.

21. Elkholy, "The Arab-Americans," 5.

22. I am influenced by Matthew Shannon's study of Iranian students at American and

European universities in the 1960s, in which he emphasizes the students' collaboration with New Left groups in their host countries and views them as pivotal actors in cultivating "New Left internationalism." Shannon, "'Contacts with the Opposition.'"

23. Naff, *Becoming American*; Orfalea, *Before the Flames*, 141; Suleiman, "Arab-Americans and the Political Process," 42–45. Such studies argued that most of the first-wavers maintained a private identity attached to their homeland, but even then it was parochial and attuned to their specific nation, village, or sect of origin, not a consciousness of Arab-ness. Their organizations, according to the prevailing conception, were social in nature, not political.

24. Davidson, "Debating Palestine"; Bawardi, *The Making of Arab Americans*.

25. Gualtieri, *Between Arab and White*, 14. Also see McAlister, *Epic Encounters*, 38.

26. Cainkar, "Palestinian Women in the United States," 103–5.

27. Shakir, *Bint Arab*, 126. Also see Suleiman, "Arab-Americans and the Political Process," 46; Abu-Laban, "The Coexistence of Cohorts," 53; Cainkar, "Palestinian Women in American Society," 92; Abraham, "Arabs in America," 18–19.

28. Gualtieri, *Between Arab and White*, 162, 169.

29. Abdulhadi, "Activism and Exile"; Orfalea, *The Arab Americans*, 189–90; Abu-Laban, "The Coexistence of Cohorts," 55–56; Cainkar, "Palestinian Women in the United States," 106; Abraham, "Arabs in America," 19.

30. Suleiman, "Arab-Americans and the Political Process," 46–47; Shakir, *Bint Arab*, 96; Christison, "On Being Palestinian," 106–7; Ahmed, interview with author.

31. Shakir, *Bint Arab*, 85. Also see Suleiman and Abu-Laban, "Introduction," 4; Aswad, "Introduction and Overview," 1–2; and David, "The Creation of 'Arab American,'" 846.

32. Abraham, "Arab-American Marginality"; also see Suleiman, "The Arab American Left," 247.

33. Suleiman and Abu-Laban, "Introduction," 5; Said, *Orientalism*; Stockton, "Ethnic Archetypes"; Suleiman, *The Arabs in the Mind of America*; Ghareeb, *Split Vision*; Shaheen, "ABSCAM"; Joseph, "Against the Grain."

34. McAlister, *Epic Encounters*, 38–39.

35. Kayyali, *The Arab Americans*, 105; Suleiman, "A History of Arab-American Political Participation," 5; Gualtieri, *Between Arab and White*, 17. Yvonne Haddad has pointed out that their claiming of an Arab American identity was a double-edged sword because while it made them more visible targets of Arabophobic animosity, it also gave them "security," a feeling of "belonging," and a "common sense of pride." See Haddad, "Maintaining the Faith of the Fathers," 79–80.

36. Cainkar, "Immigrants," 183.

37. Shryock, "The Moral Analogies of Race," 102. On racial identity formation, see Lee, *Building a Latino Civil Rights Movement*, 4–9.

38. Naber, "Introduction"; Samhan, "Not Quite White"; Samhan, "Politics and Exclusion"; Salaita, *Anti-Arab Racism*, 13; Abraham, "Anti-Arab Racism," 179–80; Hatem, "Political and Cultural Representations of Arabs," 20.

39. Cainkar, "Thinking Outside the Box," 47–49.

40. Salaita, *Anti-Arab Racism*, 77.

41. Liu, Geron, and Lai, *The Snake Dance*, xv, 30; Pulido, *Black, Brown*, 107, 136.

42. Pulido, *Black, Brown*, 47, 173. On Puerto Ricans' and other Latinos' campaigns against urban renewal plans that would destroy their neighborhoods, see Glasser, "From 'Rich Port' to Bridgeport"; Rodríguez, "Saving the *Parcela*"; and Fernández, "The Young Lords." These studies also discuss the Puerto Rican activists' establishment of community centers to augment their community organizing. On community centers founded by Asian American activists in this period, see Liu, Geron, and Lai, *The Snake Dance*, 4, 69. Liu examines Asian American activists who "formed anti-imperialist organizations that combined disseminating political analysis with essential services to establish contact with their communities" (4).

43. Liu, Geron, and Lai, *The Snake Dance*, xvi, 68. Leaders of the Puerto Rican Socialist Party in the United States prioritized independence for the island and believed that organizing Puerto Ricans residing in the United States would be the decisive strategy. But newer, grassroots members of the party wanted to place more focus on the rights of Puerto Ricans on the American mainland, in what they called a "dual priority" strategy. This debate during the 1970s about priorities in the diaspora caused ongoing tension in the organization, similar to tensions manifest in some Arab American organizations of the era. In contrast, the Puerto Rican activist group the Young Lords, while also closely linked to the struggle for island independence, emphasized revolutionary struggle on the mainland. See Torres, "Introduction," and Velázquez, "Coming Full Circle." In *Puerto Rican Citizen*, Lorrin Thomas provides more historical background on Puerto Ricans' dual engagement with island and mainland politics, demonstrating that Puerto Ricans living in New York City throughout the twentieth century were deeply attentive to "everyday concerns of working people as well as autonomy for Puerto Rico" (39). He also discusses Americans' cultural and political prejudice against Puerto Ricans living in America, attitudes that were exacerbated by the violent actions of Puerto Rican extremists living in New York City, including an assassination attempt on President Harry Truman. As with Arab Americans, Puerto Rican Americans' activism was undertaken against a backdrop of "terrorism." On the militant Puerto Rican liberation group Fuerzas Armadas de Liberación Nacional (FALN) and the series of bombings it perpetrated in the United States in the 1970s, see Starr, "Hit Them Harder."

44. Pulido, *Black, Brown*, 125–28, 170–71.

45. Mantler, *Power to the Poor*, 4; Smith, *Hippies*, 11; Pulido, *Black, Brown*, 56–58; Whitaker, "Great Expectations," 89–94; Foley, *Quest for Equality*; Behnken, "The Movement in the Mirror"; Fernández, "The Young Lords," 81.

46. Smith, *Hippies*, 6, 13.

47. Fernández, "Denise Oliver," 272; Ramos, "Not Similar Enough," 38; Pulido, *Black, Brown*, 33. Also see Fujino, "The Black Liberation Movement"; Fujino, "Grassroots Leadership"; Starr, "Hit Them Harder"; Williams, *From the Bullet to the Ballot*; Kochiyama, "A Quick Reflection"; Springer, *Living for the Revolution*; and Thomas, *Puerto Rican Citizen*, 222–38. Thomas points out that the African American and Puerto Rican communities in New York City harbored considerable hostility toward each other, yet "at the level of radical activism, ties between African American and Puerto Rican youth were stronger than they had ever been by 1970" (234). In fact, many young Puerto Rican activists were so inspired by black nationalism that they came to perceive themselves as similarly "black."

48. Smith, *Hippies*, 15; Pulido, *Black, Brown*, 156.

49. Young, *Soul Power*, 2. Katsiaficas, *The Imagination of the New Left*, is a rare example of a study that incorporates the Palestinian resistance movement into its analysis of the late-1960s global left. Brick and Phelps, in *Radicals in America*, 239, also incorporate a brief discussion of how the Arab-Israeli conflict split the American Left, a topic I explore in chapter 3.

50. Near the beginning of her study, Pulido, *Black, Brown*, includes population data for each ethnic group in Los Angeles in 1970 and lists the following groups in descending order: White, Hispanic, African American, Asian American, Middle Eastern, American Indian, and other. She discusses American Indians in Los Angeles and explains why she did not select them as a focus for one of the book's case studies, but she does not include a similar discussion of "Middle Easterners" and why they are not a part of the book's analysis, even though her data demonstrates that more "Middle Easterners" lived in Los Angeles than American Indians. Pulido does, however, once mention Arab Americans in passing when listing "smaller groups," including Filipinos and Vietnamese, inspired by Black Power (5, 42, 91).

51. Young, "American Blacks"; Newby, "Afro-Americans and Arabs"; McAlister, *Epic Encounters*; Feldman, "Representing Permanent War"; Daulatzai, *Black Star*; Meghelli, "From Harlem to Algiers"; Lubin, *Geographies of Liberation*.

52. Saliba, "Resisting Invisibility," 307–8; Shohat and Alsultany, "Cultural Politics," 21–22.

53. Aswad, "The Southeast Dearborn Arab Community"; Terry, "Community and Political Activism," 241–43; Abraham, "A Survey of the Arab-American Community"; Shryock and Abraham, "On Margins and Mainstreams"; Rignall, "Arab American Identity in Detroit"; Stiffler and Rignall, "'You Are Our Homeland.'"

Chapter 1

1. Bawardi, *The Making of Arab Americans*; Davidson, "Debating Palestine"; Suleiman, "Arab-Americans and the Political Process," 45; Gualtieri, *Between Arab and White*, 165–66; Beverly, "Shaking Off the Sheikh," 14, 17; Hussaini, "The Impact of the Arab-Israeli Conflict," 205.

2. Beverly, "Shaking Off the Sheikh," 14; Naber, *Arab America*, 43.

3. Smith, *Palestine*, 281–90; Tessler, *A History of the Israeli-Palestinian Conflict*, 381–97.

4. Farsoun and Aruri, *Palestine and the Palestinians*, 177, 180–81.

5. The PLO was founded by the League of Arab States in 1964 in an effort to co-opt the Palestinian resistance. The Arab League sponsors of the PLO viewed Palestinian nationalism as a constituent of the broader movement for Arab nationalism, whereas Fatah resisted the subordination of Palestinian nationalism to the pan-Arab cause and to the direction of the Arab League. Fatah gained particular prestige as a result of the 1968 Battle of Karameh in which PLO forces, with Fatah fighters at the forefront, along with the Jordanian military, inflicted heavy losses on Israeli forces that were trying to destroy a Fatah base in Jordan. See Smith, *Palestine*, 372–74; Tessler, *A History of the Israeli-Palestinian Conflict*, 374–75, 425–26; and Dawisha, *Arab Nationalism*, 258. On the formation of other fedayeen factions, chiefly the Marxist Popular Front for the Liberation of Palestine and the Democratic Front for the Liberation of Palestine, see Farsoun and Aruri, *Palestine and the Palestinians*, 182–97, and Chamberlin, *The Global Offensive*, 72, 117.

6. The PLO's increasing strength and influence proved threatening to the Jordanian government, led by King Hussein. In what is called "Black September" by Palestinians and their supporters, in September 1970 the Jordanian military attacked PLO forces based in Jordan. At the conclusion of the ten-month war, the Jordanian government expelled the PLO from its country. Shortly after, the PLO moved its headquarters to Lebanon, and eventually its presence produced tension there as well and was one contributor to the long Lebanese Civil War. See Farsoun and Aruri, *Palestine and the Palestinians*, 187; Chamberlin, *The Global Offensive*, 121; and Dawisha, *Arab Nationalism*, 270.

7. AAUG, *The First Decade*, 3; Aruri, "AAUG," 35; Bashshur, "Unfulfilled Expectations," 8; Hussaini, "The Impact of the Arab-Israeli Conflict," 207.

8. After deliberation, the AAUG soon created an affiliate membership category for non-Arabs. See Board Meeting Minutes, Dec. 1967, in AAUGP, box 23, folder Board Meeting Minutes, 1967; Board Meeting Minutes, 22 Sept. 1968, AAUGP, box 23, folder Board Meeting Minutes, 1968.

9. Mattson, *Intellectuals in Action*, 9–10.

10. Mattson, "Between Despair and Hope," 40.

11. "Resolutions," in AAUG, *The First Decade*, 49.

12. Talhami, "A Cultural, Not a Political Lobby," 129.

13. Shain, "Arab Americans," 52; Hagopian, "Minority Rights," 110–11; Jabara, interview with Terry, JTP, box 1; Peter Tanous, President of NAAA, to Friends, 29 May 1973, AJP, box 12, folder Activities–National Association of Arab Americans–Correspondence; "NAAA Today–Two Years

of Growth and Accomplishment," pamphlet, n.d., in PAAA; Khoury, "The Arab Lobby." Also see the packet of notes from several meetings held in the period October 1971 to April 1972 to discuss formation of the NAAA, in AAUGP, box 43, folder NAAA.

14. Orfalea, *The Arab Americans*, 218–19.

15. Tuma, "The Palestinians in America"; Abdulhadi, "Activism and Exile," 234–37. In the nondated "Survey of Arab American Political Opinions" (likely written between 1984 and 1986), James Zogby noted that the American Federation of Ramallah, Palestine, constituted "the largest and most active grouping of Palestinians in the U.S." In BAP, box 1, folder Clippings–Discrimination, 1977–1986.

16. Hussaini, "The Impact of the Arab-Israeli Conflict," 211; Wigle and Abraham, "Arab Nationalism," 295–96; Khoury, interview with author.

17. Hussaini, "The Impact of the Arab-Israeli Conflict," 211. Also in this period, the PLO-sponsored Institute for Palestine Studies started the *Journal of Palestine Studies* with its publication based in American universities. Like the AAUG, it was aimed at a more academic audience, but it served as another expression of political support in the United States for the Palestinian cause. According to Tuma, "The Palestinians in America," the journal has been "the most effective . . . periodical in English on the Palestinian problem," and it "has filled a big information gap relating to the Palestinian cause."

18. Initiated in 1968, *Free Palestine* was published in London, England, and edited by Aziz M. Yafi. In the middle of 1969 the paper moved to Washington, D.C., with Jabara as its editor. Its May 1971 issue contained the following note: "The editors thought it appropriate to restate the paper's policy and re-express the function we hope it has served in the U.S. *Free Palestine* was conceived and actualized by a handful of supporters of the Palestinian revolution who are, by no means, partisans of any of the Palestine commando organizations. The paper is definitely not an official organ of any organization anywhere, nor is it published in the interests of any foreign entity." It published monthly issues until April 1972, then revived in 1976 with an unnamed editor, and its duration is unclear.

19. Hussaini, "The Impact of the Arab-Israeli Conflict," 209; David G. Nes, "Report on Visit to Texas, Arizona, California, and Colorado," 2–16 Nov. 1970, in FSP, http://content.lib.utah.edu/cdm/ref/collection/uu-fasc/id/961 (accessed 11 June 2013). Examples of other Palestinian aid organizations established in the late 1960s and 1970s were Najda, Project Riayat, Palestine Aid Society, and Pal-Aid International. The United States Organization for Medical and Educational Needs (US-OMEN), based in California, was founded earlier in the 1960s, but after 1967 its focus became provision of aid to Palestinians. Arab Americans also were involved in the Palestine Red Crescent Society, a humanitarian aid organization based in the Arab world.

20. Abdulhadi, "Activism and Exile," 237; Naber, *Arab America*, 50.

21. Hussaini, "The Impact of the Arab-Israeli Conflict," 213; Kayyali, *The Arab Americans*, 112; "Midwest Federation Calls for Recognition of Palestine Liberation Organization," AN, Sept. 1974; "Crusade to Save America Urged: Award Recipient Maria Challenges Arab Americans," press release, in AJP, box 12, folder Activities–NAAA–Membership Guidelines Binder; Garrett and Purpura, *Frank Maria*, 396–97. The federation's call for recognition of the PLO coincided with the UN General Assembly's decision that year to recognize the PLO as the representative organization for Palestinians and to grant the PLO nonstate observer status. For more on Frank Maria's political work, see ibid., 280–86, 515, 571.

22. "Metropolitan Shaheen Gives $5000 to Help Refugees," *Heritage*, 7 June 1968; "Antiochians Call for Recognition of PLO," AN, Sept. 1974; Garrett and Purpura, *Frank Maria*, 386–87. During the Lebanese Civil War in the early 1980s, Maronite Christians, who generally had been nonpolitical, formed the American Lebanese League to urge American support for Maronite interests and against the PLO and Syria. See Haddad, "Maintaining the Faith," 81.

23. Howell, *Old Islam in Detroit*, 155, 158–60, 188; Abdo Elkholy, *The Arab Moslems*, 48–49; "Resolution of Federation on Palestine Not Political but Humanitarian Stand," *FIA Journal*, July–Sept. 1965, in Aliya Hassen Papers, box 1, folder Federation of Islamic Associations–F.I.A. Journals 1965.

24. Also in the early 1970s, the FIA initiated a project aimed at refuting the American media's distorted stereotypes of Muslims. In the *Muslim Star*, see the following articles: "FIA Established Office to Refuse Ignorance or Bias on Islam," May 1971; "The Arabs and Israel: Vietnam in Reverse," and "U.S. to Resume Delivery of Phantom Jets to Israel," Feb. 1972; "Protest in New York Times Sponsored Jointly by FIA," and M. Cherif Bassiouni, "The Arab-Americans: Future Political Force," Aug. 1972; reprint of ad in *NYT*, "Is the Nixon Administration Playing Politics with Civil Liberties?" Oct. 1972, all found in IMJCP, box 8, subseries Zehia Kahil, folder *Muslim Star*. Another Muslim periodical, the newspaper *Al-Islaah* [The Reform], published in New York City, also began to run overtly political articles in the early 1970s. For example, see John Thomas Church, "The Bankruptcy of Zionism," 31 Mar. 1971, and Dan Borman, "Zionism Attempts Control of U.S. Policy," 21 Apr. 1971.

25. Bulletin of the Islamic Center, Aug. 1974, in IMJCP, box 9, folder Bulletin of the Islamic Center in Washington, D.C.

26. Haddad, "Maintaining the Faith," 75–76.

27. AAUG, *The First Decade*, 5–6. The initial meeting at which the AAUG was conceived occurred at Rashid Bashshur's home in Ann Arbor.

28. Abu-Lughod, Presidential Statement, AAUG Convention, 5 Dec. 1969, Wayne State University, Detroit, Mich., in AAUGP, box 14, folder 11: Correspondence President, 1969 (Abu-Lughod).

29. Hagopian, "Reversing Injustice," 60–61; Suleiman, "'I Come to Bury Caesar,'" 79–80.

30. Suleiman, "'I Come to Bury Caesar,'" 77; AAUG, *The First Decade*, 5–6, Abu-Lughod quoted on page 6; AAUG Board Meeting Minutes, 22 Sept. 1968; Bashshur, "Unfulfilled Expectations," 10.

31. Terry, "The AAUG," 3. Terry does admit that the organization sometimes overlooked women's issues. On the involvement of women in AAUG leadership positions, also see Hagopian, "Reversing Injustice," 65.

32. Bassiouni's address in "Annual Convention Draws Record Attendance," *AN*, Dec. 1970; Suleiman, "'I Come to Bury Caesar,'" 80.

33. Terry, "Community and Political Activism," 246–47.

34. Jabara, "The AAUG," 17; Suleiman, "'I Come to Bury Caesar,'" 79–80; Beverly, "Shaking Off the Sheikh," 9–10.

35. Abu-Laban, "Reflections on the Rise," 47.

36. Hagopian, "Reversing Injustice," 58; Adnan Aswad and Barbara Aswad, interview with author; Fauzi Najjar, "AAUG: The First Year," *AN*, Mar. 1971; Bashshur, "Unfulfilled Expectations," 11.

37. Hagopian, "Reversing Injustice," 58–59; Bashshur, "Unfulfilled Expectations," 8; Jabara, "The AAUG," 15. Simultaneously, the League of Arab States was promoting an information campaign in the United States, intended to "defend the Arabs against malicious attacks, especially from Zionists in the West, and to convey to the world the picture of an Arab world working for progress, welfare, and stability." In *The Arabs in the Mind of America*, 161–70, AAUG scholar Michael Suleiman studied the Arab League's campaign and judged it to be ineffective.

38. AAUG Board Meeting Minutes, 22 Sept. 1968, and AAUG Annual Report, Dec. 1969, in AAUGP, box 23, folder Board Meeting Minutes, 1969; Moughrabi, "Remembering the AAUG," 99; Jabara, "A Strategy for Political Effectiveness," 202.

39. Terry, "The AAUG," 2; AAUG Annual Report, Dec. 1969; AAUG, *The First Decade*, 8,

20, 36; Jabara, interview with author. To further promote the collection of knowledge and establish their community's legitimacy, the AAUG established an archive on Arab Americans at the University of Minnesota in the early 1970s. See Board Meeting Minutes, Nov. 1, 1970, in AAUGP, box 23, folder Board Meeting Minutes, 1970.

40. Examples of publications by Medina University Press International, located in Wilmette, Illinois, are Waines, *The Unholy War*, and Jabara and Terry, eds. *The Arab World*, which features an introduction by the editors that extolled the Palestinian Liberation Movement as a revolutionary people's struggle directed not only against Israel but also against conservative Arab regimes. This collection contains Edward Said, "The Palestinian Perspective," and Noam Chomsky, "The Radical Perspective." Aruri's edited volume, *Middle East Crucible*, includes Edward Said, "Shattered Myths," and Eqbal Ahmad, "What Washington Wants." Zogby, *Perspectives on Palestinian Arabs*, features an article by the noted Israeli leftist attorney Felicia Langer, "Israeli Violations of Human Rights in the Occupied Arab Territories."

41. Publications Committee Report, Apr. 1974, in AAUGP, box 23, folder Board Meeting Minutes, 1974; AAUG Board Meeting Minutes, 16 Oct. 1975, in box 23, folder Board Meeting Minutes, 1975.

42. AAUG Board Meeting Minutes, 20 Apr. 1974, AAUGP, box 23, folder Board Meeting Minutes, 1974. One member of the board, Fauzi Najjar, objected to the relationship with MERIP because he feared political retribution, especially revocation of the organization's tax-exempt status by the federal government; however, Farsoun, Jabara, and Abu-Lughod spoke strongly in favor of supporting MERIP, and the motion passed.

43. Terry, "The AAUG," 2; Suleiman, "'I Come to Bury Caesar,'" 80–81; Bassiouni, "The AAUG," 24. Talhami, "A Cultural, Not a Political Lobby," 127, remembers: "Indeed, what we struggled to accomplish was the creation of a legitimate voice capable of presenting issues of the Arab World empathetically, not negatively, as was customary in the American academy." My review of the contents of MESA's *International Journal of Middle East Studies*, which began publication in 1970, reveals that its first article relevant to Israel or Palestine was published in 1972 (Donald L. Losman, "The Arab Boycott of Israel"), and over the remainder of the 1970s, it published three articles about Israel and only one article about Palestine (Michael Cohen, "Secret Diplomacy and Rebellion in Palestine, 1936–1939," July 1977). Janice Terry remembers a "marked contrast" between AAUG conventions (which she calls "informative and exciting") and MESA conferences. She found it telling that the MESA conference held in December 1967, six months after the June War, included no discussion of the Arab-Israeli conflict. See Terry, "The AAUG," 1.

44. Khoury, "The AAUG in My Eyes," 168; Barbara Aswad, interview with author; Joel Beinin, interview with author.

45. "The First Annual Convention," *AN*, Jan. 1969. Papers from the first convention were published in the collection Elaine C. Hagopian and Ann Paden, *The Arab Americans*. Papers from the seventh convention were published in the collection in Abu-Laban and Zeadey, *Arabs in America*.

46. "Successful Detroit Convention Establishes Solid Base for AAUG," *AN*, Dec. 1969; "Text of Statement Released at Close of Second Annual Convention," *AN*, Mar. 1970; Shain, "Arab Americans," 50.

47. AAUG, Minutes of the Meeting of the General Assembly, 7 Dec. 1969, Detroit, Mich., in AAUGP, box 26, folder General Assembly Meeting Minutes, 1969.

48. "Two Lines in the Palestine Support Movement," *CSMEL Newsletter*, Feb. 1970, in Committee to Support Middle East Liberation Papers, SPC.

49. Seth S. King, "Arab-American Meeting Hears Chomsky," reprinted from *NYT* in *AN*, Dec. 1970.

50. Telegrams in AAUGP, box 28, folder Correspondence Abdeen Jabara, President, 1972.

51. "Resolutions, 5th Annual Convention, 1972," in AAUGP, box 26, folder General Assembly Resolution, 1972.

52. Quote from "Text of Statement"; Chamberlin, *The Global Offensive*, 61–65.

53. "Text of Statement"; Aruri, "AAUG," 38.

54. Bassiouni, "The AAUG," 24–25; Hagopian, "Reversing Injustice," 60; Jabara, interview with author; Barbara Aswad, interview with author; Nassar, "Ibrahim Abu-Lughod."

55. Abu-Lughod, Presidential Statement.

56. Jabara, interview with author; Jabara, Presidential Statement, AAUG Convention, 11 Nov. 1972, Berkeley, California, in AAUGP, box 14, folder 4: Correspondence President,1972 (Jabara); AAUG, *The First Decade*, 21–22; "Arab Group in US Hails Guerrillas," *NYT*, 13 Nov. 1972; Gualtieri, *Between Arab and White*, 174.

57. Moughrabi, "Remembering the AAUG," 98; Aruri, "AAUG," 38.

58. "Two Lines in the Palestine Support Movement"; Aruri, "AAUG," 39.

59. "Annual Convention Draws Record Attendance."

60. Aruri, "AAUG," 40; King, "Arab-American Meeting Hears Chomsky"; AAUG, *The First Decade*, 27–29, 39.

61. Jabara, "The AAUG," 17; AAUG, *The First Decade*, 21; Hagopian, "Reversing Injustice," 61; Suleiman, "'I Come to Bury Caesar,'" 85; Abu-Laban, "Reflections on the Rise," 49.

62. Correspondence between Jabara and Walid Khadduri, 1972, in AAUGP, box 6, folder Project with Institute of Palestine Studies; "AAUG Conference in Kuwait—A Great Success," *AN*, Mar. 1976; "Sponsorship Project for Palestinian Children," *AN*, Sept. 1969; Jabara, Presidential Statement.

63. Hagopian, "Reversing Injustice," 63–65.

64. Jabara's statement in AAUG Board Meeting Minutes, 1 Dec. 1973, in AAUGP, box 23, folder Board Meeting Minutes, 1973; Link Committee report in AAUG Board Meeting Minutes, 3 Aug. 1974, box 23, folder Board Meeting Minutes, 1974.

65. "Needed: A Nixon Declaration for Five Million Jewish Christian and Moslem Palestinians," *NYT*, 2 Nov. 1969; AAUG Annual Report, Dec. 1969; "An Open Letter," *WP*, 5 Nov. 1971; Jabara's correspondence with the Secretaries of State and Defense, in AAUG Board Meeting Minutes, 23 Apr. 1972, AAUGP, box 23, folder Board Meeting Minutes, 1972. Also see Hatem, "Political and Cultural Representations of Arabs," 19.

66. AAUG, *The First Decade*, 26; AAUG Board Meeting Minutes, 20 Apr. 1974.

67. Report of Chairman of Committee on the Future of the Association, 14 Apr. 1973, in AAUGP, box 23, folder Board Meeting Minutes, 1973.

68. Abu-Lughod to Members of the Committee on the Future of the Association, 25 July 1973, in AAUGP, box 46, folder AAUG, NAAA, Ramallah Cooperation. At the time of its founding, NAAA leader F. K. Taima wrote to Abdeen Jabara, then serving as AAUG president, inviting him to the inaugural meeting. Taima avowed that "the Association doesn't seek to compete with, nor delineate the role of . . . the AAUG" and expressed his hope that the two organizations could work together. See Taima to Jabara, 4 May 1972, in AAUGP, box 43, folder NAAA.

69. Abu-Lughod to Members of the Committee.

70. AAUG, *The First Decade*, 36; "U.S. Aid to Israel Protested Nationally: 60 Rallies in 34 Cities," *AN*, Dec. 1973; AAUG Board Meeting Minutes, 16 Oct. 1975, AAUGP, box 23, folder Board Meeting Minutes, 1975; "Palestine Lives," *AN*, June 1978.

71. The AAUG did not disband until 2007, but since the 1990s its only function had been to publish the academic journal *Arab Studies Quarterly*, which it began in 1979.

72. Hagopian was president in 1976. Hatem, "How the Gulf War Changed the AAUG's Discourse"; Jabara, "A Strategy for Political Effectiveness," 202; Suleiman, "'I Come to Bury Caesar,'" 83, 87–88; Bassiouni, "The AAUG," 26; Terry, "The AAUG," 3.

73. "Women Hold Up Half the Sky," *AN*, June 1978; "Results of the Questionnaire," n.d., in AAUGP, box 88, folder Women's Caucus Members and Questionnaires; "Synopsis of Minutes of Women's Caucus," AAUG Annual Convention, 28 Oct. 1989, in AAUGP, box 88, folder Women's Committee, 1979–80. The AAUG's Committee on the Status of Women, the Women's Caucus, and the Women's Task Force were different names for essentially the same entity.

74. "Results of the Questionnaire"; Ismail to Task Force Members, 31 Mar. 1979, in AAUGP, box 88, folder Women's Committee, 1979–80. See also AAUG Women's Caucus Meeting, 10 Nov. 1979, in NAP, box 2, folder AAUG.

75. "Results of the Questionnaire"; "Synopsis of Minutes"; Ismail newsletters to Task Force members, 12 Jan. 1979, 31 Mar. 1979, 10 June 1979, in AAUGP, box 88, folder Women's Committee, 1979–80.

76. Moughrabi to Ismail, 6 Dec. 1978, in AAUGP box 88, folder Women's Committee, 1979–80.

77. Barbara Aswad, interview with author; Khoury, interview with author; Jabara, interview with author.

78. Bashshur, "Unfulfilled Expectations," 13; Nakhleh, "AAUG," 110.

79. Jabara, interview with Terry; Suleiman, "'I Come to Bury Caesar,'" 79.

80. Bassiouni, "The AAUG," 30–31; Hagopian, "Reversing Injustice," 66, 70; Aruri, "AAUG," 45.

81. Suleiman, "'I Come to Bury Caesar,'" 83–86; Aruri, "AAUG," 42.

82. Bashshur, "Unfulfilled Expectations," 12–13; Adnan Aswad, interview with author.

83. Jabara, interview with author.

84. Jabara, "Arab-Americans and the U.S. Policy Process," *AN*, Sept. 1978.

85. Ibid.

86. Hagopian, "Reversing Injustice," 70, 72; Terry, "The AAUG," 3–4; Jabara, "AAUG," 17–18; Abu-Laban, "Reflections on the Rise," 50.

87. Jabara, "AAUG," 18; Hagopian, "Reversing Injustice," 61; Terry, "The AAUG," 2; Aruri, "AAUG," 44; Suleiman, "'I Come to Bury Caesar,'" 81, 86–90.

88. Abu-Laban, "Reflections on the Rise," 50; Hagopian, "Reversing Injustice," 72; Jabara, "AAUG," 17; Beverly, "Shaking Off the Sheikh," 9, 34–35; Suleiman, "Arab-Americans and the Political Process," 47–48.

89. Abu-Laban, "Reflections on the Rise," 50.

Chapter 2

1. Ahmed, interview with author. Ahmed helped to establish OAS chapters at Henry Ford Community College and the University of Michigan–Dearborn. Hanania, interview with author.

2. Fatah, which formed in 1959 and advocated Palestinian armed struggle against Israel, was the largest guerrilla faction. Another faction associated with the PLO was the Popular Front for the Liberation of Palestine (PFLP), which differed from Fatah in its more avid commitment to inciting revolutionary movements throughout the Arab world and its adherence to Marxist-Leninism. In the early 1970s, the PFLP engaged in airplane hijackings and other terrorist actions outside of Palestine and Israel, further separating it from Fatah, which remained focused on armed struggle in Palestine. Another faction split from the PFLP in 1969, eventually calling itself the Democratic Front for the Liberation of Palestine (DFLP). This group of fedayeen was also Marxist-Leninist but claimed to be more grassroots than the PFLP in its orientation toward the Palestinian people.

3. Anderson, *The Movement and the Sixties*, 49, 65, 130; Gosse, *Rethinking the New Left*, 64–65; Cohen, "Prophetic Minority"; Rodríguez-Morazzani, "Political Cultures of the Puerto Rican Left"; Liu, Geron, and Lai, *The Snake Dance*.

4. Gosse, *Rethinking the New Left*, 195; Varon, *Bringing the War Home*, 1, 7; Shannon, "'Contacts with the Opposition,'" 5, 15.

5. Naber, *Arab America*, 49.

6. OAS, *Young Arab Speaks*.

7. Haddad, "Nationalist and Islamist Tendencies," 147; Notes on the OAS, unpublished, n.d., NAP, box 13, folder Organization of Arab Students (2); OAS, *Yearbook*, 6.

8. In a sample of 62 Arab students at California universities in the late 1950s, the greatest number came from Iraq (21) followed by Egypt (13). See Gezi, "The Acculturation of Middle Eastern Arab Students," 49–50. A study of Arab students at American universities in the 1970s revealed that most came from Lebanon and Egypt in the early part of the decade, whereas by the late 1970s the number of Saudi Arabian and Libyan students spiked. Palestine was not included as a country category in the study, but students listed as coming from Jordan also increased over the course of the 1970s. See Charbaji, "Academic and Social Problems," 3.

9. Edward B. Fiske, "Arab and Iranian Students Increasing at U.S. Colleges," *NYT*, 28 Mar. 1975; Garrett and Purpura, *Frank Maria*, 223–24; Nimer, "The Americanization of Islamism"; OAS, *Yearbook*. In 1960, the Columbia University and University of Michigan chapters were led by female presidents. The University of Michigan chapter's report in the OAS *Yearbook* stated, "In keeping with the tradition of encouraging Arab girls to take part in club affairs, the club elected its third lady president." In the late 1960s, Wayne State University's OAS chapter was led by Soraya Obaid. Barbara Aswad, interview with author.

10. *Young Arab Speaks*, iv, 70–72; OAS, *Yearbook*, 5, 11.

11. OAS, *Yearbook*.

12. OAS, *Yearbook*; Ziyad Husami, OAS Newsletter Committee Chairman, to Fayez Sayegh, 25 Jan. 1963, in FSP, box 243, folder Organization of Arab Students in the United States. Husami stated that the OAS newsletter's circulation in 1963 was seven thousand recipients.

13. *Arab Journal*, vol. II (1965)–vol. VI (1969).

14. OAS, *Yearbook*; D. W. Phillips, North Carolina State Social Director, to Fawzy Hammad, Arab Club, 14 Dec. 1959, in Arab Club Records, Correspondence File, North Carolina State University Student and Other Organizations, Special Collections Research Center, North Carolina State University Libraries, Raleigh, North Carolina.

15. "Arab Students Picket Dinner," *LAT*, 12 Oct. 1964; Irving Spiegel, "Rabbi Contends Arab Students Foster Sentiment against Israel," *NYT*, 14 Sept. 1964. Many of the Arab student groups affiliated with the OAS were named Arab Student Association or Arab Student Club.

16. OAS, *Yearbook*; "Turkish Java?," *Daily Collegian* [Wayne State University], 1 May 1969.

17. Haddad, "Maintaining the Faith," 75–76; Howell, *Old Islam in Detroit*, 202–6; Curtis, "Islamism and Its African American Muslim Critics," 689; Algar, *Wahhabism*, 50–51. According to Haddad, conservative Islamists established the MSA to challenge the Federation of Islamic Associations, which it believed had become too Americanized. The MSA was intended to be "an alternative umbrella organization with a mandate to propagate true Islam" (75). Later, in the 1980s, the MSA became more open to participating in American society and politics. Curtis argues that the MSA was "one of the most successful immigrant-led organizations in propagating Islamist ideas throughout North America" (689). Also see "Al-Mumineen Mosque Welcomes Convention of Muslim Students," *Muslim Star*, Oct. 1966, about the fourth annual convention of the MSA held at the University of Michigan. The *Muslim Star* issue is located in IMJCP, box 8, folder *Muslim Star*.

18. Shakir, *Bint Arab*, 96; Hussaini, "The Impact of the Arab-Israeli Conflict," 207–8.

19. Hussaini, 207–8; "Resume of Resolutions"; "The Palestinian Revolution: Message from the Palestine National Liberation Movement (Fateh) to the 17th Annual Convention of Arab Students in the United States and Canada," Ann Arbor, Mich., 26–31 August 1968, SCL-UM.

20. For example, the following publications were distributed as flyers on the UC-Berkeley campus: "Statement by Al-Fateh to the United Nations General Assembly," Oct. 1968; "To Our African Brothers: Message from the Palestine National Liberation Movement (Fateh) to the African Cultural Festival held in Algeria—July 27, 1969"; "News of the Palestinian Resistance Movement," *Al-Hadaf* [PFLP], 6 Nov. 1971, all in ASAR. At the University of Michigan, flyers included "The Position of Al-Fateh," 15 Oct. 1969, in WSP, box 1, folder Organization of Arab Students, 1969.

21. Abdulhadi, "Activism and Exile," 235–36; Abraham, unpublished notes, NAP, box 13, folder Organization of Arab Students (2); Abraham, "From Campus to Coffeehouse," 5–6. According to Abraham, the new OAS constitution "read more like a manifesto of a political party than a student organization."

22. Declassified FBI and ADL documents, http://www.irmep.org/ila/ADL/1199215—-62-NY-10686—-Section2.pdf, 156, 169, 178, 180 (accessed 18 July 2014). Ironically, along with monitoring the OAS, the FBI was also monitoring the ADL, which is how it obtained this ADL report on the OAS convention. The FBI became concerned that the ADL was passing this information to Israel and was thereby violating the Foreign Agents Registration Act. See "The FBI and the Anti-Defamation League." The program for the OAS convention held at Ohio State in August 1969 can be found in the Michael Suleiman Collection, Arab American National Museum, Dearborn, Mich., box 35, subseries 2–5-1.

23. United Press International, "Ford: Mideast Agitators on U.S. Campuses," *Sandusky Register*, 25 Apr. 1969 (accessed online); Forster, letter to the editor of the *NYT*, 28 May 1969; Haddad, *Not Quite American?*, 20; Hussaini, "The Impact of the Arab-Israeli Conflict," 216–17. Also see Boris Smolar, "New Arab-American Effort Bears Watching by U.S. Jews," *Cleveland Jewish News*, 3 Aug. 1973, in AJP, box 12, folder Activities—NAAA—Press Clippings.

24. Seymour Hersh, "Alien-Radical Tie Disputed by CIA," *NYT*, 25 May 1973; Gessert, "A Non-Arab Looks," 23.

25. FBI, "Fedayeen Impact," http://www.governmentattic.org/2docs/FBI_Monograph_Fedayeen-Impact_1970.pdf.

26. "Resume of Resolutions." On the tie between socialism and Arab American activism, see Naber, *Arab America*, 43.

27. Abraham, interview with author; "Policy Statement of the OAS"; Abraham, "From Campus to Coffeehouse," 5–8. According to Abraham, besides the fedayeen, the only Arab political groups favored by the OAS by the early 1970s were the Iraqi Baath Party and the Marxist government of South Yemen.

28. Abudayyeh, interview with author, 14 Sept. 2015; Naber, *Arab America*, 43–44.

29. "Activities of OAS Chapters," *OAS News*, Mar.–Apr. 1969; "Demonstration and Fund Raising at Oswego," *AN*, Mar. 1969; "Arabs Protest Israel Event," *Chicago Tribune*, 19 May 1969. Also see Ivan C. Brandon, "Protesting Students Seize Arab Office," *WP*, 29 Mar. 1972; "Protest Israel War Salesman," *Committee to Support Middle East Liberation Newsletter*, Feb. 1970, in Committee to Support Middle East Liberation Records, SPC. "Protest $1000 a plate fund raising dinner for Zionist aggression," flyer, 13 Nov. 1973, which called for picketing at a hotel in San Francisco, and "Mass Rally in Union Square in Support of the Palestinian Revolution," flyer, n.d., which contained information about carpools from Berkeley and San Jose State to San Francisco, both in IACR.

30. "Arab Students Stage Sit-In," *Free Palestine*, June 1969.

31. "Chants for Al-Fateh Mark Teach-In at Columbia," *Free Palestine*, June 1969; "Members in the News," *AN*, June 1969; "Perspective for Peace in the Middle East, talk by Dr. Ibrahim Abu-Lughod," flyer, 7 Feb. 1969, in WSP. In 1969 AAUG members spoke at teach-ins held at Columbia University, Brown University, the University of Pennsylvania, Ohio State, the Uni-

versity of Nebraska, the University of Michigan, Wayne State University, and the University of Wisconsin. See AAUG annual report, Dec. 1969, AAUGP, Eastern Michigan University Library, box 23, folder Board Meeting Minutes, 1969.

32. Collections of flyers in WSP; OAS records, University of Kansas, University Archives, Student Organization Records, Record Group 67/9; IACR and ASAR.

33. IACR and ASAR.

34. "Press Ignores UC Arabs' Rap," *Berkeley Barb*, 7–13 July 1967; IACR, ASAR, and Liberation Support Movement Records 1967–1974, in SPC; Iranian Student Association and Arab Students in North California, "Dhofar: Revolution and Politics of Oil in the Persian-Arabian Gulf," pamphlet, 1974, in SCL-UM; Matin-Asgari, *Iranian Student Opposition*, 135. I have found evidence of General Union of Palestine Students presence at a few American universities later in the 1970s and 1980s.

35. IACR.

36. Abraham, "From Campus to Coffeehouse," 7–13.

37. Nabeel Abraham, interview with Terry, JTP, box 1; Abraham, interview with author.

38. Abraham, interview with Terry; Abraham, interview with author; Abraham, "To Palestine and Back," 453.

39. Nawash, interview with Terry, JTP, box 1.

40. Khoury, interview with Terry, JTP, box 1.

41. Khoury, interview with author; Abraham, "To Palestine and Back," 452–53; Abraham, "From Campus to Coffeehouse," 3, 7, 10. When Abraham joined Wayne State's OAS in 1968, the leaders were Obaid from Saudi Arabia, Riad Karaoui from Lebanon, and Khoury, Nawash, and Muhsen Munem, all Palestinian. Secondary players were two Jordanian siblings who supported the Baath Party.

42. Abraham, interview with author; Khoury, interview with author; Wigle and Abraham, "Arab Nationalism," 295; "Blacks and Arabs to Protest Israeli Speaker," *SE*, 4 June 1968; Soraya Obaid, "The Truth behind Begin and Zionism," *SE*, 6 June 1968; Niko Boyias, "Arab Supporters Demonstrate," *SE*, 27 Jan. 1969.

43. Khoury, interview with author; Abraham, interview with author; Barbara Aswad, interview with author.

44. Barbara Aswad, interview with author; Georgakas and Surkin, *Detroit*, 45; Hamlin, interview with author; Thompson, *Whose Detroit?*, 101; Abraham, interview with author.

45. In *SE*, see Habib Fakhouri, "Arabs Protest 'Racist Israel,'" letter to the editor, 12 Oct. 1967; Fakhouri, "Semite Attacks Israeli Religion," 20 May 1968; Muhsen A. Munem, letter to the editor, 5 Feb. 1969; Soraya Obaid, "Arab Students Protest Discrimination," 6 Feb. 1969; OAS, letter to the editor, 21 Feb. 1969.

46. "Student Head 'Frustrated'—Talks of 'Guerrilla' War," *SE*, 28 May 1968; Nabeel Abraham, "The World's Oppressed Speak," *SE*, 10 Jan. 1969.

47. "Blacks and Arabs to Protest"; Boyias, "Arab Supporters Demonstrate."

48. Khoury, interview with author; Abraham, interview with author. Abraham participated in an antiwar occupation of the Wayne State president's office and spent the whole time arguing with an SDS student who was pro-Israel.

49. Abraham, "From Campus to Coffeehouse," 14.

50. Abraham, interview with author; Khoury, interview with author.

51. Letters to the editor in *SE*: Amos Traub, 6 June 1968; J. S. Cohen, "Unfortunate Distortion in Israeli Article," 6 June 1968; Rachel Malkin, 27 June 1968; David Elazar, Wayne State reference librarian, 13 Jan. 1969; Nancy Stein, 15 Jan. 1969; Leonard Simons, Helen Shiffman, and Martin N. Fealk, 29 Jan. 1969; Abba Binder and Mel Krugel of Hashomer Hatzair, 5 Feb. 1969; and Karen Amin, 19 Feb. 1969.

52. Georgakas and Surkin, *Detroit*, 48, 52; Nick Medvecky, "Al-Fatah," *SE*, 8 Jan. 1969; Boyias, "Arab Supporters Demonstrate"; "Fatah, the Palestine National Liberation Movement," *SE*, 7 Feb. 1969. On the heels of that article and demonstration, in early February a conflict broke out when Wayne State librarians, one of whom was an outspoken Zionist named David Elazar, tried to remove the OAS's material from its showcase in the library, and ultimately the director of the library allowed the materials to remain in the name of academic freedom. See Obaid, "Arab Students Protest Discrimination," and Abraham, interview with author.

53. Keast, letter to the editor, *SE*, 10 Feb. 1969. Also see the Wayne State University Board of Governors, Official Proceedings, 13 Feb. 1969, vol. 13, 1968–1969, in Walter P. Reuther Library.

54. "Keast Blasts South End as Spiteful," *Detroit News*, 10 Feb. 1969; "Radical Editor Can Hold Job, WSU Admits," *Detroit News*, 12 Feb. 1969; "Head of Wayne State Scores School Paper as Hitler-Like," *NYT*, 11 Feb. 1969; Anthony Ripley, "Wayne State Suspends Student Paper to Bar 'Damage' to School," *NYT*, 13 July 1969.

55. Hamlin, interview with author; Georgakas and Surkin, *Detroit*, 52–54; Hamlin, "We Continue the Struggle," *SE*, 7 Mar. 1969. Thompson views the conflict over the *South End's* editorship as part of the "war for the control of the Motor City" between the radicals (mainly black militants) and the corporations and mainstream unions. Thompson, *Whose Detroit?*, 101–2.

56. Maureen Hallett, "Arab Israeli Forum Tomorrow," *SE*, 11 Feb. 1969.

57. "Commemorative Issue on the Arab Struggle," *SE*, 15 May 1969; Nick Medvecky, "relaxes the tension in me . . . not the middle east," *SE*, 1 Oct. 1969; "Forum Today to Protest Government Harassment of Arabs," *SE*, 7 Dec. 1972; OAS, letter to the editor, *SE*, 8 Dec. 1972; Georgakas and Surkin, *Detroit*, 58, 62.

58. Nawash, interview with Terry; Abraham, interview with author; Khoury, interview with author.

59. Another student active in this organizing was Muhsen Munem. Abraham, "From Campus to Coffeehouse," 17–21; Ahmed, interview with author; Abraham, interview with author; Nawash, interview with Terry.

60. Abraham, interview with author; Ahmed, "Ishmael Ahmed," 28.

61. Abraham, "From Campus to Coffeehouse," 23; Abraham, interview with author.

62. Abraham, interview with author; Abraham, interview with Terry; Khoury, interview with author.

63. Abudayyeh, interview with author, 14 Sept. 2015.

64. Bassiouni, *The Civil Rights of Arab-Americans*; "Forum Today to Protest Government Harassment of Arabs"; Jabara to Ahmed Shalaby, 1 Feb. 1973, in AJP, box 9, folder Activities—Harassment of Arab Americans—Correspondence.

65. "U.S. Aid to Israel Protested Nationally: 60 Rallies in 34 Cities," *AN*, Dec. 1973. According to Haddad, the Muslim Student Association grew in membership and became more active after the October War. See Haddad, "American Foreign Policy," 226. The following year, Muslim students associated with the Muslim Brotherhood established another organization, the Muslim Arab Youth Association, as a rival organization to the secular OAS. See Nimer, "The Americanization of Islamism."

66. OAS, *Arab Student Bulletin*, Sept. 1976 and Dec. 1976; "Arab Student Meet Begins in Long Beach Today," *Long Beach Press-Telegram*, 29 Aug. 1976, clipping in FSP, box 386, folder 1.

67. Middle Eastern Student Groups Papers, University of California–Santa Barbara Library, Special Collections, Student Organizations Collection, series 1, box 2; OAS, "The Lebanese Crisis: A Socio-Economic Background," pamphlet, 1976, in SCL-UM; "Chapter Action on Human Rights," *AN*, June 1977; "Protesters Disrupt Talk by Israel's President at U. of Michigan," *NYT*, 14 Mar. 1975; "Massive Demonstration Climaxes Northwestern," *AN*, June 1978. Also see Arab

Club Records at Special Collections Research Center, North Carolina State University Libraries, for evidence of the activities of that OAS affiliate during the mid-1970s.

68. "Arab Students under Attack," *Arab Student Bulletin*, Mar.–Apr. 1977. Another conflict broke out at the University of Maryland in 1976, but this time it was between Jewish students and the Black Student Union (BSU) on campus. During a BSU-sponsored event that featured a speaker from the Organization for All African Peoples Revolutionary Party who denounced Zionism, Jewish students ripped down the BSU's inflammatory flyers, and a "shouting match" between the BSU and Jewish students ensued. See "BSU Forum Draws Jewish Students' Anger," *Diamondback*, 12 Nov. 1976, reprinted in *Palestine Digest*, Nov. 1976.

69. "MSU Student Tortured in Israeli Jail," *Michigan Free Press*, 29 Jan. 1978; Peter C. Gavrilovich, "MSU Student Held by Israelis," *Detroit Free Press*, 18 Jan. 1978; John Masterson and Barbara Thibeault, letter to the editor, *NYT*, 15 June 1978. See materials on Sami Esmail in AAUGP, box 90, folder PHRC. I discuss the establishment of the PHRC in chapter 7.

70. At Ohio State, the chapter of the National Committee to Defend the Human Rights of Sami Esmail changed its name to the Palestinian Human Rights Committee and became loosely affiliated with the Palestine Human Rights Campaign.

71. O'Laughlin and Murphy, interview with author; Palestinian Human Rights Committee Records, Student Organizations, Ohio State University Archives, Columbus, Ohio; "To Stop the Deportation of Elias Ayoub," *PHRC Bulletin*, n.d., in AJP, box 13, folder Palestine Human Rights Campaign—Bulletin; Stanley Diamond, Noam Chomsky, William Sloane Coffin Jr., Edward W. Said, and Ramsey Clark, "Facing Deportation," *New York Times Review of Books*, 1 Apr. 1982.

72. O'Laughlin and Murphy, interview with author.

73. Beinin, interview with author.

74. "News about the Organization," *Arab Student Bulletin*, July-August-September 1982; OAS, "The Latest Israeli Invasion of Lebanon," pamphlet, n.d., in PAAA.

75. For the "crash-and-burn" characterization of the movements, see Echols, *Shaky Ground*, 51, and Mattson, *Intellectuals in Action*, 7. For an analysis of OAS's organizational weaknesses in the 1970s, see Nabeel Abraham's unpublished notes on the OAS, n.d., NAP, box 13, folder Organization of Arab Students (2).

76. Hatem, "Political and Cultural Representations of Arabs," 22. Also in this period, the General Union of Palestinian Students became more established in American universities. See Abdulhadi, "Activism and Exile," 238; Greenberg, *The Dangers of Dissent*, 138; and AAUGP, box 44, folder General Union of Palestine Students.

Chapter 3

1. A subset of the broader political left, the New Left manifested in the 1960s and 1970s as both an American and a global phenomenon. The New Left was characterized by young people's involvement and more focused attention on issues of racial justice and, over time, women's rights and gay rights, rather than the classic Marxist analysis of class struggle and adherence to rigid doctrine that had characterized the "Old" Left. In the American context, most scholars use the term to refer mainly to white students. See, for instance, McMillian, "Introduction," 6. However, a few historians use "New Left" more broadly to describe all the movements on the left in the sixties, including the civil rights movement. See Gosse, *Rethinking the New Left*, 4–6. By the late 1960s, the New Left grew less distinct from other elements of the Left and adhered to a stricter Marxist, sometimes Maoist, perspective. Therefore, at times I use "Left" and "New Left" interchangeably. Katsiaficas, *The Imagination of the New Left*, discusses the global New Left, in which he includes the Palestinian Movement.

2. Chamberlin, *The Global Offensive*, 40, 52, 61–65, 258. Palestinian guerrillas trained with

the FLN in Algeria and with the army of the People's Republic of China. The Vietnamese National Liberation Front proclaimed its support for the Palestinian resistance, and the Cuban government provided material assistance to the fedayeen.

3. Greenberg, *Troubling the Waters*; Newby, "Afro-Americans and Arabs," 52–54; Newsome, "International Issues," 22–23; Yaqub, "'Our Declaration of Independence.'"

4. Weisbord and Kazarian Jr., *Israel in the Black American Perspective*, 14, 17, 31; Lubin, *Geographies of Liberation*, 5–6. Both books emphasize that African American leaders, including Ralph Bunche, Paul Robeson, DuBois, Bayard Rustin, A. Philip Randolph, Martin Luther King Jr., and John Lewis, at times took strong stances supporting Israel. On NAACP support for Israel in the 1950s, see Greenberg, *Troubling the Waters*, 121.

5. Lubin, *Geographies of Liberation*, 8–10; Feldman, "Representing Permanent War," 199–201; McAlister, *Epic Encounters*, 87–88; O'Dell quoted in Singh, "'Learn Your Horn,'" 44–45. In his memoir, Stokely Carmichael (Kwame Ture) recalls that when he was in high school in the late 1950s and involved with the Young Communist League, he followed the official Communist Party line of supporting Israel as a revolutionary state. His realization of Israeli injustice toward Palestinians came in the early 1960s from reading articles about the Palestinians in *Muhammad Speaks*, the publication of the Nation of Islam. See Carmichael, *Ready for Revolution*, 93, 557.

6. McAlister, *Epic Encounters*, 89–91; Marable, *Malcolm X*, 119–20.

7. Feldman, "Representing Permanent War," 202–3; Daulatzai, *Black Star*, 23–28; McAlister, *Epic Encounters*, 89–91.

8. Meghelli, "From Harlem to Algiers," 102–5.

9. McAlister, *Epic Encounters*, 91–96; Curtis, "Islamism," 684–85; Daulatzai, *Black Star*, xv, 18.

10. Young, "American Blacks," 75; Newsome, "International Issues," 35. Malcolm X quoted in Daulatzai, *Black Star*, 41–42, and in Weisbord and Kazarian, *Israel in the Black American Perspective*, 45.

11. Curtis, "Islamism," 689–92, 697–99; Aliya Hassen Papers, BHL, box 1, folder Malcolm X–Articles and Correspondence 1959–1965; Ahmed, interview with author; Howell, *Old Islam in Detroit*, 193; Kelley, "Muslims in Los Angeles," 151–52. After Elijah Muhammad's death in 1975, his son Warith Deen Mohammed aligned the NOI more closely with orthodox Sunni Islam, embracing a more universal Islam and encouraging interactions with immigrant Muslims.

12. Carson, *In Struggle*, 191–92, 198; Greenberg, *Troubling the Waters*, 205; Lubin, *Geographies of Liberation*, 120.

13. Feldman, "Representing Permanent War," 210–11; Carson, *In Struggle*, 266.

14. Forman, *The Making of Black Revolutionaries*, 493–96; Carson, *In Struggle*, 267–68.

15. "Third World Round Up, the Palestinian Problem: Test Your Knowledge," *SNCC Newsletter*, June–July 1967, 4–5; Feldman, "Representing Permanent War," 215–20; Newsome, "International Issues," 36; Lubin, *Geographies of Liberation*, 122.

16. "Third World Round Up"; Feldman, "Representing Permanent War," 217; Carson, *In Struggle*, 267. According to Carmichael, he had been a member of Minor's Palestine study group (although he does not use her name in his memoir), and along with other SNCC members, he helped her draft a position paper on the Israeli-Palestinian conflict for internal circulation in SNCC. But in a process that he states became "short-circuited," this draft became the article published in the June–July newsletter before it was vetted for public distribution. See Carmichael, *Ready for Revolution*, 558–61.

17. "SNCC and the Jews," *Newsweek*, 28 Aug. 1967; Gene Roberts, "SNCC Charges Israel Atrocities," *NYT*, 15 Aug. 1967; Kathleen Teltsch, "SNCC Criticized for Israel Stand," *NYT*, 16 Aug. 1967; Feldman, "Representing Permanent War," 213.

18. Roberts, "SNCC Charges"; Teltsch, "SNCC Criticized"; Carson, *In Struggle*, 268.

19. Forman, *The Making of Black Revolutionaries*, 496–97; Carmichael, *Ready for Revolution*, 560–61.

20. "Resume of Resolutions"; Young, "American Blacks," 76.

21. Young, "American Blacks," 78–79; Weisbord and Kazarian, *Israel in the Black American Perspective*, 36; Carmichael, "The Black American,"139–41; "Carmichael Says Negroes to Help Arabs," *Chicago Tribune*, 28 Aug. 1968.

22. Weisbord and Stein, *Bittersweet Encounter*, 104; Carson, *In Struggle*, 268; Young, "American Blacks," 78.

23. Weiss, "From Mississippi to Gaza," http://mondoweiss.net/2014/06/mississippi-reflects-struggle.

24. Carson, *In Struggle*, 268–69; Greenberg, *Troubling the Waters*, 11–12; Newsome, "International Issues," 25, 38; Newby, "Afro-Americans and Arabs," 53–54; Forman, *The Making of Black Revolutionaries*, 496.

25. Lubin, *Geographies of Liberation*, 121–23.

26. Field Marshall DC, "Zionism (Kosher Nationalism) + Imperialism = Fascism," *Black Panther*, 30 Aug. 1969; "Eldridge Warmly Received by the People of Algiers," *Black Panther*, 9 Aug. 1969. Other examples of pro-Palestinian reporting in the *Black Panther* include "Mao Condemns U.S.-Israeli Link," 16 Nov. 1968; "Palestine Guerillas vs. Israeli Pigs," 4 Jan. 1969; "Fatah's Spokesman," 4 Jan. 1969; and "Al Fath Speaks," 9 Aug. 1969.

27. Newton, "On the Middle East," 193–94, 196. On the BPP's criticism of Arab nationalism, see Lubin, *Geographies of Liberation*, 122.

28. Hamlin, interview with author; John Watson to Muhammad Kenyatta, 7 Apr. 1971, in Dan Georgakas Papers, RL, box 1, folder Black Star Productions correspondence.

29. Hall, "On the Tail of the Panther"; Marvin Garson, "What Happened in Chicago—An Analysis: The Whites: A Clown Show," *Berkeley Barb*, 15–21 Sept. 1967.

30. Garson, "What Happened in Chicago"; Carmichael, "The Black American," 140; Jabara, "The American Left," 178–79; Stork, "The American New Left," 67.

31. Garson, "What Happened in Chicago"; James Ridgeway, "Freak Out in Chicago: The National Conference of New Politics," *New Republic*, 16 Sept. 1967, 9–12; Podhoretz, *Breaking Ranks*, 335; Vaisse, *Neoconservatism*, 61; Jabara, "The American Left," 179.

32. Weisbord and Kazarian, *Israel in the Black American Perspective*, 38–39; Lubin, *Geographies of Liberation*, 118.

33. "An Appeal by Black Americans for United States Support for Israel," advertisement, *NYT*, 28 June 1970.

34. "An Appeal by Black Americans against United States Support of the Zionist Government of Israel," advertisement, *NYT*, 1 Nov. 1970.

35. Weisbord and Kazarian, *Israel in the Black American Perspective*, 48. After some black leaders associated with the convention, principally Gary mayor Richard Hatcher, disavowed the anti-Israel resolution, it was later watered down. See "Israel-South Africa Ties Exposed by AAUG Delegates," *AN*, July 1972.

36. "To Our African Brothers: Message from the Palestine National Liberation Movement (Fateh) to the African Cultural Festival Held in Algeria," 27 July 1969, ASAR; "Israel-South Africa Ties"; "Seminar on Israel, South Africa Diamond Industries Held," *AN*, July 1972; Iris Southall, "Madison Area Committee on Southern Africa," *AN*, Mar. 1971.

37. Juan Williams, "African, Arab Groups Stage Rally," *WP*, 14 May 1978; Yaqub, "'Our Declaration of Independence,'" 18–19.

38. "An Appeal by Black Americans"; "Shirley Chisholm Speaks Out," *Palestinian Voice*, Apr. 1972; "Chisholm Endorses Palestinian Rights in Position Paper," *AN*, Apr. 1972.

39. Unknown to Abdeen Jabara, 23 Mar. 1972, and Jabara to Congressional Black Caucus

Members, 27 Mar. 1972, in AAUGP, box 28, folder Correspondence, Abdeen Jabara, President 1972"; "Shirley Chisholm Disavows View of Black Caucus," *AN*, June 1972; "Americans Lose Arab Goodwill, Trust–Chisholm," *AN*, July 1972.

40. Farsoun, Farsoun, and Ajay, "Mid-East Perspectives," 94; Jabara, "The American Left," 171; Chomsky, "Israel and the New Left," 199; Stork, "The American New Left," 65.

41. Marvin Garson, "The Ombilical," *Berkeley Barb*, 16–22 June 1967; "Catch 8 ½," *Berkeley Barb*, 30 June–6 July 1967.

42. Saks, "Israel and the New Left."

43. I. F. Stone, "The Future of Israel," *Ramparts*, July 1967. The next month, Stone's piece critical of Israel in the *New York Review of Books* attracted considerable attention and controversy. Stone, "Holy War," 3 Aug. 1967. Paul Jacobs's contribution to the *Ramparts* discussion of the conflict was similar to Stone's in both supporting Israel's existence and calling on Israel to initiate a two-state solution. Jacobs, "A Time to Heal," *Ramparts*, July 1967. Also see Stork, "The American New Left," 65.

44. In *Ramparts*, Michael Walzer and Martin Peretz, "Israel Is Not Vietnam," July 1967; Maurice Zeitlin, "The Post-War Israeli Left," Jan. 1968; Michael P. Lerner, "Ephemera: Marx and the Zionists," Sept. 1969; and Sol Stern, "My Jewish Problem—and Ours," Aug. 1971. Also see Jabara, "The American Left," 172–73.

45. Robert Scheer, "Foreign News: A Territorial Imperative," *Ramparts*, Nov. 1969; Jabara, "The American Left," 174–76; Stetler, *Palestine*. Other pro-Palestinian pieces in *Ramparts* included Joe Stork, "The Battle of Amman," Sept. 1972; Fawaz Turki, "Thoughts of a Palestinian Exile," Sept. 1972; and Noam Chomsky, "The Mideast: Dark at the End of the Tunnel," Jan. 1973.

46. The paper, founded in 1948, originally was titled the *National Guardian* but changed its leadership and name in 1968 to signal a shift from Old Left to New Left orientation. Elbaum, *Revolution in the Air*, 61; Jabara, "The American Left," 182.

47. Radical Education Project pamphlets: Israeli Socialist Organization, "The Other Israel: A Critique of Zionist History and Policy," 1968; "They Say All the Women Must Be Commandoes," n.d.; Fatah, "Towards a Democratic State in Palestine," n.d. "Arab Women Fight," *New Left Notes*, 8 Mar. 1969. An undated compilation of essays by SDS members includes both pro-Zionist and anti-Zionist views. The anthology, titled *SDS* (in the online database "The Sixties: Primary Documents and Personal Narratives, 1960 to 1974," Alexander Street Press, alexanderstreet.com), includes essays such as Alan Schreck, "Zionism: A Racist Ideology: A Challenge," and Robert Steinhorn, "Golda as Fascist." On SDS's Radical Education Project, see Sale, *SDS*, 288–89, 395.

48. Ryan and Cavalletto, interview with author.

49. Ibid.; Stork, "The American New Left," 65. Examples of LNS articles on the Arab-Israeli conflict during this period are Yehuda Krantz, "Middle East: The Refugee Problem," 21 Nov. 1968; "Al-Fatah Threatens Hussein," 25 Apr. 1969; "Demonstrations Banned in Israel," 3 May 1969; Mark Feinstein, "Middle East Crisis" (a four-part series), July through Aug. 1969; "The Making of Refugees: How the Palestinians Were Driven from Their Land," 27 Oct. 1973; "Demonstrators Protest 'Salute to Israel,'" 16 June 1976; and "Israeli Arms Exports Grow, Sales to South Africa Increase," 18 Jan. 1977. In *A New Dawn*, 180–81, Slonecker states that Ryan and Cavalletto were able to convince the LNS to take a strong "pro-Palestinian line," yet some members of the collective were very uncomfortable with that position. For more discussion of the LNS and Ryan's and Cavalletto's participation, see McMillian, *Smoking Typewriters*, 147–48, 152.

50. "For Peace and Reconciliation," *Link*, Sept./Oct. 1970.

51. Committee to Support Middle East Liberation Records, 1967–1969, in SPC.

52. Jabara, "The American Left," 171–72; "Tri-Con Vows Support for NLF's Anywhere," *Berkeley Barb*, 29 July 1966. Friends of the Tri-Con Progressive Students Committee, "Vietnam-Palestine One Struggle," flyer, in IACR; Liberation Support Movement, "Films of Liberation," flyer, in

Liberation Support Movement Records, SPC. Columbia Anti-Imperialist Movement Records, 1971–1973, University Protest and Activism Collection, Series VIII, Columbia University Rare Book and Manuscript Library, box 10, folder 2.

53. Jabara, "The American Left," 171–72; "Hillel Foundation Calls for Student Unity on War," *Spartan Daily*, 31 May 1972 (in "The Sixties: Primary Documents and Personal Narratives, 1960 to 1974," online database, Alexander Street Press, alexanderstreet.com, accessed 16 July 2012); Stork, "The American New Left," 65.

54. Chomsky, "Israel and the New Left"; Seth King, "Arab-American Meeting Hears Chomsky," *NYT*, 2 Nov. 1970. In what was known as the "Mideast Pentagon Papers" case, Chomsky joined with such other clergy and scholars associated with the peace movement as Howard Zinn to file suit against the federal government to compel the release of the U.S. government's contingency plans for military intervention in the Middle East. Represented by Abdeen Jabara, the plaintiffs were ultimately unsuccessful. See "What You Don't Know Does Hurt You," *AN*, Dec. 1971, and "Mideast Pentagon Papers Linked to Current Threats," *AN*, Aug. 1973.

55. AAUG, *The First Decade*, 27–29; "Berrigan Speech Sparks U.S. Debate," *AN*, Mar. 1974; Paul Jacobs, "Some of His Best Friends Were," *Ramparts*, Apr. 1974.

56. Timothy Leary, "The P.O.W. Communiqué," 1970, www.luminist.org/archives/leary_POW .htm (accessed 13 Nov. 2013); Albert quoted in Greenfield, *Timothy Leary*, 407. For more discussion of Leary's attempt to meet with Fatah, see Leary, *Confessions*, 170–78; Jennifer Dohrn, "Getting High with Jennifer," *Good Times*, 8 Jan. 1971, behistory.weebly.com/tim-leary.html (accessed 11 Nov. 2013). Jennifer Dohrn accompanied Leary on the delegation from Algeria to Beirut.

57. Bernadine Dohrn, "Communique #4 from The Weatherman Underground," www.anti authoritarian.net/sds_wuo/weather/wuo_communique_4.txt (accessed 11 Nov. 2013).

58. Jabara, interview with author, 23 July 2012; Jabara, "The American Left," 182–85; Farsoun, Farsoun, and Ajay, "Mid-East Perspectives," 100–103, 110–12; Robert Langston, "Lebanon: A Developing Social Revolution," *Militant* 14 Nov. 1969 (in "The Sixties: Primary Documents and Personal Narratives, 1960 to 1974," online database, Alexander Street Press, alexanderstreet. com, accessed 14 July 2012); "Stop the Anti-Arab Witch Hunt," and Peter Buch, "Imperialism and the Arab Revolution," *Young Socialist*, Nov. 1972, both in AJP, box 13, folder Operation Boulder—Press Clippings 1972–9. At Wayne State University, the Socialist Workers Party and its affiliated Young Socialist Alliance cosponsored demonstrations with the Organization of Arab Students (Arab Student Association). See "Blacks and Arabs to Protest Israeli Speaker," *SE*, 4 June 1968, and Nikos Boyias, "Arab Supporters Demonstrate," *SE*, 27 Jan. 1969. At Berkeley, representatives of the Progressive Labor Party and the Socialist Workers Party occasionally spoke at the Arab Student Association's events. See "Palestine Week Activities," flyer, n.d., ASAR, and "Mass Rally in Union Square in Support of the Palestinian Revolution," flyer, n.d., IACR.

59. Farsoun, Farsoun, and Ajay, "Mid-East Perspectives," 96–98; 107–10, 116–17. Other progressive, but not revolutionary, American organizations took varying positions on the Palestinian question in this period. The New American Movement generally supported Palestinian rights, the Social Democratic Party (associated with Michael Harrington) advocated U.S. support for Israel, and the Socialist Labor Party attempted to maintain a neutral stance.

60. Issues of the *Eldon Spark*: "Why the Arabs and the Jews Are at War," 21 Sept. 1972; "War in the Mid-East," 18 Oct. 1973; "Middle-East Massacres," 5 June 1974; "Who Are the Terrorists?," 27 Nov. 1974, all in UAW Collection, Eldon Wildcat Records, folders Eldon Spark 1972, Eldon Spark 1973, and Eldon Spark 1974, RL; Beinin, interview with author, 5 July 2012.

61. Many pro-Arab organizations that originated in the United States in the late 1960s and early 1970s had considerable involvement from Americans who were not of Arab heritage. A prime example was the American Committee for Justice in the Middle East (ACJME), based in Boulder, Colorado. The committee was led by such individuals as Bernice Espy Hicks, an

American woman who became interested in Arab world issues when she hosted Arab exchange students in the 1950s and then traveled to Jordan in the early 1960s and visited Palestinian refugee camps, and it published a newsletter, along with position papers on Middle East issues that supported the Palestinian cause, and had a mailing list of several thousand people. Americans for Middle East Understanding (AMEU), founded in 1968 and based in New York City, was an ecumenical Christian group with a pro-Palestinian stance. It was initially led by non–Arab Americans who were academics, professionals, and businesspeople who had associations with the Middle East. Americans for Middle East Understanding published a monthly newsletter, the *Link*, that sought to inform its audience, mainly churchgoing Americans, about the Arab perspective on Middle East conflicts. See "Bernice Espy Hicks: A Profile," *AN*, June 1976; "Who's Who in AMEU?," *Link*, Sept. 1968, www.ameu.org (accessed 28 Jan. 2013). A similar organization that was established in the early 1950s was the American Friends of the Middle East (AFME). One of its founders was Frank Maria, a prominent Syrian American leader. A cofounder was the prominent journalist Dorothy Thompson, who was ostracized from the American press after she expressed a pro-Palestinian stance in the late 1940s. Consisting mainly of non-Arab academics, clergy, and professionals, the AFME supported Arab nationalism and concentrated on fostering cultural exchange between the United States and the Arab world, along with humanitarian and other assistance projects in the Middle East, through the 1970s. It should also be noted that the AFME was funded by the CIA. See Carenen, *The Fervent Embrace*, 87, 100–101, and Garrett and Purpura, *Frank Maria*, 129–31; on the AFME as a CIA front group, see Wilford, *America's Great Game*, 117–31.

62. Interview with Beinin, who called MERIP "the most important Left organization that focused on the Middle East." See the list of staff members in *MERIP Reports* 1 (Aug. 1971): 1; Sheila Ryan and Joe Stork, "U.S. and Jordan: Thrice Rescued Throne," *MERIP Reports* 2 (Feb. 1972): 3–11; Ryan, "Constructing a New Imperialism: Israel and the West Bank," *MERIP Reports* 9 (May 1972): 3–11. After a couple of years, a few Arab Americans joined the staff of *MERIP Reports*, such as Palestinian American sociologist Samih Farsoun. Later in the 1970s, Joel Beinin joined MERIP.

63. Ryan and Cavalletto, interview with author; "Judge Frees Sheila Ryan," *WP*, 17 Dec. 1967, discusses her arrest for participating in a 1965 civil rights sit-in at the White House.

64. "Demonstrate June 13" and "PLO Representative Addresses NYC Rally," *Palestine!*, 10 June 1976; "N.Y. Protest Hits Zionist Parade," *Palestine!*, July–Aug. 1976.

65. Ryan and Cavalletto, interview with author.

66. Third World Liberation Front at University of California–Berkeley, Vertical File, SCL-UM; Fujino, "The Black Liberation Movement"; Third World Coalition Records, University Protest and Activism Collection, Series VIII, Columbia University Rare Book and Manuscript Library, box 14, folder 16; Beinin, interview with author; Jabara, interview with author; Jabara, "The American Left," 185–86.

67. Stork, "The American New Left," 64–65, 68–69.

68. Chomsky, "Israel and the New Left," 200–202, 205–6, 211.

69. Klinghoffer, *Vietnam, Jews*, 161; Vaisse, *Neoconservatism*, 61–62; Podhoretz, *Breaking Ranks*, 335; Brick and Phelps, *Radicals in America*, 239.

70. Abba Binder and Mel Krugel, letter to the editor, *SE*, 5 Feb. 1969; Sol Stern, "My Jewish Problem—and Ours," *Ramparts*, Aug. 1971.

71. Stern, "My Jewish Problem"; Ehrman, *The Rise of Neoconservatism*, 38–41; Vaisse, *Neoconservatism*, 10, 58, 61–63. One sign of Jewish progressives' shift to conservatism was New Left intellectual Martin Peretz walking out of the Conference of New Politics and later assuming editorship of the *New Republic*, using the magazine to assert pro-Israel views. Another sign was

Norman Podhoretz's transformation of the Jewish magazine *Commentary* into a neoconservative publication in the 1970s.

72. Chertoff, "The New Left," 172, 175; Glazer, "Jewish Interests," 159–60; Lipset, "'The Socialism of Fools,'" 118–23. Also see Avineri, "Israel and the New Left."

73. Stork and Theberge, "Any Arab," 6; David Young, "Arabs in U.S. Accuse F.B.I. of Spying on Them," *Chicago Tribune*, 13 July 1975; FBI, "Fedayeen Impact," http://www.governmentattic.org/docs/FBI_Monograph_Fedayeen_Impact_1970.pdf ; United Press International, "Ford: Mideast Agitators on U.S. Campuses," *Sandusky Register*, 25 Apr. 1969, http://NewspaperArchive.com.

74. Suleiman, "The Arab American Left," 233.

75. Ahmed, interview with author; Ahmed, interview with Terry, JTP, box 1; Ahmed, "Ismael Ahmed," 28.

76. Ahmed, interview with author; Ahmed, interview with Terry; *Stillborn Press*, Feb. 1971, in HAP, box 1, folder SEDCC Newsletters & Flyers 1970–1975.

77. Ahmed, interview with author; Ahmed, interview with Terry.

78. Abraham, interview with author; Abraham, "To Palestine and Back," 452.

79. Nawash, interview with Terry, JTP, box 1; Khoury, interview with author.

80. Jabara, interview with Terry, JTP, box 1.

81. Ibid.; Jabara, interview with author. See, for example, "Anti-Vietnam War Activists Urge U.S. to Stay Out of Mideast War: Parallels Drawn to U.S. War in Vietnam," n.d., in AJP, box 13, folder UAW Arab Workers Caucus-Miscellaneous (c. 1973–4).

82. Fernandez, "Denise Oliver"; Fujino, "Grassroots Leadership"; Fujino, "The Black Liberation Movement."

83. Smith, *Hippies*, 10–11.

84. Ibid., 11.

85. Jabara, Presidential Address to AAUG Convention, Berkeley, California, 11 Nov. 1972, in AAUGP, box 14, folder Correspondence President—1972 (Jabara); Suleiman, "Arab Americans and the Political Process," 47; Cainkar, "Thinking Outside the Box," 80. According to Jabara in his interview with me, a few early AAUG members wanted the organization to be a "much more mainstream organization in the United States" that identified with and appealed to the people in power: white Americans. But the organization chose to align itself with Third World peoples and advocate a radical anti-imperialist ideology. As a result, some AAUG members who sought the "mainstream" orientation ended up leaving the organization.

86. Abu Shanab, "Repression at Home," *Action*, 16 Feb. 1970, University of North Carolina–Charlotte Special Collections Library, American New Left Collection, folder Palestinians.

87. Pulido, *Black, Brown*, 136–37, 155–59.

88. Gualtieri, *Between Arab and White*, 11; Cainkar, "Thinking Outside the Box," 46–47.

89. Abu-Laban, "The Coexistence of Cohorts," 55–56; Abraham, "Arabs in America," 19.

90. Samhan, "Politics and Exclusion"; Salaita, *Anti-Arab Racism*, 13; Abraham, "Anti-Arab Racism," 179–80.

91. Abraham, "Anti-Arab Racism,"180–89; Cainkar, "Thinking Outside the Box," 47; Shryock, "The Moral Analogies of Race," 95; Gualtieri, *Between Arab and White*, 180; Shain, "Arab Americans," 47–48; Naber, *Arab America*, 39.

92. "Arab Group in U.S. Hails Guerrillas," *NYT*, 13 Nov. 1972.

93. Georgakas, "Arab Workers," 16–17; Georgakas and Surkin, *Detroit*, 68.

94. Ahmed, interview with Terry.

95. Ahmed, interview with author; Jabara, interview with author. These perceptions of racial identity are further complicated by the diversity among ethnic groups from the Arab world.

Iraqi Chaldeans, for example, have been resistant to characterization as "Arab." See Sengstock, "Detroit's Iraqi-Chaldeans."

96. Most of the Arab American gas station and convenience store owners in the Detroit metropolitan area were Iraqi Chaldean Americans. In the 1980s and 1990s, robberies and violence exacerbated the conflicts between African Americans and Arab Americans, and in 2001 one activist black organization mobilized a boycott of Chaldean gas stations. See David, "Behind the Bulletproof Glass," 167–71; Darden and Thomas, *Detroit*, 181–98; and Cainkar, "Immigrants," 193.

97. Jabara, interview with author; Armand Gebert, "Store Slaying Fuels Tensions," *Detroit News*, 26 Oct. 1980.

98. House, interview with author.

99. Hamlin, interview with author.

100. Ahmed, interview with author; Abraham, interview with author; Khoury, interview with author.

101. Barbara Aswad, interview with author.

102. Pulido, *Black, Brown*, 4, 33; Brilliant, *The Color of America*, 6–9.

103. Pulido, *Black, Brown*, 47–52; Thomas, *Puerto Rican Citizen*, 229, 234; Glasser, "From 'Rich Port' to Bridgeport," 192–93.

104. Pulido, *Black, Brown*, 56–58, 125–26; Thomas, *Puerto Rican Citizen*, 234. One of the Los Angeles organizations that Pulido studies, the Centros de Accion Social Autonomo (CASA), embraced a form of transnationalism that caused it to focus exclusively on Mexican immigrants and developments in Mexico. Practicing its politics in an insular, isolationist vein, even CASA's leaders did not seek interactions with African American and Asian American activists in the area.

105. Smith, *Hippies*, 11.

106. Fernandez, "Denise Oliver"; Smith, *Hippies*, 13.

Chapter 4

1. Kaiser, "R.F.K. Must Die," 530; Ayton, *The Forgotten Terrorist*; Michael R. Fischbach, "First Shot in Terror War Killed RFK," *LAT*, 2 June 2003. For an interpretation similar to Ayton's, see Gil Troy, "How Come We Don't Call RFK's Assassination Palestinian Terrorism?," *History News Network*, 6 June 2013, http://hnn.us/gil_troy/articles/152145.html (accessed 12 June 2013). A book that discusses the "patsy" theory is Moldea, *The Killing of Robert F. Kennedy*. The documentary *RFK Must Die* advances conspiracy theories about the assassination and ignores Arab political motives.

2. Jabara, foreword to "Lost Significance of Sirhan's Case."

3. Ayton, *The Forgotten Terrorist*, 51–53.

4. Ibid., 51–54; Jabara, foreword to "Lost Significance of Sirhan's Case," 2.

5. Moldea, *The Killing of Robert F. Kennedy*, 121; Jansen, *Why Robert Kennedy*, 143–44; Ayton, *The Forgotten Terrorist*, 215. It is under dispute whether Sirhan was involved in the OAS while at Pasadena City College. Ayton states that while it was not recognized as an official student organization, the OAS did operate a chapter there, and Sirhan was active in it for a while. See Ayton, *The Forgotten Terrorist*, 210, 243. In a long profile of Sirhan, *Los Angeles Times* reporters talked to a man who said he was a friend of the Sirhan family and attended OAS meetings with Sirhan and his two brothers. See Robert C. Toth and Dave Smith, "Sirhan—The Wanderer—Never Found His Way," *LAT*, 5 Jan. 1969. However, no other journalists or researchers have confirmed his membership, and in fact an officer of the national OAS wrote a letter to the editor of the *Washington Post* denying that Sirhan was ever a member of the organization. See Walid Khadduri, letter to the editor, *WP*, 9 June 1968.

6. See pages from Sirhan's notebook in the appendix to Kaiser, "R.F.K. Must Die," 383–97; Ayton, *The Forgotten Terrorist*, 67.

7. Brown, *The Presidency on Trial*, 44.

8. Jansen, *Why Robert Kennedy*, 186–88, 190; "HHH Said Near Nomination," with picture of Kennedy captioned "Bobby Says Shalom," *Pasadena Independent*, 27 May 1968, http://NewspaperArchive.com (accessed 8 Apr. 2013); Richard Harwood, "Kennedy Declares U.S. Should Defend Israel," *WP*, 27 May 1968; Ayton, *The Forgotten Terrorist*, 44–46.

9. Sirhan quoted in Jansen, *Why Robert Kennedy*, 193–94; notebook pages in Kaiser, *"R.F.K. Must Die."*

10. Ayton, *The Forgotten Terrorist*, 27, 75–83; Jansen, *Why Robert Kennedy*, 225; Jabara, foreword to "Lost Significance of Sirhan's Case," 3.

11. David Lawrence, "Paradoxical Bob," *Pasadena Independent Star-News*, 26 May 1968, http://NewspaperArchive.com.

12. Harry F. Rosenthal [Associated Press], "Prosecution Says Sirhan Told Reason," *Denver Post*, 14 Feb. 1969, in FSP, box 13, folder 4: Sirhan Sirhan Trial; George Lardner Jr., "Sirhan Motive Called Political," *WP*, 29 Mar. 1969; "Studies in Killing," *Newsweek*, 31 Mar. 1969.

13. United Press International, "Sirhan's Lawyer Asks Life Term," *Ogden (Utah) Standard-Examiner*, 11 Apr. 1969; "Sirhan Case May Go to Jury Monday," *Evening Star*, 12 Apr. 1969, clippings in FSP.

14. Kaiser, *"R.F.K. Must Die,"* 231.

15. Jabara, foreword to Jansen, *Why Robert Kennedy*, 8. In his preparation for the Sirhan trial, Jabara collected the following articles and essays: H. Edward Ransford, "Isolation, Powerlessness, and Violence: A Study of Attitudes and Participation in the Watts Riot," *American Journal of Sociology* (1968); Marvin E. Olsen, "Two Categories of Political Alienation," *Social Forces* (1969); Allen D. Grimshaw, "Relationships among Prejudice, Discrimination, Social Tension, and Social Violence," *Journal of Intergroup Relations* (1961); Frantz Fanon, "Colonial War and Mental Disorders," from *The Wretched of the Earth* (1961). See AJP, box 1, folders 1 and 9.

16. "Months of Conflicting Testimony Accent the Basic Disagreements," *National Observer*, 14 Apr. 1969; Douglas E. Kneeland, "Sirhan Trial Seen Plodding Along in World of Own," *NYT*, 2 Feb. 1969. Jabara was convinced that Berman, a Jew, was not comfortable highlighting the importance of Palestinian nationalism in Sirhan's mental makeup. Jabara, interview with author; Jabara, foreword to Jansen, *Why Robert Kennedy*, 10. Jabara prepared a long list of voir dire questions about Palestine and Israel for Sirhan's attorneys to ask potential jurors. According to Jabara, the attorneys ignored them. See Jabara, voir dire questions, FSP. An article in the *Los Angeles Herald-Examiner* reported that "Jabara is a source of friction in the Sirhan defense battery. To Parsons, he is a valued consultant. To Berman and Cooper he is often a thorn in the side." See John Douglas, "Trial Spotlight to Turn on Sirhan Slaying Story," *Los Angeles Herald-Examiner*, n.d., FSP. Jabara sent the *Herald-Examiner* article to Fayez Sayegh, an Arab diplomat working with the Arab Information Center of the Arab League, accompanied by a handwritten note: "This article will give you some of the flavor of the problems I've faced out here. However, I think we have had some effect although less than hoped for or expected."

17. "Doesn't Recall Killing, Sirhan Tells RFK Jury," *Evening Star*, 7 Mar. 1969, in FSP. According to *Newsweek*, Sirhan's testimony about the 1948 war contributed to the jury's perception that he was mentally unstable. See "Sirhan: Tragedy of the Absurd," *Newsweek*, 24 Mar. 1969.

18. Sirhan's testimony in "Lost Significance of Sirhan's Case," 5–16.

19. "Sirhan Begs for Execution," *Evening Star*, 1 Mar. 1969, in FSP.

20. "The Story of Sirhan Sirhan," *WP*, 10 Mar. 1969.

21. Jabara, foreword to Jansen, *Why Robert Kennedy*, 11–12; Jabara, foreword to "Lost Significance of Sirhan's Case," 3–5; Jabara, interview with author.

22. Jabara, foreword to "Lost Significance of Sirhan's Case," 3. Making a similar case in his

foreword to Jansen's book, Jabara drew on the writings of Frantz Fanon and Edward Said to explain the psychological state of colonized people.

23. Jansen, *Why Robert Kennedy*, 17, 231–32.

24. Lukas, "Why Robert Kennedy Was Killed."

25. Mehdi, *Kennedy and Sirhan: Why?*, 9, 31.

26. Jansen, *Why Robert Kennedy*, 214; Ayton, *The Forgotten Terrorist*, 246, 233.

27. For examples of this media coverage, see Jane E. Brody, "In the Mind of the Assassin," *NYT*, 9 June 1968; "The Trial of Sirhan Sirhan," *WP*, 7 Jan. 1969; George Lardner, "RFK Slaying Is Reenacted by Hypnosis," *WP*, 9 Mar. 1969; "All the Elements," *Newsweek*, 10 Mar. 1969; "The Sirhan Case," *Time*, 21 Mar. 1969; Linda Mathews, "Sirhan in Trance on Assassination Night," *LAT*, 27 Mar. 1969; and Jansen, *Why Robert Kennedy*, 211.

28. "Crime Bill Passed, but Johnson Calls Gun Curbs Weak," *WP*, 7 June 1968; "Yorty Claims Red Groups Inflamed Assassin," *WP*, 7 June 1968.

29. I examined approximately 150 newspaper and magazine reports of the assassination and trial, from June 1968 to June 1973. Most appeared in major newspapers such as the *Washington Post*, *Los Angeles Times*, and *New York Times*, along with national news magazines *Newsweek*, *Time*, and *Life*. My sample also included the reporting provided by the *Evening Star*, a Washington, D.C., daily, and the *Ogden (UT) Standard-Examiner*. Over one hundred articles from these two newspapers, along with a few other newspapers, mainly from AP and UPI sources, were collected in a clippings file on the Sirhan case in the Fayez Sayegh Papers at the Marriott Library, University of Utah.

30. Said, *Orientalism*; Suleiman, *The Arabs in the Mind of America*.

31. "For Perspective and Determination," *Time*, 14 June 1968; Paul O'Brien, "Ray, Sirhan—What Possessed Them?," *Life*, 21 June 1969; "Smiling Through," *Newsweek*, 27 Jan. 1969. Also see "RFK Suspect Identified as an Arab," *Chicago Tribune*, 6 June 1968.

32. "The Intricate Puzzle of Sirhan Sirhan," *WP*, 9 June 1968.

33. Toth and Smith, "Sirhan—The Wanderer."

34. "A Year Nearer the Next War," *Economist*, 8 June 1968; Harry F. Rosenthal [Associated Press], "Prosecution Says Sirhan Told Reason," *Denver Post*, 14 Feb. 1969, FSP.

35. Seymour Korman, "Sirhan Admits under Oath That He Shot RFK," *Chicago Tribune*, 4 Mar. 1969; Associated Press, "Sirhan Testifies of Decision to Kill Kennedy," *Evening Star*, 5 Mar. 1969, FSP. Also see Korman, "Defense Counsel Depicts Sirhan as Man Out of Touch with Reality," *Chicago Tribune*, 15 Feb. 1969; "The Wanderer," *Newsweek*, 13 Jan. 1969; George Lardner, "Agitated Sirhan Tells Court of Urge to Kill RFK in May," *WP*, 5 Mar. 1969; Lacey Fosburgh, "Sirhan Tells Court Why He Wanted to Kill Kennedy," *NYT*, 5 Mar. 1969; and Douglas Robinson, "Sirhan Is Enraged by Opinion He Lied," *NYT*, 2 Apr. 1969.

36. For example, George Lardner, "Mention of Execution Jars Sirhan," *WP*, 14 Jan. 1969; Associated Press, "Sirhan 'Trance' Told by Counsel," *Ogden (Utah) Standard-Examiner*, 14 Feb. 1969, FSP.

37. Frank Mankiewicz and Tom Braden, "Rogers Backed but Judge Rejected Sirhan Guilty Plea for Life Term," *WP*, 26 Feb. 1969. I have not found corroboration of the meeting between the Los Angeles district attorney and the secretary of state.

38. Douglas E. Kneeland, "Sirhan Trial Seen Plodding Along in World of Own," *NYT*, 2 Feb. 1969; Ellen Zurkey, "Detroiter Fights to Save Sirhan," *Detroit Free Press*, 4 July 1969; "Sirhan Voices Regret at Having Killed Kennedy," *NYT*, 3 June 1969; Sirhan's NBC interview quoted in Kaiser, *"R.F.K. Must Die,"* 350–53.

39. "Who Seeks the Blood of This Boy?," press release, 26 June 1968, and John M. Lawrence to Al Matthews, 13 June 1968, in AJP, box 13, folder Organizing Committee for Clemency for Sirhan; Correspondence between Hagopian and Jabara, 1–2 July 1968, and Jabara to Lawrence,

3 July 1968, in AAUGP, box 16, folder 12. Also see Paul Coates, "Clemency for Sirhan or Wheels within Wheels," *LAT*, 15 July 1968, and Kaiser, *"R.F.K. Must Die,"* 125–27. It appears that Lawrence had anti-Semitic tendencies and was unbalanced. See additional materials from Lawrence to Jabara in AAUGP, box 31.

40. The reproduced telegram appears to be a paid advertisement by Mehdi. See *Al-Islaah*, 7 May 1969 and 31 May 1969.

41. "One More Chapter in a Tragedy of Our Time," *Middle East Newsletter*, June–July 1968, in JTP, box 1, folder Publications—The Middle East Newsletter; Robert Fraga, "Sirhan/Kennedy: An Essay on Political Violence," *Middle East Newsletter*, Apr. 1969, in AJP, box 1, folder 8: Litigation—Sirhan Defense—Press Clippings.

42. "Arab Press Plays Up Sirhan's Anti-Zionism," *NYT*, 10 Mar. 1969; "Trials: Verdict on Sirhan," *Newsweek*, 28 Apr. 1969, 41; William Tuohy, "Posters in Arab Nations Depict Sirhan as Hero," *LAT*, 9 Apr. 1969. The poster can be viewed on the Palestine Poster Project website, http://www.palestineposterproject.org/poster/sirhan-bishara-sirhan (accessed 20 Nov. 2013.)

43. Naftali, *Blind Spot*, 69; Fischbach, "First Shot."

44. Jabara, interview with author.

45. Shihab, *Sirhan*, 4. But Shihab himself was not persuaded that Sirhan acted out of a political motive.

46. Mahmoud Abdel-Hadi, "Assassinations: Sirhan's Motives," reprinted in *Ramparts*, Sept. 1968.

47. Rubin, *Do It*, 150–51.

48. Ahmed, interview with author; Aswad and Aswad, interview with author; "Father of Sirhan Asks, 'What Do You Think I Feel?'" *WP*, 7 June 1968.

49. E-mail from Ron Amen to Sally Howell, 6 May 2011, in author's possession. George Khoury remembers that most Arab Americans he knew at the time were in such disbelief that they did not believe that Sirhan committed the murder. Khoury, interview with author.

50. Jabara, interview with author.

51. United Press International, "Ford: Mideast Agitators on U.S. Campuses," *Sandusky Register*, 25 Apr. 1969, http://NewspaperArchive.com.

52. Max Lerner, "Attacks on Airliners Must Stop," *LAT*, 20 Feb. 1969.

53. Khoury, interview with author; Aswad and Aswad, interview with author; "Operation Arab: Silencing Voices of Truth in Fear," *AN*, June 1973.

Chapter 5

1. Samhan, "Politics and Exclusion," 17; Jamal, "Civil Liberties," 116–17; Naber, *Arab America*, 39. Also see Shryock, "The Moral Analogies of Race," 98.

2. Bashshur, "Unfulfilled Expectations," 13.

3. In *Enemies*, 313–14, 321–23, Tim Weiner briefly discusses the FBI's illegal efforts to thwart Arab terrorists in the 1970s but does not explore Operation Boulder. See Naftali, *Blind Spot*, 58–60, 67–70. Prominent studies of the national security state that do not mention its treatment of Arabs and Arab Americans include Theoharis, *Spying on Americans*, and *The FBI and American Democracy*; Greenberg, *The Dangers of Dissent*; and Scott, *Reining in the State*. For example, nearly all studies of the federal government's investigative apparatus rely on journalist Seymour Hersh's exposés of FBI and CIA activities published in the *New York Times* in 1973 and 1974 (discussed later in this chapter), but they ignore Hersh's mention of "potential Arab saboteurs" alongside the Black Panthers and antiwar groups as targets included in secret agency documents.

4. United Press International, "Ford: Mideast Agitators on U.S. Campuses," *Sandusky Register*, 25 Apr. 1969, http://NewspaperArchive.com.

5. Irving Spiegel, "Pro-Arab Groups in U.S. Assailed," *NYT*, 21 Apr. 1969; Arnold Forster,

letter to the editor, *NYT*, 28 May 1969. See Shannon, "'Contacts with the Opposition,'" on the U.S. government monitoring and infiltration of Iranian student groups in the United States during the 1960s.

6. Hussaini, "The Impact of the Arab-Israeli Conflict," 216–17; Fischbach, "Government Pressures," 89; Haddad, *Not Quite American?*, 20.

7. Seymour Hersh, "Alien-Radical Tie Disputed by CIA," *NYT*, 25 May 1973; Gessert, "A Non-Arab Looks," 23. In violation of the National Security Act of 1947, in the late 1960s the CIA began Operation CHAOS in which it surveilled American political dissenters, purportedly seeking connections between U.S. activists and foreign subversives. See Theoharis, *Spying on Americans*, 131, 178.

8. Seymour Hersh, "Nixon '70 Domestic Security Plan Detailed," *NYT*, 24 May 1973.

9. FBI, "Fedayeen Impact," http://www.governmentattic.org/docs/FBI_Monograph_Fedayeen_Impact_1970.pdf; quote from FBI, "The Fedayeen Terrorist," http://www.governmentattic.org/docs/FBI_Monograph_Fedayeen_Terrorist_June-1970.pdf; Gessert, "A Non-Arab Looks," 21–23.

10. Jabara, "Operation Arab," 7.

11. "Complaint," *Abdeen Jabara, Plaintiff vs. Manufacturer's National Bank of Detroit*, 10 May 1972, in AJP, box 2, folder Litigation–Jabara v Manufacturer's National Bank of Detroit, Court Documents; "Abdeen Jabara Discusses Lawsuit against FBI," *AN*, Sept. 1979. Jabara states that the FBI's inquiry to the bank was triggered by a payment he made to the Organization of Arab Students, which was a loan to help the OAS hold its annual convention. Jabara, interview with author; Jabara interview, *Tracked in America*, http://www.trackedinamerica.org/timeline/civil_rights/jabara/.

12. For Nixon's reaction to the Munich massacre and his political calculations behind the creation of the Cabinet Committee, see Nixon White House Tapes, NPL, Tape 771, Conversation 2, 6 Sept. 1972, http://www.nixonlibrary.gov/forresearchers/find/tapes/tape771/tape771.php. (accessed 12 Apr. 2013).

13. Nixon, Memo to Secretary of State, 25 Sept. 1972, *The American Presidency Project*, UC-Santa Barbara, http://www.presidency.ucsb.edu/ws/?pid=3596 (accessed 13 Apr. 2013); Nixon White House Tapes, NPL, Tape 786, Conversation 5, 25 Sept. 1972, http://www.nixonlibrary.gov/forresearchers/find/tapes/tape786/786-005.mp3 (accessed 13 Apr. 2013). Also represented on the Cabinet Committee were the Department of Treasury, the Department of Defense, the Justice Department, the Department of Transportation, the U.S. ambassador to the United Nations, the CIA, and the president's assistants for national security and for domestic affairs. Also see Naftali, *Blind Spot*, 58–60. Bizarrely, it seems that Nixon may also have been influenced by his secretary Rosemary Woods, who informed him shortly after the Munich massacre that psychic Jeanne Dixon had told her there would soon be a terrorist attack on Israeli officials in the United States and advised him to respond preemptively. See Nixon White House Tapes, NPL, Tape 783, Conversation 25, 19 Sept. 1972 https://www.nixonlibrary.gov/forresearchers/find/tapes/tape783/783-025.mp3 (accessed 13 Apr. 2013).

14. Naftali, *Blind Spot*, 59–60.

15. Cabinet Committee to Combat Terrorism (CCCT) Working Group, minutes of 22 Mar. 1973 meeting, in NPL, White House Special Files, State Member and Office Files, Richard C. Tufaro, Subject Files 1972–3, CCCT Working Group, box 1, in Salim Yaqub's personal collection (hereafter Tufaro files).

16. Secretary of State William Rogers, Memo to President Nixon, 18 Sept. 1972, National Archives, RG 59.

17. CCCT Working Group, Minutes of 10 Oct. and 12 Oct. 1972 meetings, Tufaro files, box 1. The Committee also showed concern about the activities of the Jewish Defense League. See

Department of Justice memo to CCCT, 24 Nov. 1972, box 3, and CCCT Working Group, Minutes of 24 Jan. 1973 meeting, Tufaro files, box 1.

18. CCCT Working Group, Minutes of 6 Dec. 1972 and 7 Mar. 1973 meetings, Tufaro files, box 1; Acting Director of FBI to White House situation room, re: Arab Terrorism, Mar. 1973, Tufaro files, box 3; quote from FBI to U.S. Attorney General Edward Levi, 28 Apr. 1975, in National Archives, RG 60: Department of Justice, box 32, Subject Files of Attorney General Levi, folder Counter-Intelligence—Arabs.

19. "U.S. Checks Arabs to Block Terror," *NYT*, 5 Oct. 1972; "US Measures against Terror," *Newsweek*, 16 Oct. 1972; Jabara to AAUG Members and Friends, 24 Oct. 1972, in AJP, box 10, folder Activities-Harassment of Arab Americans–Correspondence.

20. Stork and Theberge, "Any Arab," 3; Saikowski, "Arabs in U.S."

21. Rogers, Memo to Nixon, 21 Sept. 1972, National Archives, RG 59; CCCT Working Group, Minutes of 22 Mar. 1973 meeting, Tufaro files, box 1; Sarafa, "The 'Chilling Effect,'" 48; Naftali, *Blind Spot*, 68; Saikowski, "Arabs in U.S."; Mosher, "Arabs Taste." The federal government was also reluctant to grant U.S. citizenship to politically active Arabs who applied for naturalization during the Operation Boulder period. See Jabara to Senator James Abourezk, 3 June 1974, in AJP, box 9, folder Activities Harassment of Arab Americans–Correspondence.

22. Jabara, "Operation Arab," 9; Saikowksi, "Arabs in U.S."

23. Jabara, "Operation Arab," 9; Saikowski, "Arabs in U.S."; Rogers, Memo to Nixon, 21 Sept. 1972.

24. Department of State, Memo of Conversation, Re: INS Handling of Arab Students, 20 Feb. 1973, in Tufaro files, box 2; Betty Edwards, "Victims in the War on Terrorism," *Palestinian Voice*, 16 Apr. 1973, clipping in FSP, box 355, folder 15. There are disputes in the records about how many Arab students were affected by Operation Boulder. According to Saikowski's January 1973 piece in the *Christian Science Monitor*, INS official James Greene told her 9,000 Arab students were presently in the United States, and the INS had screened 3,500 of them and begun deportation proceedings against 106. In *MERIP Reports*, journalists Joe Stork and René Theberge reported that the U.S. government had deported 78 Arab immigrants between September and December 1972. In his *National Observer* article, Lawrence Mosher reported that 6,300 Arab students were in the United States in the fall of 1972.

25. Saikowski, "Arabs in U.S."

26. The reason for this emphasis is unknown. Perhaps it is because Sirhan Sirhan had resided in that area.

27. Walt Murray, "U.S. Checking Arab Students in Colleges," *Long Beach Independent Press-Telegram*, 8 Nov. 1972, in AJP, box 13, folder Operation Boulder–Press Clippings 1972–9; Stork and Theberge, "Any Arab," 4. In April 1973, Edwards, "Victims in the War on Terrorism," quoted the Los Angeles district INS director stating that between 300 and 500 Arab students in the area had been questioned.

28. Edwards, "Victims in the War on Terrorism"; Stork and Theberge, "Any Arab."

29. "Meeting of Foreign Student Advisors with Mr. Salturelli, Immigration Investigations and Travel Control Representative at the Immigration Service Office in Detroit," 7 Nov. 1972, in AJP, box 13, folder Operation Boulder–Correspondence and Miscellaneous; Rachael Kamel, "U-M Collaborates in US Surveillances of Arab Students," *Michigan Free Press*, 20 Oct. 1975, in AJP, box 10, folder Activities–Harassment of Arab Americans, Press Clippings.

30. Organization of Arab Students, Wayne State University, to Members and Friends, 20 Nov. 1972, in AJP, box 10, folder Activities-Harassment of Arab Americans-Correspondence.

31. Quoted in Edwards, "Victims in the War on Terrorism." Also see Fischbach, "Government Pressures," 90.

32. Gessert, "A Non-Arab Looks," 18.

33. Bassiouni, "The AAUG," 28; Mosher, "Arabs Taste."

34. AJP, box 10, folder Activities-Harassment of Arab Americans–Correspondence and folder Activities-Harassment of Arab Americans–Testimonials and Misc., and box 13, folder Operation Boulder–Correspondence and Miscellaneous; Ahmed, interview with author. ACCESS is Arab Community Center for Economic and Social Services. AACC is American Arab Coordinating Committee. The Red Crescent is a humanitarian organization based in Syria that is affiliated with the International Red Cross. UHLF is United Holy Land Fund.

35. Bassiouni, "The AAUG," 29.

36. Jabara, "IRS Proposes"; Theoharis, *Spying on Americans*, 189.

37. Nicholas Horrock, "New Senate Panel May Study F.B.I. Drive on Arab Terrorism," *NYT*, 13 Feb. 1975; Wilson, "Buggings"; Weiner, *Enemies*, 292–95, 313–14. As part of its investigation of the FBI's illegal activities, the Senate's Select Committee to Study Governmental Operations with Respect to Intelligence Activities, led by Senator Frank Church, learned in its 1975 hearings of the FBI's 1972 burglary of the Arab Information Center.

38. Rogers to Nixon, 29 Mar. 1973, and CCCT Working Group, Minutes of 18 Apr. 1973 meeting, both in Tufaro files, box 1.

39. Rogers to Nixon, 8 Jan. 1973, Foreign Relations of the United States, U.S. Department of State, Office of Historian, http://history.state.gov/historicaldocuments/frus1969–76ve03/d203 (accessed 12 Apr. 2013); Bill Richards and LaBarbara Bowman, "Slaying of Alon Activated U.S. Watch for Terrorists," *WP*, 4 July 1973.

40. Paul Magnusson, "NSA Tapped Six Overseas Messages by Attorney for Sirhan, FBI Reveals," *WP*, 3 Aug. 1977; George Lardner Jr., "U.S. Fights Efforts of Terrorists," *WP*, 18 Mar. 1973, reported that the FBI quickly identified Khalid Al-Jawary, a member of Black September who entered the United States through Canada, as the perpetrator. According to Tim Weiner, *Enemies*, 321–23, the FBI suspected Al-Jawary, also known as Khalid Mohammed al-Jessem, of both attacks but did not have the evidence to convict him at the time; the U.S. federal government finally convicted him of the Meir bomb plot in 1993. The assassination of Alon remains officially unsolved. "Terrorist Freed after Sixteen Years," *LAT*, 27 Feb. 2009.

41. Bassiouni, introduction to *The Civil Rights of Arab-Americans*, vi.

42. Jabara, "Investigating the FBI/CIA Apparatus: Will It Include the Arab-Americans?," speech delivered to Illinois AAUG, Chicago, Illinois, 8 Mar. 1975, in AJP, box 10, folder Activities–Harassment of Arab Americans–Testimonials and Misc.; David Young, "Arabs in U.S. Accuse F.B.I. of Spying on Them, *Chicago Tribune*, 13 July 1975; Saikowski, "Arabs in U.S."; Hagopian, "Minority Rights," 101.

43. Stork and Theberge, "Any Arab," 5.

44. On the comparison with Japanese American internment, see Bassiouni to Nixon, 11 Oct. 1972, reprinted in Bassiouni, *The Civil Rights of Arab-Americans*, 28; Hagopian, "Minority Rights," 97; Saikowksi, "Arabs in U.S."; Stork and Theberge, "Any Arab," 3; Mosher, "Arabs Taste."

45. Dan Georgakas, "New Racist Attacks on Arabs Here," *Guardian Independent Radical Newsweekly*, 3 Jan. 1973, in AJP, box 13, folder Operation Boulder–Press Clippings 1972–9; Stork and Theberge, "Any Arab," 6.

46. Murray, "U.S. Checking Arab Students"; Edwards, "Victims in the War on Terrorism."

47. Stork and Theberge, "Any Arab," 6; Young, "Arabs in U.S. Accuse F.B.I."; Young, "Arabs, Jews Wage War on the Propaganda Front," *Chicago Tribune*, 27 July 1975.

48. Jabara, "Investigating the FBI/CIA Apparatus"; Hagopian, "Minority Rights," 101. Seymour Hersh reported that in 1970, after receiving intelligence from foreign sources indicating that Arab students in the U.S. were receiving funds from Arab governments, Nixon officials asked

Leonard Garment, Nixon's adviser for civil rights and Jewish affairs, to contact Israeli intelligence sources to gather more information. See Hersh, "Nixon '70 Domestic Security Plan."

49. "AAUG Defends Rights of Arabs," *AN*, Mar. 1973.

50. AAUG Board Meeting Minutes, 1 Dec. 1972 and 20 Jan. 1973, in AAUGP, box 23.

51. Jabara, Telegram to Rogers, in AJP, box 10, folder Activities-Harassment of Arab Americans–Correspondence; Bassiouni's correspondence with Nixon and Gray is reprinted in Bassiouni, *The Civil Rights of Arab-Americans*, 28–30. Also see Jabara, Bassiouni, and Omar Ghobashy to U.S. Attorney General, 8 Feb. 1974, in Bassiouni, *The Civil Rights of Arab-Americans*, 86–90.

52. Greene, Associate Commissioner of INS, to Jabara, 1 Nov. 1972 and 24 Nov. 1972, in AJP, box 9, folder Activities–Harassment of Arab Americans–Correspondence; Saikowski, "Arabs in U.S."

53. Farrell to Hart, 20 Dec. 1972, in AJP, box 13, folder Operation Boulder–Correspondence and Miscellaneous; Hart to Farrell, 29 Dec. 1972, and Hart to Jabara, 29 Dec. 1972, in AJP, box 9, folder Activities–Harassment of Arab Americans–Correspondence. Bassiouni also met with U.S. Attorney General Edward Levy and Senator Bill Saxbe (R-OH), urging them to end the operation. See Bassiouni, "The AAUG," 28.

54. Abourezk to Clarence Kelley, Director of FBI, 8 Nov. 1973; Hassan Husseini to Abourezk, 1 Dec. 1973; Jabara to Abourezk, 3 June 1974, all in AJP, box 9, folder Activities—Harassment of Arab Americans–Correspondence.

55. Jabara to AAUG Members and Friends, 5 Oct. 1972, in AJP, box 10, folder Activities—Harassment of Arab Americans–Correspondence.

56. Jabara to Mel Wolfe, 9 Oct. 1972, and Aryeh Neier, ACLU, to Richard Kleindienst, U.S. Attorney General, 16 Oct. 1972, both in AJP, box 13, folder Operation Boulder–Correspondence and Miscellaneous.

57. Steve Hollopeter, NLG and Community Legal Assistance Center, Los Angeles, to Jabara, 27 Oct. 1972, in AJP, box 10, folder Activities-Harassment of Arab Americans—Correspondence; Hollopeter to Jabara, 8 Dec. 1972, in AJP, box 9, folder Activities- Harassment of Arab Americans—Correspondence; Newsletter of the Immigration Law Panel, South California Chapter of the NLG, Jan. 1973 and Feb. 1973, in AJP, box 13, folder Operation Boulder–Press Clippings; NLG newsletter, Jan. 1973, in Bassiouni, *The Civil Rights of Arab-Americans*, 34.

58. "Is the Nixon Administration Playing Politics with Civil Liberties?," *NYT*, 29 Oct. 1972; Hagopian, "Minority Rights," 102–3. Other sponsors of the ad included the Action Committee on Arab-American Relations (New York City), the Ad Hoc Committee for Lebanon (Washington, D.C.), the American-Arab Yemeni Benevolent Society (Dearborn, Mich.), the American-Arabic Association (Boston), the Cleveland Council on Arab-American Relations, and the World Lebanese Cultural Union, Washington, D.C., chapter.

59. Mehdi quoted in John L. Hess, "Mideast Tensions Afflicting the Arab Communities Here," *NYT*, 7 Oct. 1972; "A Suspicious Blaze Burns Arab Office," *NYT*, 4 June 1974. A few years earlier, Mehdi was physically assaulted, allegedly by members of the Jewish Defense League. See Robert D. McFadden, "Police Are Posted Outside Arab National and Business Offices Here," *NYT*, 24 May 1970.

60. Arab American Congress for Palestine to U.S. Attorney General, n.d., in AJP, box 9, folder Activities–Harassment of Arab Americans—Correspondence. For the FBI's reaction to this letter, see FBI to Attorney General Levi, 28 Apr. 1975, in ibid.

61. "Forum Today to Protest Government Harassment of Arabs," *SE*, 7 Dec. 1972, and Press Release, Organization of Arab Students, 8 Jan. 1973, both in AJP, box 13, folder Operation Boulder–Press Clippings.

62. Socialist Workers Party, Press Release, 10 Oct. 1972, in AJP, box 13, folder Operation Boul-

der–Press Clippings; Young Socialist National Convention Program, Cleveland, Ohio, 23–26 Nov. 1972, in AJP, box 10, folder Activities-Harassment of Arab Americans–Correspondence; also see Georgakas, "New Racist Attacks on Arabs Here."

63. Theoharis, *Spying on Americans*, 121–25, discusses the information sharing between the NSA, FBI, and CIA, a program formalized in 1969 under the code name MINARET.

64. "FBI Admits Surveillance in Court Suit by Jabara," *AN*, June 1974; Horrock, "New Senate Panel"; Yoder, "Breach of Privilege," https://www.nlg.org/sites/default/files/Breach%20of%20Privilege%20COLOR_3.pdf. The FBI stated that the government did not bug Jabara's phone but that his conversations had been picked up when he spoke with people who were targets of NSA wiretapping. See Ronald Kessler, "FBI Admits Monitoring Mich. Lawyer," *WP*, 5 Feb. 1975.

65. Jabara, "Abdeen Jabara"; "Abdeen Jabara Discusses Lawsuit against FBI," *AN*, Sept. 1979; Hagopian, "Minority Rights," 101–2; Billy Bowles and Susan Brown, "FBI Admits Wiretapping Detroit Arab Spokesman," *Detroit Free Press*, 22 May 1974; Magnusson, "NSA Tapped Six Overseas Messages." In 1982 a federal appeals court overturned Judge Freeman's ruling in Jabara's case, deciding that the NSA could legally eavesdrop on Americans' overseas communications without a warrant and supply the intercepted information to the FBI. In 1984 the FBI agreed to destroy all its files on Jabara and admitted again that Jabara had not broken any laws. See David Burnham, "Court Says U.S. Spy Agency Can Tap Overseas Messages," *NYT*, 7 Nov. 1982, and Smith, *Notebook of a Sixties Lawyer*, 91.

66. Kessler, "FBI Admits Monitoring"; Horrock, "New Senate Panel."

67. Theoharis, *The FBI and American Democracy*, 121–30; Weiner, *Enemies*, 289–95, 335. The Church committee's official title was the U.S. Senate Select Committee to Study Governmental Operations with Respect to Intelligence Activities.

68. "Berrigan, Jabara on Rights," *AN*, June 1974. See materials in AJP, box 2, folder Litigation—Police Surveillance (Benkert et al. vs. Michigan State Police)–Court Documents, and box 13, folder Operation Boulder–Court Cases Involving Investigation and Harassment. For example, Jabara researched the case of a Philadelphia antiwar group charging illegal surveillance and infiltration by the FBI, *Philadelphia Resistance v. John Mitchell, Attorney General*, as well as another case in Pennsylvania in which a coalition of peace and black rights organizations were suing the FBI.

69. Jabara, "Investigating the FBI/CIA Apparatus"; Hersh, "Nixon '70 Domestic Security Plan" and "Alien-Radical Tie." In their *MERIP* article, "Any Arab," Stork and Theberge similarly placed the operation in the context of past and ongoing federal government practices, calling the harassment of Arab Americans "no surprise." "Operation Boulder," they continued, "is different from previous cases only in its degree of coordination between international and domestic agencies of surveillance and in the blatant manner in which it has been carried out" (13).

70. Bassiouni, introduction to *The Civil Rights of Arab-Americans*, vii–viii.

71. Jabara, interview with author; Jabara to Ahmed Shalaby, 1 Feb. 1973, in AJP, box 9, folder Activities-Harassment of Arab Americans–Correspondence.

72. In a subsequent author conversation with Jabara, he emphasized how helpful the ACLU has been to him and to Arab Americans generally over the past forty years.

73. Jabara, interview with author; Bassiouni, "The AAUG"; Jabara, "Investigating the FBI/CIA Apparatus."

74. Fischbach, "Government Pressures," 88.

75. Ihsan Diab quoted in Mosher, "Arabs Taste"; Hussaini, "The Impact of the Arab-Israeli Conflict," 218–19; Young, "Arabs in U.S. Accuse F.B.I."

76. Hoffacker to Brown, 23 Apr. 1974, Foreign Relations of the United States, U.S. Department of State, Office of Historian, http://history.state.gov/historicaldocuments/frus1969–76ve03/d214 (accessed 13 Apr. 2013).

77. "A Plan to Screen Terrorists Ends," *NYT*, 24 Apr. 1975.

78. Matt Ross, People's Law Office, to NLG Middle East Subcommittee, 25 Feb. 1979, in AJP, box 12, folder NLG Middle East Delegation correspondence; Jabara, "Action Alert: FBI Surveillance and Harassment," 7 Aug. 1980, in NAP, box 2, folder AAUG, 1978–2001 (2). Also see Jim Zogby, "Senate Sub-Committee on Security and Terrorism: A Threat to Arab-Americans?," 17 Feb. 1981, and Mowahid Shah, "The FBI and the Civil Rights of Arab-Americans," *ADC Issues* no. 5, n.d., both in NAP, box 2, folder ADC 1981–2003.

79. "Always, It's the Homeland, Even in U.S.," *Detroit Free Press*, 17 Sept. 1982.

80. Lamya Shihadeh, "Arab Discrimination," *SE*, 28 Jan. 1986, clipping in BAP, box 1, folder Clippings: Discrimination 1977–1986; Ahmed, interview with author; Samhan, "Politics and Exclusion," 17; "ADC Remembers Alex Odeh," *ADC Newsletter*, 11 Oct. 2005, http://www.adc.org/index.php?id=2626 (accessed 4 May 2013).

81. Hagopian, "Minority Rights," 106; Bassiouni, *The Civil Rights of Arab-Americans*, 48.

Chapter 6

1. Ahmed, interview with author.

2. Fernández, "The Young Lords," 65–68, 71; Rodríguez, "Saving the *Parcela*," 211–14; Glasser, "From 'Rich Port' to Bridgeport," 192–93; Torres, "Introduction," 8.

3. Abraham, Abraham, and Aswad, "The Southend," 166–71; Ahmed, "Ishmael Ahmed," 28.

4. Abraham, Abraham, and Aswad, "The Southend," 166–71.

5. Aswad, "The Southeast Dearborn Arab Community," 53–59; Wigle and Abraham, "Arab Nationalism," 282. Abraham, Abraham, and Aswad report that two of the coffeehouses were Lebanese, three were Palestinian, and five were dominated by Yemeni patrons ("The Southend," 176).

6. Aswad, "The Southeast Dearborn Arab Community," 70–72.

7. "Detroit Arabs Fight City Hall," *AN*, Aug. 1973; Aswad quoted in Debby Allen, "The South End Talks to Barbara Aswad," *SE*, 15 Mar. 1973.

8. Jabara, interview with author; Aswad, "The Southeast Dearborn Arab Community," 59; Malek, *A Country Called Amreeka*, 61; Unis, interview with Terry, in JTP, box 1. Howell, "Southend Struggles," 52, while acknowledging growing anti-Arab prejudice in Dearborn, discounts it as a motive for the city's neighborhood removal plan.

9. Aswad, "The Southeast Dearborn Arab Community," 64; Ahmed, interview with author.

10. Howell, "Southend Struggles," 48. See materials about the library branch and the Salina school in HAP, box 1, folder Neighborhood Information 1970–1975.

11. Malek, *A Country Called Amreeka*, 65–66; SEDCC Newsletter, Sept. 1971, in HAP, box 1. Several non-Arab community activists were also instrumental in the SEDCC's campaign.

12. These flyers and similar materials are in HAP, box 1, folder Neighborhood Information 1967–1970, folder Neighborhood Information 1970–1975, folder Notebook—notes of SEDCC ca. 1972–1974, and folder SEDCC Newsletters & Flyers 1970–1975.

13. Joyce Hagelthorn, "Protesting Southenders Storm Council," *Dearborn Press*, 23 Sept. 1971, and "Angry Residents March on City," *Dearborn Press*, 9 Dec. 1971, both in BAP, box 1, folder Clippings–City of Dearborn 1971–1980. SEDCC to Dearborn City Council, 21 Sept. 1971, in BAP, box 2, folder Southeast Dearborn Community Council 1967–1977.

14. Aswad, interview with author; Khoury, interview with author; Abraham, interview with author; "Southeast Dearborn Questionnaire," BAP, box 2, folder Southeast Dearborn Community Council 1967–1977.

15. Aswad, "The Southeast Dearborn Arab Community," 69, 79.

16. Ibid., 79; Allen, "The South End Talks to Barbara Aswad"; "Detroit Arabs Fight City Hall."

17. Abdeen Jabara, Presidential Statement, AAUG Convention, 11 Nov. 1972, Berkeley, California, in AAUGP, box 14, folder 4: Correspondence President–1972 (Jabara); "You CAN Fight City

Hall: It Can be Done with Community Action," *AN*, Dec. 1971; "Detroit Arabs Fight City Hall," *AN*, Aug.1973; "Detroit's Dearborn Arabs Defeat City Hall," *AN*, Oct. 1973; Jabara, "Workers, Community Mobilized in Detroit," *AN*, June 1974; "Program of Fifth Annual AAUG Convention," Nov. 1972, *AN*, Oct. 1972; Aswad, "The Southeast Dearborn Arab Community," 76.

18. Ahmed, interview with author; Aswad, "The Southeast Dearborn Arab Community," 75–76; Barbara Aswad, interview with author.

19. Ahmed, "Ishmael Ahmed," 27–28; Ahmed, interview with Terry, in JTP, box 1; Ahmed, interview with author. Two of his brothers were in the U.S. Army, one serving in Vietnam and the other in Korea; when Ahmed was drafted, he was initially ordered to Vietnam, but his family informed their congressman, John Dingell, that one of his brothers was serving in Vietnam, and his orders were changed to Korea.

20. Ahmed, "Ishmael Ahmed," 28; Ahmed, interview with author; Ahmed, interview with Terry; Abraham, interview with author.

21. Rignall, "Building the Infrastructure," 55–56; Abraham, "National and Local Politics," 128; Ahmed, interview with author; Aswad, interview with author; Khoury, interview with author. The founders' origin stories place different emphases on who was most crucial in the creation of ACCESS. Khoury argues that the Palestinian student activists provided the vital push for the center; Aswad and Rignall stress the role of the SEDCC activists; and Ahmed claims that Jabara's ability to bring together the "street activists" and the AAUG was what provided the key organizing ingredient for its genesis.

22. According to Barbara Aswad, members of a leftist organization that included African Americans and "women in overalls" were helping to paint the first community center on Dix Avenue, which she thinks bothered "some of the local people" and led them to burn down the center. She speculates that both "religion and maybe some racism" fueled opposition to the center among some Arabs in the neighborhood. Aswad, interview with author.

23. ACCESS brochure, n.d., in BAP, box 2, folder ACCESS 1975–1979; "ACCESS Helps Workers with Services," *AN*, Oct. 1973; Almaklani, interview with author; Khoury, interview with author; Khoury, interview with Terry, JTP, box 1; Ahmed, interview with author.

24. See Jabara's notes on the interrogations in AJP, box 10, folder Activities-Harassment of Arab Americans–Correspondence (1972–1973); Bassiouni, *The Civil Rights of Arab-Americans*.

25. Amen et al. v. City of Dearborn et al., 363 F. Supp. 1267 (E.D. Mich.1973); "Detroit Arabs Fight City Hall"; John Cusumano, "Southend Renewal Ruled 'Illegal,'" *Dearborn Press*, 16 Aug. 1973; "South End Court Order Favors Area Residents," *Dearborn Guide*, 16 Aug. 1973; Louis Heldman, "Renewal Plan Ruled Illegal in Dearborn," *Detroit Free Press*, 15 Aug. 1973, clippings in BAP, box 1, folder Clippings–City of Dearborn 1971–1980. The case went back to court in 1976, and the appeals court overturned the 1973 ruling, but only on jurisdictional grounds, and remanded the case back to district court. Amen et al., Plaintiffs-Appellees v. City of Dearborn et al., Defendants-Appellants, 532 F.2d 554 (6th Circ., 1976). On remand, the district court reaffirmed its original ruling, thus the city appealed again, resulting in a 1983 appeals court case that upheld most of the district court's decision. Amen et al., Plaintiffs-Appellees-Cross-Appellants v. City of Dearborn et al., Defendants-Appellants-Cross-Appellees, 718 F.2d 789 (6th Circ., 1983).

26. Aswad, "The Southeast Dearborn Arab Community," 75; Robinson, "An American Grass-Roots Community Organization as a Vehicle for Change: From Arab Politics to American Politics," n.d., in HAP, box 1, folder SEDCC–Collected Research on Arab Americans and Urban Renewal.

27. Malek, *A Country Called Amreeka*, 66–67.

28. Ibid., 64, 68; Ahmed, interview with author.

29. Abraham, "National and Local Politics," 20–21, 23, 30, 35–36, 43; Abraham, "The Yemeni Immigrant Community," 124, 128. Yemenis also lived in other pockets of Detroit in the

1970s, such as the Poletown neighborhood. The majority of the Yemenis living in Detroit and Dearborn were from North Yemen, and a minority was from South Yemen. Both leftist and rightist Yemeni political factions were represented among the immigrants, and they often came into conflict. While Abraham argues that Yemenis were indifferent to the Southend struggle against urban removal, Yemeni activist Ali Baleed Almaklani claims that although Yemeni involvement was not widespread, a few of them did participate in resisting the city's plan. Almaklani, interview with author.

30. Abraham, "National and Local Politics," 127–31. In *Arab America*, Nadine Naber writes about similar leftist Arab groups, which were tied to parties and factions in the Arab world, being established in the San Francisco Bay Area by Arab American activists in the 1970s.

31. Georgakas and Surkin, *Detroit*, 67; Almaklani, interview with author; "Detroit Yemeni Robbed and Killed," *Muslim Star*, Oct. 1973, in Aliya Hassen Papers, box 1, folder Federation of Islamic Associations, BHL.

32. Malek, *A Country Called Amreeka*, 68; Abraham, "National and Local Politics," 131–32; Wigle and Abraham, "Arab Nationalism," 289–90. The other AACC subcommittees were the Medical Committee, Public Relations Committee, and Financial Committee.

33. Malek, *A Country Called Amreeka*, 68–70; Georgakas and Surkin, *Detroit*, 65; Almaklani, interview with author. "Southend Rally Nets $25,000," *Dearborn Press*, 18 Oct. 1973, and Randy C. MacIntosh, "Arabs Protest U.S. Role in Mideast," *Dearborn Times-Herald*, 17 Oct. 1973, in Sally Howell's personal collection. Wigle and Abraham, "Arab Nationalism," 298, state that over $60,000 was raised at the rally, and the Islamic Center subsequently held a meeting at which an additional $20,000 was raised to support the Arab nations at war.

34. Malek, *A Country Called Amreeka*, 70; Ahmed, "Organizing an Arab Workers Caucus," 19.

35. Ahmed, "Organizing an Arab Workers Caucus," 18; Georgakas, "Arab Workers,"16.

36. Georgakas, "Arab Workers,"16; Beinin, interview with author. The Revolutionary Union became the Revolutionary Communist Party.

37. Wigle and Abraham, "Arab Nationalism," 287; Georgakas and Surkin, *Detroit*, 40, 65; "DRUM's Program," n.d., and "Stages of Action," n.d., in Dodge Revolutionary Union Movement (DRUM) Records, box 1, folder 1; DRUM Slate campaign materials, in DRUM Records, box 1, folder 9; "Pigs in the Polls," flyer, 1970, in DRUM Records, box 1, folder 10, all in RL; Mohamed Saddiq, interview with Nabeel Abraham, 6 Oct. 1976, in NAP, box 21, folder Abraham Dissertation–The Union & Yemenis, 1976.

38. Aswad, "The Southeast Dearborn Arab Community," 66; Jabara, "Workers, Community Mobilized in Detroit," *AN*, June 1974; Hamlin, interview with author.

39. Quotation from Malek, *A Country Called Amreeka*, 73; Abraham, "National and Local Politics," 133; Ahmed, "Organizing an Arab Workers Caucus," 19.

40. Ahmed, "Organizing an Arab Workers Caucus,"19; Malek, *A Country Called Amreeka*, 73; Georgakas and Surkin, *Detroit*, 65. The leftist organization Spark, which was simultaneously organizing in the Dodge Main plant, circulated material supportive of the demonstration. Spark printed an article in its newsletter charging that the leaders of the UAW local at Dodge Main had put out a leaflet in Arabic "to tell the many Arabian workers NOT TO LEAVE THEIR JOBS—THE STRIKE WAS CALLED OFF." Spark questioned: "Why is it that information in Arabic has ONLY come from the Local when the Local wanted to *keep the lines going*?"(emphasis in original). See "They Are Concerned!," *Dodge Workers Speak*, 7 Nov. 1973, in UAW Local 3 Records, RL, box 21.

41. "Is the UAW Leadership Acting in the Interests of Its Members?," *Detroit Free Press*, n.d., in AJP, box 13, folder UAW Arab Workers Caucus Press Clippings, 1973.

42. Abraham, interview with author; Jabara, interview with author; Malek, *A Country Called Amreeka*, 74; Letter to President of Local, 23 Nov. 1973, in AJP, box 13, folder UAW Arab Workers Caucus–Miscellaneous; Hamlin, interview with author. In "Workers, Community Mobilized,"

Jabara claimed that 2,500 people participated in the Cobo protest. The Trotskyist Revolutionary Socialist League said that its members joined the protest, and then two of them went to the ACCESS office to talk about socialist revolution in the Arab world. See "Discussion with Arab Workers," *Torch*, n.d., in NAP, box 20, folder Dearborn (1).

43. Tim McNulty, "B'nai B'rith Fetes Woodcock as Arabs Stage a Protest," *Detroit Free Press*, n.d., and Gerald L. Nelson, "Top B'nai B'rith Award Presented to Woodcock," *Detroit News*, n.d., clippings in Don Unis Papers, BHL; Malek, *A Country Called Amreeka*, 75–76; Georgakas and Surkin, *Detroit*, 65; Jabara, interview with author.

44. Jabara, "Workers, Community Mobilized"; Malek, *A Country Called Amreeka*, 76–77.

45. Ahmed, "Organizing an Arab Workers Caucus," 20; Abraham, interview with author; Abraham, "National and Local Politics," 135–36. An AWC organizing flyer issued in 1974 stated: "Nearly 700 Arab and Black auto Workers in our Local 3 Dodge Main plant were given warning notices, because they demonstrated against Leonard Woodcock's giving union money to buy Israeli war bonds" and demanded that Local 3 " fight to remove company warnings from all 700 workers files." See AWC flyer, UAW Local 3 Records, box 22, folder 43. In their Dodge Main newsletter, Spark stated, "Last week management went around harassing the Arabian workers because of their protest. The foremen gave out more than 700 write-ups to the Arabian workers. These workers were threatened with one or three days off if they should protest again. . . . By threatening the Arabian workers this way, Chrysler is threatening ALL workers." See "Chrysler Threatens Everyone," *Dodge Workers Speak*, 19 Dec. 1973, in UAW Local 3 Records, box 21, folder 39.

46. Abraham, "National and Local Politics," 136–38, and interview with author.

47. Ahmed, "Organizing an Arab Workers Caucus," 19. Nabeel Abraham's dissertation details behind-the-scenes factionalism in the AWC in the months after the Woodcock protest. The divisions replicated the factional turmoil in the Palestinian resistance movement after the October War between the "PLO camp" (which included the Democratic Front for the Liberation of Palestine) and the "rejectionist camp" (which included the Popular Front for the Liberation of Palestine). In the AWC, the Yemeni leftists joined the rejectionist camp. See Abraham, "National and Local Politics," 140–41.

48. According to Ismael Ahmed, in 1975 the UAW continued to hold Israeli bonds worth $780,000, in "Organizing an Arab Workers Caucus," 20; AWC pamphlet, n.d., in AJP, box 13, folder UAW Arab Workers Caucus Miscellaneous. Arab American workers at the Dodge Main plant were also active in other dissident groups that were organizing in the plant to challenge UAW Local 3. See issues of the newsletter *Strike Back* in UAW Local 3 Records, box 21, folder 39, and issues of the newsletter *Voice of Chrysler Workers*, and flyers "The People's Choice for Delegates," n.d., and "Local 3 Action Group," n.d., in UAW Local 3 Records, box 22, folder 43.

49. Arab Workers Caucus, "The Basis for Unity: Our General Call," n.d., in AJP, box 13, folder UAW Arab Workers Caucus—Articles & Papers.

50. "UAW Arab Workers Caucus Program," in Ahmed, "Organizing an Arab Workers Caucus," 21.

51. Ahmed, "Organizing an Arab Workers Caucus," 20. On the United National Caucus, see Thompson, *Whose Detroit?*, 181–83.

52. "Arab Caucus Pickets UAW," *AN*, June 1974; UAW, "Daily Summary: 24th Constitutional Convention of the UAW," 2 June 1974, in NAP, box 20, folder Dearborn (1). See also "Post Mortem on the UAW Convention," *Voice of Chrysler Workers*, n.d., which criticizes the failure of Local 3's leaders to support the Israeli bond resolution, along with other resolutions proposed by rank-and-file groups. In UAW Local 3 Records, box 22, folder 43.

53. AWC, "Auto Worker's Report," n.d., in NAP, box 20, folder Dearborn (1); Ahmed, "Organizing an Arab Workers Caucus," 22.

54. Issues of *Eldon Spark*: "War in the Mid-East," 18 Oct. 1973; "Middle-East Massacres," 5 June 1974; "Who Are the Terrorists?," 27 Nov. 1974, all in RL, UAW Collection, Eldon Wildcat Records, folders Eldon Spark 1973 and Eldon Spark 1974. It is not clear whether Eldon Wildcat and its publication *Spark* is related to the organization Spark operating in the Dodge Main plant.

55. "Workers of All Lands, Unite!" *Eldon Spark*, 26 Mar. 1975, in RL, UAW Collection, Eldon Wildcat Records, folder Eldon Spark 1975; also see "UAW Supports Israel," *Eldon Spark*, 18 Oct. 1973, condemning UAW's purchase of Israeli bonds, in folder Eldon Spark 1973.

56. "No More Racist Killer Cops!," *Eldon Spark*, 7 May 1975, and "Racist Murders in Dearborn," *Eldon Spark*, 17 June 1976, in RL, UAW Collection, Eldon Wildcat Records, folders Eldon Spark 1975 and Eldon Spark 1976. In his study of these murders, Nabeel Abraham was not able to confirm the motives. He found that the rumor on the streets was that the crimes were attributable to the workers' involvement in the vice world. See materials in NAP, box 21, folder Dissertation–Yemeni Killings in Detroit, 1976; Abraham, interview with author.

57. Dodge Main Workers Committee leaflet, 1977, in RL, UAW Local 3 Records, box 45, folder 3.

58. Beinin, interview with author. While organizing for the RCP in Detroit, Beinin also edited the party's newsletter, the *Worker*. Palestinian brothers who owned a grocery store near Beinin's residence in Southwest Detroit were sympathetic to the Popular Front for the Liberation of Palestine and helped him translate articles into Arabic to print in the newsletter. Besides organizing in plants, Beinin spoke with Arab immigrants in the community and sold the newsletter in the Arab cafes along Dix Avenue in the Southend. He remembers: "It wasn't a difficult sell. The people there were supportive of both Palestinian liberation and the rights of workers in auto plants."

59. Abraham, "Detroit's Yemeni Workers," 8; Abraham, interview with author; Beinin, letter to the editor, *MERIP Reports*, 26; Abraham, letter to the editor, *MERIP Reports*, 25. See also Abraham, "The Yemeni Immigrant Community," 128, and "National and Local Politics," 35–37. Abraham predicted, however, that despite their intentions to resettle in their homeland (which he calls "the myth of return"), most of the Yemenis would end up bringing their families to the United States and establishing residency, and in fact a trend of permanent settlement could already be discerned. A decade later the prediction became established fact.

60. Beinin, interview with author; Khoury, interview with author; Ahmed, interview with author.

61. Ahmed, interview with author; Ahmed, interview with Terry; ACCESS brochure, n.d., in BAP, box 2, folder ACCESS 1975–1979; Unis, interview with Terry. Leaders of ACCESS were central to the Arab Mobilization Committee that was housed in the Hashemite Hall during the period of organizing around the war that October, and they found themselves splitting their time between the Hashemite Hall and the center on Vernor Avenue a few miles away. By the end of the year, ACCESS leaders decided to move ACCESS to the Hashemite Hall, which was better located to serve the Southend community. The Salina Street building was owned by the Yemeni Benevolent Association, which let ACCESS use it for free (later, ACCESS paid rent). The Salina Street building burned down in 1983.

62. Aswad and Gray, "Challenges to the Arab-American Family," 224; Khoury, interview with author; Ahmed, interview with author. Ahmed states that the Black Panthers advised ACCESS activists to refuse outside funding—advice that "we took to heart for several years," until they realized that the center could not grow and expand its service mission unless it sought outside support.

63. Ahmed, interview with author; Unis, interview with Terry.

64. "Who We Are," *Arab Center*, Dec. 1975. Also see the Oct. 1976 and Jan.–Feb. 1977 issues of *Arab Center*, all in NAP, box 23, folder 23: ACCESS (1).

65. Khoury, interview with author; Khoury, interview with Terry.

66. Nawash, interview with Terry, in JTP, box 1; Abraham, interview with author; Jabara, interview with author. See Linda Harsant and Helen Niemiec, "Pro Palestine Rally Held at City Hall," *Dearborn Press*, 20 May 1976, clipping in Sally Howell's personal collection; Lawrence Chakur and Kathy Horak, "Pro-Arab Backers March through City," *Dearborn Press*, 18 May 1978, clipping in Don Unis Papers, BHL.

67. Khoury, interview with author; Khoury to ACCESS Advisory Board, 20 June 1979, in BAP, box 2, folder ACCESS 1975–1979; Ahmed, interview with author; Ahmed, "Ishmael Ahmed," 30; Nawash, interview with Terry. On the Arab World Festival in 1973 through 1976, see materials in IMJCP, Subsection: Zehia Kahil, , box 8.

68. Ahmed, interview with author.

69. Payne, "Men Led, but Women Organized"; Frost, *"An Interracial Movement of the Poor,"* 69.

70. Ahmed, interview with author; Ahmed, "Ishmael Ahmed," 29.

71. Ahmed, interview with author; Aswad, interview with author; Aswad and Gray, "Challenges to the Arab-American Family," 225. Nevertheless, conflict did materialize between ACCESS and some members of the Southeast Dearborn Community Council. Abraham characterizes the conflict as a "turf battle" between two organizations competing for resources in the Southend. Abraham, interview with author.

72. ACCESS brochure, n.d., in BAP, box 2, folder ACCESS 1975–1979; Ahmed, interview with author; Douglas Ilka, "How Arab Throngs Vie for New Mecca in Dearborn Homes," *Detroit News*, 24 Apr. 1977, clipping in BAP, box 1, folder Clippings–Immigrants 1978–1986; "The South End . . . A Mid-East Melting Pot," *Ford Estate*, 27 July 1978, clipping in Don Unis Papers, BHL; Kathy Horak, "Residents Express Fear, Anger and Understanding," *Dearborn Press and Guide*, 17 Aug. 1978, clipping in Sally Howell's personal collection.

73. "Defend the Arab Center (ACCESS)," leaflet, Dec. 1977, in BAP, box 2, folder ACCESS 1975–1979; Amen quoted in "Affirmative Injunction? Preferential Hiring of Arabs as Police Termed Unconstitutional," *Dearborn Press*, n.d., clipping in BAP, box 1, folder Clippings: Discrimination 1977–1986.

74. Borrajo quoted in Diane Katz, "Dearborn Arabs Seeking Power of Ballot," 9 Sept. 1984, *Detroit News*, clipping in Imam Mohamad Jawad Chirri Papers, box 6, folder Newspaper clippings on ICA & Islam in Detroit/Dearborn Area.

75. ACCESS letter to members, n.d. [Aug. 1979], in BAP, box 2, folder ACCESS 1975–1979.

76. Unis, interview with Terry; Terry, "Community and Political Activism," 249; Rignall, "Building the Infrastructure," 56; Khoury, interview with author. The Southeast Dearborn Community Council was also receiving government funding in the early 1980s, including a multimillion-dollar HUD grant and city block grants. Increasingly, SEDCC and ACCESS were competing for government grants, a competition in which ACCESS prevailed, and SEDCC had collapsed by 1986. See Howell, "Southend Struggles," 54; HAP, box 1, folder SEDCC Petition to Stop Closure, 1986.

77. Ahmed, interview with Terry.

78. Aswad and Gray, "Challenges to the Arab American Family," 225; Jabara, interview with author; Khoury, interview with author; Rignall, "Building the Infrastructure," 56; Aswad, "How a Dearborn Community Gained."

Chapter 7

1. Naber, *Arab America*, 36–37; Akram and Johnson, "Race and Civil Rights," 17; Ghareeb, *Split Vision*; "Arab Baiting: ADC Mounts the Challenge," *ADC Reports*, Feb. 1984, 3–7, NAP, box 2, folder ADC 1981–2003; Findley, *They Dare to Speak*, 288–93.

2. Abourezk, *Advise and Dissent*, 253; Fischbach, "Government Pressures," 94–95; Jim Zogby, "Senate Sub-Committee on Security and Terrorism: A Threat to Arab-Americans?," 17 Feb. 1981,

and Mowahid Shah, "The FBI and the Civil Rights of Arab-Americans," *ADC Issues* no. 5, n.d., both in NAP, box 2, folder ADC 1981–2003.

3. Abraham, "Anti-Arab Racism," 199–203; Peter H. King, "The LA 8: 18 Years of Waiting for a Gavel to Fall," *LAT*, 29 June 2005; "The Case of the L.A. 8," http://www.democracynow.org/2007/11/2/the_case_of_the_la8_u. (accessed 10 June 2015).

4. Abraham, "Anti-Arab Racism"; Akram and Johnson, "Race and Civil Rights," 12–13; Findley, *They Dare to Speak*, 35; David Newell, "Arab Bashing in America," *Newsweek*, 20 Jan. 1986.

5. Samhan, "Politics and Exclusion," 11, 25. Also see Samhan, "Losing the Battle," 134.

6. The OAS maintained its radical (at least rhetorical) stance and close alignment with the fedayeen factions. Compared with the late 1960s–early 1970s, the OAS was fading from many American campuses, and according to some reports it was weakened by internal factionalism. By the 1980s the General Union of Palestinian Students (GUPS) was becoming more of a presence at American universities. See Nabeel Abraham, notes on OAS, n.d. in NAP, box 13, folder Organization of Arab Students (2); Materials in AAUGP, box 44, folder General Union of Palestine Students; Turki, *Soul in Exile*, 119.

7. Marrar, *The Arab Lobby*, 89, 94; Yaqub, "'Our Declaration of Independence,'" 13.

8. Turki, *Soul in Exile*, 194. See also Nasser Aruri, telegram to Yasser Arafat, 5 Nov. 1983, in AAUGP, box 53, folder PLO. Abraham, "The PLO at the Crossroads," discusses the increasing constraints on the Palestinian Resistance and its shift from offensive assaults at its primary enemy, Israel, to a defensive "rear-guard action" against Arab foes. At the leadership level, the PLO was shifting to more pragmatic diplomatic avenues, less likely to capture militants' imaginations.

9. Shain, "Arab Americans," 50–51.

10. Yaqub, "'Our Declaration of Independence,'" 13, 18–21.

11. Naber, *Arab America*, 49–50; Marrar, *The Arab Lobby*, 32, 91–93; Brick and Phelps, *Radicals in America*, 239.

12. Abraham, "Arab-American Marginality"; Haddad, "American Foreign Policy," 227–30; "Always, It's the Homeland, Even in U.S.," *Detroit Free Press*, 17 Sept. 1982; Cainkar, "Palestinian Women in the United States," 20, 106–7, 127–33.

13. Samhan, "Losing the Battle," 140–43.

14. See issues of NAAA's *Counterpoint*, such as "On Turning Frogs into Princes: Why President Carter Is Right in Opposing Israel's Settlement Policy," Mar. 1978; "Paying for Middle East 'Peace,'" May 1979; "Israel: A 'Strategic Asset' to America?," June 1979, along with "Statement of the NAAA on the Israel Occupation of South Lebanon," 21 May 1978, all in AAUGP, box 43, folder NAAA.

15. Nick Thimmesch, "The Arabs in Washington," *Saturday Evening Post*, May/June 1979; Sharabi to Carter, 5 Dec. 1978, in AAUGP, box 43, folder NAAA. Nothing ever came of this request.

16. Suleiman to Joe Baroody, 5 Aug. 1977; Hagopian to Baroody, 1 Nov. 1977; Hagopian to AAUG Board of Directors, Re: Meetings with NAAA and Ramallah Federation Reps, 1 Nov. 1977, all in AAUGP, box 43, folder NAAA.

17. Thimmesch, "The Arabs in Washington"; Sheba Mittelman, American Jewish Committee, "Arab Americans and Their Organizations: A Fact Sheet," 15 May 1978, in AAUGP, box 43, folder NAAA.

18. Hagopian to Baroody, 1 Nov. 1977; "Camp David One Year Later," *Counterpoint (NAAA)*, Sept. 1979, in AAUGP, box 64, folder NAAA (II). Furthermore, in the 1980s the NAAA was warmer to the Reagan administration than were the AAUG and the ADC, although the NAAA did seek political influence with both Democratic and Republican political officials. The American Ramallah Federation, which shared many members and leaders (such as Joe Baroody) in common with the NAAA, hewed Republican and supported Ronald Reagan's campaign. See

the statement about the NAAA delegation meeting with President Reagan on 16 Jan. 1984, in AAUGP, box 64, folder NAAA (I); Reagan-Bush '84 Campaign Committee press release, 17 Oct. 1984, in AAUGP, box 44, folder American Ramallah Federation.

19. George to Baroody, 24 Mar. 1978; Moughrabi to Baroody, 3 Apr. 1978; Hagopian to Baroody, 13 Apr. 1978, all in AAUGP, box 43, folder NAAA. Although this collaboration failed, in 1982 the NAAA and the AAUG, along with the ADC and the Palestine Congress of North America, met at least twice to coordinate support for congressional candidates. See memos in AAUGP, box 43, folder Coordinating Efforts. In 2000 the NAAA merged with the ADC.

20. For example, see AAUG, Press Release on Elias Ayoub case, 25 July 1979, in NAP, box 2, folder AAUG 1978–2001 (1); "American Blacks, Latinos, Educators Form Delegation to Lebanon," *AN*, July 1979; Materials in AAUGP, box 69, folder Mayors Delegation 1983.

21. Bassiouni, "The AAUG," 30; Hagopian, "Reversing Injustice," 70; Abdeen Jabara, e-mail message to author, 26 July 2015; Marrar, *The Arab Lobby*, 89; Yaqub, "'Our Declaration of Independence,'" 18.

22. Compare the resolutions in AAUG, *The First Decade*, 49, with the resolutions from AAUG's Annual Convention in 1983, in AAUGP, box 117, folder Sixteenth Annual Convention Resolutions; Shain, "Arab Americans," 50–51.

23. "What Is the PHRC?," n.d., in AJP, box 13, folder Palestine Human Rights Campaign–Bulletin; "Chapter Action on Human Rights," *AN*, June 1977; Jabara, interview with Terry, in JTP, box 1; Jabara to AAUG members, June 1980, in AAUGP, box 90, folder PHRC.

24. For example, see "Isa Hanna: An American in Israel's Jails," *PHRC Action Alert*, 25 Jan. 1980, and "The Case of Ziad Abu Eain," *PHRC Bulletin*, Jan. 1980, in AJP, box 13, folder Palestine Human Rights Campaign–Bulletin. Jabara served as an attorney on Eain's defense committee. See associated materials in AJP, boxes 6, 7, 8, and 9. Despite widespread protest by Arab American and human rights groups, as well as by the UN General Assembly, the United States allowed Israel to extradite Eain (whose name is also spelled Ein).

25. Zogby quoted in "What Worked for Vietnam . . . Can Work for Palestine Too," *Middle East*, Mar. 1980, 26–27, clipping in AJP, box 13, folder Palestine Human Rights Campaign–Bulletin. Also see *Palestine Human Rights Bulletin* from the 1980s in JTP, box 1, folder Palestine Human Rights Bulletin/Newsletter 1980–1989. Later in the 1980s, Presbyterian minister Donald Wagner became head of the PHRC, and the organization grew more distant from the AAUG, as detected in correspondence evincing friction over PHRC's inclusion in AAUG conventions, located in AAUGP, box 92, folder PHRC.

26. Terry, "Community and Political Activism," 247; Jabara, "A Strategy for Political Effectiveness," 203; Jabara, interview with author; "Abourezk under Zionist Attack, *AN*, Mar. 1974; "Abourezk Blasts Israel for Terrorism Bombings, *AN*, June 1974; "Anti-Arab Attacks Called Politicians' Ploy," *AN*, Sept. 1974; Abourezk, *Advise and Dissent*, 182.

27. Shaheen, "ABSCAM"; Jabara, interview with Terry; Beverly, "Shaking Off the Sheikh," 39; Abourezk, *Advise and Dissent*, 254.

28. Abourezk, "Arabs"; Beverly, "Shaking Off the Sheikh," 40–41.

29. Ghassan Bishara, "James Abourezk: Building Up Grass-roots Support," *Middle East*, July 1983; Jabara, interview with Terry; Shain, "Arab Americans," 47–48. On the weakness of the "Arab lobby," see Terry, *U.S. Foreign Policy*, 52–67.

30. "Arab Baiting"; "Coalition Work" in Wingfield, "ADC"; Suleiman, "The Arab American Left," 238.

31. Beverly, "Shaking Off the Sheikh," 41–57; Armand Gebert, "New Group to Attack Slurs at Arabs," *Detroit News*, 30 Mar. 1981; Wingfield, "ADC," 7–9; Zogby to NAC Members, 12 Aug. 1982, and *ADC Reports*, May–June 1983, in NAP, box 2, folder ADC 1981–2003; Matt Moffett,

"Minority Push: Arab Americans Seek to Fight Stereotyping and Get Political Voice," *Wall Street Journal*, 30 Aug. 1984.

32. Jabara, interview with author; James Zogby statement, Save Lebanon Project, 14 Feb. 1983, in ADC Papers, PAAA; Terry, "Community and Political Activism," 247; Harold Samhat, President ADC Greater Detroit Chapter, to Thomas Bray, *Detroit News* editor, n.d., in JTP, box 1, folder ADC Misc. Also see ADC Alert: "Arab-Americans Respond to Israeli Invasion," 7 June 1982, in ADC Papers, PAAA. Another organization that experienced a surge in this period was the November 29th Coalition for Palestine, formed in 1981, which staged demonstrations protesting Israel's invasion of Lebanon that involved endorsement of and participation by many organizations representing people of color and international Third World groups. See Abdulhadi, "Activism and Exile," 240.

33. Ad Hoc Coalition against Terrorism in America, "Don't Let Terrorism Spread into America," *NYT*, 5 Jan. 1986; Tom Hundley, "Dozens from State Sign Ad for Arab Americans," *Detroit Free Press*, n.d., clipping in BAP, box 1, folder Clippings—Immigrants 1978–1986; McMahon, "Abdeen Jabara."

34. Turki, "The Passions of Exile"; "Palestinians in America Organize New Council," *AN*, Mar. 1979. Speakers at the New York City Congress included Edward Said, Ibrahim Abu-Lughod, and Fayez Sayegh. The initial name proposed for the organization was the Palestine American Congress, but at the 1979 convention it was changed to Palestine Congress of North America. Palestine American Congress, "Organization Registration Kit," n.d., in PAAA. See also materials in AAUGP, box 104, folder Palestine Congress of North America.

35. As recounted in Wingfield's "ADC," 17–18, a conflict developed between Abourezk and Zogby over the amount of time that Zogby devoted to the Jesse Jackson campaign in 1984, which Abourezk felt interfered with Zogby's duties as ADC executive director. Supported by the ADC Board, Abourezk dismissed Zogby from his ADC position.

36. Samhan, "Arab Americans," 229–30; Ahmed, "Michigan Arab Americans," 47; Dressler quoted in Lamya Shihadeh, "Arab Americans Fight against Discrimination," *SE*, 29 Jan. 1986, clipping in BAP, box 1, folder Clippings: Discrimination 1977–1986.

37. Zogby to Susan Ziadeh, 1 Aug. 1986; Zogby to Mujid Kazimi, 27 Feb. 1987; quotation from *Issues '88*, Dec./Jan. 1988; AAI Action Alert: "Building a Movement on Palestinian Rights: A Plan of Action," n.d., all in AAUGP, box 44, folder Arab American Institute; Samhan, "Arab Americans," 230.

38. Zogby, "Survey of Arab American Political Opinions," n.d., in BPA, box 1, folder Clippings: Discrimination 1977–1986; Ahmed, "Michigan Arab Americans," 47; Ahmed, interview with Terry, JTP, box 1; Abdulhadi, "Activism and Exile," 238. Also see Samhan, "Losing the Battle."

39. Jabara, "Arab-Americans and the U.S. Policy Process," *AN*, Sept. 1978.

40. Jabara, "Israel and Human Rights"; Ross, "Abdeen Jabara." When the Detroit chapter submitted the resolution, the NLG leadership told Jabara that members needed more information about the subject and asked him to write an article for the newsletter. After he submitted his article, the leadership then told him they would not publish it unless they could find a member to write a companion article presenting an opposing view. Finally, a year later, the NLG newsletter published Jabara's piece on its own. Still, the resolution did not go forward. See Jabara, "The Guild in Palestine," and interview with Jabara, *Law and Disorder Radio*, http://lawanddisorder.org/.

41. Jabara, "The Guild in Palestine"; Jabara, interview with author; "Abdeen Jabara," *National Lawyers Guild—New York City News*. Also see correspondence and reports in AJP, box 12, folders Activities–NLG Middle East Delegation–Correspondence, 1975, 1977, and 1978. After the 1970s, the NLG continued to sponsor trips to the Occupied Territories, issued more reports on Israel's policies toward Palestinians, and passed more resolutions calling for Palestinian rights.

42. UN General Assembly Resolution 3379, http://www.un.org/documents/ga/res/30/ares30.htm (accessed 8 June 2016). For the AAUG position supporting the resolution, see Jabara, *Zionism and Racism*.

43. Newsome, "International Issues," 33–34; Weisbord and Kazarian, *Israel in the Black American Perspective*, 51, 53; Zogby and O'Dell, *Afro-Americans*. In 1975 many mainstream black leaders were affiliated with the Black Americans in Support of Israel Committee, but within a couple of years, some of its key members, such as Andrew Young and Walter Fauntroy, were criticizing Zionism.

44. "What is the PHRC?," n.d., in AJP, box 13, folder Palestine Human Rights Campaign–Bulletin; "Chapter Action on Human Rights," *AN*, June 1977.

45. Jabara, interview with Terry.

46. "The La Grange Declaration: Palestinian-Israeli Conflict: Responsibilities for the Christian Church" and "What Worked for Vietnam," *Palestine Human Rights Bulletin*, May 1980, in AJP, box 13, folder Palestine Human Rights Campaign–Bulletin; Jim Zogby, Jack O'Dell, Dave Dellinger, Paul Meyer, and Abdeen Jabara to MEPAC [Middle East Peace Action Coalition] members, 20 Aug. 1980, in AJP, box 13, folder Palestine Human Rights Campaign–Correspondence; Zogby and Jabara, "Recent Growth of the PHRC," *Palestine Human Rights Bulletin*, May 1980, in PAAA. The PHRC also received support from the leftist group New American Movement. See Robert Shaffer to PHRC, 4 June 1980, in AJP, box 13, folder Palestine Human Rights Campaign–Correspondence.

47. Zogby and O'Dell, *Afro-Americans*, 5; "American Blacks, Latinos, Educators Form Delegation to Lebanon," *AN*, July 1979; O'Dell to Nabeel Abraham, 3 Mar. 1980, in AAUGP, box 68, folder Black Caucus Project, 1980; Singh, "'Learn Your Horn,'" 43.

48. DeRoche, *Andrew Young*, 110–11; Yaqub, "'Our Declaration of Independence,'" 20; Gualtieri, *Between Arab and White*, 175–76; "AAUG Statement," *AN*, Sept. 1979.

49. When Secretary of State Cyrus Vance first asked Young about his meeting with Terzi, Young dishonestly replied that it was a chance social encounter. Young later admitted that it was a formal meeting at which policy procedures were discussed. Carter thus reprimanded him not only for breaching American protocol about meeting with PLO representatives but also for lying about the nature of the meeting. See DeRoche, *Andrew Young*, 111–12.

50. Yaqub, "'Our Declaration of Independence,'" 20–21; Weisbord and Kazarian, *Israel in the Black American Perspective*, 124–27; DeRoche, *Andrew Young*, 113–14; "11 Jewish Groups Reject Criticism from Blacks, but Urge Cooperation," *NYT*, 24 Aug. 1979; "Young's Role in U.N. Could Bring about More P.L.O. Contact," *NYT*, 17 Aug. 1979; Gualtieri, *Between Arab and White*, 176. Gualtieri, as do Weisbord and Kazarian, demonstrates that not all black leaders blamed Jews for what happened to Young. Young himself denied that Jewish influence compelled his resignation.

51. Weisbord and Kazarian, *Israel in the Black American Perspective*, 136–37; Ehrman, *The Rise of Neoconservatism*, 126; Thomas A. Johnson, "Black Leaders Air Grievances," *NYT*, 23 Aug. 1979; Roger Wilkins, "Black Leaders' Meeting: 'Watershed' Effort for Unanimity," *NYT*, 24 Aug. 1979. Other moderate black organizations, such as the Progressive National Baptist Convention, the Black Theology Project, and Transafrica, issued statements supporting Young and criticizing U.S. support of Israel. See Zogby and O'Dell, *Afro-Americans*, 25–39.

52. Johnson, "Black Leaders Air Grievances"; Wilkins, "Black Leaders' Meeting." Also see Ida Lewis, editorial in *Encore*, 4 Sept. 1979. But G. James Fleming, "Unfortunate: The Making of Black-Jewish 'Rift,'" *Afro-American*, 1 Sept. 1979, presented an alternative perspective by a black scholar, arguing that African Americans should maintain an alliance with Jews and not become unduly upset by Young's dismissal. Both article clippings in AAUGP, box 68, folder Black Press on Arab Issues 1979.

53. "AAUG Statement."

54. Walters, "The Black Initiatives," 4–5; Walter E. Fauntroy, "Report to Congress," in Zogby and O'Dell, *Afro-Americans*, 7–9; "10 Blacks from U.S. Tour South Lebanon, Meet with Guerrillas," *NYT*, 20 Sept. 1979; Weisbord and Kazarian, *Israel in the Black American Perspective*, 143. Lowery felt that their meeting with Israeli officials was unproductive.

55. "Jackson Calls for Mideast 'Justice,'" *NYT*, 28 Sept. 1979; "Jackson, in Beirut, Urges P.L.O. to Halt Terrorism," *NYT*, 29 Sept. 1979; "Jackson and Arafat Confer in Lebanon," *NYT*, 30 Sept. 1979; Singh, "'Learn Your Horn,'" 43–44; Weisbord and Kazarian, *Israel in the Black American Perspective*, 154; Yaqub, "'Our Declaration of Independence,'" 21; Stanford, *Beyond the Boundaries*, 56–60.

56. Nathaniel Sheppard, "Arab Groups in U.S. Seek to Woo Blacks," *NYT*, 20 Oct. 1979; Jackson, "The Challenge to Live in One World," in Zogby and O'Dell, *Afro-Americans*, 13; "Black Leaders to Address Convention," *AN*, Sept. 1979; Yaqub, "'Our Declaration of Independence,'" 22.

57. Materials in AAUGP, box 89, folder Congress on Racial Equality. The Arab League had a separate initiative to provide funding to African American organizations and institutions called the Black America Project. It is unclear how much funding actually materialized. See materials in AAUGP, box 68, folder Black America Project.

58. Sheppard, "Arab Groups." Along with the PHRC and the AAUG, Sheppard's article related attempts by M. T. Mehdi of the American-Arab Relations Committee and Jawad George of the PCNA to make connections with African American organizations. Mehdi reported that the NAACP and the Urban League would not respond to him.

59. Cainkar, "Immigrants," 193.

60. Jabara, interview with author; Armand Gebert, "Blacks, Arabs Start 'Coalition,'" *Detroit News*, 2 Oct. 1982; "Testimonial to Congressman John Conyers from the Arab American Community of Metropolitan Detroit," 30 Nov. 1984, in AJP, box 9, folder Activities–Detroit Arab American Community–Misc (1975–1979); "Congressman Crockett Decries U.S. Involvement in Lebanon," press release, n.d., and "American Arabs for the Re-election of Congressman George W. Crockett Jr. Reception of July 19, 1982," in NAP, box 7, folder George Crockett.

61. Abourezk, "Arabs"; Jackson quoted in Garrett and Purpura, *Frank Maria*, 618.

62. Marisa Tamari to Abbas Al Nasrawi, 15 Feb. 1984, in AAUGP, box 68, folder Jesse Jackson Presidential Campaign; Shain, "Arab Americans," 50–51; Suleiman, "The Arab American Left," 238; Abdulhadi, "Activism and Exile," 238.

63. Democratic parties in Iowa, Minnesota, Vermont, Maine, Oregon, and Washington adopted the resolution calling for a Palestinian state in the West Bank and the Gaza Strip. The Republican Party did not feature a similar Middle East peace initiative or debate in 1988. See Samhan, "Arab Americans," 239, 247.

64. "Proposal for Seminar for Senior Staff of Congressional Black Caucus and Executive Directors in National Black Leadership Roundtable," n.d., and Leila McDowell to PCNA Staff, 9 Mar. 1981, in AAUGP, box 68, folder Black Caucus Project, 1980.

65. Yaqub, "'Our Declaration of Independence,'" 23–24.

66. Samhan, "Not Quite White," 214.

67. Majaj, "Arab-American Ethnicity," 322. With Abdeen Jabara leading the way, Arab American activists in the Detroit area, particularly at ACCESS and in the Detroit AAUG chapter, were key participants in the census reclassification effort during the mid-1980s. Jabara worked with Michigan congressman Carl Purcell in the failed attempt. See Jabara, interview with author; Warren Brown, "Detroit: Arabs' Mecca in the Midwest," *WP*, 30 Oct. 1978; "Chapter Notes," *AN*, Apr. 1982; Luther Keith, "Detroit Area Arabs Not a 'Minority,'" *Detroit News*, n.d., clipping in Sally Howell's personal collection. A prevalent claim to whiteness also has affected many Hispanics' uneasiness about census classifications. See Almaguer, "Race."

68. Wingfield, "ADC," 74–75; Samhan, "Not Quite White," 222–24. When the federal gov-

ernment (specifically the Office of Management and Budget) considered removing the ancestry question from the 1990 census and again from the 2000 census, the AAI headed a multiethnic coalition that helped ensure its continued inclusion. Without an Arab racial category on the census, the ancestry question has been the only way to track and count Arab Americans. See Zogby memo, 20 June 1986, in AAUGP, box 44, folder Arab American Institute.

69. One of the plaintiffs in the suit that resulted in the Supreme Court decision was Majid Ghaidan Khazraji, who claimed he was denied tenure at St. Francis College due to his Arab ethnicity. He was supported in the suit by the ADC. Another plaintiff was a Jewish congregation in Silver Spring, Maryland, which had been the target of neo-Nazis harassment. See "Justices Will Rule on Arab's Charge of Bias," *LAT*, 6 Oct. 1986; "Where Race Means More Than Color," *NYT*, 30 May 1987; and "Ruling Hands Ethnic Groups a Powerful Tool against Bias," *Orlando Sentinel*, 19 May 1987.

70. Stanford, *Beyond the Boundaries*, 60. Feeling this pressure, in the 1988 campaign Jackson backtracked on his stated support for the PLO, which then caused the ADC to register its protest. See ADC Press Release, "Arab Americans Critical of Jackson Flip-Flop on Palestinian Issue," 12 Apr. 1988, and Abourezk to Abraham, 26 July 1988. However, the AAI stood by Jackson during this controversy, with Zogby explaining: "The media reports of a shift in Jesse Jackson's position on the Middle East are grossly exaggerated and appear designed to corner him in New York. Jackson was attempting, as he said, to detach the emotional issue of the PLO from the substantive issue of the Palestinian people's right to self-determination." Zogby memo, 14 Apr. 1988. All documents in NAP, box 11, folder Jesse Jackson. See also Samhan, "Arab Americans," 237.

71. Samhan, "Politics and Exclusion," 21–25; Untitled AAUG document attached to "Proposal for Seminar for Senior Staff of Congressional Black Caucus," n.d., in AAUGP, box 68, folder Black Caucus Project, 1980.

72. Abraham, "Anti-Arab Racism," 196–97; Findley, *They Dare to Speak*, 287–88. On Joe Kennedy returning James Abourezk's campaign donation, see Abourezk, *Advise and Dissent*, 257. During his 1984 campaign, Democratic presidential candidate Gary Hart sought to disassociate himself from any possible Arab "taint" by paying off a large loan he had earlier taken from a bank that may have been tied to Arab interests.

73. Wingfield to Mujid S. Kazimi, 16 Dec. 1986, in AAUGP, box 44, folder ADC.

74. Khoury, "The Arab Lobby," 389–90; Elbaum, *Revolution in the Air*, 266; Katsiaficas, *The Imagination of the New Left*, 191; "New England-wide March and Rally," flyer, 22 Sept. 1984, AAUGP, box 44, folder ADC; Abdulhadi, "Activism and Exile," 240.

75. Ismail to Samih Farsoun, 3 May 1978, and Ismail to Women's Task Force Members, 10 June 1979, in AAUGP, box 88, folder Women's Committee 1979–80; AAUG 1981 Convention Resolutions, in AAUGP, box 116, folder General Assembly Resolution.

76. Letty Cottin Pogrebin, "Anti-Semitism in the Women's Movement," *Ms.*, June 1982, 45–48, 62–72; Hatem, "The Invisible American Half," http://www.haussite.net/haus.0/SCRIPT/txt2001/01/hatem.HTML. For their part, women pro-Palestinian activists in AAUG, MERIP, the Palestine Solidarity Committee, and Najda were disturbed that the U.S. delegation to the UN conference in Copenhagen had voted down "its own resolution against racism because of clauses supporting the rights of Palestinian women." Penny Johnson of the AAUG suggested they write "a letter of protest to Sarah Weddington [who headed the U.S. delegation] . . . . Hopefully we could contact some of the . . . American black women in the delegation who pressed for the anti-racism resolution." See Johnson, 4 Aug. 1980, in AAUGP, box 88, folder Women's Committee 1979–80.

77. Al-Hibri, "Tear Off Your Western Veil"; Haddad, "In Search of Home"; Ahmed, *A Border Passage*, 291–92. Also see Abdulhadi, "Gender," and Ahmed, "Western Ethnocentrism."

78. Haddad, "In Search of Home," 220–21; Haddad, "Anti-Arab Racism," *off our backs*, Mar. 1983.

79. "Perspectives by American Women of Color," *off our backs*, Oct. 1982; Haddad, letter to editor, in "Anti-Arab Racism," and Jordan, "Apologies to All the People in Lebanon," *off our backs*, Mar. 1983. In her letter to the journal, Haddad was also upset that the editors had attributed her presentation to Azizah Al-Hibri, another woman who attended the conference, and in other instances had misspelled her name. She noted that she had subscribed to *off our backs* for ten years and expected the journal would get her identity and name correct.

80. Haddad, "In Search of Home," 222–23; Shakir, *Bint Arab*, 105–6; Hatem, "How the Gulf War Changed the AAUG's Discourse," 279, 286–88; Hatem, "The Invisible American Half."

81. Slade, "The Image." Furthermore, 70 percent of those polled believed that Iran was an Arab country. In *The Fervent Embrace*, 196–97, Carenen cites research showing "57 percent of Americans sided with Israel, whereas only 16 percent sided with the Palestinians" in the 1980s.

82. McAlister, *Epic Encounters*, 193–95, 233. Mearsheimer and Walt, *The Israel Lobby*, 45, 144, place the instances when Reagan questioned Israel or supported Arab interests in the context of the administration's, not to mention Congress's, overwhelming support for Israel. Also see Ginsberg, *The Fatal Embrace*, 184–223; Little, *American Orientalism*, 110; Marrar, *The Arab Lobby*, 30.

83. Samhan, "Arab Americans," 229; Joseph, "Against the Grain," 266; Little, *American Orientalism*, 110–12, 292–97.

84. Abraham, "The Gulf Crisis."

85. McAlister, *Epic Encounters*, 200; Hatem, "Political and Cultural Representations of Arabs," 22. The shift from secular to Islamic organizing was fostered by the arrival of increasing numbers of Muslim immigrants in these years. An example of an Arab American leader who made this transition was Dr. M. T. Mehdi, the Iraqi American who founded and led the secular Action Committee on American-Arab Relations in the 1960s (discussed in chapter 5). By the 1990s his identity and political leadership had become "grounded in Islam," and he founded the National Council for Islamic Affairs. See Haddad, *Not Quite American?*, 34–35.

86. Shryock, Abraham, and Howell, "The Terror Decade."

Conclusion

1. Haddad, "Inventing and Re-inventing the Arab American Identity," 117; Pulcini, "Trends in Research," 38–41.
2. Howell, *Old Islam in Detroit*; Bawardi, *The Making of Arab Americans*.
3. Schiller, Basch, and Blanc-Szanton, "Transnationalism."
4. Pulcini, "Trends in Research," 59.
5. Aruri, "AAUG," 44–46; Kayyali, *The Arab Americans*, 106–7; Shain, "Arab Americans," 53.
6. Abraham, "Arab-American Marginality"; Shain, "Arab Americans," 47–50; Hanania, interview with author.
7. Suleiman, "'I Come to Bury Caesar,'" 85.
8. Gitlin, *The Sixties*.
9. For example, see Foley, *Quest for Equality*, and Behnken, "The Movement in the Mirror."
10. American New Leftists did idealize Algerian revolutionaries, but they seemed to regard Algerians as different and separate from Arab nationalist revolutionaries. See Abdulhadi, "Gender."
11. Abu-Lughod, preface to *The Arab Americans*, v. Also see McAlister, *Epic Encounters*, 39.
12. Said, "Conspiracy of Praise," 30. For an analysis of how charges of anti-Semitism stifle political expression and scholarship, see Butler, *Precarious Life*, 100–127.
13. Samhan, "Losing the Battle," 140, 143.
14. Feldman, *Shadow Over Palestine*, 150.

15. US Campaign to End the Israeli Occupation, http://www.endtheoccupation.org/ (accessed 5 Jan. 2016); Baker, "Palestinians Express 'Solidarity,'" https://electronicintifada.net/blogs/rana-baker/palestinians-express-solidarity-people-ferguson-mike-brown-statement. Also see "Black Solidarity with Palestine," http://www.blackforpalestine.com/ (accessed 19 Sept. 2015).

16. Students for Justice in Palestine, whose chapters adopt various titles, converges with the Palestine Solidarity Movement, another university student organization, founded in 2000. Norton, "Academia," http://mondoweiss.net/2014/10/battleground-palestinian-solidarity; Youmans and Muaddi, "The Growing Israel Divestment Movement," http://www.counterpunch.org/2006/01/24/the-growing-israel-divestment-movement/.

17. The BDS Movement, "Introducing the BDS Movement," n.d., http://www.bdsmovement.net/bdsintro (accessed 17 Sept. 2015); Dawson and Mullen, *Against Apartheid*; Green, "The Real Issues in the Salaita Case," http://mondoweiss.net/2014/09/neoliberalism-corporate-university; Salaita, *Uncivil Rites*.

BIBLIOGRAPHY

Manuscript Collections
Arab American National Museum, Dearborn, Mich.
   Michael Suleiman Collection
Bancroft Library, University of California–Berkeley, Berkeley, Calif.
   The Social Protest Collection, Subseries 6.3: Foreign Movements, 1961–1982 (microfilm)
      Arab Student Association Records, 1968–1974
      Committee to Support Middle East Liberation Records, 1967–1969
      Israeli-Arab conflict Records, 1969–1973
      Liberation Support Movement Records, 1967–1974
Bentley Historical Library, University of Michigan, Ann Arbor, Mich.
   Nabeel Abraham Papers
   Barbara C. Aswad Papers
   Helen Atwell Papers
   Imam Mohamad Jawad Chirri Papers
   Aliya Hassen Papers
   Abdeen Jabara Papers
   Palestine Solidarity Committee, University of Michigan Chapter Papers, 1986–1988
   Wystan Stevens Papers
   Janice Terry Papers
   Donald Unis Papers
Columbia University Rare Book and Manuscript Library, University Archives, New York, N.Y.
   Columbia University Anti-Imperialist Movement Records, 1971–1973, University Protest and Activism Collection, Series VIII
   Third World Coalition Records, 1970–1972, University Protest and Activism Collection, Series VIII
Marriott Library, University of Utah, Salt Lake City, Utah
   Fayez Sayegh Papers
Michigan State University Library, East Lansing, Mich.
   Pamphlets about Arab-American Associations Collection, digitized microfilm, Middle East Microform Project
      American-Arab Anti-Discrimination Committee Papers, 1980–1990
      Palestine Human Rights Campaign Records, 1980–1987
National Archives and Records Administration, College Park, Md.
   Department of Justice Records, RG 60
   Department of State General Records, RG 59
Nixon Presidential Library, Yorba Linda, Calif.
   Nixon White House Tapes, http://www.nixonlibrary.gov/forresearchers/find/tapes/
   White House Special Files, State Member and Office Files, Richard C. Tufaro (Personal collection of Salim Yaqub)

Special Collections Library, Eastern Michigan University, Ypsilanti, Mich.
    Association of Arab American University Graduates Papers
Special Collections Library, University of Michigan, Ann Arbor, Mich.
    Organization of Arab Students at University of Michigan, Vertical File
    Third World Liberation Front at University of California–Berkeley, Vertical File
Special Collections Library, University of North Carolina–Charlotte
    American New Left Collection
Special Collections Research Center, North Carolina State University Libraries, Raleigh, N.C.
    Arab Club Records
University of California–Santa Barbara Library, Santa Barbara, Calif.
    Middle Eastern Student Groups Papers, Student Organizations Collection
University of Kansas Archives, Lawrence, Kans.
    Organization of Arab Students Records, Student Organization Records
Walter P. Reuther Library, Wayne State University, Detroit, Mich.
    Detroit Revolutionary Movement Records
    UAW Local 3 Records
    UAW Collection, Eldon Wildcat Records
    Wayne State University Board of Governors, Official Proceedings

Interviews with Author
Abraham, Nabeel. 20 August 2012. Dearborn, Mich.
Abudayyeh, Khairy. 10 and 14 September 2015. Telephone.
Ahmed, Ismael. 22 May 2012. Dearborn, Mich.
Almaklani, Ali Baleed. 29 April 2013. Dearborn, Mich.
Aswad, Barbara C., and Adnan Aswad. 24 August 2012. Holly, Mich.
Beinin, Joel. 5 July 2012. Telephone.
Hamlin, Mike. 16 June 2012. Detroit, Mich.
Hanania, Ray. 16 July 2015. Telephone.
House, Gloria. 21 June 2012. Dearborn, Mich.
Jabara, Abdeen. 23 July 2012. Plymouth, Mich.
Khoury, George. 16 July 2012. Royal Oak, Mich.
O'Laughlin, Mike, and Janice Murphy. 18 June 2012. Telephone.
Ryan, Sheila, and George Cavalletto. 4 September 2012. Telephone.

Interviews with Janice Terry, in Janice Terry Papers, Bentley Historical Library, University of Michigan, Ann Arbor, Michigan
Abraham, Nabeel. 26 August 1996.
Ahmed, Ismael. 12 June 1996.
Jabara, Abdeen. 20 July 1994.
Khoury, George. 31 July 1994.
Nawash, Hasan. 7 August 1996.
Unis, Don. 29 July 1996.

Specialized Periodicals
AAUG Newsletter, in AAUG Papers, Special Collections Library, Eastern Michigan University, Ypsilanti, Mich.
Action (Action Committee on American-Arab Relations), in Special Collections Library, University of Michigan, Ann Arbor, Mich.

ADC Reports (American Arab Anti-Discrimination Committee), in Nabeel Abraham Papers, Bentley Historical Library, University of Michigan.
Al-Islaah, microfilm in Immigration History Research Center, University of Minnesota, Minneapolis, Minnesota.
Arab Journal (Organization of Arab Students), in University of Wisconsin–Madison Library.
Arab Student Bulletin (Organization of Arab Students), in Special Collections Library, University of Michigan.
Berkeley Barb, in "The Sixties: Primary Documents and Personal Narratives, 1960 to 1974," online database, Alexander Street Press, alexanderstreet.com. Accessed 14 July 2012.
Black Panther, in "Black Thought and Culture," online database, Alexander Street Press, alexanderstreet.com. Accessed 14 July 2012.
Daily Collegian, in Walter P. Reuther Library, Wayne State University.
Eldon Spark, in UAW Papers, Walter P. Reuther Library, Wayne State University.
Free Palestine, in Special Collections Library, University of Michigan.
Heritage, in Immigration History Research Center, University of Minnesota.
Liberation News Service, http://www.lns-archive.org/.
Link (Americans for Middle East Understanding), http://www.ameu.org.
MERIP Reports, JSTOR, http://www.jstor.org.
New Left Notes (Students for a Democratic Society), in "The Sixties: Primary Documents and Personal Narratives, 1960 to 1974," online database, Alexander Street Press, alexanderstreet.com. Accessed 14 July 2012.
OAS News, in Special Collections Library, University of Michigan.
Palestine! (Palestine Solidarity Committee), in Special Collections Library, University of Michigan, and in Janice Terry Papers, Bentley Historical Library, University of Michigan.
Palestine Digest (Arab Information Center of the League of Arab States), in Special Collections Library, University of Michigan.
Palestine Issue (Palestine Liberation Organization in New York), in Special Collections Library, University of Michigan.
Palestinian Voice, in the Immigration History Research Collection, University of Minnesota.
PHRC Bulletin (Palestinian Human Rights Campaign), in Abdeen Jabara Papers and Janice Terry Papers, Bentley Historical Library, University of Michigan.
Ramparts, in "The Sixties: Primary Documents and Personal Narratives, 1960 to 1974," online database, Alexander Street Press, alexanderstreet.com. Accessed 14 July 2012.
SNCC Newsletter, in Special Collections Library, University of Michigan.
South End, in Walter P. Reuther Library, Wayne State University.

Published Sources

"Abdeen Jabara." *National Lawyers Guild—New York City News*, Summer 2013, 10.
Abdulhadi, Rabab. "Activism and Exile: Palestinianness and the Politics of Solidarity." In *Local Actions: Cultural Activism, Power, and Public Life in America*, edited by Melissa Checker and Maggie Fishman, 231–54. New York: Columbia University Press, 2004.
———. "Gender, Resistance, and Liberation in 1960s Palestine: Living under Occupation." *Against the Current* 27 (July/Aug. 2012): 15–20.
Abourezk, James G. *Advise and Dissent: Memoirs of South Dakota and the U.S. Senate*. Chicago: Lawrence Hill Books, 1989.
Abraham, Nabeel. "Anti-Arab Racism and Violence in the United States." In *The Development of Arab-American Identity*, edited by Ernest McCarus, 155–215. Ann Arbor: University of Michigan Press, 1994.

———. "Arab-American Marginality: Mythos and Praxis." In *Arab Americans: Continuity and Change*, edited by Baha Abu-Laban and Michael W. Suleiman, 17–44. Belmont, Mass.: Association of Arab American University Graduates, 1989.

———. "Arabs in America: An Overview." In *The Arab World and Arab Americans: Understanding a Neglected Minority*, edited by Sameer Y. Abraham and Nabeel Abraham, 17–22. Detroit: Center for Urban Studies, Wayne State University Press, 1981.

———. "Detroit's Yemeni Workers." *MERIP Reports* 57 (May 1977): 3–9, 13.

———. "The Gulf Crisis and Anti-Arab Racism in America." In *Collateral Damage: The New World Order at Home and Abroad*, edited by Cynthia Peters, 255–78. Boston: South End Press, 1992.

———. Letter to the editor. *MERIP Reports* 60 (September 1977): 25.

———. "To Palestine and Back: Quest for Place." In *Arab Detroit: From Margin to Mainstream*, edited by Nabeel Abraham and Andrew Shryock, 425–62. Detroit: Wayne State University Press, 2000.

———. "The Yemeni Immigrant Community of Detroit: Background, Emigration, and Community Life." In *Arabs in the New World: Studies on Arab-American Communities*, edited by Sameer Y. Abraham and Nabeel Abraham, 110–31. Detroit: Wayne State University Press, 1983.

Abraham, Sameer. "The PLO at the Crossroads: Moderation, Encirclement, Future Prospects." *MERIP Reports* 80 (September 1979): 5–13, 26.

———. "A Survey of the Arab-American Community in Metropolitan Detroit." In *The Arab World and Arab Americans: Understanding a Neglected Minority*, edited by Sameer Y. Abraham and Nabeel Abraham, 23–33. Detroit: Center for Urban Studies, Wayne State University Press, 1981.

Abraham, Sameer Y., Nabeel Abraham, and Barbara C. Aswad. "The Southend: An Arab Muslim Working-Class Community." In *Arabs in the New World: Studies on Arab-American Communities*, edited by Sameer Y. Abraham and Nabeel Abraham, 164–84. Detroit: Wayne State University Press, 1983.

Abu-Laban, Baha. "Reflections on the Rise and Decline of an Arab-American Organization." *Arab Studies Quarterly* 29 (Summer–Fall 2007): 47–56.

Abu-Laban, Baha, and Faith T. Zeadey, eds. *Arabs in America: Myths and Realities*. Wilmette, Ill.: Medina University Press International, 1975.

Abu-Laban, Sharon McIrvin. "The Coexistence of Cohorts: Identity and Adaptation among Arab-American Muslims." In *Arab Americans: Continuity and Change*, edited by Baha Abu-Laban and Michael W. Suleiman, 45–63. Belmont, Mass.: Association of Arab American University Graduates, 1989.

Abu-Lughod, Ibrahim. Preface to *The Arab Americans: Studies in Assimilation*, edited by Elaine C. Hagopian and Ann Paden. Wilmette, Ill.: Medina University Press International, 1969.

Abu-Lughod, Lila, and Ahmad H. Sa'di. "Introduction: The Claims of Memory." In *Nakba: Palestine, 1948, and the Claims of Memory*, edited by Ahmad H. Sa'di and Lila Abu-Lughod, 1–26. New York: Columbia University Press, 2007.

Ahmed, Ismael. "Ishmael Ahmed." In *Detroit Lives*, edited by Robert H. Mast, 27–32. Philadelphia: Temple University Press, 1994.

———. "Michigan Arab Americans: A Case Study of Electoral and Non-Electoral Empowerment." In *American Arabs and Political Participation, Proceedings of a Conference Sponsored by the Division of United States Studies, Woodrow Wilson International Center for Scholars*, edited by Philippa Strum, 41–52, 5 May 2006.

———. "Organizing an Arab Workers Caucus." *MERIP Reports* 34 (January 1975): 17–22.

Ahmed, Leila. *A Border Passage: From Cairo to America—A Woman's Journey*. New York: Farrar, Straus and Giroux, 1999.

———. "Western Ethnocentrism and Perceptions of the Harem." *Feminist Studies* 8 (Autumn 1982): 521–34.

Akram, Susan M., and Kevin R. Johnson. "Race and Civil Rights Pre-September 11, 2001: The Targeting of Arabs and Muslims." In *Civil Rights in Peril: The Targeting of Arabs and Muslims*, edited by Elaine C. Hagopian, 9–26. Chicago: Haymarket Books, 2004.

Algar, Hamid. *Wahhabism: A Critical Essay*. Oneonta, N.Y.: Islamic Publications International, 2002.

Al-Hibri, Azizah. "Tear Off Your Western Veil." In *Food for Our Grandmothers: Writings by Arab-America and Arab-Canadian Feminists*, edited by Joanna Kadi, 160–64. Boston: South End Press, 1994.

Almaguer, Tomas. "Race, Racialization, and Latino Populations in the United States." In *Racial Formation in the Twenty-First Century*, edited by Daniel Martinez HoSang, Oneka LaBennett, and Laura Pulido, 143–61. Berkeley: University of California Press, 2012.

Anderson, Terry H. *The Movement and the Sixties: Protest in America from Greensboro to Wounded Knee*. New York: Oxford University Press, 1995.

Aruri, Naseer H. "AAUG: A Memoir." *Arab Studies Quarterly* 29 (Summer–Fall 2007): 33–46.

———, ed. *Middle East Crucible: Studies on the Arab-Israeli War of October 1973*. Wilmette, Ill.: Medina University Press International, 1975.

Association of Arab American University Graduates. *The First Decade, 1967–1977*. Detroit: Association of Arab American University Graduates, 1977.

Aswad, Barbara C. "How a Dearborn Community Gained the ACCESS It Needed." *Dearborn Historian* 51 (Winter 2014): 9–15.

———. "Introduction and Overview." In *Arabic Speaking Communities in American Cities*, edited by Barbara C. Aswad, 1–17. New York: Center for Migration Studies of New York and Association of Arab American University Graduates, 1974.

———. "The Southeast Dearborn Arab Community Struggles for Survival against Urban 'Renewal.'" In *Arabic Speaking Communities in American Cities*, edited by Barbara C. Aswad, 53–84. New York: Center for Migration Studies of New York and Association of Arab American University Graduates, 1974.

Aswad, Barbara C., and Nancy Adadow Gray. "Challenges to the Arab-American Family and ACCESS." In *Family and Gender among American Muslims: Issues Facing Middle Eastern Immigrants and Their Descendants*, edited by Barbara C. Aswad and Barbara Bilge, 223–40. Philadelphia: Temple University Press, 1996.

Avineri, Shlomo. "Israel and the New Left." *Society* 7 (July 1970): 79–83.

Ayton, Mel. *The Forgotten Terrorist: Sirhan Sirhan and the Assassination of Robert F. Kennedy*. Washington, D.C.: Potomac Books, 2007.

Bakalian, Anny, and Medhi Bozorgmehr. *Backlash 9/11: Middle Eastern and Muslim Americans Respond*. Berkeley: University of California Press, 2009.

Baker, Rana. "Palestinians Express 'Solidarity with the People of Ferguson' in Mike Brown Statement." *Electronic Intifada*, 15 August 2014. https://electronicintifada.net/blogs/rana-baker/palestinians-express-solidarity-people-ferguson-mike-brown-statement. Accessed 15 September 2015.

Baker, Wayne, and Andrew Shryock. "Citizenship and Crisis." In *Citizenship and Crisis: Arab Detroit after 9/11*, by Detroit Arab American Study Team, 3–32. New York: Russell Sage Foundation, 2009.

Bashshur, Rashid. "Unfulfilled Expectations: The Genesis and Demise of the AAUG." *Arab Studies Quarterly* 29 (Summer–Fall 2007): 7–13.

Bassiouni, M. Cherif. "The AAUG: Reflections on a Lost Opportunity." *Arab Studies Quarterly* 29 (Summer–Fall 2007): 21–32.

———, ed. *The Civil Rights of Arab-Americans: "The Special Measures."* North Dartmouth, Mass.: Association of Arab American University Graduates, 1974.

Bawardi, Hani J. *The Making of Arab Americans: From Syrian Nationalism to U.S. Citizenship.* Austin: University of Texas Press, 2014.

Behnken, Brian D. "Introduction." In *The Struggle in Black and Brown: African American and Mexican American Relations during the Civil Rights Era*, edited by Brian D. Behnken, 1–18. Lincoln: University of Nebraska Press, 2011.

———. "The Movement in the Mirror: Civil Rights and the Causes of Black-Brown Disunity in Texas." In *The Struggle in Black and Brown: African American and Mexican American Relations during the Civil Rights Era*, edited by Brian D. Behnken, 49–77. Lincoln: University of Nebraska Press, 2011.

Beinin, Joel. Letter to the editor. *MERIP Reports* 59 (August 1977): 26.

Bisharat, Mary. "Yemeni Farmworkers in California." *MERIP Reports* 34 (January 1975): 22–26.

Brick, Howard, and Christopher Phelps. *Radicals in America: The U.S. Left since the Second World War.* New York: Cambridge University Press, 2015.

Brilliant, Mark. *The Color of America Has Changed: How Racial Diversity Shaped Civil Rights Reform in California, 1941–1978.* New York: Oxford University Press, 2010.

Brown, Stuart Gerry. *The Presidency on Trial: Robert Kennedy's 1968 Campaign and Afterwards.* Honolulu: University of Hawai'i Press, 1972.

Butler, Judith. *Precarious Life: The Powers of Mourning and Violence.* London: Verso Press, 2004.

Cainkar, Louise. "Immigrants from the Arab World." In *The New Chicago: A Social and Cultural Analysis*, edited by John P. Koval, Larry Bennett, Michael I. J. Bennett, Fassil Demissie, Roberta Garner, and Kiljoong Kim, 182–96. Philadelphia: Temple University Press, 2006.

———. "Palestinian Women in American Society: The Interaction of Social Class, Culture, and Politics." In *The Development of Arab-American Identity*, edited by Ernest McCarus, 85–105. Ann Arbor: University of Michigan Press, 1994.

———. "Thinking Outside the Box: Arabs and Race in the United States." In *Race and Arab Americans before and after 9/11: From Invisible Citizens to Visible Subjects*, edited by Amaney Jamal and Nadine Naber, 46–80. Syracuse, N.Y.: Syracuse University Press, 2008.

Camarillo, Albert. "Blacks, Latinos, and the New Racial Frontier in American Cities of Color: California's Emerging Minority-Majority Cities." In *African American Urban History since World War II*, edited by Kenneth L. Kusmer and Joe W. Trotter, 39–59. Chicago: University of Chicago Press, 2009.

Carenen, Caitlin. *The Fervent Embrace: Liberal Protestants, Evangelicals, and Israel.* New York: New York University Press, 2012.

Carmichael, Stokely. "The Black American and Palestinian Revolutions." In *Stokely Speaks: Black Power Back to Pan-Africanism*, 131–43. New York: Random House, 1971.

———, with Ekwueme Michael Thelwell. *Ready for Revolution: The Life and Struggles of Stokely Carmichael (Kwame Ture).* New York: Scribner, 2003.

Carson, Clayborne. *In Struggle: SNCC and the Black Awakening of the 1960s.* Cambridge, Mass.: Harvard University Press, 1995.

"The Case of the L.A. 8: U.S. Drops 20-Year Effort to Deport Arab Americans for Supporting Palestinian National Rights." *Democracy Now*, 2 November 2007. http://www.democracynow.org/2007/11/2/the_case_of_the_la8_u. Accessed 10 June 2015.

Chamberlin, Paul Thomas. *The Global Offensive: The United States, the Palestine Liberation Organization, and the Making of the Post–Cold War Order.* New York: Oxford University Press, 2012.

Chertoff, Mordecai S. "The New Left and the Newer Leftists." In *The New Left and the Jews,* edited by Mordecai S. Chertoff, 166–96. New York: Pitman Publishing, 1971.

Chomsky, Noam. "Israel and the New Left." In *The New Left and the Jews,* edited by Mordecai S. Chertoff, 197–228. New York: Pitman Publishing, 1971.

Christison, Kathleen. "On Being Palestinian in a Nation Fixated on Israel." In *American Arabs and Political Participation, Proceedings of a Conference Sponsored by the Division of United States Studies, Woodrow Wilson International Center for Scholars,* edited by Philippa Strum, 101–16, 5 May 2006. https://www.wilsoncenter.org/sites/default/files/DUSS_Arab _America.pdf. Accessed 8 May 2012.

Cohen, Robert. "Prophetic Minority versus Recalcitrant Majority: Southern Student Dissent and the Struggle for Progressive Change in the 1960s." Introduction to *Rebellion in Black and White: Southern Student Activism in the 1960s,* edited by Robert Cohen and David J. Snyder, 1–42. Baltimore: The Johns Hopkins University Press, 2013.

Curtis, Edward E., IV. "Islamism and Its African American Muslim Critics: Black Muslims in the Era of the Arab Cold War." *American Quarterly* 59 (September 2007): 683–709.

Darden, Joe T., and Richard W. Thomas. *Detroit: Race Riots, Racial Conflicts, and Efforts to Bridge the Racial Divide.* East Lansing: Michigan State University Press, 2013.

Daulatzai, Sohail. *Black Star, Crescent Moon: The Muslim International and Black Freedom beyond America.* Minneapolis: University of Minnesota Press, 2012.

David, Gary. "Behind the Bulletproof Glass: Iraqi Chaldean Store Ownership in Metropolitan Detroit." In *Arab Detroit: From Margin to Mainstream,* edited by Nabeel Abraham and Andrew Shryock, 151–78. Detroit: Wayne State University Press, 2000.

———. "The Creation of 'Arab American': Political Activism and Ethnic (Dis)Unity." *Critical Sociology* 33 (2007): 833–62.

Davidson, Lawrence. "Debating Palestine: Arab-American Challenges to Zionism, 1917–1932." In *Arabs in America: Building a New Future,* edited by Michael W. Suleiman, 227–40. Philadelphia: Temple University Press, 1999.

Dawisha, Adeed. *Arab Nationalism in the Twentieth Century: From Triumph to Despair.* Princeton, N.J.: Princeton University Press, 2003.

Dawson, Ashley, and Bill V. Mullen, eds. *Against Apartheid: The Case for Boycotting Israeli Universities.* Chicago: Haymarket Books, 2015.

DeRoche, Andrew J. *Andrew Young: Civil Rights Ambassador.* Wilmington, Del.: Scholarly Resources, 2003.

Dirlik, Arif. "The Third World." In *1968: The World Transformed,* edited by Carole Fink, Philipp Gassert, and Detlef Junker, 295–317. Cambridge: Cambridge University Press, 1998.

Echols, Alice. *Shaky Ground: The Sixties and Its Aftershocks.* New York: Columbia University Press, 2002.

Ehrman, John. *The Rise of Neoconservatism: Intellectuals and Foreign Affairs, 1945–1994.* New Haven, Conn.: Yale University Press, 1995.

Elbaum, Max. *Revolution in the Air: Sixties Radicals Turn to Lenin, Mao and Che.* London: Verso Press, 2002.

Elkholy, Abdo A. "The Arab-Americans: Nationalism and Traditional Preservations." In *The Arab Americans: Studies in Assimilation,* edited by Elaine C. Hagopian and Ann Paden, 3–17. Wilmette, Ill.: Medina University Press International, 1969.

———. *The Arab Moslems in the United States: Religion and Assimilation.* New Haven: College and University Press, 1966.

Farsoun, Karen, Samih Farsoun, and Alex Ajay. "Mid-East Perspectives from the American Left." *Journal of Palestine Studies* 4 (Fall 1974): 94–119.

Farsoun, Samih, and Naseer H. Aruri. *Palestine and the Palestinians: A Social and Political History*, 2nd ed. Boulder, Colo.: Westview Press, 2006.

"The FBI and the Anti-Defamation League." The Institute for Research: Middle Eastern Policy. The Israel Lobby Archive. http://www.irmep.org/ila/ADL/. Accessed 18 July 2014.

Feldman, Keith P. "Representing Permanent War: Black Power's Palestine and the End(s) of Civil Rights." *CR: The New Centennial Review* 8 (Fall 2008): 193–231.

———. *A Shadow Over Palestine: The Imperial Life of Race in America*. Minneapolis: University of Minnesota Press, 2015.

Fernández, Johanna. "Denise Oliver and the Young Lords Party: Stretching the Political Boundaries of Struggle." In *Want to Start a Revolution? Radical Women in the Black Freedom Struggle*, edited by Dayo F. Gore, Jeanne Theoharis, and Komozi Woodard, 271–93. New York: New York University Press, 2009.

———. "The Young Lords and the Postwar City: Notes on the Geographical and Structural Reconfigurations of Contemporary Urban Life." In *African American Urban History since World War II*, edited by Kenneth L. Kusmer and Joe W. Trotter, 60–82. Chicago: University of Chicago Press, 2009.

Findley, Paul. *They Dare to Speak: People and Institutions Confront Israel's Lobby*. Westport, Conn.: Lawrence Hill, 1985.

Fischbach, Michael R. "Government Pressures against Arabs in the United States." *Journal of Palestine Studies* 14 (Spring 1985): 87–100.

Foley, Neil. *Quest for Equality: The Failed Promise of Black-Brown Solidarity*. Cambridge, Mass.: Harvard University Press, 2010.

Forman, James. *The Making of Black Revolutionaries*. Seattle: University of Washington Press, 1997. Originally published 1972.

Francos, Ania. "The Palestinian Revolution and the Third World." In *The Palestinian Resistance to Israeli Occupation*, edited by Naseer Aruri, 32–48. Wilmette, Ill.: Medina University Press International, 1970.

Friedlander, Jonathan, ed. *Sojourners and Settlers: The Yemeni Immigrant Experience*. Salt Lake City: University of Utah Press, 1988.

Frost, Jennifer. *"An Interracial Movement of the Poor": Community Organizing and the New Left in the 1960s*. New York: New York University Press, 2001.

Fujino, Diane C. "The Black Liberation Movement and Japanese American Activism: The Radical Activism of Richard Aoki and Yuri Kochiyama." In *Afro Asia: Revolutionary Political and Cultural Connections between African Americans and Asian Americans*, edited by Fred Ho and Bill V. Mullen, 165–97. Durham, N.C.: Duke University Press, 2008.

———. "Grassroots Leadership and Afro-Asian Solidarities: Yuri Kochiyama's Humanizing Radicalism." In *Want to Start a Revolution? Radical Women in the Black Freedom Struggle*, edited by Dayo F. Gore, Jeanne Theoharis, and Komozi Woodard, 294–316. New York: New York University Press, 2009.

Garrett, Paul D., and Kathleen A. Purpura. *Frank Maria: A Search for Justice and Peace in the Middle East*. Bloomington, Ind.: Author House, 2007.

Georgakas, Dan. "Arab Workers in Detroit." *MERIP Reports* 34 (January 1975): 13–17.

Georgakas, Dan, and Marvin Surkin. *Detroit: I Do Mind Dying: A Study in Urban Revolution*, 3rd ed. Chicago: Haymarket Press, 2012.

Gessert, Charles R. "A Non-Arab Looks at an Anti-Arab-American Policy." In *The Civil Rights of Arab-Americans: "The Special Measures,"* edited by M. C. Bassiouni, 16–27. North Dartmouth, Mass.: Association of Arab American University Graduates, 1974.

Ghareeb, Edmund, ed. *Split Vision: The Portrayal of Arabs in the American Media.* Washington, D.C.: American Arab Affairs Council, 1983.

Ginsberg, Benjamin. *The Fatal Embrace: Jews and the State.* Chicago: University of Chicago Press, 1993.

Gitlin, Todd. *The Sixties: Years of Hope, Days of Rage.* New York: Bantam Books, 1987.

Glasser, Ruth. "From 'Rich Port' to Bridgeport: Puerto Ricans in Connecticut." In *The Puerto Rican Diaspora: Historical Perspectives*, edited by Carmen Teresa Whalen and Victor Vazquez-Hernandez, 174–99. Philadelphia: Temple University Press, 2005.

Glazer, Nathan. "Jewish Interests and the New Left." In *The New Left and the Jews*, edited by Mordecai S. Chertoff, 152–65. New York: Pitman Publishing, 1971.

Goldman, Shalom. *Zeal for Zion: Christians, Jews, and the Idea of the Promised Land.* Chapel Hill: University of North Carolina Press, 2009.

Gosse, Van. *Rethinking the New Left: An Interpretative History.* New York: Palgrave Macmillan, 2005.

Green, David. "The Real Issues in the Salaita Case: Palestine, Neoliberalism, and the Corporate University." *Mondoweiss*, 8 September 2014. http://mondoweiss.net/2014/09/neoliberalism-corporate-university. Accessed 17 September 2015.

Greenberg, Cheryl Lynn. *Troubling the Waters: Black-Jewish Relations in the American Century.* Princeton, N.J.: Princeton University Press, 2006.

Greenberg, Ivan. *The Dangers of Dissent: The FBI and Civil Liberties since 1965.* Lanham, Md.: Lexington, 2010.

Greenfield, Robert. *Timothy Leary: A Biography.* Orlando: Harcourt, 2006.

Gualtieri, Sarah. *Between Arab and White: Race and Ethnicity in the Early Syrian American Diaspora.* Berkeley: University of California Press, 2009.

Haddad, Carol. "In Search of Home." In *Food for Our Grandmothers: Writings by Arab-American and Arab-Canadian Feminists*, edited by Joanna Kadi, 218–23. Boston: South End Press, 1994.

Haddad, Yvonne. "American Foreign Policy in the Middle East and Its Impact on the Identity of Arab Muslims in the United States." In *Muslims of America*, edited by Yvonne Haddad, 217–35. New York: Oxford University Press, 1993.

———. "Inventing and Re-inventing the Arab American Identity." In *A Community of Many Worlds: Arab Americans in New York City*, edited by Kathleen Benson and Philip M. Kayal, 109–23. Syracuse, N.Y.: Syracuse University Press, 2002.

———. "Maintaining the Faith of the Fathers: Dilemmas of Religious Identity in the Christian and Muslim Arab American Communities." In *The Development of Arab-American Identity*, edited by Ernest McCarus, 61–84. Ann Arbor: University of Michigan Press, 1994.

———. "Nationalist and Islamist Tendencies in Contemporary Arab American Communities." In *Arab Nationalism and the Future of the Arab World*, edited by Hani Faris, 141–59. Belmont, Mass.: Association of Arab American University Graduates, 1986.

———. *Not Quite American? The Shaping of Arab and Muslim Identity in the United States.* Waco, Tex.: Baylor University Press, 2004.

Hagopian, Elaine. "Minority Rights in a Nation-State: The Nixon Administration's Campaign against the Arab Americans." *Journal of Palestine Studies* 5 (Fall 1975): 97–114.

———. "Reversing Injustice: On Utopian Activism." *Arab Studies Quarterly* 29 (Summer–Fall 2007): 57–73.

Hagopian, Elaine C., and Ann Paden, eds. *The Arab Americans: Studies in Assimilation.* AAUG Monograph Series. Wilmette, Ill.: Medina University Press International, 1969.

Hall, Simon. "On the Tail of the Panther: Black Power and the 1967 Convention of the National Conference for New Politics." *Journal of American Studies* 37 (April 2003): 59–78.

Hatem, Mervat F. "How the Gulf War Changed the AAUG's Discourse on Arab Nationalism and Gender Politics." *Middle East Journal* 55 (Spring 2001): 277–96.

———. "The Invisible American Half: Arab American Hybridity and Feminist Discourses in the 1990s," 1998. http://www.haussite.net/haus.0/SCRIPT/txt2001/01/hatem.HTML. Accessed 3 April 2015.

———. "The Political and Cultural Representations of Arabs, Arab Americans, and Arab American Feminisms after September 11, 2001." In *Arab and Arab American Feminisms: Gender, Violence, and Belonging*, edited by Rabab Abdulhadi, Evelyn Alsultany, and Nadine Naber, 10–28. Syracuse, N.Y.: Syracuse University Press, 2011.

Ho, Fred, and Bill V. Mullen, eds. *Afro Asia: Revolutionary Political and Cultural Connections between African Americans and Asian Americans*. Durham, N.C.: Duke University Press, 2008.

HoSang, Daniel Martinez, Oneka LaBennett, and Laura Pulido, eds. *Racial Formation in the Twenty-First Century*. Berkeley: University of California Press, 2012.

Howell, Sally. *Old Islam in Detroit: Rediscovering the Muslim American Past*. New York: Oxford University Press, 2014.

———. "Southend Struggles: Converging Narratives of an Arab/Muslim American Enclave." *Mashriq & Mahjar* 3, no. 1 (2015): 41–64. http://lebanesestudies.ojs.chass.ncsu.edu/index.php/mashriq/article/view/63. Accessed 12 November 2015.

Hussaini, Hatem I. "The Impact of the Arab-Israeli Conflict on Arab Communities in the United States." In *Settler Regimes in Africa and the Arab World: The Illusion of Endurance*, edited by Ibrahim Abu-Lughod and Baha Abu-Laban, 201–20. Wilmette, Ill.: Medina University Press International, 1974.

Jabara, Abdeen. "The AAUG: Aspirations and Failures." *Arab Studies Quarterly* 29 (Summer–Fall 2007): 15–19.

———. "Abdeen Jabara: Targeting Palestinian Activists." *Tracked in America*, American Civil Liberties Union. http://www.trackedinamerica.org/timeline/civil_rights/jabara/. Accessed 18 July 2012.

———. "The American Left and the June Conflict." In *The Arab-Israeli Confrontation of June 1967: An Arab Perspective*, edited by Ibrahim Abu-Lughod, 169–90. Evanston, Ill.: Northwestern University Press, 1970.

———. Foreword to *Why Robert Kennedy Was Killed: The Story of Two Victims*, by Godfrey Jansen. New York: Third Press, 1970.

———. "The Guild in Palestine: A History." *Guild Practitioner* 63 (Fall 2006): 193–99.

———. Interview. *Law and Disorder Radio*. http://lawanddisorder.org/2016/01/law-and-disorder-january-11-2016/. Accessed 11 January 2016.

———. "IRS Proposes to Revoke AAUG Tax Exemption: Another Form of Political Harassment." In *The Civil Rights of Arab-Americans: "The Special Measures,"* edited by M. C. Bassiouni, 49–54. North Dartmouth, Mass.: Association of Arab American University Graduates, 1974.

———. "Israel and Human Rights." *Guild Practitioner* 29 (1970).

———. "Operation Arab: The Nixon Administration's Measures in the United States after Munich." *The Civil Rights of Arab-Americans: "The Special Measures,"* edited by M. C. Bassiouni, 1–15. North Dartmouth, Mass.: Association of Arab American University Graduates, 1974.

———. "A Strategy for Political Effectiveness." In *Arab Americans: Continuity and Change*, edited by Baha Abu-Laban and Michael W. Suleiman, 201–5. Belmont, Mass.: Association of Arab American University Graduates, 1989.

———. *Zionism and Racism*. AAUG Occasional Papers, No. 3, 1976. Special Collections Library, Eastern Michigan University, Ypsilanti, Michigan.

Jabara, Abdeen, and Janice Terry, eds. *The Arab World: From Nationalism to Revolution*, AAUG Monograph Series, No. 3. Wilmette, Ill.: Medina University Press International, 1971.

Jamal, Amaney. "Civil Liberties and the Otherization of Arab and Muslim Americans." In *Race and Arab Americans before and after 9/11: From Invisible Citizens to Visible Subjects*, edited by Amaney Jamal and Nadine Naber, 114–30. Syracuse, N.Y.: Syracuse University Press, 2008.

Jansen, Godfrey. *Why Robert Kennedy Was Killed: The Story of Two Victims*. New York: Third Press, 1970.

Joseph, Suad. "Against the Grain of the Nation—the Arab-." In *Arabs in America: Building a New Future*, edited by Michael W. Suleiman, 257–71. Philadelphia: Temple University Press, 1999.

Judis, John B. *Genesis: Truman, American Jews, and the Origins of the Arab/Israeli Conflict*. New York: Farrar, Straus and Giroux, 2014.

———. "Zionist Movement: How AIPAC Is Severing Its Historical Roots—and Weakening Its Influence." *Foreign Policy*, 27 February 2014. http://foreignpolicy.com/2014/02/27/zionist-movement/. Accessed 12 May 2015.

Kaiser, Robert Blair. *"R.F.K. Must Die": A History of the Robert Kennedy Assassination and Its Aftermath*. New York: E. P. Dutton, 1970.

Katsiaficas, George. *The Imagination of the New Left: A Global Analysis of 1968*. Cambridge, Mass.: South End Press, 1987.

Kayyali, Randa A. *The Arab Americans*. Westport, Conn.: Greenwood Press, 2006.

Kelley, Robin D. G., and Betsy Esch. "Black Like Mao: Red China and Black Revolution." In *Afro Asia: Revolutionary Political and Cultural Connections between African Americans and Asian Americans*, edited by Fred Ho and Bill V. Mullen, 97–154. Durham, N.C.: Duke University Press, 2008.

Kelley, Ron. "Muslims in Los Angeles." In *Muslim Communities in North America*, edited by Yvonne Yazbeck Haddad and Jane Idleman Smith, 135–67. Albany: State University of New York Press, 1994.

Khoury, Nabeel A. "The Arab Lobby: Problems and Prospects." *Middle East Journal* 41 (Summer 1987): 379–96.

Khoury, Nabil Elie. "The AAUG in My Eyes." *Arab Studies Quarterly* 29 (Summer–Fall 2007): 165–72.

Klinghoffer, Judith. *Vietnam, Jews, and the Middle East: Unintended Consequences*. New York: St. Martin's Press, 1999.

Kochiyama, Yuri. "A Quick Reflection." *Amerasia* 15 (1989): 99–102.

Leary, Timothy. *Confessions of a Hope Fiend*. New York: Bantam Books, 1973.

Lee, Sonia Song-Ha. *Building a Latino Civil Rights Movement: Puerto Ricans, African Americans, and the Pursuit of Racial Justice in New York City*. Chapel Hill: University of North Carolina Press, 2014.

Lipset, Seymour Martin. "'The Socialism of Fools': The Left, the Jews, and Israel." In *The New Left and the Jews*, edited by Mordecai S. Chertoff, 103–31. New York: Pitman Publishing, 1971.

Little, Douglas. *American Orientalism: The United States and the Middle East since 1945*. Chapel Hill: University of North Carolina Press, 2002.

Liu, Michael, Kim Geron, and Tracy Lai. *The Snake Dance of Asian American Activism: Community, Vision, and Power*. Lanham, Md.: Lexington Books, 2008.

Lubin, Alex. *Geographies of Liberation: The Making of an Afro-Arab Political Imaginary*. Chapel Hill: University of North Carolina Press, 2014.

Lukas, J. Anthony. "Why Robert Kennedy Was Killed." Review of Godfrey Jansen, *Why Robert Kennedy Was Killed: A Story of Two Victims*. In *New York Times Book Review*, 2 May 1971.

Majaj, Lisa Suhair. "Arab-American Ethnicity: Locations, Coalitions, and Cultural Negotiations." In *Arabs in America: Building a New Future*, edited by Michael W. Suleiman, 320–36. Philadelphia: Temple University Press, 1999.

Malek, Alia. *A Country Called Amreeka: U.S. History Retold through Arab-American Lives*. New York: Free Press, 2009.

Mantler, Gordon K. *Power to the Poor: Black-Brown Coalition and the Fight for Economic Justice, 1960–1974*. Chapel Hill: University of North Carolina Press, 2013.

Marable, Manning. *Malcolm X: A Life of Reinvention*. New York: Viking, 2011.

Marrar, Khalil. *The Arab Lobby and US Foreign Policy: The Two-State Solution*. London: Routledge, 2009.

Matin-Asgari, Afshin. *Iranian Student Opposition to the Shah*. Costa Mesa, Calif.: Mazda Publishers, 2002.

Mattson, Kevin. "Between Despair and Hope: Revisiting *Studies on the Left*." In *The New Left Revisited*, edited by John McMillian and Paul Buhle, 28–47. Philadelphia: Temple University Press, 2003.

——. *Intellectuals in Action: The Origins of the New Left and Radical Liberalism, 1945–1970*. University Park: Pennsylvania State University Press, 2002.

McAlister, Melani. *Epic Encounters: Culture, Media, and U.S. Interests in the Middle East, 1945–2000*. Berkeley: University of California Press, 2001.

McMahon, Janet. "Abdeen Jabara." *Washington Report on Middle East Affairs*, 30 September 1990, 29.

McMillian, John. "Introduction: 'You Didn't Have to Be There': Revisiting the New Left Consensus." In *The New Left Revisited*, edited by John McMillian and Paul Buhle, 1–8. Philadelphia: Temple University Press, 2003.

——. *Smoking Typewriters: The Sixties Underground Press and the Rise of Alternative Media in America*. New York: Oxford University Press, 2011.

Mearsheimer, John J., and Stephen M. Walt. *The Israel Lobby and U.S. Foreign Policy*. New York: Farrar, Straus and Giroux, 2008.

Meghelli, Samir. "From Harlem to Algiers: Transnational Solidarities between the African American Freedom Movement and Algeria, 1962–1978." In *Black Routes to Islam*, edited by Manning Marable and Hishaam D. Aidi, 99–119. New York: Palgrave Macmillan, 2009.

Mehdi, M. T. *Kennedy and Sirhan: Why?* New York: New World Press, 1968.

Moldea, Dan. *The Killing of Robert F. Kennedy: An Investigation of Motive, Means, and Opportunity*. New York: W. W. Norton, 1995.

Mosher, Lawrence. "Arabs Taste U.S. 'Terror.'" *National Observer*, 18 November 1972.

Moughrabi, Fouad. "Remembering the AAUG." *Arab Studies Quarterly* 29 (Summer–Fall 2007): 97–103.

Naber, Nadine. *Arab America: Gender, Cultural Politics, and Activism*. New York: New York University Press, 2012.

——. "Introduction: Arab Americans and U.S. Racial Formations." In *Race and Arab Americans before and after 9/11: From Invisible Citizens to Visible Subjects*, edited by Amaney Jamal and Nadine Naber, 1–45. Syracuse, N.Y.: Syracuse University Press, 2008.

Naff, Alixa. *Becoming American: The Early Arab Immigrant Experience*. Carbondale, Ill.: Southern Illinois University Press, 1993.

Naftali, Timothy. *Blind Spot: The Secret History of American Counterterrorism*. New York: Basic Books, 2005.

Nakhleh, Khalil. "AAUG: A Personal Introspection." *Arab Studies Quarterly* 29 (Summer–Fall 2007): 105–10.

Nassar, Jamal R. "Ibrahim Abu-Lughod: The Legacy of an Activist Scholar and Teacher." *Arab Studies Quarterly* 26 (Fall 2004): 23–24.

Newby, Robert. "Afro-Americans and Arabs: An Alliance in the Making?" *Journal of Palestine Studies* 10 (Winter 1981): 50–58.

Newsome, Yvonne D. "International Issues and Domestic Ethnic Relations: African Americans, American Jews, and the Israel-South Africa Debate." *International Journal of Politics, Culture, and Society* 5 (Autumn 1991): 19–48.

Newton, Huey. "On the Middle East: September 5, 1970." In *To Die for the People: The Writings of Huey P. Newton*, 191–96. New York: Vintage Books, 1972.

Nimer, Mohamed. "The Americanization of Islamism." *American Interest* 6 (July 2011). http://www.the-american-interest.com/2011/07/01/the-americanization-of-islamism/. Accessed 14 May 2012.

Norton, Ben. "Academia, the 'Battleground' in the Palestinian Solidarity Movement." *Mondoweiss*, 9 October 2014. http://mondoweiss.net/2014/10/battleground-palestinian-solidarity. Accessed 18 September 2015.

Ogbar, Jeffrey O. G. *Black Power: Radical Politics and African American Identity*. Baltimore, Md.: Johns Hopkins University Press, 2004.

Omi, Michael, and Howard Winant. *Racial Formation in the United States: From the 1960s to the 1990s*. 2nd ed. New York: Routledge, 1994.

Orfalea, Gregory. *The Arab Americans: A History*. Northampton, Mass.: Olive Branch Press, 2006.

——. *Before the Flames: A Quest for the History of Arab Americans*. Austin: University of Texas Press, 1988.

Organization of Arab Students in the United States and Canada. *Yearbook*. New York, 1961. Special Collections Library, University of Michigan, Ann Arbor, Michigan.

——. *Young Arab Speaks: A Symposium, the Proceedings of the First Arab Student Convention*. New York: Organization of Arab Students, 1953.

Payne, Charles. "Men Led, but Women Organized: Movement Participation of Women in the Mississippi Delta." In *Women in the Civil Rights Movement: Trailblazers and Torchbearers, 1941–1965*, edited by Vicki L. Crawford, Jacqueline Anne Rouse, and Barbara Woods, 1–12. Brooklyn, N.Y.: Carlson Publishing, 1990.

Podhoretz, Norman. *Breaking Ranks: A Political Memoir*. New York: Harper and Row, 1979.

"Policy Statement of the OAS, November 10, 1967." *Arab Journal* 5 (Summer 1968): 79–80.

Pulcini, Theodore. "Trends in Research on Arab Americans." *Journal of American Ethnic History* 12 (Summer 1993): 27–60.

Pulido, Laura. *Black, Brown, Yellow, and Left: Radical Activism in Los Angeles*. Berkeley: University of California Press, 2006.

Ramos, Lisa Y. "Not Similar Enough: Mexican American and African American Civil Rights Struggles in the 1940s." In *The Struggle in Black and Brown: African American and Mexican American Relations during the Civil Rights Era*, edited by Brian D. Behnken, 19–48. Lincoln: University of Nebraska Press, 2011.

"Resume of Resolutions, 16th Annual Convention, Aug. 28–Sept. 2, 1967." *Arab Journal* 4 (Fall 1967): 80–82.

RFK Must Die: The Assassination of Bobby Kennedy. Directed by Shane O'Sullivan. DVD. E2 Films, 2007.

Rignall, Karen. "Building the Infrastructure of Arab American Identity in Detroit: A Short History of ACCESS and the Community It Serves." In *Arab Detroit: From Margin to*

Mainstream, edited by Nabeel Abraham and Andrew Shryock, 49–60. Detroit: Wayne State University Press, 2000.

Rodriguez, Félix V. Matos. "Saving the *Parcela*: A Short History of Boston's Puerto Rican Community." In *The Puerto Rican Diaspora: Historical Perspectives*, edited by Carmen Teresa Whalen and Victor Vazquez-Hernandez, 200–226. Philadelphia: Temple University Press, 2005.

Rodríguez-Morazzani, Roberto P. "Political Cultures of the Puerto Rican Left in the United States." In *The Puerto Rican Movement: Voices from the Diaspora*, edited by Andrés Torres and José E. Velázquez, 25–47. Philadelphia: Temple University Press, 1998.

Ross, Matt. "Abdeen Jabara." *NLG-NYC Spring Fling Program*, 14 June 2013, 13–15.

Rubin, Jerry. *Do It: Scenarios of the Revolution*. New York: Simon and Schuster, 1970.

Sa'di, Ahmad H. "Afterword: Reflections on Representation, History, and Moral Accountability." In *Nakba: Palestine, 1948, and the Claims of Memory*, edited by Ahmad H. Sa'di and Lila Abu-Lughod, 285–314. New York: Columbia University Press, 2007.

Sa'di, Ahmad H., and Lila Abu-Lughod, eds. *Nakba: Palestine, 1948, and the Claims of Memory*. New York: Columbia University Press, 2007.

Said, Edward. "The Arab Portrayed." In *The Arab-Israeli Confrontation of June 1967: An Arab Perspective*, edited by Ibrahim Abu-Lughod, 1–9. Evanston, Ill.: Northwestern University Press, 1970.

———. "Conspiracy of Praise." In *Blaming the Victims: Spurious Scholarship and the Palestinian Question*, edited by Edward Said and Christopher Hitchens, 23–31. London: Verso Press, 1988.

———. *Orientalism*. New York: Vintage Books, 1978.

Saikowski, Charlotte. "Arabs in U.S. Cite Harassment." *Christian Science Monitor*, 22 January 1973.

Saks, Robert. "Israel and the New Left." *Journal of Jewish Communal Service* 45 (Winter 1968): 139–46.

Salaita, Steven. *Anti-Arab Racism in the USA: Where It Comes From and What It Means for Politics Today*. London: Pluto Press, 2006.

———. *Uncivil Rites: Palestine and the Limits of Academic Freedom*. Chicago: Haymarket Press, 2015.

Sale, Kirkpatrick. *SDS*. New York: Random House, 1973.

Saliba, Therese. "Resisting Invisibility: Arab Americans in Academia and Activism." In *Arabs in America: Building a New Future*, edited by Michael W. Suleiman, 304–19. Philadelphia: Temple University Press, 1999.

Samhan, Helen Hatab. "Arab Americans and the Elections of 1988: A Constituency Comes of Age." In *Arab Americans: Continuity and Change*, edited by Baha Abu-Laban and Michael W. Suleiman, 227–50. Belmont, Mass.: Association of Arab American University Graduates, 1989.

———. "Losing the Battle: How Political Activism Guarantees Ethnic Integration (in Spite of Defeats along the Way)." In *American Arabs and Political Participation, Proceedings of a Conference Sponsored by the Division of United States Studies, Woodrow Wilson International Center for Scholars*, edited by Philippa Strum, 131–45, 5 May 2006. https://www.wilsoncenter.org/sites/default/files/DUSS_Arab_America.pdf. Accessed 8 May 2012.

———. "Not Quite White: Race Classification and the Arab-American Experience." In *Arabs in America: Building a New Future*, edited by Michael W. Suleiman, 209–26. Philadelphia: Temple University Press, 1999.

———. "Politics and Exclusion: The Arab American Experience." *Journal of Palestine Studies* 16 (Winter 1987): 11–28.

Schiller, Nina Glick, Linda Basch, and Cristina Blanc-Szanton. "Transnationalism: A New Analytic Framework for Understanding Migration." *Annals of the New York Academy of Sciences* 645 (1992): 1–24.

Schopmeyer, Kim. "A Demographic Portrait of Arab Detroit." In *Arab Detroit: From Margin to Mainstream*, edited by Nabeel Abraham and Andrew Shryock, 61–68. Detroit: Wayne State University Press, 2000.

Scott, Katherine A. *Reining in the State: Civil Society and Congress in the Vietnam and Watergate Eras*. Lawrence: University Press of Kansas, 2013.

Sengstock, Mary C. "Detroit's Iraqi-Chaldeans: A Conflicting Conception of Identity." In *Arabs in the New World: Studies on Arab-American Communities*, edited by Sameer Y. Abraham and Nabeel Abraham, 135–46. Detroit: Wayne State University Press, 1983.

Shain, Yossi. "Arab Americans at a Crossroads." *Journal of Palestine Studies* 25 (Spring 1996): 47–59.

Shain, Yossi, and Aharon Barth. "Diasporas and International Relations Theory." *International Organization* 57 (2003): 449–79.

Shakir, Evelyn. *Bint Arab: Arab and Arab American Women in the United States*. Westport, Conn.: Praeger, 1997.

Shannon, Matthew. "'Contacts with the Opposition': American Foreign Relations, the Iranian Student Movement, and the Global Sixties." *The Sixties: A Journal of History, Politics, and Culture* 4 (June 2011): 1–29.

Shihab, Aziz. *Sirhan*. San Antonio: Naylor Company, 1969.

Shlaim, Avi. "The War of the Israeli Historians." *Annales* 59 (January–February 2004): 161–67.

Shohat, Ella, and Evelyn Alsultany. "The Cultural Politics of 'the Middle East' in the Americas: An Introduction." In *Between the Middle East and the Americas: The Cultural Politics of Diaspora*, edited by Evelyn Alsultany and Ella Shohat, 3–41. Ann Arbor: University of Michigan Press, 2013.

Shryock, Andrew. "The Moral Analogies of Race: Arab American Identity, Color Politics, and the Limits of Racialized Citizenship." In *Race and Arab Americans before and after 9/11: From Invisible Citizens to Visible Subjects*, edited by Amaney Jamal and Nadine Naber, 81–113. Syracuse, N.Y.: Syracuse University Press, 2008.

Shryock, Andrew, and Nabeel Abraham. "On Margins and Mainstreams." In *Arab Detroit: From Margin to Mainstream*, edited by Nabeel Abraham and Andrew Shryock, 15–35. Detroit: Wayne State University Press, 2000.

Shryock, Andrew, and Ann Chih Lin. "Arab American Identities in Question." In *Citizenship and Crisis: Arab Detroit after 9/11*, by Detroit Arab American Study Team, 35–68. New York: Russell Sage Foundation, 2009.

Shryock, Andrew, Nabeel Abraham, and Sally Howell. "The Terror Decade in Arab Detroit: An Introduction." In *Arab Detroit 9/11: Life in the Terror Decade*, edited by Nabeel Abraham, Sally Howell, and Andrew Shryock, 1–25. Detroit: Wayne State University Press, 2011.

Singh, Nikhil Pal. "'Learn Your Horn': Jack O'Dell and the Long Civil Rights Movement." In *Climbin' Jacob's Ladder: The Black Freedom Movement Writings of Jack O'Dell*, edited by Nikhil Pal Singh, 1–68. Berkeley: University of California Press, 2010.

Slade, Shelley. "The Image of the Arab in America: Analysis of a Poll on American Attitudes." *Middle East Journal* 35 (Spring 1981): 143–62.

Slonecker, Blake. *A New Dawn for the New Left: Liberation News Service, Montague Farm, and the Long Sixties*. New York: Palgrave Macmillan, 2012.

Smith, Charles D. *Palestine and the Arab-Israeli Conflict*. 4th ed. Boston: Bedford St. Martin's, 2001.

Smith, Sherry L. *Hippies, Indians, and the Fight for Red Power*. New York: Oxford University Press, 2012.

Smith, Michael Steven. *Notebook of a Sixties Lawyer: An Unrepentant Memoir and Selected Writings*. Brooklyn, N.Y.: Smyrna Press, 1992.

Springer, Kimberly. *Living for the Revolution: Black Feminist Organizations, 1968–1980*. Durham, N.C.: Duke University Press, 2005.

Stanford, Karin. *Beyond the Boundaries: Reverend Jesse Jackson in International Affairs*. Albany: State University of New York Press, 1997.

Starr, Meg. "Hit Them Harder: Leadership, Solidarity, and the Puerto Rican Independence Movement." In *The Hidden 1970s: Histories of Radicalism*, edited by Dan Berger, 135–54. New Brunswick, N.J.: Rutgers University Press, 2010.

Stetler, Russell, ed. *Palestine: The Arab-Israeli Conflict*. San Francisco: Ramparts Press, 1972.

Stiffler, Matthew Jaber, and Karen Rignall. "'You Are Our Homeland': How a Cozy Enclave Made Dearborn a Prime Destination for Arabs." *Dearborn Historian* 50 (Summer 2013): 69–82.

Stockton, Ronald. "Ethnic Archetypes and the Arab Image." In *The Development of Arab-American Identity*, edited by Ernest McCarus, 119–53. Ann Arbor: University of Michigan Press, 1994.

Stork, Joe. "The American New Left and Palestine." *Journal of Palestine Studies* 2 (Autumn 1972): 64–69.

Stork, Joe, and René Theberge. "Any Arab or Others of a Suspicious Nature." *MERIP Reports* 14 (February 1973): 3–6, 13.

Suleiman, Michael. "The Arab American Left." In *The Immigrant Left in the United States*, edited by Paul Buhle and Dan Georgakas, 233–55. Albany: State University of New York Press, 1996.

———. "Arab-Americans and the Political Process." In *The Development of Arab-American Identity*, edited by Ernest McCarus, 37–60. Ann Arbor: University of Michigan Press, 1994.

———. *The Arabs in the Mind of America*. Brattleboro, Vt.: Amana Books, 1988.

———. "A History of Arab-American Political Participation." In *American Arabs and Political Participation, Proceedings of a Conference Sponsored by the Division of United States Studies, Woodrow Wilson International Center for Scholars*, edited by Philippa Strum, 3–26, 5 May 2006. https://www.wilsoncenter.org/sites/default/files/DUSS_Arab_America.pdf. Accessed 8 May 2012.

———. "'I Come to Bury Caesar, Not to Praise Him': An Assessment of the AAUG as an Example of an Activist Arab-American Organization." *Arab Studies Quarterly* 29 (Summer–Fall 2007): 75–96.

Suleiman, Michael W. and Baha Abu-Laban. "Introduction." In *Arab Americans: Continuity and Change*, edited by Baha Abu-Laban and Michael W. Suleiman, 1–16. Belmont, Mass.: Association of Arab American University Graduates, 1989.

Talhami, Ghada Hashem. "A Cultural, Not a Political Lobby: The Mixed Legacy of a Grand Plan." *Arab Studies Quarterly* 29 (Summer–Fall 2007): 125–37.

Terry, Janice J. "The AAUG: An Activist, Academic Organization." *Arab Studies Quarterly* 29 (Summer–Fall 2007): 1–5.

———. "Community and Political Activism among Arab Americans in Detroit." In *Arabs in America: Building a New Future*, edited by Michael W. Suleiman, 241–54. Philadelphia: Temple University Press, 1999.

———. *U.S. Foreign Policy in the Middle East: The Role of Lobbies and Special Interest Groups*. London: Pluto Press, 2005.

Tessler, Mark. *A History of the Israeli-Palestinian Conflict,* 2nd ed. Bloomington: Indiana University Press, 2009.

Theoharis, Athan. *The FBI and American Democracy: A Brief Critical History.* Lawrence: University Press of Kansas, 2004.

———. *Spying on Americans: Political Surveillance from Hoover to the Huston Plan.* Philadelphia: Temple University Press, 1978.

Thomas, Lorrin. *Puerto Rican Citizen: History and Political Identity in Twentieth-Century New York City.* Chicago: University of Chicago Press, 2010.

Thompson, Heather Ann. *Whose Detroit? Politics, Labor, and Race in a Modern American City.* Ithaca, N.Y.: Cornell University Press, 2001.

Torres, Andrés. "Introduction: Political Radicalism in the Diaspora—The Puerto Rican Experience." In *The Puerto Rican Movement: Voices from the Diaspora,* edited by Andrés Torres and José E. Velázquez, 1–22. Philadelphia: Temple University Press, 1998.

Tuma, Elias H. "The Palestinians in America." *Link,* July/August 1981, 1–2. http://www.ameu.org/getattachment/e45fc4da-7b75-45b2-ad4d-79896c7dc951/The-Palestinians-in-America.aspx. Accessed 10 April 2012.

Turki, Fawaz. "The Passions of Exile: The Palestine Congress of North America." *Journal of Palestine Studies* 9 (Summer 1980): 17–43.

———. *Soul in Exile: Lives of a Palestinian Revolutionary.* New York: Monthly Review Press, 1988.

Vaisse, Justin. *Neoconservatism: The Biography of a Movement.* Translated by Arthur Goldhammer. Cambridge, Mass.: Harvard University Press, 2010.

Varon, Jeremy. *Bringing the War Home: The Weather Underground, the Red Army Faction, and Revolutionary Violence in the Sixties and Seventies.* Berkeley: University of California Press, 2004.

Velázquez, José E. "Coming Full Circle: The Puerto Rican Socialist Branch, U.S. Branch." In *The Puerto Rican Movement: Voices from the Diaspora,* edited by Andrés Torres and José E. Velázquez, 48–68. Philadelphia: Temple University Press, 1998.

Waines, David. *The Unholy War: Israel and Palestine, 1897–1971.* Wilmette, Ill.: Medina University Press International, 1971.

Walters, Ronald W. "The Black Initiatives in the Middle East." *Journal of Palestine Studies* 10 (Winter 1981): 3–13.

Weiner, Tim. *Enemies: A History of the FBI.* New York: Random House, 2012.

Weisbord, Robert G., and Arthur Stein. *Bittersweet Encounter: The Afro-American and the American Jew.* Westport, Conn.: Negro Universities Press, 1970.

Weisbord, Robert G., and Richard Kazarian Jr. *Israel in the Black American Perspective.* Westport, Conn.: Greenwood Press, 1985.

Weiss, Philip. "From Mississippi to Gaza: Dorothy Zellner Reflects on 50 Years of Struggle." *Mondoweiss,* 24 June 2014. http://mondoweiss.net/2014/06/mississippi-reflects-struggle. Accessed 26 June 2014.

Werbner, Pnina. "Introduction: The Materiality of Diaspora—Between Aesthetic and 'Real' Politics." *Diaspora* 9, no. 1 (2000): 5–20.

Whitaker, Matthew C. "Great Expectations: African Americans and Latino Relations in Phoenix since World War II." In *African American Urban History since World War II,* edited by Kenneth L. Kusmer and Joe W. Trotter, 83–97. Chicago: University of Chicago Press, 2009.

Wigle, Laurel D., and Sameer Y. Abraham. "Arab Nationalism in America: The Dearborn Arab Community." In *Immigrants and Migrants: The Detroit Ethnic Experience,* edited by David W. Hartman, 279–302. Detroit: Wayne State University Press, 1974.

Wilford, Hugh. *America's Great Game: The CIA's Secret Arabists and the Shaping of the Modern Middle East*. New York: Basic Books, 2013.

Williams, Jakobi. *From the Bullet to the Ballot: The Illinois Chapter of the Black Panther Party and Racial Coalition Politics in Chicago*. Chapel Hill: University of North Carolina Press, 2013.

Wilson, James Q. "Buggings, Break-Ins, and the FBI." *Commentary*, 1 June 1978. https://www.commentarymagazine.com/articles/buggings-break-ins-the-fbi/. Accessed 25 July 2012.

Yaqub, Salim. "'Our Declaration of Independence': African Americans, Arab Americans, and the Arab-Israeli Conflict, 1967–1979." *Mashriq & Mahjar* 3, no. 1 (2015): 12–29. http://lebanesestudies.ojs.chass.ncsu.edu/index.php/mashriq/article/view/61/121. Accessed 25 November 2015.

Yoder, Traci. "Breach of Privilege: Spying on Lawyers in the United States." A National Lawyers Guild Report, April 2014. https://www.nlg.org/sites/default/files/Breach%20of%20Privilege%20COLOR_3.pdf. Accessed 12 May 2014.

Youmans, Will, and Nadeem Muaddi. "The Growing Israel Divestment Movement." *Counterpunch*, 24 January 2006. http://www.counterpunch.org/2006/01/24/the-growing-israel-divestment-movement/. Accessed 17 September 2015.

Young, Cynthia A. *Soul Power: Culture, Radicalism, and the Making of a U.S. Third World Left*. Durham, N.C.: Duke University Press, 2006.

Young, Lewis. "American Blacks and the Arab-Israeli Conflict." *Journal of Palestine Studies* 2 (Fall 1972): 70–85.

Zogby, James, ed., *Perspectives on Palestinian Arabs and Israeli Jews*. Wilmette, Ill.: Medina University Press International, 1977.

Zogby, James, and Jack O'Dell, eds. *Afro-Americans Stand Up for Middle East Peace*. Washington, D.C.: Palestine Human Rights Campaign, 1980.

Unpublished Sources

Abourezk, James. "Arabs: The Convenient Scapegoat." Pamphlet by the American Anti-Discrimination Committee, 3 May 1980. Pamphlets about Arab-American Associations Collection, Michigan State University Library.

Abraham, Nabeel. "From Campus to Coffeehouse: The Spread of Palestinian Diaspora Politics (1968–1978)." Presentation at the Organization of American Historians Conference, Washington, D.C., 12 April 2002.

———. "National and Local Politics: A Study of Political Conflict in the Yemeni Immigrant Community of Detroit, Michigan." Ph.D. diss., University of Michigan, 1978.

Beverly, Philip. "Shaking Off the Sheikh: How Two Major Arab American Organizations Combatted Arab Stereotypes, 1967–1990." M.A. thesis, New York University, April 2012.

Cainkar, Louise. "Palestinian Women in the United States: Coping with Tradition, Change, and Alienation." Ph.D. diss., Northwestern University, 1988.

Charbaji, Abdulrazzak. "Academic and Social Problems Facing Arab Students on American Campuses." Ph.D. diss., University of Northern Colorado, 1978. Michael Suleiman Collection, Arab American National Museum, Dearborn, Michigan.

Federal Bureau of Investigation. "The Fedayeen Terrorist—A Profile." June 1970. http://www.governmentattic.org/docs/FBI_Monograph_Fedayeen_Terrorist_June-1970.pdf. Accessed 14 June 2012.

———. "Fedayeen Impact—Middle East and United States, June 1970." http://www.governmentattic.org/2docs/FBI_Monograph_Fedayeen-Impact_1970.pdf. Accessed 14 June 2012.

Gezi, Khalil Ismail. "The Acculturation of Middle Eastern Arab Students in Selected American Colleges and Universities." Ph.D. diss., Stanford University, 1959. Michael Suleiman Collection, Arab American National Museum, Dearborn, Mich.

Jabara, Abdeen. Foreword to "The Lost Significance of Sirhan's Case." Pamphlet by the Organization of Arab Students, University of Southern California, 1969. Abdeen Jabara Papers, Bentley Historical Library, University of Michigan, Ann Arbor.

Sarafa, Randall S. "The 'Chilling Effect': The Nixon Administration's Operation Boulder and the Repression of Arab Americans." B.A. thesis. Harvard College, 2009.

Shaheen, Jack. "ABSCAM: Arabiaphobia in America." ADC Issues no. 1, n.d. (Pamphlets about Arab-American Associations collection.)

Wingfield, Marvin. "ADC: The Struggle for Arab American Civil Rights." Washington, D.C.: ADC Research Institute, 2011.

INDEX

Abdulhadi, Rabab, 25–26, 212, 224
Abernathy, Ralph, 207, 216
Abourezk, James, 156, 208–9, 221, 277 (n. 35)
Abraham, Nabeel, 16; scholarship on Arab and Yemeni Americans, 9, 179–80, 181, 187–88, 192, 195, 201; as a student activist, 61–62, 63–64, 66–67, 70–72, 106–7, 108, 115, 173; views on Organization of Arab Students, 50, 54, 56
Abraham, Sameer, 66, 169
ABSCAM affair, 201, 208, 210
Abudayyeh, Khairy, 16, 56–57, 72
Abu-Laban, Baha, 29, 45, 46
Abu-Lughod, Ibrahim, 28, 35, 38–39, 57, 108, 234, 277 (n. 34)
Action Committee on American-Arab Relations (ACAAR), 110, 132, 157–58, 267 (n. 58), 279 (n. 58)
Ad Hoc Committee on the Middle East, 96
African Americans: Arab Americans and, 1–2, 12, 18, 67–68, 80, 83, 114–15; Arab World and, 15, 81–83, 85, 87–88, 90, 279 (n. 57); attitudes toward Israel, 80–81, 82, 85–86, 87, 203, 254 (n. 4); delegations to Middle East, 205, 217, 219–20, 279 (n. 54); Jews and, 80–81, 87–88, 103, 218–19, 220, 278 (nn. 50, 52). *See also* Anti-Semitism: African Americans accused of and defense against
African liberation movements, 35, 51, 60, 69, 81, 84, 91, 97
African Students Union, 51
Afro-Asian Conference (Bandung, Indonesia), 81, 107
Ahmad, Eqbal, 36
Ahmed, Ismael, 16, 47, 140, 151, 178, 212, 270 (n. 19); ACCESS and, 177, 193, 194, 196–97; activism in the Southend, 106, 174, 176, 179 (ill.); Arab Workers Caucus and, 106, 182, 184, 190; leftist and civil rights coalitions and, 71, 105–6, 108–9, 113, 114–15, 175–76, 194

Ahmed, Leila, 226
al-Assad, Hafez, 73
Aldamalani, David, 150
al-Fatah. *See* Fatah
Algeria, 5, 51, 88, 98; independence movement, 51, 52, 60, 66, 81–82, 107, 127, 253–54 (n. 2)
Algerian National Liberation Front (FLN). *See* Algeria: independence movement
Al-Hibri, Azizah, 226
Ali, Muhammad, 85
Ali, Noble Drew, 83
Al-Islaah, 137
All African People's Revolutionary Party, 91, 215, 253 (n. 68)
All Palestine Congress, 211
Almaklani, Ali Baleed, 182, 270–71 (n. 29)
Almulaiki, Ahmed Ali, 180
Al-Mu'mineen Mosque, 83
Alwan, Pierre, 150–51
Amen, Alan, 171, 175, 178–79, 182, 184, 185, 198
Amen, Katherine, 171, 196
Amen, Ron, 140
American-Arab Anti-Discrimination Committee (ADC), 18, 45, 163, 201, 202, 207–10, 211, 212, 221, 222–24, 227, 231, 235, 236, 277 (n. 35)
American Arab Coordinating Committee (AACC), 1, 180–81, 184–85, 271 (n. 32)
American bias against Arabs, 4, 9, 10, 15, 142, 147, 153, 164, 197, 200, 201–3, 208, 209, 226, 228–29, 234, 240 (n. 10), 281 (n. 81). *See also* Arab Americans: racism against

American Civil Liberties Union (ACLU), 156, 157, 158, 159, 161, 268 (n. 72)
American Committee for Justice in the Middle East, 257–58 (n. 61)
American Federation of Ramallah, 25–26, 205, 244 (n. 15), 275–76 (n. 18)
American Friends of the Middle East, 52, 257–58 (n. 61)
American Indians, 91, 208; activism of, 13, 14, 100, 109–10, 160
American Israel Public Affairs Committee (AIPAC), 25, 52, 55, 145, 201
American Jewish Committee (AJC), 205, 208
American Lebanese League, 244 (n. 22)
American Left, 3, 5, 23, 98–99, 224, 257 (n. 59); and the labor movement, 99, 101, 168, 169, 183–84, 188, 190, 191–92, 271 (n. 40), 273 (n. 58). *See also* Association of Arab American University Graduates: the American and Third World Left and; Civil rights movements, comparative; League for Revolutionary Black Workers; New Left
American Moslem Society mosque, 182
Americans for Justice in the Middle East, 137–38
Americans for Middle East Understanding, 257–58 (n. 61)
American Zionist Federation, 218
Amin, Karen, 68
Anderson, Terry, 48
Ann Arbor, Mich., 27, 50, 54, 77, 87, 106
Anti-Arab attitudes. *See* American bias against Arabs; Arab Americans: racism against
Anti-Defamation League (ADL), 54–55, 85, 145, 154, 201, 250 (n. 22)
Anti-Draft Union, 66
Anti-imperialism, 6, 12, 23–24, 33–36, 56, 59–60, 71, 74, 79, 81, 84–5, 87, 94, 96, 105, 108, 176, 189, 190, 227, 230, 232
Anti-Imperialist Movement (Columbia University), 97
Anti-Muslim attitudes, 11, 226, 228, 236
Antiochian Orthodox Christian Archdiocese, 26, 157
Anti-Semitism, 4, 225; African Americans accused of and defense against, 68, 69, 85–86, 88, 89, 104, 218, 223; Arab Americans and allies accused of, 55, 202, 223, 234, 281 (n. 12); leftists accused of, 97, 102, 226; Palestinians viewed as anti-Semitic, 80, 134
Anti–Vietnam War movement, 14, 31, 59–60, 89, 94, 96–97, 102, 121, 160, 162, 216
Aoki, Richard, 109
Arab American Action Network, 236
Arab American activists: African American civil rights movement and, 12–13, 62, 78, 79, 93, 105–8, 176, 177, 185, 196, 209, 214–17, 219–24, 228, 235, 279 (n. 58); antiwar movement and, 62, 66, 107–8, 176, 177, 206; civil rights for Arab Americans and, 3, 4, 5, 10, 12, 18, 112, 164, 195–96, 202, 204; coalitions with American leftists, 3, 10, 14, 47, 77–78, 79–80, 93, 100–101, 105–11, 113, 116–17, 144, 161–62, 164, 189, 196, 213, 224, 227, 230, 231, 233–34; coalitions with liberals, 204, 207, 209, 210, 213–17, 223–24, 228; deradicalization of, 5, 10, 202, 213, 228, 235; feminism and, 66–67, 225, 224–27, 280 (n. 76), 281 (n. 79); Islam and, 229, 240 (n. 18), 245 (n. 24), 281 (n. 79); internal divisions, 3, 231; mainstream American politics and, 10, 18, 46, 198–99, 202, 203–4, 211–13, 220–22, 229, 231–32, 235, 276 (n. 19), 280 (n. 72); moderates of, 5, 27, 202, 209, 222; protest of civil liberties violations, 105, 112, 141, 144, 153–58, 161–62, 163–64; protest of UAW's Israeli bonds, 1–2, 18, 182, 184–88, 189–90, 192, 233, 236, 271 (n. 40), 271–72 (n. 42), 272 (nn. 45, 48); response to Arab-Israeli War of 1967, 8, 22, 53, 61–62, 176, 178; response to Sirhan Sirhan, 122–23, 133, 138, 140, 141–42; secularism and, 6, 21, 29, 77, 167, 177, 229; transnationalism of, 3, 9–10, 11, 21, 79, 109, 164, 167–68, 174, 177, 178, 189, 193, 199–200, 210, 231; under surveillance or investigation, 104, 109, 144, 150–52, 159, 163, 177. *See also* American-Arab Anti-Discrimination Committee; Association of Arab American University Graduates: internal divisions of; Association of Arab American University Graduates: women and; Civil rights movement: stance on

304 INDEX

Israel-Palestine conflict; National Association of Arab Americans; Southend: struggle against urban renewal
Arab American Congress for Palestine (AACP), 26, 61, 63, 158
Arab American Institute (AAI), 18, 45, 211–12, 221, 222–23, 229, 231, 236, 279–80 (n. 67), 280 (n. 70)
Arab American Left. *See* Arab American activists; Association of Arab American University Graduates; Organization of Arab Students
Arab Americans: absence from scholarly accounts, 14–15, 234–35, 242 (n. 50), 263 (n. 3); Arab diaspora and, 5–6, 7–8, 9, 11; assimilation and, 7–8, 9, 112, 234; autoworkers, 1, 7, 99, 101, 106, 113, 168, 180, 182–84, 188–93; Christian, 7, 63, 114, 169; civil liberties of, 17, 104, 143, 145, 147, 150–51, 153, 157–58, 162–64, 233, 289 (n. 69); first wave of immigrants to U.S., 7–8, 9, 71; identity, ethnic and racial, 5–8, 9, 11, 62, 110–13, 162, 164, 167–68, 182, 200, 209, 222–23, 230, 240 (n. 19), 241 (n. 23), 241 (n. 35), 259–60 (n. 95), 279 (n. 67); interactions with African Americans, 15, 80, 105, 112–15, 182–84, 185–87, 192, 220–21, 260 (n. 96), 270 (n. 22); internal divisions of, 3, 6, 10, 16, 181, 192–93, 229; isolationism, 9, 13, 162, 164, 203, 229; Muslim, 8–9, 61, 77, 83, 111, 169, 229; racism against, 11, 112, 143, 157, 164, 171, 191, 195, 197–98, 208, 233; second wave of immigrants to U.S., 8, 71; stereotyped as terrorist, 17, 121, 141, 144, 153, 202; third generation, 9, 113, 169, 171, 176, 178, 197, 200; third wave of immigrants to U.S., 8–9, 70–71, 111–12, 169, 171, 176, 182, 197, 200; violence against, 158, 163, 200, 201, 210, 267 (n. 59); working-class, 29, 167, 169, 176, 177, 182, 189, 193, 194, 195. *See also* Dearborn, Mich.: Arab Americans in; Detroit, Mich.: Arab Americans in; Yemeni Americans: violence against
Arab-American Voter Registration and Education Committee, 198
Arab Club. *See* Organization of Arab Students: campus chapters of
Arab Community Center (Chicago), 72, 221
Arab Community Center for Economic and Social Services (ACCESS) (Dearborn, Mich.), 12, 18, 83, 109, 178, 273 (n. 61); formation of, 106, 176–77, 270 (n. 21); later changes in, 168, 190, 198–99, 202, 212, 273 (n. 62), 274 (n. 71); political activism and, 72, 112, 167, 177, 180, 181, 185, 193–98, 200, 270 (n. 22), 271–72 (n. 42); services of, 177, 193–94, 195–96, 200
Arab immigration to the United States. *See* Arab Americans
Arab Information Center, 51, 52, 152
Arab-Israeli War of 1948, 4, 22, 81, 240 (n. 8). See also *Nakba*
Arab-Israeli War of 1967, 1–18 passim, 23, 25, 26, 27, 28, 33, 46, 47, 49, 53, 57, 61, 79–102 passim, 121, 125, 128, 143, 144, 174, 176, 178, 230, 232, 233; events of, 21–22
Arab-Israeli War of 1973. *See* October War of 1973
Arab Journal (Organization of Arab Students), 51–52
Arab League. *See* League of Arab States
Arab Mobilization Committee (AMC), 181–82, 193
Arab nationalism, 21–23, 27, 63, 107, 134–35, 187–88, 200, 230. *See also* Association of Arab American University Graduates: Arab nationalism and
Arab National League, 2, 21
Arab nations, conservative regimes, 23, 31, 33, 37, 44, 56, 88, 95, 98, 102, 230
Arab Spring, 231
Arab Student Association. *See* Organization or Arab Students: campus chapters of
Arab students in the U.S., 6, 9, 16, 17, 47–48, 50, 75–77, 97, 98, 114, 143, 190, 207, 248 (n. 8); under government investigation, 70, 73, 144, 145, 148, 149–50, 154, 265 (nn. 24, 27), 266–67 (n. 48). *See also* Organization of Arab Students
Arab Studies Quarterly (Association of Arab American University Graduates), 31, 52, 247 (n. 71)
Arab Workers Caucus (AWC), 2, 18, 106, 168, 184, 191, 192, 193, 197, 200, 230, 233, 272 (nn. 45, 47)
Arab World Festivals (Detroit), 196
Arafat, Yasser, 22, 70, 77, 217, 220

Aruri, Naseer, 22, 35, 36, 110, 211
Asian Americans: activism, 6, 12–14, 111, 183, 241 (n. 42). *See also* Japanese Americans
Association of Arab American University Graduates (AAUG), 15–17, 21, 26, 47, 121, 137, 142, 177, 202, 203, 231; advocacy tactics of, 31, 38, 39–40, 232; African Americans and, 35–36, 43–44, 91–93, 217, 219, 220, 221, 222, 223; the American and Third World Left and, 23–24, 31–32, 33, 34–36, 42–43, 46, 48, 97, 108, 110, 116, 232, 259 (n. 85); Arab American identity and, 23, 24, 29, 45–46, 112, 245–46 (n. 39); Arab nationalism and, 24, 33–34, 48; civil liberties and, 144, 151–52, 155–57, 160, 163; decline of, 40, 44–45, 232, 247 (n. 71); formation of, 8, 27–28, 144; intellectual approach of, 23–24, 28, 30, 32, 45; internal divisions of, 24–25, 32, 40–43, 206, 232, 246 (n. 42), 259 (n. 85); membership of, 23, 28–30, 32, 39, 40–42, 48, 209, 243 (n. 8); moderation in the 1980s, 204–6; *Newsletter*, 31, 43–44, 73, 175, 213; policy advocacy by, 28, 29, 38–39, 44, 232; relation to Arab nations, 28, 33–34, 37, 43, 44, 220; relation to other Arab American organizations, 38–39, 45, 48, 57, 67, 157, 175, 205, 206, 208, 211, 215, 233, 247 (n. 68), 250–51 (n. 31), 276 (nn. 19, 25); scholarship and publications of, 23, 30, 31–32, 206, 234, 246 (nn. 40, 43); stance on Palestine and Israel, 24, 28, 32–35, 39, 41–42, 48, 79, 204, 219; transnationalism of, 24, 28, 37, 42, 46; women and, 29, 40–41, 225, 227, 245 (n. 31)
Aswad, Adnan, 16, 30, 43, 140, 141
Aswad, Barbara, 16, 32, 65, 115, 140, 141, 170, 173–75, 177, 178, 194, 196, 199
Atwell, Helen, 171, 178, 196
Ayoub, Elias, 76
Ayton, Mel, 122, 133
Azzah, Jamil, 151

Baath Party (Iraq), 250 (n. 27), 251 (n. 41)
Baldwin, James, 81
Balfour Declaration (1917), 57
Barkey, Jeanne, 227
Bashshur, Rashid, 22, 28, 30, 43

Bassiouni, M. Cherif, 27, 29, 32, 38, 151–52, 155–56, 160–61, 164
Battle of Algiers, The (1966), 60, 71, 82, 98
Bawardi, Hani, 2
Beal, Frances, 91
Becker, Iris, 173
Begin, Menachem, 64, 66, 75, 77, 138, 220
Beinin, Joel, 16, 77, 99, 101, 191–93, 258 (n. 62), 273 (n. 58)
Beirut, Lebanon, 36, 58, 98, 108
Beit Hanina Club, 195
Bella, Ahmed Ben, 82
Ben-Gurion, David, 52
Benkert et al. v. Michigan State Police, 159
Berkeley Barb, The, 90, 94
Berman, Emile Zola, 127–28, 261 (n. 16)
Berrigan, Daniel, 36, 97, 160, 207
Berrigan, Philip, 160
Birzeit University, 37
Black Americans in Support of Israel, 278 (n. 43)
Black Lives Matter movement, 236
Black Muslims, 82–83, 176. *See also* Nation of Islam
Black nationalism, 12, 14, 65, 68, 71; Arab American organizations and, 86–87, 89; civil liberties and, 144; stance on Israel and Palestine, 15, 36, 65–67, 79–80, 81–82, 84–92, 104, 114, 116, 203, 215, 218, 234, 253 (n. 68), 254 (n. 5); the Third World and, 81–82, 84–85, 88–89. *See also* Anti-Semitism: African Americans accused of and defense against; Arab American activists: African American civil rights movement and; Association of Arab American University Graduates: African Americans and; Organization of Arab Students: African Americans and
Black Panther Party, 14, 60, 83–84, 88, 94, 97, 98, 100, 106, 110, 145, 160, 168, 176, 194, 273 (n. 62)
Black Power. *See* Black nationalism
Black September, 10, 138, 144, 147, 148, 152, 153, 266 (n. 40)
Black Student Union, 60, 91, 253 (n. 68)
Black Theology Project, 216
B'nai B'rith, 1, 52, 184
Boggs, Grace Lee, 91
Boggs, James, 91

Bond, Julian, 218, 223
Borrajo, Joseph, 198
Boycott Divestment and Sanctions campaign (BDS), 236–37
Brown, H. Rap, 84, 98
Brown, Stuart Gerry, 125
Buch, Peter, 98
Bush, George H. W., 229

Cabinet Committee to Combat Terrorism, 17, 143–44, 147–48, 152, 153, 155, 157, 160, 264 (n. 13)
Cainkar, Louise, 8, 11, 110, 220
Cambodia, 59, 67
Camp David Accords (1978), 76–77, 205, 211
Carmichael, Stokely, 36, 86, 87, 89, 91, 254 (nn. 5, 16)
Carson, Clayborne, 88
Carter, Jimmy, 76–77, 204, 205, 216, 217, 218, 219
Cass Tech High School (Detroit), 61, 107
Cavalletto, George, 16, 95–96, 97, 99–100, 256 (n. 49)
Center for Urban Law and Housing (Wayne County, Mich.), 171
Central Intelligence Agency (CIA), 55, 145–46, 148, 154, 205, 257–58 (n. 61), 264 (n. 7)
Centros de Accion Social Autonomo (CASA), 13, 260 (n. 104)
Chaldean Americans, 114, 192–93, 259–60, 260 (n. 96)
Chamberlin, Paul Thomas, 79
Chertoff, Mordecai, 104
Chevrolet, 107
Chicago, Ill., Arab Americans in, 8, 26, 28, 47, 51, 57, 72, 151, 158, 220, 221, 239 (n. 4)
Chicago Tribune, 135, 154
Chicanos. *See* Latino Americans
China, People's Republic of, 56, 80, 253–54 (n. 2)
Chinese Revolution, 66
Chisholm, Shirley, 92–93, 222
Chomsky, Noam, 36, 96, 97, 102, 207, 257 (n. 54)
Christian Science Monitor, 64, 207
Chrysler, 69, 99, 183, 190, 191, 192
Church, Frank, 160, 162, 266 (n. 37)
Church Senate committee. *See* Church, Frank

Civil rights movement, 48, 79–80; stance on Israel and Palestine, 79, 81, 90, 92–93, 203, 214–23, 227, 228, 278 (nn. 43, 51)
Civil rights movements, comparative, 6, 12–14, 48–49, 105, 109, 111, 115–16, 194, 233, 242 (n. 47), 260 (n. 104)
Clark, Harry W., 69
Clark, Kenneth, 219
Clark, Ramsey, 216
Cleaver, Eldridge, 88, 139
Clergy and Laity Concerned (about Vietnam), 216
Cleveland, Ohio, 26
Coalition for an Anti-Imperialist Movement, 96
Coalition for a New Foreign and Military Policy, 224
Cockrel, Ken, 66
Coffin, William Sloan, 36
COINTELPRO (counterintelligence program), 104, 146, 159–60
Commentary, 258–59 (n. 71)
Committee of Black Americans for Truth about the Middle East, 91
Committee on New Alternatives in the Middle East, 96
Committee to Support Middle East Liberation (CSMEL), 33, 96
Committee to Support the Omani Revolution (CSOR), 180
Communist Party USA (CPUSA), 98
Confederation of Iranian Students National Union, 60
Congressional Black Caucus (CBC), 91, 93, 218, 222, 223
Congress on Racial Equality (CORE), 80, 83, 220
Conyers, John, 90, 207, 216, 220
Cooper, Grant B., 127–28
Crockett, George, 220–21
Cuba, 5, 14, 60, 79, 106, 113, 253–54 (n. 2)

Daifullah, Nagi, 180, 189
Davis, Angela, 98
Dayan, Moshe, 85, 96
Dearborn, Mich., 71, 105, 187; Arab Americans in, 1, 15–16, 17, 26, 49, 61, 83, 112, 140, 151, 164, 178
Dellinger, Dave, 207, 216

INDEX 307

Democratic Committee for Palestine, 26
Democratic Front for the Liberation of Palestine, 48, 64, 96, 98, 248 (n. 2)
Democratic Party, 92, 125, 126, Arab Americans and, 209, 211–12, 221–22, 223, 235, 279 (n. 63)
Detroit, Mich., 1, 26, 32, 36, 47, 64–66, 69–70, 74, 83, 89, 105–8, 114–15, 116, 144, 146, 150, 153, 158, 161, 170, 177, 184–87, 194, 199; Arab Americans in, 15–16, 61–63, 99, 101, 151, 163, 175, 179–80, 183–84, 187, 190, 191, 192–93, 196, 210, 229, 239 (n. 4), 260 (n. 96), 270–71 (n. 29), 273 (n. 58); police of, 144, 159, 180, 191; riot/rebellion of 1967 and, 65, 170
Detroit Free Press, 163, 186
Detroit News, 68, 197, 198
Detroit Yemen Society, 180
Detroit Yemeni Association, 157
Diab, Ihsan, 151
Dodge Main auto plant (Detroit), 65–66, 179, 183, 185, 187–88, 191, 272 (nn. 45, 48)
Dodge Revolutionary Union Movement (DRUM). *See* Revolutionary Union Movements
Dorosh, Walter, 187
Dressler, Mark, 211
DuBois, Shirley Graham, 36
DuBois, W. E. B., 80
Dukakis, Michael, 222
Durham, Jimmy, 100

Eain, Ziad Abu, 207, 276 (n. 24)
Eban, Abba, 133
Economist, The, 135
Egypt, 8, 21–22, 33, 34, 50, 56, 64, 87, 139, 178, 187, 211
Egyptian students in the U.S., 56, 60, 64
Elbaum, Max, 224
El-Kotob, Essam, 149–50
Equal Rights Amendment, 225
Esmail, Sami, 75–76, 207
Exodus (1960), 52

Faisal, Dauod Ahmed, 83
Fanon, Frantz (*The Wretched of the Earth*), 82, 84, 127
Farrell, Raymond, 156

Farsoun, Samih, 32, 211, 258 (n. 62)
Fatah, 22, 48, 53–55, 57, 58, 64, 66, 68–70, 79, 88, 89, 91, 95–96, 98, 100, 126, 146, 148, 150, 151, 243 (n. 5), 248 (n. 2)
Fauntroy, Walter, 216, 219
Featherstone, Ralph, 86
Fedayeen. *See* Palestinian resistance groups
Federal Bureau of Investigation (FBI), 250 (n. 22); surveillance or investigation of Arab students and Arab Americans, 17, 55, 104, 109, 145–52, 154, 155, 156, 158–59, 162, 163, 201, 263 (n. 3), 264 (n. 11), 266 (n. 37); surveillance or investigation of New Left and African Americans, 104, 109, 144, 145, 146, 159–60, 216
Federation of Islamic Associations (FIA), 27, 157, 240 (n. 18), 245 (n. 24)
Feinberg, Marion, 99
Feldman, Keith, 85
Feminism, 76; Third World, 14, 91, 95, 226. *See also* Arab American activists: feminism and
Feminist Arab-American Network (FAN), 227
Ferguson, Mo., 236
Fernández, Johanna, 13–14, 116, 168
Fifth Estate, The, 63, 67
First Intifada, 203
Fischbach, Michael, 122
Fitts, David, 126
Ford, Gerald, 55, 140, 145, 205
Ford Motor Company, 170, 194; Arab American workers of, 7, 182, 190, 192; Rouge auto plant (Dearborn, Mich.), 70, 167, 169, 182, 192
Forman, James, 84, 86, 87, 88
Forster, Arnold, 55, 145
Franco, Ania, 36, 95
Freedomways, 216
Freeman, Ralph, 158–59, 177–78
Free Palestine, 26, 57, 244 (n. 18)
Fromm, Eric, 96
Frost, Jennifer, 196

Garvey, Marcus, 80
Gatch, John, 162–63
Gay rights movement, 67, 115, 227
Gaza. *See* Palestine: occupied territories

General Union of Palestine Students (GUPS), 60, 251 (n. 34), 253 (n. 76), 275 (n. 6)
Georgakas, Dan, 69–70, 113, 182–83
George, Jawad, 211
George, Minor, 26
Geron, Kim, 13
Glazer, Nathan, 104
Goldberg, Arthur, 128
Gonzalez, Corky, 109
Goode, W. Wilson, 223
Goodman, Ernest, 108
Gray, L. Patrick, 155
Gray, Nancy Adadow, 194, 199
Greek students in the U.S., 66
Greene, James, 155–56
Gregory, Dick, 109
Gualtieri, Sarah, 7–8, 111
Guardian, The, 95, 256 (n. 46)
Guevara, Che, 106

Haddad, Carol, 226–27, 281 (n. 79)
Haddad, Yvonne, 50
Hagopian, Elaine, 28, 30, 37, 40, 44–45, 137, 164, 205, 247 (n. 72)
Hamlin, Mike, 16, 65, 69, 114–15, 184, 187
Hanania, Ray, 16, 47
Harkin, Tom, 207
Hart, Gary, 280 (n. 72)
Hart, Philip, 156
Hashemite Hall (Dearborn, Mich.), 181, 193, 273 (n. 61)
Hashomer Hatzair, 103
Hassen, Aliya, 83, 151, 176, 193, 196
Hatem, Mervat, 40–41, 226, 227
Hersh, Seymour, 146, 266–67 (n. 48)
Hillel, 60
Hispanic Americans. *See* Latino Americans
Histadrut, 189, 190
Holocaust, 4, 81, 227
House, Gloria, 16, 114
Howell, Sally, 83
Hubbard, Orville, 170
Human rights organizations, 75, 84, 206, 215–16. *See also* Palestine Human Rights Campaign; Palestinians: human rights of
Hussaini, Hatem, 53
Hussein (king of Jordan), 33
Husseini, Hassan, 156

Huston, Tom Charles, 160
Huston Plan, 160

Immigration and Nationality Act (1965), 8, 111
Immigration and Naturalization Service (INS), 17, 73, 76, 147, 148, 149–51, 155–56, 162
Inner City Voice, 65
Innis, Roy, 220
Institute for Palestine Studies (Beirut), 37, 99, 244 (n. 17)
Institute of African Studies, 36
Institute of Arab American Affairs, 2, 21
Internal Revenue Service (IRS), 152, 155
Iran, 11, 49, 101, 157, 231; hostage crisis, 228, 229; students, 49, 60, 97, 148, 190, 240–41 (n. 22), 263–64 (n. 5)
Iranian Students Association, 51, 60
Iran-Iraq War, 8
Iraq, 8
Iraq War, 231
Ireland, Jill, 227
Islamic Center (Washington, D.C.), 27
Islamic Foundation of South California, 154
Islamic Society of North America, 27
Islamophobia. *See* Anti-Muslim attitudes
Ismail, Noha, 41, 225
Israel, 4, 25, 60–61, 75, 76, 167, 187, 218, 225; American attitudes toward, 4, 8, 32, 110, 203, 204, 213, 215, 228, 240 (n. 10), 281 (n. 81); Arab American criticism of, 1, 3–4, 15, 27, 28, 30, 31, 33, 52, 57, 60, 64, 66, 70, 205, 207; bonds of, 52, 110; embassy in the U.S., 52, 152–53; intelligence officials of, 104, 135, 152, 154, 217; Mission to the United Nations, 96; U.S. relationship with, 21, 23, 28, 38, 64, 85, 88, 90, 103, 121, 125, 128, 133, 147–48, 150, 154–55, 181–82, 203, 205, 210, 212, 229, 232, 266–67 (n. 48), 276 (n. 24). *See also* African Americans: attitudes toward Israel; Arab American activists: protest of UAW's Israeli bonds; South Africa: relation to Israel
Israelis: leftists, 36, 64, 76, 93; students in the U.S., 52, 67–68, 77
Israel Public Affairs Committee. *See* American Israel Public Affairs Committee

INDEX 309

Jabara, Abdeen, 16, 26, 113, 199, 231, 235, 279 (n. 67); American-Arab Anti-Discrimination Committee and, 207, 208, 210; Association of Arab American University Graduates and, 31, 34, 35–36, 37, 38, 42, 43–44, 45, 93, 140, 144, 152, 155–56, 175; civil liberties issues and, 38, 144, 146, 149, 150, 151–53, 154–56, 158–62, 177, 264 (n. 11), 268 (n. 65); coalitions with leftists and civil rights activists, 35–36, 43–44, 67, 68, 70, 90, 92 (ill.), 93, 101–2, 107–9, 114, 115, 156, 159–62, 213–14, 220–21, 257 (n. 54), 277 (n. 40); Palestine Human Rights Campaign and, 76, 206; Sirhan Sirhan's attorney, 121, 127–28, 129–30, 132, 133, 136, 137, 138, 140, 142, 261 (n. 16); Southend of Dearborn and, 175, 177, 182, 197

Jackson, Jacqueline, 220

Jackson, Jesse, 211, 212, 216, 219–21, 223, 228, 280 (n. 70); National Rainbow Coalition and, 18, 209, 212, 216–17, 221

Jacobs, Paul, 256 (n. 43)

Jamal, Amaney, 143

Jansen, Godfrey, 132, 133

Japanese Americans, 109, 110; internment of in World War II, 153

Jerusalem, 25, 63, 124, 135

Jewish Americans, 4, 67–69, 87–88, 102–3, 134–35, 147, 148, 205, 211, 218, 223, 223, 225–26; leftists, 51, 89–90, 94–95, 97, 99–100, 102–3, 192; neoconservatives, 103–4, 258–59 (n. 71); students, 60–61, 67–68, 75, 97, 98, 103, 253 (n. 68); support for Palestine, 87, 214. *See also* African Americans: Jews and; B'nai B'rith; Israelis: leftist

Jewish Defense League (JDL), 163, 201, 210, 264 (n. 17), 267 (n. 59)

Jewish Information Society, 75

Jewish Radical, 60

Johnson, Grantland, 223

Johnson, Lyndon, 4, 90, 128, 134, 145

Jordan, 21–22, 56, 59, 64, 68, 70, 133, 138, 150; Palestinians in, 22, 33, 63, 95, 98, 243 (n. 6)

Jordan, June, 227

Jordan, Vernon, 218

Journal of Palestine Studies, 234, 244 (n. 17)

Judis, John B., 4

June War. *See* Arab-Israeli War of 1967

Kaiser, Robert, 122

Katsiaficas, George, 224

Katzir, Ephraim, 74

Keast, William, 68–69

Kennedy, Joe, 223

Kennedy John F., 123, 133

Kennedy, Robert F.: assassination by Sirhan Sirhan, 14, 17, 121–23, 126, 128, 129, 130, 139, 141, 260 (n. 1); stance on Israel and Palestine, 125–26, 132, 134, 135–36

Khartoum, Sudan, 138

Khoury, George, 16, 26, 63, 67, 70–72, 107, 115, 141, 173, 177, 193, 194, 195

King, Coretta Scott, 218

King, Martin Luther, Jr., 82, 86, 90, 121, 133, 134

Kissinger, Henry, 147, 205

Klinghoffer, Judith, 102

Kochiyama, Yuri, 109

Kuwait, 37

Lai, Tracy, 13

Langer, Felicia, 36

Latin Americans for Social Development (LA SED), 106, 194

Latin American liberation movements, 84, 97

Latino Americans, 12, 14, 91, 100, 111, 115, 183, 217, 221, 223

Lawrence, John M., 137, 262–63 (n. 39)

League of Arab States, 51, 55, 73–74, 85, 243 (n. 5); 245 (n. 37), 279 (n. 57)

League of Revolutionary Black Workers, 65–66, 88–89, 98, 106, 114, 168, 183, 188

Leary, Timothy, 97–98

Lebanese Americans, 8, 27, 35, 70, 150, 169, 171, 192–93, 205, 207, 244 (n. 22)

Lebanese Communist Party, 49

Lebanese Mission to the U.S., 57

Lebanon, 8, 56, 64, 98, 216, 217, 228; Civil war and Syrian invasion of, 42, 73–74, 195, 197, 231; Israeli invasion of (1982), 77, 203, 210, 224, 226, 228, 277 (n. 32); Palestinians in, 22, 203, 243 (n. 6)

Lerner, Michael P., 95
Liberation News Service (LNS), 95–96, 97, 99, 256 (n. 49)
Liberation Support Movement, 60, 97
Libya, 228
Lipset, Seymour Martin, 104
Liu, Michael, 13
Los Angeles, 15, 26, 40, 52, 74, 110–11, 121, 126, 127, 134, 150, 201, 239 (n. 4)
Los Angeles Eight (L.A. 8), 201
Los Angeles Times, 135, 141
Lowery, Joseph, 216, 219, 220
Lubin, Alex, 88
Luce, Don, 216
Lukas, J. Anthony, 132

Madison Area Committee on Southern Africa, 91
Malek, Alia, 178
Maoist groups, 95, 98–99, 183, 253 (n. 1)
Maria, Frank, 26, 257–58 (n. 61)
Marxism, 5, 12, 33, 49, 65, 71, 98, 189, 202
Masterson, John, 75
Mattson, Kevin, 23
Mazey, Emil, 187
McAlister, Melani, 81, 228
McKee, Peggy, 76
McMahon, Janet, 210
Medina University Press, 31, 32
Medvecky, Nick, 68, 70
Mehdi, Mohammed T., 110, 132–33, 137, 142, 157–58, 267 (n. 59), 281 (n. 85). *See also* Action Committee on American-Arab Relations (ACAAR)
Meir, Golda, 152
Menon, Krishna, 36
MERIP Reports, 31, 67, 99, 154, 192, 234, 258 (n. 62)
Methodist Federation for Social Action, 216
Mexican Americans. *See* Latino Americans
Michigan Chronicle, 185
Michigan State Police, 144, 159
Middle East Newsletter (Americans for Justice in the Middle East), 137–38
Middle East Peace Action Coalition, 216
Middle East Research and Information Project (MERIP), 31–32, 99, 102. *See also* *MERIP Reports*

Middle East Studies Association (MESA), 32, 246 (n. 43)
Midwest Federation of American Syrian-Lebanese Clubs, 26–27
Minor, Ethel, 85, 86, 254 (n. 16)
Mobilization to End the War in Vietnam, 97
Mondale, Walter, 223
Moorish Science Temple, 83
Mosher, Lawrence, 151
Moughrabi, Fouad, 31, 36, 41
Ms. magazine, 225–26, 227
Muhammad, Elijah, 82, 83
Muhammad Speaks (Nation of Islam), 82, 87, 254 (n. 5)
Munem, Muhsen, 251 (n. 41), 252 (n. 59)
Munich Olympics: massacre of Israeli athletes (1972), 17, 73, 144, 147, 148, 151, 152, 153, 155
Murphy, Janice, 76
Muslim Americans, 27, 53. *See also* Arab Americans: Muslim; Arab American activists: Islam and
Muslim Brotherhood, 53, 252 (n. 65)
Muslim Star (Federation of Islamic Associations), 27
Muslim Student Association (MSA), 27, 53, 77, 249 (n. 17), 252 (n. 65)

Naber, Nadine, 49, 57, 143
Naftali, Timothy, 145
Najjar, Fauzi, 30
Nakba, 4, 39, 85, 124, 128, 129
Nasser, Gamal Abdel, 8, 21, 22, 61, 63, 81, 85, 107, 125
Nation of Islam (NOI), 82–83, 85, 254 (n. 11)
National Association for the Advancement of Colored People (NAACP), 80, 90, 218
National Association of Arab Americans (NAAA), 25, 26, 38–39, 202, 204–5, 211, 240 (n. 5), 247 (n. 68), 275 (n. 18)
National Black Political Convention (Gary, Ind.), 91, 255 (n. 35)
National Broadcasting Company (NBC), 136, 148
National Committee to Defend the Rights of Sami Esmail, 75
National Conference for New Politics convention (Chicago), 91, 255 (n. 35)

National Council for Islamic Affairs, 281 (n. 85)
National Lawyers Guild (NLG), 67, 108, 156–57, 161, 163, 213–14, 277 (n. 40), 277 (n. 41)
National Liberation Front (Vietnam), 35, 56, 59, 60, 94, 98, 106, 253–54 (n. 2)
National Organization for Women, 227
National Peace Action Coalition, 108
National Security Agency (NSA), 145, 152–53, 159, 268 (nn. 63, 65)
National Women's Studies Association (NWSA), 226–27
Native Americans. *See* American Indians
Nawash, Hasan, 62–64, 66, 70–71, 106, 107, 115, 195, 196
Near East Report (American Israel Public Affairs Committee), 55, 145, 208
Neoconservative movement, 90, 103–4, 228
Neveh Shalom Temple (Portland, Ore.), 125
New American Movement, 216, 257 (n. 59), 278 (n. 46)
New Left, 23, 34, 47–49, 59–60, 77, 79, 110, 196, 233, 236; description of, 253 (n. 1); positions on Israel and Palestine, 80, 89–90, 93–104, 116–17; under surveillance, 104, 109, 144, 159–60, 162, 264 (n. 7), 268 (n. 68)
New Republic, The, 90, 258–59 (n. 71)
New Right, 228
Newsreel, 71
Newsweek, 126–27, 134, 138, 201
New Syria Party, 2
Newton, Huey, 88
New York City, 26, 50, 51, 52, 74, 83, 99–100, 110, 137, 152, 158, 176, 211, 218, 219, 224, 239 (n. 4)
New York Times, 27, 33, 38, 55, 85–86, 90, 91, 136, 146, 148, 155, 157, 162, 207, 210, 220
New York Times Book Review, 132
Nixon, Richard, 4, 38, 60, 147, 148, 149, 150, 155, 264 (n. 13), 264 (n. 17); presidential administration of, 17, 55, 144, 145, 146, 147, 152, 154–55, 157, 158, 160, 164, 266–67 (n. 48)
Non-Aligned Movement, 81, 107
Northwestern University, 35, 74
November 29th Coalition for Palestine, 277 (n. 32)

Obaid, Soraya, 64, 249 (n. 9)
Ocean Hill-Brownsville schools dispute, 88
October War of 1973, 1, 22, 25, 32; demonstrations, 1, 39–40, 73, 74 (ill.), 167, 178–82, 184, 187, 193, 198, 199, 271 (n. 33)
Odeh, Alex, 163, 201, 210
Odeh, Camilia, 221
O'Dell, Jack, 80–81, 207, 216–17
off our backs, 227
Ohio State University, 51, 54, 73, 76, 91
Oil of the Middle East, 4, 61, 201; embargo of, 203, 228
O'Laughlin, Mike, 76–77
Oliver, Denise, 13, 109
Oman, 71, 74
Operation Boulder, 17, 73, 104, 143–44, 147–51, 153, 154–58, 161, 162–63, 164, 265 (nn. 21, 24), 268 (n. 69)
Operation PUSH, 81, 209, 216–17, 219–20, 221
Orfalea, Gregory, 25
Organization of Arab Students, 15, 17, 21, 30, 35, 46, 121, 202, 231; activism in the community, 49, 70–72, 175, 176; advocacy tactics and style, 48, 51–52, 57–60, 64, 73–75, 230, 250 (n. 29); African Americans and, 56, 60, 65–67, 77, 86–87, 91, 115, 215; American Left, students, and civil rights movement and, 47–49, 55, 59–63, 65–70, 72, 75, 77–78, 107, 109, 116, 145, 233, 257 (n. 58); Arab nationalism and, 49, 50–51, 56; Arab nations and, 50–51, 55, 56, 145, 250 (n. 27); Association of Arab American University Graduates and, 48, 57, 250–51 (n. 31); before 1967, 50–53; campus chapters of, 49, 51–53, 57–60, 73–75, 248 (n. 1); internal divisions of, 48, 56–57, 65, 72, 77, 275 (n. 6); membership of, 47–48, 49–50, 56–57, 64, 75, 232, 249 (n. 12); Palestinian resistance groups and, 48, 53–55, 57–59, 64–65, 68, 70–71, 145–46, 180, 250 (n. 20), 275 (n. 6); response to Arab-Israeli War of 1967, 53–54; stance on Palestine, 49, 50–51, 54, 57, 63, 77, 79; Third World left and, 56, 59–60, 66, 74, 145, 233; transnationalism of, 48, 49, 71; under surveillance or investigation, 54–56, 145–46, 150, 158, 163, 250 (n. 22); Wayne State University chapter of, 16, 17,

312 INDEX

49, 56, 61–68, 70–72, 73, 106, 107, 109, 115, 150, 158, 175, 176, 190, 251 (n. 41), 252 (n. 52); women and, 50, 64, 249 (n. 9)
Organizing Committee for Clemency for Sirhan, 137
Orientalism, 4, 6, 10, 30, 31, 52, 112, 134, 138, 141, 143, 226
Oslo Accords (1993), 231
Oswald, Lee Harvey, 134-139

Pakistani Students Association, 51
Palestine: British Mandate, 35; occupied territories, 4, 22, 63, 87, 205, 214, 219, 228, 236
Palestine Arab Fund, 26
Palestine Committee (Boston, Mass.), 26
Palestine Congress of North America (PCNA), 210–11, 222, 277 (n. 34), 279 (n. 58)
Palestine Day, 51, 106, 195
Palestine House (Washington, D.C.), 26
Palestine Human Rights Campaign (PHRC), 18, 45, 47, 76–77, 163, 202, 206–21 passim, 276 (n. 25)
Palestine Liberation Organization (PLO), 22, 24, 26, 27, 32, 33, 41, 48, 55, 56, 57–58, 73, 91, 99, 100–101, 138, 211, 214, 215, 217, 218, 219–20, 225, 243 (nn. 5, 6), 275 (n. 8)
Palestine National Council, 206, 228
Palestine question: two-state solution, 202, 206, 214, 228
Palestine Red Crescent Society, 244 (n. 19)
Palestine Research Center, 36, 99, 108
Palestine Solidarity Committee, 99–101, 233
Palestine Solidarity Movement, 282 (n. 16)
Palestine Week, 58, 60
Palestinian, The (1977), 40
Palestinian Americans, 8, 25–26, 47, 61–63, 70, 72, 114, 169, 178, 210–11, 212
Palestinian resistance movement, 3, 22, 33, 54, 56, 64, 66, 70, 74, 79, 83, 202–3. *See also* Palestine Liberation Organization; Palestinians: resistance groups
Palestinians: human rights of, 76, 205, 207, 210, 214, 276 (n. 24); refugees or displacement of, 4, 8, 21–22, 26, 27, 50, 60, 79, 81, 90, 95, 124, 135, 233; resistance groups (fedayeen), 5, 22, 32, 53–59, 64, 79, 89, 95–96, 98, 145, 152, 169, 176, 180, 195, 248 (n. 2), 253–54 (n. 2); students in the U.S., 54, 64, 85
Palestinian solidarity movement, 14, 36, 77, 94, 117, 224, 236, 277 (n. 32). *See also* Palestine Solidarity Committee
Pan-African Cultural Festival (Algeria), 91
Pan-Arabism. *See* Arab nationalism
Parsons, Russell, 127
Pasadena, Calif., 124. *See also* Sirhan, Sirhan: Los Angeles area and
Peace movement, 204, 206, 215–16, 223–24. *See also* Anti–Vietnam War movement
People's Exchange (Dearborn, Mich.), 71, 105
Peretz, Martin, 95, 258–59 (n. 71)
Persian Gulf War, 229, 231
Podhoretz, Norman, 258–59 (n. 71)
Pogrebin, Letty Cottin, 225
Popular Front for the Liberation of Palestine (PFLP), 10, 48, 64, 70–71, 75–76, 89, 96, 99, 148, 201, 248 (n. 2), 273 (n. 58)
Progressive Labor Party, 60, 98
Protocol (1984), 209
Puerto Ricans, 91; activism of, 6, 13–14, 100, 109, 115–16, 168, 241 (n. 42), 242 (nn. 43, 47). *See also* Young Lords
Pulcini, Theodore, 231
Pulido, Laura, 12, 14–15, 110–11, 115

Rabin, Yitzhak, 64, 66, 68
Radical Education Project, 95, 256 (n. 47)
Ramallah Federation. *See* American Federation of Ramallah
Ramparts, 94–95, 102, 256 (n. 43)
Randolph, A. Philip, 85, 90
Rauf, Muhammad Abdul, 27
Ray, James Earl, 134
Raza Unida, 216
Reagan, Ronald, 228–29, 281 (n. 82)
Redgrave, Vanessa, 40
Red Power. *See* American Indians: activism of
Red Scare, 154
Republican Party, 228; Arab Americans and, 25, 205, 211, 229, 235, 274–75 (n. 18), 279 (n. 63)
Revolutionary Communist Party, 99, 101, 183, 191–92
Revolutionary Socialist League, 271–72 (n. 42)

Revolutionary Union. *See* Revolutionary Communist Party
Revolutionary Union Movements (RUMs), 65–66, 107, 168, 183–84
Revolution until Victory (1974), 74
Rignall, Karen, 199
Rogers, William, 136, 148, 149, 155
Rubin, Jerry, 139
Rustin, Bayard, 85
Ryan, Sheila, 16, 95–96, 97, 99–101, 102, 256 (n. 49), 258 (n. 63)

Sadat, Anwar, 77
Said, Edward, 36, 207, 277 (n. 34)
Samhan, Helen Hatab, 143, 201–2, 235
San Bernardino attack (2015), 236
San Francisco, 26, 49, 74, 143, 271 (n. 30)
San Jose State, 97
Saturday Evening Post, 205, 208
Saudi Arabia, 53, 64
Save Lebanon Project, 210
Sayegh, Fayz, 32, 85, 277 (n. 34)
Scheer, Robert, 89–90, 95
Seale, Bobby, 106
Seeger, Pete, 207
September 11th (2001), 10, 114, 141, 145, 229, 236
Shafer, Lou, 99
Shahak, Israel, 36
Shaheen, Jack, 208
Shain, Yossi, 112, 206
Shair, Kamal A., 50
Shakir, Evelyn, 53
Shannon, Matthew, 49
Sharabi, Hisham, 204, 205
Shattuck, John, 159
Shihab, Aziz, 138, 263 (n. 45)
Sirhan, Bishara, 124
Sirhan, Mary, 124, 135
Sirhan, Sirhan, 14, 17; American Left's response to, 139; American media coverage of, 123, 126, 132, 133–37, 138, 141, 262 (n. 29); Arab Americans' response to, 122, 123, 140, 263 (n. 49); Arab world reaction to, 122–23, 138; attitude toward U.S. political leaders and Robert F. Kennedy, 121, 124, 125–26, 128, 136; defense attorneys of, 126–30, 132, 261 (n. 16); family of, 124, 133, 135; impact on American attitudes toward Arabs, 121, 123, 135, 136–37, 141–42, 145, 234; Los Angeles area and, 124–25; mentally ill, 121, 122, 127–28, 129, 132, 133; mysticism and, 125; Organization of Arab Students and, 130, 131 (ill.), 140, 142, 260 (n. 5); political stance on Israel and Palestine, 121, 122, 123, 125, 126, 127–28, 130, 132, 133, 135; political stances, 124, 125; prosecution of, 126–29, 130; supporters of, 137–39; trial testimony of, 128–29, 130, 135–36, 261 (n. 17); verdict and sentence, 129, 130, 137; youth in Palestine, 121, 124, 127–28, 129, 135. *See also* Arab American activists: response to Sirhan, Sirhan
Smith, Sherry, 13–14, 109, 116
Social Democratic Party, 257 (n. 59)
Socialist Labor Party, 257 (n. 59)
Socialist Workers Party (SWP), 67, 98, 108, 145, 158, 160, 257 (n. 58)
Sojourners Magazine, 216
South Africa, 217; relation to Israel, 36, 91, 185–86, 203, 215, 219, 228
Southeast Dearborn Community Council (SEDCC), 171–75, 176, 177–78, 179 (ill.), 274 (nn. 71, 76)
South End, The (Wayne State University), 65–70, 89, 103, 114, 158, 252 (n. 55)
Southend of Dearborn, Mich., 17–18, 61, 70–72, 74, 151, 169, 179, 180–82, 197, 199–200, 269 (n. 5), 273 (n. 58); struggle against urban renewal in, 106, 167, 168, 170–78, 197, 198, 269 (n. 8), 270 (n. 25), 270–71 (n. 29)
Southern Christian Leadership Conference (SCLC), 90, 160, 215–21 passim
Soviet Union, 4, 56, 98–99
Spark, 271 (n. 40), 272 (n. 45), 273 (n. 54)
Spark. See Wildcat
State Street Mosque (Brooklyn, N.Y.), 83
Stern, Sol, 95, 103
Stillborn Press (Dearborn, Mich.), 106
Stone, I. F., 94, 96, 207, 256 (n. 43)
Stork, Joe, 102, 150, 153, 154
Student Nonviolent Coordinating Committee (SNCC), 48, 80, 83–88, 94, 114, 218, 254 (n. 47)
Students for a Democratic Society (SDS), 48–49, 67, 77, 95, 106, 107, 160, 232, 256 (n. 47)

Students for Justice in Palestine, 236
Suez Crisis (1956), 81
Suleiman, Michael, 2, 32, 42, 45, 105, 205, 232
Sullivan, Bill, 160
Sunni Islam, 82–83, 254 (n. 11)
Surkin, Marvin, 69–70, 113, 183
Syria, 7, 21–22, 33, 178; Civil War in, 231, 236
Syrian Americans, 7–8, 27, 28, 111

Taam, Milt, 99
Talhami, Ghada Hashem, 24
Tamari, Marisa, 221
Terrorism, 163, 242 (n. 43); accusations of, 55, 121, 122, 138, 140–41, 143, 151, 153, 157–58, 162, 163, 207, 217, 223, 225; Palestinian, 4, 10, 17, 141, 143, 147, 148, 152–53, 228, 266 (n. 40)
Terry, Janice, 29, 31, 32, 45, 63, 107
Terzi, Zehdi, 217, 219
Theberge, Rene, 150, 153, 154
Thibeault, Barbara, 75
Thimmesch, Nick, 205
Third World Coalition (Columbia University), 101
Third World Left, 5, 12–15, 17, 24, 49, 79, 84, 93, 95, 98–99, 100–101, 107, 109, 113, 116, 189, 203, 224, 233, 242 (n. 49)
Third World Liberation Front (San Francisco), 14, 101
Third World nationalism. *See* Third World Left
Third World Women's Alliance, 91
Thomas, Lorrin, 116
Thompson, Dorothy, 257–58 (n. 61)
Time, 134
Transnationalism. *See* Arab American activists: transnationalism of; Association of Arab American University Graduates: transnationalism of; Organization of Arab Students: transnationalism of
Traub, Amos, 67–68
Tricontinental Progressive Students (University of California–Berkeley), 60, 97
Tripp, Luke, 65
Tsemel, Lea, 76
Turki, Fawaz, 40, 74, 202

Union of American Hebrew Congregations, 224
Unis, Don, 151, 171, 193, 194, 197
United Arab Republic Day, 51
United Automobile Workers (UAW), 69, 194; African American workers and, 65, 183, 185; Arab American workers and, 1–2, 168, 183, 187–90, 191, 192, 193, 199, 271 (n. 40), 272 (nn. 48, 52); Israel and, 168, 184, 185–87, 189–90; Local 600 (Dearborn) of, 2, 182, 187, 199. *See also* Arab American activists: protest UAW's Israeli bonds
United Holy Land Fund, 26, 162
United Methodist Church, 216
United National Caucus, 190
United Nations, 50; General Assembly Resolution 3379 (1975), 215; Palestine Liberation Organization and, 217, 244 (n. 21); Security Council Resolution 242 (1967), 39; U.S. ambassadors to, 128, 217; U.S. Mission to, 96
U.S. Campaign to End the Israeli Occupation, 236
U.S. Census: and Arab Americans, 11, 222–23, 279–80 (n. 67)
U.S. policy toward the Middle East, 22, 25, 27, 31, 38, 44, 136, 202, 205, 208, 219, 220, 236. *See also* Israel: U.S. relationship with
U.S. State Department, 147, 162–63, 217. *See also* Rogers, William
University of California–Berkeley, 16, 57–61, 97, 132, 236
University of California v. Bakke (1978), 218
University of Kansas, 16, 57–58, 73
University of Michigan, 35, 57–58, 74, 77, 107
Urban League, 80, 90, 218

Vaisse, Justin, 90
Venceremos Brigade, 14, 100, 106, 113
Viet Cong. *See* National Liberation Front (Vietnam)
Vietnam War, 13, 35, 36, 60, 68, 84, 137, 185, 228. *See also* Anti–Vietnam War movement

Wagner, Donald, 276 (n. 25)
Wahhabism, 53

Walker, Herbert, 137
Walters, Ron, 207
Walzer, Michael, 95
Washington, D.C., 25, 26, 27, 32, 74, 91, 145, 210, 211
Washington, Harold, 220
Washington Post, 38, 126, 129, 134–35, 136, 140, 154, 159, 207
Watson, John, 65–66, 68–69, 89
Wayne State University, 32, 35, 57, 68–69, 103, 107, 114–15, 160, 173, 181, 236. *See also* Organization of Arab Students: Wayne State University chapter of
Weather Underground (the Weathermen), 97–98
Weiner, Tim, 144–45
West Bank. *See* Palestine: occupied territories
White Panthers, 106, 176
Wigle, Lauren, 169
Wildcat, 99, 191, 273 (n. 54)
Wilkins, Roger, 218
Will, Donald, 216
Williams, Faye, 223
Wingfield, Marvin, 224
Wise, Stanley, 84, 86
Wolfe, Mel, 156
Wolfe, Milton, 218
Women against Rape (WAR), 76
Woodcock, Leonard, 1, 184–87, 188
Workers World Party, 98
Wright, Richard, 81

X, Malcolm, 82–83, 84, 176

Yaqub, Salim, 203
Yemen, 8, 180
Yemeni Americans, 7, 8, 273 (n. 59); Arab world politics of, 71, 174, 180, 270–71 (n. 29); labor and UAW Israeli bonds protest and, 177, 182, 183, 184, 185, 187–88, 192; settlement in Detroit and Dearborn, 70, 169, 170–71, 179–80, 270–71 (n. 29); Southend protest, ACCESS and, 177, 178, 180, 197, 270–71 (n. 29); violence against, 180, 189, 191, 273 (n. 56)
Yemeni Arab Association, 180
Yemeni Benevolent Society, 180
Yorty, Sam, 134
Young, Andrew, 217–19, 220, 228, 278 (nn. 49, 50, 51, 52)
Young, Coleman, 216
Young, Cynthia, 14–15
Young, Whitney, 85, 90
Young Lords, 109, 168
Young Socialist Alliance, 60, 66, 68, 158
Youth against War and Fascism, 96, 98, 108
Youth Committee for Peace and Democracy in the Middle East, 60–61

Zeitlin, Maurice, 95
Zellner, Dorothy, 87
Zinn, Howard, 257 (n. 54)
Zionism, 4, 22; African Americans and, 80, 82, 85, 86, 87, 88, 90; American Left and, 60, 67–68, 89, 94, 99, 101, 104, 234; curtailment of Arab Americans, 52, 54–55, 164, 158, 159; opposition to by Arab Americans, 24, 27, 30, 33, 74, 122, 128, 132, 133, 188–89, 190; political power in U.S., 44, 232; representation of Arabs, 31, 38
Zogby, James, 76, 206, 207, 208, 210, 211–12, 217, 221, 222, 224, 228, 235, 277 (n. 35), 280 (n. 70)